WILLIAM CONRAD

A LIFE & CAREER

by CHARLES TRANBERG

WILLIAM CONRAD: A LIFE & CAREER
©2018 CHARLES TRANBERG

ALL RIGHTS RESERVED.

No part of this book may be reproduced in any form or by any means, electronic, mechanical, digital, photocopying, or recording, except for in the inclusion of a review, without permission in writing from the publisher.

Published in the USA by:

BEARMANOR MEDIA
P.O. BOX 71426
ALBANY, GEORGIA 31708
www.BearManorMedia.com

ISBN: 978-1-62933-271-0 (alk. paper)

DESIGN AND LAYOUT: VALERIE THOMPSON

TABLE OF CONTENTS

INTRODUCTION & ACKNOWLEDGMENTS . . . 1

CHAPTER ONE—BEGINNINGS:
THE EMERGENCE OF A RADIO ACTOR . . . 5

CHAPTER TWO—MOVIE TOUGH GUY . . . 15

CHAPTER THREE—GUNSMOKE . . . 27

CHAPTER FOUR—THE RIDE BACK . . . 61

CHAPTER FIVE—WARNER BROTHERS . . . 75

PHOTO GALLERY . . . 105

CHAPTER SIX—CANNON . . . 125

CHAPTER SEVEN—NERO WOLFE . . . 151

CHAPTER EIGHT—JAKE AND THE FATMAN . . . 167

EPILOGUE . . . 187

SELECTED RADIO CREDITS OF WILLIAM CONRAD . . . 189

SELECTED TV GUEST ROLES . . . 291

BIBLIOGRAPHY . . . 399

SOURCES . . . 403

INDEX . . . 417

INTRODUCTION & ACKNOWLEDGMENTS

William Conrad had a fascinating career. He began as a teenager in radio and after the interruption of World War II he quickly established himself as one of the top voices of West Coast radio drama. He was much in demand on shows like *The Whistler, Escape, Suspense* and many others. He once boasted (with some justification) that he worked on over 7000 radio shows. While his radio work from 1946-1951 was substantial—he didn't find his peak as a radio star until he was selected to play Marshal Matt Dillon on the radio version of *Gunsmoke* (1952-1961).

Matt Dillon was an iconic role and what makes it even more impressive is that he took it on in the waning days of radio drama. Not that radio wasn't still a force—but more and more people were getting their entertainment from that new-fangled medium of television. Even after *Gunsmoke* transitioned to television in 1955, the radio show was still a success and lasted another six years with Conrad's sardonic, world weary Matt Dillon competing against the more white bread, heroic version of television. For many people who began with *Gunsmoke* on radio there was no competition—William Conrad was Matt Dillon.

Along with radio he was a sought-after character actor in films. Between 1946 and 1959 Conrad acted in twenty-five films often as a villain or the best friend of the hero. He worked with top directors and in support of some of the biggest stars in Hollywood. Among his films were *The Killers, Body and Soul* and such noir classics as *Tension, One Way Street, Cry Danger, The Racket,* and *5 Against the House.*

Not that he would boycott television. Even after he was by-passed by for the television part of Matt Dillon (TV being a visual medium thought that Conrad was too short, fat, and bald to play Dillon) he began working on television as an actor, producer and director starting in the late 1950's. By the early sixties he virtually stopped acting all together to become first, Jack Webb's partner in running the television division of Warner Brothers. He then became the head of his own 'B' movie unit at Warner Brothers in the mid-sixties producing ten films for a million dollars or less. Along with his producing and directing duties he also still lent his voice to such projects as the classic *Rocky and Bullwinkle Show* and gave the weekly narration for *The Fugitive* which introduced him to the world of Quinn Martin Productions.

It was for producer Quinn Martin that he began his own successful television show in 1971 as the private detective *Cannon*. Frank Cannon was a man who enjoyed the best—food, wine, boats and cars. A former cop he took on assignments for the money it provided him to indulge in the finer things in life. There had not been a lead in a detective show quite like him before. That he wasn't the classic television leading man is an understatement—he was balding and overweight, and yet audiences and not a few women identified with him. He had charisma—something that the real life Conrad had in spades.

After that Conrad took on other television projects including a short-lived run as Rex Stout's *Nero Wolfe*. He also began to appear on the stage in a series of plays. By the late 80's he returned to television in his next famous role as former cop J.L. McCabe in *Jake and the Fatman*. You can guess which part he played. Unlike *Cannon* where Conrad was the whole show (except for guest stars) he had a young, good-looking assistant to back him up and perform the chases and fist fights that he used to do as Cannon. Part of this was due to his increasingly poor health. Within two-years of the end of *Jake and the Fatman* Conrad would be dead.

Bill Conrad was a fascinating man in real life. As stated he was a man who exuded charisma. He had many friends—and yet, as he once told Leonard Maltin, he couldn't understand why anybody would want to be his friend. His looks may not have been his ticket to stardom but they didn't stop him from fascinating women. He married three times and had lovers. He was an often profane man—four letter words were just part of his everyday language and yet he could recite poetry and Shakespeare with ease. He had many interests and often they came before those of his own family—including his only son, Christopher—who he loved, but didn't feel that he was a particularly good father to.

I'm quite fortunate to have had many people connected with Bill Conrad share their recollections of this fascinating man. At the top of the list is his son **Christopher Conrad**. Christopher and his wife **Janet Conrad** couldn't have been more helpful. I am also thankful for Christopher for allowing me to quote from a full interview that Leonard Maltin did with Bill Conrad for his book *The Great American Broadcast* which was much more extensive than what was included in that very fine book. My thanks is also extended to the following: **Julie Adams, Richard Anderson, Kevin Butler, Alan Campbell, Paul Robert Coyle, Herb Ellis, Helen Frees, David Hedison, Ray Kemper, Michael Lange, Jimmy Lydon, Allan Miller, Kevin Moore, Robert Pine** and **Peggy Webber**. I'd also like to thank **Valerie Thompson** for her design of this book—a great job as always.

This is my eighth book and as usual I'm also indebted to my publisher, **Ben Ohmart**, for his support and for suggesting this project to me.

CHARLES TRANBERG

CHAPTER ONE
BEGINNINGS: THE EMERGENCE OF A RADIO ACTOR
1920–1946

William Conrad was born John William Cann, Jr., on September 27, 1920 in Lexington, Kentucky. His parents, John (born 1897) and Ida (born 1900) were both native Alabamians and had been married for nearly two years when "Junior," as John William was called, was born. Eventually to differentiate himself from his father Junior began to introduce himself as William Cann dropping the first name of John all together. "I remember him saying he was teased as a boy because his first name "John" was synonymous for a bathroom," Conrad's son Christopher later recalled. "Even later on he jokingly lamented after traveling through Europe that it was ironic that his name or more precisely his initials—W.C.—were still synonymous with a bathroom. I recall my mom telling him, 'Maybe that's why you're such a potty mouth.'" When he wasn't referred to as 'Junior' he began to be called 'Bill' by his friends—which stuck with him for the rest of his life.

His father and mother got jobs in a local movie theater. His father as a projectionist and his mother as a cashier. They made only a modest living and Christopher Conrad recalls his father telling how he and his friends would go to a country store to buy balls of bubble gum. He and the other boys would then climb to the roof of the store and chew the gum until it became soft. They would then dunk the gum into the a water tank which was also located on the roof. By dunking the gum into the cold water the gum hardened and the boys could then enjoy chewing it again. Money was limited and so the boys tried to make their gum last as long as possible.

At some point in the early 1930's the family moved to Bellflower, California where his father got another job as a movie theater projectionist. As a teenager Bill found work singing in a funeral parlor. It was his first professional job. "He loved singing," his son Christopher later related. Along with singing in a funeral parlor he would travel to Long Beach where he took singing lessons and sang in a choir at a local church.

Bill was in Long Beach when a 6.3 magnitude earthquake hit Southern California on Friday, March 10, 1933 (with its center in Long Beach) and ended up killing 115 people. Bill ran outside and saw the street buckling back and forth as if it were a rolling pin. Brick buildings would come crashing down when this buckling wave hit them. It was an indelible scene that Bill never forgot.

It was around this time that Bill's father died. Ida was working as a cashier at the movie theater in Bellflower that her husband had been employed as a projectionist. Bill also continued to work at the funeral parlor and do other odd jobs to help support himself and his mother.

At some point, while still in his teens, Bill decided that he could work in radio—possibly as an announcer. He visited KFOX Radio in Long Beach finding only a secretary and the station's announcer in the building. The announcer was a genial six-footer named Lou Huston, who would become a life-long friend. Huston invited Bill to sit in the booth with him and observe him at work. At one point Huston asked Bill if he wanted to give it a try. Bill was nothing if not game. He took the script and read it on the air. Afterward Bill said, "That wasn't too bad was it?" Huston later said that Bill, "learned more in ten minutes than I could in six months." Huston convinced his boss to give Bill odd jobs. "Everybody did everything," Huston later explained of those heady days of radio. "There were people who only announced, and then there were people who did announcing and went out on the street and sold shoes. We had a secretary who sang, played piano and acted in skits. That was during the Big Depression. Jobs of any kind were hard to get, so we were also driven with the idea that writing scripts and doing long announce shifts was a lot better than digging ditches..."

One day in the summer of 1938 a man from RCA (Radio Corporation of America) named Echos, who was doing a sound check at the radio station that Ida worked at in Bellflower, began a casual conversation with Bill. It was thru Echos that Bill met another man who was going to help advance Bill's career and become yet another life-long friend, Clete Roberts. Roberts was twenty-six years old and was the news director of Station KMPC Radio which was located behind a service station in Beverly Hills. KMPC was nick-named "The Station of the Stars." Roberts invited Bill (who he recalled as being young and slim, "Bill didn't start to gain weight until after World War II.") for coffee and found him to be a very enthusiastic young man with a voice that seemed tailor made for broadcasting.

Roberts arranged for Bill to meet management at KMPC in hopes of finding a position for the young man at the station. "Clete worked out a deal where I would be a clean-up man around the place," Bill later told Leonard Maltin. "I ended up living with Clete, his wife, and children for a year-and-a-half and eventually became an announcer at the station." It was easier for Conrad to live with Roberts and his family in Los Angeles than to travel to Bellflower to live with his mother—especially since Bill didn't have a car. He continued to support his mother financially.

Roberts recalled that Bill had "this big voice" that reminded him of Orson Welles. ("I was trying to sound like Welles in those days," Bill later conceded). Roberts thought he could make a newsman out of the youngster. "I took him along to Redondo Beach where the high waves were crashing against the homes there," Roberts later recalled. "I set the scene briefly, and said, 'Here's William Conrad to describe what's happening." Conrad, years later, would ruefully recall his first check from KMPC, "On the voucher it said, 'for acting, singing, directing'—two weeks. $2.50!"

While Conrad didn't really become a newsman at KMPC he did do a fair amount of announcing for the station and stayed with them until 1942—when he entered the service. It was during these early years that Bill made a realization about working in radio. "I had been poor all of my life and I thought God Dammit I could make some money at this thing," Conrad told Leonard Maltin. "I made decisions based on making money—that is why I kept myself so involved in everything."

In 1940 KMPC had the power to transmit up to 10,000 watts per day and night thanks to a transmitter that was on top of Burbank Boulevard in North Hollywood. *The Hermit's Cave* was a syndicated horror/suspense series that began in Detroit, Michigan in 1930 and moved to KMPC in 1940 where the twenty-year old Bill, now going by the last name Conrad, acted as co-producer (with Bill Forman, who would later become an announcer and lead on *The Whistler*), writer, director, and—occasionally—as an actor.

The Hermit's Cave was narrated by an old crackling voiced Hermit who would tell the audience, "Ghost stories, weird stories, and murders, too. The Hermit knows of them all. Turn out your lights. Turn them out...and listen as the Hermit tells you the story." While Conrad did sometimes work as an actor on *The Hermit's Cave* he was most happy being a director. "I had always hoped to be a director when I began in radio," he later told a reporter. In addition to all of this Conrad also began taking courses in drama and literature at Fullerton College.

It was while working on *The Hermit's Cave* that Conrad became acquainted with another great radio voice and actor, John Dehner, who assumed the voice of the old hermit in 1942. They would work together many times over the next twenty-years in numerous radio programs. John Dunning in his Encyclopedia of Radio would accurately state that the West Coast version of *The Hermit's Cave* was "a training ground of sorts for young actors with network aspirations." It should also be noted that the music on *The Hermit's Cave* (including the macabre organ tones) was by Rex Koury, who would later compose the theme to *Gunsmoke*.

It was during this period that Conrad began dating June Nelson, a fellow student at Fullerton College, who had aspirations of becoming a school teacher. Many people thought it was a case of opposites attracting—since Bill was outgoing, loud, and often profane. June, in contrast, was a gentle and shy brunette. Complicating matters for Bill was that the United States was at war and able bodied young men were being called upon to serve their county—Bill was no exception. In 1943 he began basic training at Luke Air Force Base near Phoenix, Arizona. It was while training at Luke that Bill and June were married.

He became a pilot and enjoyed flying immensely—he would continue to do so as a hobby for years after leaving the service. His son, Christopher, has few WWII anecdotes to offer about his dad, but does recall that as a pilot Bill buzzed the Golden Gate Bridge and then a small town north of San Francisco—in which he succeeded in breaking a bunch of windows. Christopher recalls his dad telling him that he got called on the carpet for that. Initially Conrad was to be a fighter pilot with the U.S. Army Air Force—but he was ultimately grounded due to night blindness.

Most of his service career was spent from 1944-1946 as a member of the Armed Forces Radio Network. With his experience in radio prior to the war he often produced and directed a series of programs for service personnel. Bill also worked on a short-lived public affairs program titled *Destination Tomorrow* which only ran for about fifteen episodes from January to March of 1945. Bill was an announcer and occasional actor on the program which also featured Jack Moyles (who later became best known to radio listeners as Rocky Jordan) playing FDR. The show discussed and dramatized issues of the day. Among the issues highlighted on various episodes were 1) Does man only do his best for war? 2) The right to a useful job (following the war for returning service men and a G.I. Bill of Rights) 3) The right of a family to a decent home? 4) The right of good health and medical treatment (a discussion of National Health Insurance) 5) The right of 'freedom of economic fear' such as unemployment, disability, illness, old age 6) The right to a good education.

Destination Tomorrow was narrated by Chet Huntley, a Montana born newsman associated with CBS News and station KNX since 1939 as a newscaster, correspondent and analyst. Later he would achieve national fame as the co-host of the NBC television networks very popular nightly news—*The Huntley-Brinkley Report.* Huntley and Bill became friendly acquaintances who would meet from time to time over the years (In 1980 Bill would marry Huntley's widow, Tippy). Shortly after the end of the war Bill was discharged from the service with the rank of Captain.

When he was discharged Bill and June returned to Los Angeles and for a time stayed with his old friend Clete Roberts and his family until they could get established in their own home in the San Fernando Valley. During the time that Conrad was in the service June established herself as a school teacher and was working in that field. Conrad, meanwhile, returned to WMPC, but his work during the war got him recognized and soon he was part of an integral group of young men and women who were the back bone of West Coast radio drama.

II

By the post-war period the hub of radio had moved from New York and Chicago to Los Angeles—and specifically Hollywood (in part this was true because more and more radio personalities were also big stars in movies such as Bing Crosby and Bob Hope). The area surrounding Vine Street, between Hollywood and Sunset Boulevard, was home to many of the radio shows of the day.

Bill Conrad would work at all the major radio studios in town—but it was at Columbia Square, the home of CBS Radio, in an area known as "Gower Gulch"— located between Sunset and Gower—that Conrad worked most frequently. The site of Columbia Square had a venerable past. It was built in 1938 as a CBS Radio Studio on the site of the first film company ever to be built in Hollywood. Among the gallery of stars who performed at Columbia Square were Jack Benny, Eddie Cantor, Burns and Allen, Gene Autry, Edgar Bergen, Red Skelton, Al Jolson and Ed Wynn. These were the big stars that were household names and headlined radio shows. Conrad would be included in an elite group of talented artists who worked together on some of the finest dramatic radio shows of the era. They may not have been household names but their talent made them much sought after and, in addition to Bill Conrad, the group included: Elliott Lewis, Parley Baer, Howard McNear, Herb Ellis, Hans Conried, Paul Frees, Peggy Webber, Jack Webb, Joseph Kearns, Harry Bartell, Virginia Gregg, Jeanette Nolan, and John Dehner.

The show that Bill Conrad worked most consistently during this time was *The Whistler*, a mystery-suspense anthology series which ran on CBS radio from 1942-1955. The show was hosted and narrated by "The Whistler" (such prolific radio actors as Bill Forman, Joseph Kearns and Gale Gordon performed the hosting duties over the years) whose footsteps were heard in the distance approaching while whistling a creepy tune. The listener would then hear him say his classic opening lines, "I am the Whistler, and I know many things, for I walk by night. I know many strange tales, many secrets hidden in the hearts of men and women who have stepped into the shadows. I know the nameless terrors of which they dare not speak."

Conrad maintains that *The Whistler* was his big break on network radio and tells the story about getting a call from somebody at CBS asking if he would be interested in working on *The Whistler*. Conrad, instead of jumping at the chance maintains that his first question was "how much does it pay?" It turned out to be enough and it provided him an introduction to many other shows where his distinctive voice was utilized. "From that time on I worked seven days a week while in radio," he later told Leonard Maltin. Conrad, who could be self-deprecating in many ways, maintains that his sole interest in radio was not artistic but to make money—there was, of course, truth in that—but he certainly was interested in maintaining his viability as a radio actor and in that effort became recognized as one of the finest radio talents on the West Coast.

Between March and October of 1946 Conrad made appearances on nine episodes of *The Whistler*. Many of the shows he was on during this time used him in supporting roles—often as a cop or a criminal—and he didn't always get credit at the end. One good example is **The Trigger Man (3/25/46)** in which Conrad doesn't appear until near the end—but it's a showy part. The protagonist thinks that Conrad is "Spike" a hit-man for the client that he is defending for a murder that he witnessed. But it turns out that Conrad is actually the guard that the D.A. assigned to the attorney believing that he would be a target for death by his client.

Conrad plays a cop again in **Bullet Proof (8/5/1946)** an excellent story (by Kenneth Harvey) about a woman (Mary Jane Croft) who wants to divorce her husband (Gerald Mohr) so that she can marry her lover. The husband comes up with an ingenious plan to kill her before divorcing him so that he can inherit all of her money. The plot depends on the husband devising a way to make his .45 caliber gun fire .22 caliber bullets.

It's in the middle of this episode that Bill makes his appearance playing a police detective named, ironically, William Conrad. The detective that Conrad plays is a ballistics expert. While he seems suspicious of some aspects of the crime (such as why didn't the husband wake up when the shot was fired) he seems to buy the story—that the wife was killed by a .22 bullet by a jewel thief. Eventually the husband confesses to the crime after killing a blackmailer with the same gun.

Gerald Mohr, a former member of Orson Welles' Mercury Theater, who had more than 500 radio credits, dominates this episode with an assured performance. Conrad has relatively little air time. He enters the program at mid-point for a few minutes and then appears again at the end. But he gives a completely believable performance. His voice being instantly recognizable and—at age 26—makes you believe that you are listening to an experienced police officer of many years' service. It's probably just as well that the character that Conrad plays in "Bullet Proof" is named "William Conrad" because Conrad, the actor, gets no identification in the credits (only Mohr and Croft do). But this was common for relatively young and less experienced radio actors.

Stolen Murder (8/12/46) is another gem and stars Paul Frees in a nuanced performance as a man who steals a friend's novel believing that the friend only has a short time to live. As it turns out the man was mistaken and now is expected to recover with rest and relaxation. The Frees character contrives to get his friend out of doors so he can kill him and make it look like a hunting accident. All goes according to plan—the novel becomes a best-seller and the Frees character gets rich. However, in the denouement, Conrad finally appears playing a publicist trying to get a story about the new best-selling novelist. In doing so the Conrad character eventually reveals himself to be a police officer investigating a missing persons case and the novel both in location and in characterization was close to home and so they followed the clues and found the missing man—murdered. It turns out that the plot of the friend's novel was based on a murder he committed—a murder that will now be pinned on the Frees character.

In all Conrad would work on more than thirty episodes of *The Whistler* with the bulk of these appearances being from 1946-1952.

Another popular radio show that Conrad was frequently appearing was *Favorite Story*, a transcribed syndicated series, which was produced by Frederick Ziv Productions (a company that Conrad would work for extensively on television as an actor, director and producer from the late 1950's into the early 1960's). The program was hosted by film star Ronald Colman. The show was advertised as presenting "the greatest stories of all-time, masterfully adapted by writers pre-eminent in their field." Each week some popular figure in the arts would choose his or her 'favorite story' which would then be dramatized. Several of the dramatizations were adapted by the team of Jerome Lawrence and Robert E. Lee, who would go on to write such prestigious plays as *Inherit the Wind, First Monday in October* and *Auntie Mame.*

The show was transcribed at Radio station KFI on Vermont Street in Hollywood and sponsored by Bullock's Department Store. Conrad appeared in twenty-three episodes over a two-year period in adaptations of novels by Charlotte Bronte (*Jane Eyre*), Emily Bronte (*Wuthering Heights*), Rudyard Kipling (*The Strange Mr. Bartleby*), Jane Austen (*Pride and Prejudice*), Henry Melville (*Moby Dick*), Robert Louis Stevenson (*Dr. Jekyll and Mr. Hyde*), Edgar Allen Poe (*The Tell-Tale Heart*) Henrik Isben (*The Doll's House*) among many others.

Conrad would later recall that there was only an "hour-and-a-half of rehearsals and then they put it on the air…nobody had time to think of subtlety." He later added, "I was so valuable to people they would tell me that I didn't have to make the table reading, I didn't have to make the first rehearsal; all I had to do was make the dress rehearsal. There were many times when they'd say, 'You sight read better than anybody anyway, so here's the script, everybody else is rehearsed,' and it would be go on the air."

Peggy Webber first met Conrad on Favorite Story while they were rehearsing "Jane Eyre." "I was Jane Eyre," Miss Webber recalls, "and he was Mr. Rochester. I was very impressed with his voice and ability. He was trim and nice looking—I had not seen him on any other show." (Conrad later recalled that he was a trim 165 pounds when he got out of the military. He also recalled that twice in his life he lost a hundred pounds, "but I put it back on.") As she got to know Conrad on this show (and many others over the years) she noticed a few things that fascinated her:

"I saw that he liked to look as if he were very nonchalant about 'wood shedding,' (which is a comment referring to an actor studying his script). He would work on crossword puzzles and draw cartoons instead. It was unstated behavior with more sophisticated actors, such as Hans Conried, to not mark ones script with too many pencil marks. Sometimes the role they were playing was not even circled in the margin, which was the usual way to mark a script. The lofty ones (such as Bill) showed how

astute they were and quick to perform, with what was required, but without too much display of effort."

Conrad, would later say that he could pick up a script cold (without having read it) and be able to go on the air without making any mistakes. "I'd say just tell me what the character is, or what he's called, and roughly what it's about," Conrad later told Leonard Maltin, "and that's all I need...I had a picture in my mind, but I was never consciously referring to it."

CHAPTER TWO
MOVIE TOUGH GUY
1946-1952

Between 1946 and 1959 William Conrad acted in twenty-five films. In most cases he was a member of the supporting cast. In the early 1970's Conrad gave his own take on the types of roles he played in motion pictures, "I played a lot of heavies and the leading man's best friend, which is the dullest part in the world." While Conrad is best known today for his television and radio work his film career holds its own interest not only for his work as an actor but, later, as a producer and director. Leonard Maltin once asked Conrad which took priority in his career at the time—movies or radio— and Conrad replied, "Movies were my priority always— unless it was something I was committed to do (such as *Gunsmoke*)." Conrad was a working actor and he often took anything that was offered to him. He liked to work and even in dull films he usually always enlivened the proceedings due to his presence.

Conrad acted in films which starred such Hollywood icons as Burt Lancaster, Barbara Stanwyck, Ava Gardner, Clark Gable, Joel McCrea, Ingrid Bergman, James Mason (three times), Dick Powell, Robert Mitchum, Charlton Heston, Eleanor Parker, Kim Novak, John Wayne, Susan Hayward, Anthony Quinn and Frank Sinatra. If nothing else he got his money's worth observing these Hollywood giants at work and benefited by being seen on the screen with them or at least being associated in films in which they appeared. Furthermore, for a man who was interested in directing, he had the opportunity to observe and study several outstanding film directors including Robert Siodmak, Robert Rossen, Victor Fleming, Anatole Litvak, Mervyn LeRoy, Robert Parrish, John Cromwell and Phil Karlson.

Conrad acted in several different movie genres. He appeared in westerns (*Four Faces West, Lone Star*); historical drama (*Joan of Arc*); comedies (*The Milkman*); adventures (*The Sword of Monte Cristo, The Naked Jungle*); and he even appeared in a musical (*Desert Song*). But the films he made that are among his best come under that post-World War II genre known as Film Noir. Film Noir presents characters that are cynical and sexually aggressive. They are about people who are outcasts in life who want to get ahead even if it means resorting to murder. In many cases what the 'hero' wants is a woman—one who is sometimes unhappily married—and usually one who can't be trusted. Film Noir has its roots in the German Expressionistic cinema with stark black and white cinematography and shadows. Another notable trait of Film Noir is that you are under no illusion that there will be a happy ending. Even though Film Noir has much in common with German expressionism (and found much popular success in France) the film critic Roger Ebert believes that it is, "The most American film genre, because no society would have created a world so filled with doom, fate, fear and betrayal, unless it were essentially naïve and optimistic." Among the noir films that Conrad appeared in are: *The Killers, Body and Soul, Tension, Death on a Side Street, Cry Danger, The Racket* and *Cry of the Hunted*.

The Killers, Conrad's film debut, is better known for being the first film to star Burt Lancaster. It was based on a short story by Ernest Hemingway that was published in *Scribner's* Magazine in 1927.

The prologue is brilliant. Two men, Max (Conrad) and Al (Charles McGraw), drive into the small New Jersey town of Brentwood. They are on a mission to find Ole "Swede" Andreson (Lancaster), to kill him. They go to the local diner to dig up information on the whereabouts of "the Swede" and they aren't diplomatic about it. When told that they don't have any hard liquor to serve, Max derisively says, "This is a hot town." It certainly will be *that* night. There is another diner present, Nick Adams (who in the Hemingway short story is the narrator of the story—his presence in the film much diminished), who is taken to the kitchen by Al and tied up with the cook. "What's this all about?" asks the proprietor. They admit that they have come to town to kill the Swede.

"Why—What did he ever do to you?," asks the proprietor.

"Nothing," is the reply, they have never even met him.

"He's going to see us only once," Max says.

The proprietor finally convinces Max and Al that the Swede will not be in that night, "If he's not here by six-o'clock he won't be here at all."

They take his word for it, but without Max first telling him "you gotta lot of luck" because they didn't kill him. They leave and go elsewhere to find information about the whereabouts of the Swede. After being freed, Nick sneaks over to the Swede's boarding house to warn him about the two men who are out to kill him and find that the Swede is going to take his fate laying down—literally on his bed. "There's nothing I can do about it." He wants to die because he knows he will always be a hunted man if he runs. Nick leaves and the Killers arrive and shoot half a dozen bullets into the Swede. The rest of the story unfolds mostly in flashback explaining how the Swede got into this predicament.

Conrad recalled that he auditioned for producer Mark Hellinger, who took one look at Conrad and said, "That's the guy!" Conrad and McGraw make a irritable, sarcastic and truly frightening pair. They easily admit why they are in town because they know they have nothing to fear. If anybody gets in the way they will just blow them away—like the professionals they are. They then go about their job in a workman like way—it's just another job for them. In this they foreshadow the hit men in Quentin Tarantino's *Pulp Fiction*. They dominate the first ten minutes of the film.

The film was written by John Huston and Anthony Veiller, (but it's only Veiller who is credited on screen). Huston was also slated to direct the film but then ran into a collision course with the film's producer, Mark Hellinger, which forced Huston into leaving the project. In his place Hellinger brought in Robert Siodmak as director. Siodmak was born in the United States but spent much of his early life living in Germany where he made several interesting pictures including *People on Sunday* (1930) a film he co-directed with Edgar Ulmer (and was co-written by Billy Wilder and co-photographed by Fred Zinnemann.) He was heralded by the German cinema critics of the late twenties and early thirties as an impressive director but, with the rise of Hitler, the Jewish Siodmak fled to France, where he resumed his career before finding his way to Hollywood in the early forties.

In Hollywood Siodmak signed a contract with Universal where, in addition to such stylish horror films as *Son of Dracula* and *Cobra Woman*, he became adept at directing highly imaginative and taut film noirs with B-picture budgets like *Phantom Lady, Christmas Holiday, The Suspect* and *The Dark Mirror*. But it would be *The Killers* and his follow-up film *The Spiral Staircase* that would put Siodmak (for a time) on Hollywood's A-list of directors.

Hemingway was fond of the 1946 film version of *The Killers*—despite some liberties that were taken by the filmmakers. He later called it, "the only good picture ever made of a story of mine." According to Ava Gardner, who became a close friend of the writers, "Hemingway always considered *The Killers* the best of all the many films his work inspired and after Mark Hellinger…gave him a print of his own, he'd invariably pull out a projector and show it to guests at Finca Vigia, his place in Cuba."

The Killers opened to good reviews with Lancaster, particularly, stealing the show in his film debut. *The New York Times* credited Siodmak's "restrained direction" and praised Lancaster as "lanky and wistful," Gardner as "sultry and sardonic" and O'Brien as "cool and clipped." Neither the killers of the title (Conrad and McGraw) were singled out for praise though critic Bosley Crowther did write that "several other characters are sharply and colorfully played." *Life* magazine labeled *The Killers* "a minor masterpiece." *Life* went further than that in singling out Conrad and McGraw, "With time and typecasting, you may be able to view this pair of sinister citizens with the assurance of a customer who paid for his seat and expects to be intimidated in air conditioned comfort. As of the moment, however, the chances are that they will make you feel extremely nervous." Today *The Killers* is considered one of the best of the post-war noir films.

The film was also successful with audiences. When it opened at the Winter Garden Theater in New York City it earned a robust $65,456. Per Robert Siodmak biographer Joseph Greco, "Universal was certain to recoup its $875,000 in production costs and make a sizable profit as well. It was, indeed, a phenomenal success, a rarity for a film noir, since this kind of movie was generally unpopular with American audiences."

Conrad's next film gave him more to do. *Body and Soul* stars John Garfield in a boxing drama which is based on the life of Barney Ross, a middle weight champion who became a World War II hero and then, on discharge, turned to drugs and had to claw his way back to the top. Unfortunately censorship at this time didn't allow the film to deal realistically with drug addiction, so the hero (named Charlie Davis in the film) fights to get out of the New York ghetto he was born into and ends up getting involved with gangsters. (Several years later a biography of Barney Ross would be produced by United Artists, *Monkey on My Back*, starring Cameron Mitchell with Andre De Toth directing which was more honest about his addiction).

Conrad is cast as Quinn, Charlie's fight promoter. Also in the cast is Lili Palmer as Garfield's love interest, a Greenwich Village artist. Anne Revere plays his disapproving mother (who when Charlie tells her he wants to be a fighter, replies, 'Well fight for something—not for money'). The great black actor Canada Lee plays Ben Chaplin, a boxer in an arranged fight with Charlie. It is their relationship that becomes one of the central themes of the film.

Conrad's Quinn is a gruff promoter who, in his first introduction to Charlie, is chomping on his ever present cigar while playing pool. He is dismissive of Charlie, who had just won an amateur bout. A pal of Charlie's keeps building him up to Quinn, who seemingly ignores him while concentrating on his pool moves. He is actually testing Charlie—trying to see how much he really wants it. He dismisses Charlie by saying, "Tell your boy to get an honest job."

Soon thereafter, Charlie's father dies and Charlie needs to help support his mother. For a time Charlie is determined to please his mother and go to school and lead a respectable life. But fighting is in his blood and he soon turns to Quinn, who arranges a series of fights which establish Charlie as a champ. He is in it body and soul and that includes the dark underbelly of boxing. When the champ is expected to fight the black boxer Ben Chaplin (Lee), who suffers from a blood clot in the head and has been told by doctors not to fight again (but is forced to do so to pay back a $40,000 investment), it is Charlie who is kept in the dark about Chaplin's condition—not Quinn, who is fully aware of the possibility of tragic consequences.

Meanwhile Quinn also has to deal with the fact that his floozy of a girlfriend (played by Hazel Brooks) develops a thing for Charlie—or more likely his money. She tells Quinn, "Don't romance me, Quinn, You're getting old." To which Quinn replies, with one of the best lines in the movie, "You could use a paint job yourself."

Body and Soul was produced by Garfield, who chose Robert Rossen to direct. Rossen himself was a former boxer turned writer and director and was an inspired choice to make this gritty boxing film. As a screenwriter for Warner Brothers he had several superb pictures to his credit including *A Walk in the Sun* and *The Strange Love of Martha Ivers*. *Body and Soul* would be his second film as a director (his first was a top-notch film noir with Dick Powell titled *Johnny O'Clock*).

The film was photographed by the great cinematographer James Wong Howe who, when filming the boxing sequences, would get into the ring himself wearing a pair of roller skates while holding a 16 mm camera and being pushed into position to catch the drama of the boxing scenes, some of the most effective ever photographed in a film up to that time.

Garfield pushed himself ragged for this film and at one point along the way suffered a mild heart attack. When all was said and done the film turned out to be a huge box office and critical success. The *New York Times* in its review praised Garfield for giving a "rattling good performance." (He was nominated for a Best Actor Oscar). However, critic Bosley Crowther especially praised the work of Canada Lee, "who brings to focus the horrible pathos of the cruelly exploited prizefighter…the inclusion of this portrait is one of the finer things about this film." As for Conrad—Crowther wrote that he was "revolting as a punk," which means that he got across his characterization well.

Despite the success of the film the careers of director Rossen, Garfield, Lee and Anne Revere (cast as Garfield's mother) soon were affected by the Hollywood blacklist. They each were called before the House Un-American Activities Committee. Garfield maintained his innocence and refused to name names which led to his being blacklisted with similar action taken against Lee, Revere and Rossen. Rossen directed one more big film, *All the King's Men*, before being blacklisted. But by 1953, Rossen had relented and did name names which allowed him to work again, but he chose not to return to Hollywood on any permanent basis. He would, however, direct one of his best films, *The Hustler,* in 1961. As for Garfield and Canada Lee—they would both die of heart attacks within two weeks of each other in May of 1952.

II

Sorry Wrong Number had been a hugely successful radio production written by Lucille Fletcher and presented on *Suspense*. Agnes Moorehead had made a personal triumph in playing the role of an invalid who overhears her murder being plotted over a party line on the telephone. As the tension mounts and her attempts to get help are stymied, her hysteria gradually mounts as the murderers enter her house and eventually her bedroom where she will be murdered. It was highly successful as a half-hour radio production with the focus solely on the invalid, but when Paramount decided to make a film version in 1948—the story had to be expanded and that hurt the dramatic impact. Barbara Stanwyck, one of the finest of Hollywood's actresses, was selected to play the lead role of the invalid.

The script had to be expanded from 30-minutes to 90 minutes and many characters had to be created and a reason given for why the woman is murdered (this we don't know in the radio version). It turns out that her husband (Burt Lancaster) owes a gangster named Morono (William Conrad) an IOU for $200,000—and he wants it—NOW. The husband tells Morono that he doesn't have that kind of money. Morono tells him he could collect it on his invalid wife's life insurance money. That sets the murder in motion. Morono is yet another of Conrad's heavies and he was very effective in playing such roles and with his burly looks and deep voice he seems to have become, this early in his film career, typed in such parts. He was noticed again by *New York Times* critic Bosley Crowther:

"As the ear-bending lady, however, Miss Stanwyck does a quite elaborate job of working herself into a frenzy, as well as playing a nasty dame in the previous and self-aggrandizing phases of her life. And a painfully obtuse performance as her stubborn and frustrated spouse who is driven to criminal extremities is given by Burt Lancaster. Ed Begley is uncouth as

her father, Ann Richards is prim as a school friend and Harold Vermilyea, Wendell Corey and William Conrad are intriguing in lesser roles."

After playing the small role of a prosecutor in Victor Fleming's ambitious, but generally unsatisfying, version of *Joan of Arc*, Conrad made his first movie western as a sheriff who helps Pat Garrett (Charles Bickford) track a bank robber in *Four Faces West* (1948) which starred Joel McCrea.

Tension (1949) at MGM was the kind of small scale inexpensive film that new studio production chief Dore Schary loved to make. The budget was only $682,000 and the 'stars' were talented but not huge box office names—Richard Basehart, Audrey Totter, Barry Sullivan and Cyd Charisse. Conrad plays police Lt. Edgar ("Blackie") Gonsales, the partner to Barry Sullivan's Lt. Bonnabel.

Tension tells the story of a druggist (Basehart) who becomes enraged when his wife (Totter) leaves him for another man. He soon comes up with the idea of the double murder of his wife and the man she ran off with. In doing so he needs to establish an alibi and soon comes up with a new identity. Soon, however, he finds a beautiful and sympathetic woman (Charisse) entering his life which distracts him from his initial plans. But then his wife's lover is found murdered (and, even though the Basehart character is innocent) he becomes the prime suspect in the investigation conducted by Sullivan and Conrad.

The film is a good taut 92 minutes and has uniformly good performances including a wonderful scene of Sullivan and Conrad interviewing prime suspects Basehart and Totter in their apartment. At one point Totter says the murdered man "was full of laughs" to which Conrad smirks, "He's full of lead now." The film was directed by John Berry, a member of Orson Welles' theatrical Mercury Theater, who would soon leave for France in exile after being accused of being a Communist by the House Un-American Activities Committee (HUAC).

However, Bosley Crowther in the *New York Times* wrote that *Tension* was anything but, "it rambles from one thing to another in a most unsuspenseful way and ends with a shattering revelation which you can see coming a half-hour in advance." *Variety*, however, liked the movie. It's critic writing that *Tension*, "lived up to its title. It's a tight, tersely stated melodrama that holds the attention." The film ended up grossing about $776,000 worldwide at the box office losing $229,000.

After staying on at MGM to work with Clark Gable (as a hit man) in the gambling drama *Any Number Can Play* (1949) Conrad went to Universal for *One Way Street* (1950) which was directed by Argentine director Hugo Fregonese and set mainly in Mexico. The plot deals with a doctor (James Mason) to a mob boss who steals $200,000 from the boss (the always good Dan Duryea). For good measure he runs off to Mexico with the mob boss's moll (Marta Toren). Naturally they hunt them down. Conrad is cast (fifth billed) as 'Ollie' the mob bosses right hand man. Bosley Crowther in the *New York Times* thought the film itself was "obvious and not especially exciting," but did find Conrad and actor Basil Ruysdael (who played a priest) "competent."

The Milkman (1950) (also at Universal) at least got Conrad out of crime drama and into a comedy—not that he had much to do in this story of about a dim-witted son (Donald O'Connor) of a milk company owner who gets a job as a milkman for a rival company and whose partner is another milkman on the verge of retirement (played by Jimmy Durante). And even though this is a comedy (with four songs, no less) Conrad can't escape being cast as a gangster. The film was released in New York on New Year's Day, 1951, and Bosley Crowther in the *Times* wrote that "it is painful to greet the New Year with a bleakly unfavorable report," and it goes downhill from there.

Dial 1119 is another interesting little MGM film (total budget $473,000) that featured no stars but a talented cast of character actors and up and comers. Marshall Thompson (later the star of the 1960's adventure series *Daktari*) stars as an escaped mental patient searching for a "Dr. Faron" (Sam Levene) with the intentions of killing him. He searches for Faron at his work and at the apartment complex in which he lives. He can't find him but does find a bar ("The Oasis") located across the street from the apartments which offers him a good vantage point to keep a look out for the good doctor.

There are four other people in the bar including the bar tender, "Chuckles" (played by Conrad). Unfortunately for Chuckles (and

Conrad) he is an early victim of this homicidal maniac. He recognizes the man from a television report and is shot dead while trying to phone the police.

Speaking of television when this film was produced in the early 50's the movie studios were at war with television which was taking people out of movie theaters and decreasing studio profits. It's not surprising that the television in Chuckle's bar has bad reception and Chuckles disparages the programming, "the television set cost $1400 and it's more trouble than it's worth."

Dial 1119 (1950) is a nice compact (75-minute) melodrama and it's interesting seeing the usually clean-cut Thompson playing against type. It is also interesting as the first feature film to be directed by Gerald Mayer. Mayer was the nephew of MGM studio boss Louis B. Mayer—who obviously believed in nepotism (Gerald Mayer's father Jerry Mayer was studio manager and Jack Cummings, another nephew of Mayer's, proved a successful producer for the studio). Gerald Mayer directed relatively few films but did some gritty early 50's B-plus films at Metro that are including *Dial 1119, The Sellout, Inside Straight,* and *Holiday for Sinners.* After this brief run of films directed for MGM he spent much of the rest of his career directing for television—and would go on to direct Conrad again in the short-lived *Nero Wolfe* series of the early 1980's.

From MGM Conrad returned to RKO to work with Dick Powell and Rhonda Fleming in the film noir *Cry Danger* (1951). Powell plays a man who was sentenced to life in prison for a robbery and murder he always maintained he didn't commit. After five years a witness provides him an alibi and he's released. The problem is that (unbeknown to Powell) the alibi (played by Richard Erdman, in a sensational performance) is lying—he really does think that Powell is guilty—he just wants to share in the supposedly hidden loot. Meanwhile Powell seeks out the person who really framed him. He comes to believe that a bookie named Louis Castro (Conrad) is the man. As it happens Powell gets to beat Conrad silly a couple of times in the film and torture him with a game of Russian roulette for good measure.

The director of *Cry Danger* is Robert Parrish who previously was a well-respected film editor (which included editing *Body and Soul*, for which he won an Academy Award). His directing career isn't as distinguished as his editing career but he did make a few interesting films along the way including the very gritty *The Mob* (1951) and *Saddle the Wind* (1957) a western that was written by Rod Serling and starred Robert Taylor and John Cassavetes. Incidentally the cinematographer for *Cry Danger* is Joseph F. Biroc, who photographed such diverse pictures as *It's a Wonderful Life, Bye Bye Birdie, Blazing Saddles* and *Airplane*. He won an Oscar for his camera work on *The Towering Inferno*. Conrad would use him as the director of photography on his 1957 western *The Ride Back*.

Cry Danger got some good reviews. Bosley Crowther in the *New York Times* wrote, "Looking for excitement and suspense? And perhaps a few laughs, too? Then accept this recommendation to a very tidy package of fictional extravagance called 'Cry Danger.'" Crowther congratulated Conrad on playing "the heavy with unctuous delight." *Variety* said the film had "all the ingredients for a suspenseful melodrama."

After appearing in a swashbuckler at Twentieth Century-Fox, *The Sword of Monte Cristo* (1951), Conrad moved back to RKO for *The Racket* (1951). *The Racket* was based on a 1920's stage play (which had starred Edward G. Robinson) and a silent film of the same name. The film stars three other actors who had strong ties to film noir—Robert Ryan, Robert Mitchum and Lizabeth Scott (after originally flirting with casting Shelley Winters).

Directed by John Cromwell (with uncredited help by a roster including Nicholas Ray, Tay Garnett and Mel Ferrer) it is the story of a mobster (Ryan) who has bought protection from government officials and the police in the large (unnamed) American city he controls. There is one cop (Mitchum) who is beyond his control, however. Mitchum's job isn't helped by the crooked police detective (Conrad) who is on the mobster's payroll and attempts to thwart every step he takes. Among the lead characters Ryan the crook is constantly on edge, while (as usual) Mitchum, the honest cop, is laid-back and world weary—the two crackle in their scenes together.

Of course the censors looked at the script with a fine tooth comb and found that the screenplay reached "a new low in crime screen stories"—meaning too violent and some of the characters too unsavory. For instance, in the original story, the Lizabeth Scott character (Irene) is clearly a prostitute. In the sanitized script she is a legitimate singer. Also the Breen Office wanted the ending to make clear that the character Conrad plays "Turk" gets his comeuppance at the end for killing the Ryan character—in the original script it seemed unclear what would happen to Turk.

The Racket premiered in New York in December, 1951 was panned by Bosley Crowther's in his *New York Times* review, "the only things worthy of notice about this modernized repeat of an old show are the timeliness of its general topic and the predestined clash of its stars." The direction by Cromwell was called "dismally uninspired" and the performances of Mitchum and Ryan are described as "exchanges of clichés." Perhaps mercifully Conrad is not mentioned in the review. *Variety* is more positive stating that "the old play has been handled to emphasize clear-cut action and suspense and the casting is right to stress and rough and ready toughness of the script." The performances of such supporting players as William Tallman (as a rookie cop), Ray Collins and Conrad are called, "Strong." Overall the film has more of the feel of the 1920's (when it was initially produced on the stage) than the early 50's but has enough zest and good performances to keep one interested.

Conrad next returned to MGM to play opposite Clark Gable, Ava Gardner, Broderick Crawford and, in his final film, Lionel Barrymore (as ex-president Andrew Jackson) in the western *Lone Star* (1952). The plot has Jackson sending Gable to Texas to make sure that Texans will not enter into annexation with Mexico—meanwhile finding love with Gardner and a rival in a wealthy rancher played by Crawford. Conrad has fun as a wily Frenchman in only a couple of scenes, but he makes them count. *Lone Star* is a fun, non-consequential western that made a mint for MGM (with profits of $900,000).

Two months after the premiere of *Lone Star* Conrad would make his debut in another western which would cause a sensation first on radio and then television—*Gunsmoke*. Conrad would begin a nine-year run in his most iconic radio role—U.S. Marshal Matt Dillon.

CHAPTER THREE
GUNSMOKE
1952-1955

On April 26, 1952 on CBS radio the following introduction was made to a brand new western series:

"Around Dodge City and in the territory on West, there's just one way to handle the killers and the spoilers, and that's with a U.S. Marshal and the smell of Gunsmoke! **Gunsmoke** *starring William Conrad. The transcribed story of the violence that moved West with young America, and the story of a man who moved with it."*

Then came the gruff baritone voice of Matt Dillon:

"I'm that man. Matt Dillon, United States Marshal, the first man they look for, and the last they want to meet. It's a chancy job, and it makes a man watchful, and a little lonely."

This would be the introduction to one of the most ground breaking series in all of radio—made all the more exceptional because it debuted in the waning years of radio drama—a medium done in by television. Despite this *Gunsmoke* made its mark on radio and would run for nine consecutive years with the same cast. The show transitioned to television in 1955, but the radio version was still well regarded and highly rated and the show successfully pushed on for nearly six more years despite the growing popularity of the television series. This has a great deal to do with the first rate cast selected to play the main characters as well as the ensemble stock company of well-regarded radio actors who performed year in and year out. But perhaps more than that was the integrity and realism of the scripts which caught the imagination of the public and made them think they were actually transported seventy-five years back to the frontier state of Kansas and Dodge City.

Gunsmoke became the brain child of Norman Macdonnell and John Meston who worked well together on the suspense series *Escape!* with Meston writing many of the episodes and Macdonnell directing. The two men were interested in developing a new kind of western series—an adult western—to counter such shows as *The Lone Ranger, Hopalong Cassidy, Roy Rogers* and *Gene Autry* which, in many respects, drew much of their audiences from children.

Macdonnell and Meston had certainly experimented with the adult western format in the past. For *Escape* Meston wrote a script called "Wild Jack Rhett" in which a gunfighter tames a wild west town and starred radio veteran John Dehner, who would later be one of the most frequently used of the *Gunsmoke* stock company. The episode included ample amounts of violence and bloodshed.

At another point the Macdonnell-Meston team worked on a radio series called *Romance* where in 1951 Meston wrote an episode titled "Pagosa" (produced by Macdonnell) which would have many of the ingredients that the later *Gunsmoke* would offer in style and structure as well as having William Conrad as the star (with Georgia Ellis, who would later play Miss Kitty).

As it turned out CBS was also on the lookout for a new 'adult' western series. William S. Paley, the chairman of the board of CBS, was a fan of the private eye program *The Adventures of Philip Marlowe* and suggested to a network executive that CBS develop a "Philip Marlow of the early west" type of show. The executive went to Harry Ackerman, the vice president in charge of programming for CBS radio on the West Coast, to develop this idea. "I called into action all the creative people," Ackerman later said. One of the things that Ackerman and his team did was come up with a title—"Gunsmoke." "It just popped into my head one day," Ackerman later maintained.

At this point Macdonnell and Meston came to CBS with their idea of doing an adult western and learned that the network was actively pursuing this. In fact, the network had already produced two pilots for such a series. On June 11, 1949 they taped a program which featured an actor named Rye Billsbury as "Mark" Dillon in

Mark Dillon Goes to Gouge Eye, and later the idea was re-recorded with Howard Culver as Dillon on July 15, 1949. Neither pilot seemed to satisfy the network.

Suddenly, and out of the blue, the network had an opening on its Saturday night schedule and needed a replacement series—within a week! Ackerman asked Macdonnell to produce and direct the program with the proviso that the series be named *Gunsmoke*—and that the hero be named Mark Dillon. In that week Macdonnell had to come up with a script, cast it and develop the musical theme. Interestingly Meston was not given the assignment of writing the script, but he would be the show's script editor (and ultimately its most prolific writer) and his scripts for "Pagosa" and "Wild Jack Rhett" were used as the framework. "We got Walter Brown Newman to come in, one of the better writers in town," Macdonnell later recalled. "We gave him an acetate disk of 'Pagosa' and 'Wild Jack Rhett' and said, 'This is the style, this is the color, this is the feel.' We laid out no other guidelines except that we felt Dillon should be written, be the kind of character he was, and sent Walter away…That was on a Monday." Newman was told to go for authenticity when writing his story—something that Meston, as story editor, and later as the head writer would always insist on.

Later, in an interview with Chris Lembesis, William Conrad would talk about the research which went into *Gunsmoke* that made it such an authentic show:

"Of course, there was no Matt Dillon. That was a figment of the writer's imagination. But you'd get a lot of fight from a lot of people who will tell you that they know there was. It's pretty funny. I've had several arguments with people about it who will say that they know for a fact that their grandfather was related to him. John Meston and Norman Macdonnell were very meticulous in seeing that everything was as authentic as they could possibly make it…"

As Newman got down to work Meston gave him one more bit of information—the last name of the hero—Dillon—was fine, but he felt that another first name was warranted. Meston believed that "Mark" was too contemporary of a name and felt it out of place in the 1870's. He instead suggested "Matt" and so the character of

Marshal Matt Dillon was born.

According to MacDonnell, Newman was given additional instructions regarding the script, "We made a list of every western cliché and determined to avoid them at any cost—even our jobs," Macdonnell said in a 1957 interview. "For instance, the devotion of a cowboy to his horse. That's a lot of bunk. The two things a real cowboy loves best are his saddle and hat." Secondly, "We never have action for action sake."

Next MacDonnell had to get somebody working right away on the theme music for the show—something he felt would be an important ingredient in defining the series. Composer Rex Koury was approached. Koury had been involved with composing music for many CBS radio shows over the years. Later he became the musical director at ABC on the West Coast.

Koury later said that he had never written a western theme before but that he was "game for anything." The forty-year old composer met with Macdonnell who gave him his marching orders in that he wanted something that suggested "a big, wide, open sound to it... the open spaces." Koury then asked to see the script and was astounded to learn that the script was not yet completed and that he only had about six days to get this theme written. "(It)...was written under rather frantic circumstances because I had gone to bed the night before...feeling that I knew pretty much what I wanted, and figuring I could do it rather quickly in the morning...At 8 O'clock in the morning I'm in the middle of shaving and I suddenly realize we haven't written the theme. So I grabbed a magazine, a piece of manuscript, and a pencil, and sat down in the most convenient spot (a toilet?) and that is where the *Gunsmoke* theme was actually composed."

When the theme was played for Macdonnell the producer was more than pleased. Macdonnell made arrangements for an 18-piece orchestra to record it. The actual title of the Gunsmoke theme is "Old Trails" and it suited the series to a tee, and later also became the theme of the Gunsmoke television series as well. The lyrics, written by Glenn Spencer, were never used on the radio or television show, but were used in a song recorded by Tex Ritter in 1955:

"Gunsmoke trail; oh tell me of days gone by, tho' alone you still wind your way. Are the ghostly horsemen riding, as they speed the eastern mail? It's up to you see them through the old trail.... Gunsmoke traveler, no traveler to care where you go. Sands of time are hiding your way. Bet if heaven ever let you, you could tell a rugged tale. That's why I hate to see you fade old trail...."

II

While all of this was going on, MacDonnell and Meston were working on the casting of the show. First and foremost would be the casting of Marshal Matt Dillon. "As I thought of Dillon first," Meston later said, "and as I still do, he's probably red-haired—if he has any hair at all. He'd be handsome if he had received better treatment, but his rough way of living and his enemies have given him a beat up look." For his part Macdonnell didn't think that Dillon was completely sane. "Frontier marshals were hired for only one reason—they were tough enough to frighten the inhabitants and no city had any meaner citizens that the old Dodge City. No wholly sane man would voluntarily take a job like that," Macdonnell explained. Macdonnell would also later say that Dillon was "a lonely, sad, tragic man...a quiet, unhappy confused Marshal; these days we'd send him to an analyst."

When it came to casting Dillon Macdonnell didn't want a 'cowboy' type of accent he actually wanted somebody who sounded a little like Orson Welles. Several actors were auditioned for the role among them Raymond Burr. The man who finally got the part, William Conrad, was among the last auditioned. "They auditioned everybody in town, and as a last resort, they called me and said, 'Okay, we give up. Come on in.' And I went in and read about two lines and they said, 'Okay, thank you.' And I walked out. Then the next day they called me and said, 'You have the job.'"

Of course Conrad is being typically facetious. Macdonnell and Meston both knew Conrad well and worked with him many times and had the highest regard for his talent. Meston was more enthusiastic than Macdonnell, however—but Macdonnell wasn't against Conrad.

Those who were most against the casting of William Conrad were the executives at CBS radio who wanted a big name to star in the show. They knew of Conrad as a top-notch character actor on radio but hardly a house hold name and—when he was seen on screen—it was mostly in villainous roles rather than as a hero. As the deadline was approaching Macdonnell decided to go with the known quantity—Bill Conrad. They knew he was a total professional and had one of the best voices in radio. George Walsh, who was the announcer on the radio *Gunsmoke* (and would later serve in the same capacity for a time with the television show) later said, "Conrad had a great ability in establishing character in our mind, and could be tough, hard, or sentimental."

Parley Baer, another top notch radio voice, who was well known to both Macdonnell and Meston, was chosen to play Matt Dillon's assistant—not really deputy—a character that seemed a bit dim and had a problem at times with telling the whole truth, but was totally devoted to Matt Dillon. The initial script didn't have a name for this assistant who was identified just as 'townsman.' This didn't make sense to Conrad. "I just can't say 'Hey, Townsman, Come here.' Call him Chester or something." The name struck a chord and was incorporated for the character.

Baer acknowledges that the show certainly offered plenty of action and blood shed, but he maintains that it also had its quiet moments. "It was a time of shooting and fighting," Baer told Leonard Maltin, "but conversations were not like that at that time. You figure that everything was quietly conceived and modulated out of an office or around the campfire. People lose sight of the fact that in those times; quiet was their safety, really, because even the rustle of clothing could be detected in the quiet prairie by sharp ears. That was one of the things that I think we tried to portray, that it was a time of underplay. I think we maybe overdid it at times, because it was a technique that worked."

Radio and stage veteran Howard McNear was cast as the next pivotal character— the part of Dodge City's doctor. McNear would go on to be remembered by all as the life of the *Gunsmoke* cast for his sweet natured personality. But the doctor that McNear would portray was hardly a sunny character. He was a man who came across as part vulture and part ghoul—with a love of autopsies. He also had a bit of a drinking problem. Again when it came to giving a name to "Doc" it was Bill Conrad to the rescue. Conrad knew and loved the macabre characters created by illustrator Charles Addams, which inspired the *New Yorker* cartoons and later television series *The Addams Family*, so Doc became Dr. Charles Addams on the radio show. The name fit McNear's interpretation of Doc, "because Howard always played him as though he could anticipate the taste of blood," recalled Parley Baer.

The character of Kitty Russell, the saloon working girlfriend of Matt Dillon, was not yet established in the first couple of radio shows, but she would turn up in the third episode of the series. The actress who would play her on radio, Georgia Ellis, does have a part in the first episode however, playing an old flame of Dillon's. Early on the radio Kitty moved from saloon to saloon in Dodge City and was pretty much a working girl—though one with a heart of gold. In an interview with *Time* Magazine in 1953 Macdonnell put it this way, "Kitty is just someone Matt has to visit every once in a while. We never say it, but Kitty is a prostitute, plain and simple." Amanda Blake, who would be television's Miss Kitty, would recall that Georgia Ellis had a wonderful "whiskey soaked" voice that she felt was perfect for Kitty. As for the relationship between Matt and Kitty— Ellis had this to say:

"(They) were very compatible. Yes they were lovers—the best kind. They really, truly understood one another. So there wasn't need for too much talk. I don't think there was any forgiveness to be done because I don't think Kitty was available to anybody else but Matt. Undoubtedly she had wild dreams from time to time, which she realized were completely unrealistic. But Matt could never be happy doing anything other than what he was doing, and she knew she would never be happy with Matt if he were not happy. So she was resigned to serving booze and saying, 'Be careful, Matt.' She had nothing to go back to wherever she came from. She was stuck in Dodge City and made a lot of it."

With the cast selected, theme music composed, and the first script delivered *Gunsmoke* debuted on Saturday night April 26, 1952 with an episode titled **Billy the Kid**. The story has Chester telling Matt that he has locked up a runaway—a twelve year old kid named Billy Bonny. Matt seems to take a shine to the kid (who he calls Bud) who seems to hero worship Dillon. At one point Billy proudly tells

Matt that one day he will be a famous gunfighter who will get a "bunch of notches" on his gun. "When I'm famous you can tell people you helped to get me started," young Billy tells Matt.

There is a parallel story running as well. A man is killed (thought to have been shot dead) and a mob wants to lynch the man they think murdered him. However, Doc tells Matt that the man didn't die of a gunshot wound, but actually from a stab wound caused from a Barlow knife. Meanwhile the kid's mother arrives to pick him up, but the boy has run away again. "Truth is, he's a wild one," she tells Matt. She goes on to explain that he ran away because she wouldn't buy him a gun—instead she gave the boy a Barlow knife. It was a simple yet compelling story and the radio newspaper reviewers were ecstatic about it as were radio listeners who bombarded CBS with letters praising the show. The show had what MacDonnell and Meston were driving at—honesty and authenticity.

Conrad thought the show had "realism" and, of the character he would play for the next nine years, Conrad felt that Dillon was:

"Neither a hero nor a villain, just a human being. The best of us are sometimes ashamed of our thoughts, and there are times when the worst of us can be proud of our deeds. Matt Dillon is no different. He is a law-enforcement officer who doesn't like killing. He hates the thought of bloodshed. He's underpaid (and) never liked the job, but knows it has to be done. At times he's wanted to quit—has quit. But like most people who know the difference between right and wrong—and recognizing that justice could be done by him, probably better than by anyone else available—he has always come back to his responsibility. Matt Dillon isn't perfect, but he's willing to try."

Macdonnell came to see Bill Conrad and Matt Dillon as a "study in contrast":

"Bill is one of the warmest people I've ever known, but he covers it up with a good deal of gruffness and sometimes bravado. He would rather die than let you know he's a sentimentalist. Matt's this way, too—he never shows sentimentality, except by indirection. When you first look at Bill, wearing his garden blue jeans and sporting a three day growth of beard, he looks rugged, and not exactly the picture of the

Shakespearean student he really is. Bill's interests are as varied as a desert sunset. Intellectually, Bill enjoys discussing Mozart's music, on the one hand, but isn't above playing the latest Billy May record and saying, 'Isn't that an interesting arrangement.' On the other hand, Bill skis as swiftly as a bullet, hunts and fishes as a hobby. Given a few free minutes in the script, we'll have Matt ride down to the Arkansas River to snare himself a mess of catfish—Matt loves catfish stew. But, while it's true that Bill likes the simple pleasures too, he himself is quite a gourmet."

Parley Baer, who gained great popularity as Chester, thought that there was a, "tremendously pathetic quality to Dillon...Dillon trusted Chester, Doc and Kitty as much as he dared to trust anyone... Everybody had to be honest with Dillon, because in so far as human beings are concerned, I think probably of the whole cast, Dillon was the one who was most completely honest in his dealings with lawbreakers...with the town...with everyday associates." It was Conrad's genius as a radio actor that he could play this gruff, no nonsense man with so much integrity and yet make him so completely human.

Soundman Ray Kemper, who helped make *Gunsmoke* so real to millions of radio listeners thru his sound effects, often with co-sound man Tom Hanley, maintains to this day that "Bill Conrad created the role of Matt Dillon, and in my opinion his interpretation of the U.S. Marshal was never matched." Kemper credits the overall success of the show to producer Norman Macdonnell, "Norm was very bright. He knew instinctively what he wanted to do with the show and how he wanted to present the characters. He was sharp—and a tremendous director and an all-round good guy."

Kemper is equally perceptive about the other cast members. "Parley Baer created Chester Proudfoot almost immediately as you heard it throughout the series. He was a consummate actor, and a fine man." Baer would later describe Chester as a "dependable non-thinker" and gave an example, "If we had a hypothetical case with nine desperadoes holed up, and Matt Dillon had said, 'Chester you watch the back door, and as they come out you plug number one, three, five and seven,' Chester would have said, 'Yessir.' And as they came out he would have said, 'One,' Bang! He'd have let two go, and he'd have gotten three, and he'd let four go and he'd gotten five.

Even though two and four were bearing down on him, he would have said, 'Mister Dillon said to shoot them others, so thems the ones I'm gonna shoot.'" Herb Ellis, who played various roles over the years on *Gunsmoke*, recalls that Parley Baer, "brought a unique quality to every character he played."

Conrad later contrasted the radio Chester with the TV Chester (played by the young Dennis Weaver), "We felt that he was always a middle-aged man who was not too bright...always getting into jams, and Matt was always saving him...We also felt that because of the name Proudfoot that he had a little Indian blood in him." (In the TV *Gunsmoke* Chester's last name is Goode, so that there wouldn't be any indication of Indian blood and, unlike the radio Chester, the TV Chester had a pronounced limp).

Of Georgia Ellis, Ray Kemper says she "recognized immediately that Kitty Russell was a prostitute and played the part accordingly, without being too obvious." (This is a major difference from the TV Kitty, who while a saloon gal who knows the score, isn't portrayed as a prostitute). As for Ellis herself she would simply call Kitty, "(a) very generous, loving human being. She adored the men in her life, Matt predominately, and then Chester and Doc...They (Matt and Kitty) were lovers. The best kind, because they truly understood one another, so there wasn't need for too much talk..." Of Georgia Ellis, Conrad would later say that she was a "lovely girl who was very, very good in the part. She had a sultry voice and was a great sex symbol in Dodge City."

Ray Kemper was, like all the cast and crew, clearly drawn to Howard McNear. "Howard...seemed to know instinctively the type of character needed for Doc Addams, and did it beautifully," Kemper recalled. "Bill, Parley and Georgia tagged Howie with the nickname of 'The Bird' because of his habit of getting closer and closer to anyone he was talking to and cocking his head to one side as he spoke. He would look right in your eyes and speak with great intensity. Some of what he said was a little sad, as when he told the story of accidentally flushing his canary down the toilet, but as he told it, he would look at you carefully to see what your reaction was going to be. Most people couldn't contain themselves and would break out laughing. Maybe that's why they dubbed him 'The Bird'. He told that story to anyone who would listen."

Of Howard McNear (who would become best known to television audiences for his years as Floyd the Barber on *The Andy Griffith Show*) Conrad would say, "In all the years that I've been in the business I don't think I have ever worked with a more talented man, nor have I worked with a nicer human being. Everybody who met Howard, no matter under what condition loved him. That's all you could do with Howard. He was a zany, wonderful, wild, crazy, beautiful human being." Herb Ellis echoes Conrad in saying that McNear, "was a complete joy to work with and know. He was a wonderful human being who had a great sense of humor. Everybody who knew Howard adored him."

"Howard was a thoroughly conscientious man," Parley Baer later recalled. "Prepared at all times. I've never known him to give a bad performance and I worked with him on many shows besides *Gunsmoke*. I don't know anyone who was so fondly remembered in our profession than Howard."

As an ensemble Kemper recalls that "they were all very fond of one another. I never heard a cross word spoken on those Saturday's by anyone." Parley Baer told Chuck Schaden, "*Gunsmoke* became a labor of love for all of us. We were a pretty intact group. We had the same director, same assistant director, same script girl, same engineer, same sound crew. Apart from the four regulars, there probably weren't more than twenty, twenty-five people used. It formed a tight nucleus."

Conrad would always give credit for a lot of the success of *Gunsmoke* to its sound men, Ray Kemper and Tom Hanley. "They took complete and deliberate time in setting up the sound effects, which was probably one of the secrets of show's success," Conrad told Chris Lembesis. Still later Conrad said of the sound men, "They're artists…you narrate watching what they're doing, and you're synched." Ray Kemper later described his work on developing that authentic sound on Gunsmoke to this writer:

"Tom Hanley and I were assigned as the sound effects men, although if memory serves me correctly, Clark Casey and Dave Light did the first show or two…Norman Macdonnell had worked with Tommy and me on other shows—Suspense, Romance, Escape…and he had requested us for his new show. Tom and I quickly realized that Gunsmoke was a

most unusual program. Norm wanted great realism and insisted on sound effects being an integral part of that. It was a challenge for Tommy and me and one we thoroughly enjoyed. One thing that bothered Norm immensely were the gunshots. In those days most sound men used 22 or 38 caliber revolvers filled with blanks to do a show. One would think that would be good, but every sound leaving the studio went through a limiter in Master Control and the limiter would allow the beginning of a gunshot to get through the system, then it would clip it off until the sound had been reduced to an acceptable level. The result on the air was a sound that resembled a weak cork-pop. So Tom Hanley and I gathered all the guns we could get our hands on.. We took a lot of blank ammo and brought some live rounds also. We then loaded all this in our car, along with a tape machine and headed out to the desert to an area known as Bouquet Canyon, where it was legal to shoot live ammo. Unfortunately when we returned to the studio and listened to the recorded sounds we were very disappointed. They all lacked the reverberation that gives a gunshot such a sound of authority.

We remembered that Bill Conrad had a home in the Laurel Canyon area, and to make a long story short, we wound up there with our guns and our tape machine. It was perfect—Bill's home was backed by hills that formed a small amphitheater and one gunshot proved that the reverberation was exactly what we wanted. We called the police department to get an okay to discharge fire arms loaded with blanks and they said if we cleared it with the neighbors, it was okay with them.

Back at the studio we knew we had what we wanted so we dubbed all the gunshot sounds onto MacKenzie tape cartridges, placed cue marks at the beginning of each shot or series of shots and took them to the next Gunsmoke rehearsal. We had the engineer, Bob Chadwick, feed the output of the MacKenzie tape machine directly into a line of his console, set the fader at a fixed level and threatened him with death if he sent the output through a limiter. When the shots were first heard by Norm Macdonnell in the booth, he jumped up and did a tap-dance on the console (a slight exaggeration). That's how the Gunsmoke gunshots were born and that's how they remained for the rest of the series."

It wasn't only the sound of the gunshots that made the show

seem more authentic than many other radio westerns—or most other radio shows period. "When Dillon and Chester rode the plains, the listener heard the faraway prairie wind and the dry squeak of Matt's pants against saddle leather," radio historian John Dunning wrote. "When Dillon opened the jail door, the listener heard every key drop on the ring. Dillon's spurs rang out with a dull clink-clink, missing occasionally, and the hollow boardwalk echoed dully as the nails creaked in the worn wood around them. Buckboards passed, and the listener heard extraneous dialogue in the background, just above the muted shouts of kids playing an alley. He heard noises from the next block too, where the inevitable dog was barking." Bill Ryan, who in the early fifties worked at a small CBS radio station, recalls, "I'll never forget the sound of Marshal Dillon's spurs as he strode across a plank floor after midnight."

Another ingredient in the success of the radio version of *Gunsmoke* was its stock company of top-notch radio actors who played the various guest voices each week. They were predominately west coast actors and included such fine performers as Lawrence Dobkin, John Dehner, Vic Perrin, Sam Edwards, Jack Kruschen, Virginia Gregg, Jeanette Nolan, Harry Bartell, Helen Kleeb, Virginia Christie, Joseph Kearns and Herb Ellis—many of whom had previously worked for Macdonnell on *Escape*.

John Dehner auditioned for the role of Matt Dillon (and later went on to play Paladin on radio's *Have Gun Will Travel*) recalls, "the atmosphere surrounding the radio show was, so warm and friendly you couldn't imagine. If ever there was a family, this was it. I remember them all with great affection."

Harry Bartell was another strong radio actor who appeared many times on *Gunsmoke*— including the very first episode "Billy the Kid"—where he played the newspaper editor. Of his roles on *Gunsmoke* Bartell recalled, "I played all kinds of things. I played heavies. I played goodies...I had a wider variety of characters on there than I can ever recall having done." Later (along with his good friend Vic Perrin) Bartell would even write a few *Gunsmoke* scripts. Bartell would later say that *Gunsmoke* "had an integrity which few others did." Bartell worked on both the radio and TV versions of *Gunsmoke* and says, "I believe that the radio characters were a great deal more legitimate to the time they portrayed...I believe there was more honesty in the radio show…"

If *Gunsmoke* needed a voice to play a teenager or young man they would invariably turn to Sam Edwards who recalls appearing on 60-70 percent of *Gunsmoke* episodes. Edwards is especially complimentary of William Conrad's portrayal of Matt Dillon, "Matt Dillon was first of all a human being, with human virtues and human faults," Edwards later said. "Bill Conrad's portrayal of Dillon was so believable that I could have imaged his having been a real Marshal Dillon of the era." Meston's writing also impressed Edwards, "His dialogue was so natural and easy to read the cast could read through a script one time and be ready to go on the air. In fact, many times I believe the cast could have gone on the air without a dialogue rehearsal."

Helen Kleeb (television viewers would best know her as Miss Mamie Baldwin on *The Waltons*) who played parts as varied as Indian girls, prairie women, saloon girls and towns women once said that, "Perhaps working on *Gunsmoke* was unique in that there was camaraderie in the cast that was exceptional, a relaxed atmosphere and energy that was remarkable. It was also fun."

Herb Ellis believes that "what made *Gunsmoke* such an important series on radio is the writing—you have to go to that immediately. The scripts had a different feel—the characters were deftly written and the themes were more mature than had been presented on western radio shows prior to *Gunsmoke*…they dealt with problems of the human race that people in the twentieth century could relate to like racism and war. Then you had brilliant characterizations by the actors—Bill, Parley, Howard, and Georgia—which were so true and honest."

III

Honesty and truth is what Macdonnell and Meston tried to convey with *Gunsmoke* and they were largely successful. John Meston was the most prolific script writer for the show (penning 183 radio episodes), but during the first season there were several different writers with Meston acting as the show's script editor. Yet it was Meston who captured the heart of the show. "He is a great bleeder," William Conrad would later say of Meston. "He bleeds for everybody, and perhaps that is the key to the success of the show…that it is so filled with the repulsion of man's inhumanity to man, seasoned and highlighted by red streaks of magnificent violence…and yet, the final total compassion…You add those up and they spell 'Mother.'"

Parley Baer would call Meston, "a thorough technician and writer of great integrity and accuracy." Soundman Ray Kemper recalls Meston as "short on words. He was not one who engaged in idle chit-chat. Something that would take most people three or four paragraphs to say would be said by John in one brief sentence. He was an expert at verbal editing. He was also a good listener, and had a talent for making a person talking to him feel as if he was saying something very important. John would occasionally come into the studio and sit quietly, observing and listening to the rehearsal, and he always had a kind word for Tommy (Hanley) and me."

The first script that was credited to Meston was an episode titled **"Carmen"** which was broadcast on May 31, 1952. "Carmen" involves a beautiful woman who uses her sex appeal in an attempt to lure Matt out of town to meet his death. Other significant episodes written by Meston early on include **"Never Pester Chester"** (7/5/52) in which Matt charges Chester with quieting down two seemingly rowdy, drunken cowboys who wind up nearly killing him—and reveals Matt's guilt for having allowed this to happen. **"The Lynching"** (8/16/52) explores the illegal hanging of an innocent man. **"Home Surgery"** (9/13/52) is one of the best of the first season episodes. A young girl approaches Matt Dillon out on the prairie miles from any town and tells him that her father is very sick. Matt rides out to find the critically ill man who is suffering from gangrene of the leg. If there is any chance of saving the man Matt has to amputate the leg—something that Matt has never done before. In true Meston/*Gunsmoke* style the man ends up dying anyway—with *Gunsmoke* there is never any guarantee of a happy ending. **"Overland Express"** (10/31/52) demonstrates that not all bad men are thoroughly wicked when Matt and Chester, forced to ride a stagecoach full of passengers with a prisoner, face an attack by murderous bandits—the prisoner takes up arms to help the lawmen. **"Word of Honor"** (1/10/53) gives Doc (Howard McNear) a nice showcase when he is called out to help save the life of a young kidnap victim who was shot in the back trying to escape. Doc is unable to save the young man but is released when he gives his "word of honor" to the killers that he will not reveal their identities—and Doc intends to keep his word. **Hickock** (7/25/53), like the first episode, involves a real-life historical western figure—in this case Wild Bill Hickock, who is now a sheriff who informs Matt by telegram not to allow two gunmen to leave Dodge until he arrives—in a few days—trouble is Matt finds it increasingly difficult to keep the two men from leaving when he has no cause to arrest them. "**Gone Straight**" (8/22/53) explores the quandary that Matt finds himself when he discovers that one of the most steadfast citizens of Dodge, the man responsible for a new school house, is actually a cold blooded murderer.

In addition to Meston some of the other first year writers include Herb Purdum, Les Crutchfield and Antony Ellis. Les Crutchfield contributed 81 scripts to *Gunsmoke*. Crutchfield, like Meston, was a valuable member of the team of McDonnell's *Escape* and *Romance* shows. In contrasting the *Gunsmoke* scripts of John Meston and Les Crutchfield, Macdonnell would say, "Perhaps Les did more of the light or comedy shows than John Meston." This is true, but his scripts were by no means exclusively comedic or light in nature. Among the Crutchfield output during the first season was "**Jaliscoe**" (5/10/52) which introduced the character of Kitty. **Jailbait Janet** (6/14/52) involved a young girl (played by Sammie Hill) who is captured by Matt, along with her father and brother, for robbing a train in which a man was killed. **Drop Dead** (9/20/52) explores greed when a man is unable to get his tired and dying cattle water because a rancher has a pond fenced in so that nobody can use it except himself. **Paid Killer** (1/17/53) deals with an especially determined assassin who is being paid $5000 in gold to kill Matt. Crutchfield's "**Cavalcade**" (1/31/53) is an especially interesting story because it gives the background of Doc Addams, whose real name is Calvin Moore, who had killed a wealthy man seventeen years earlier in a duel over a young woman—and had come to Dodge and changed his identity—and now his past is catching up with him. "**Cyclone**" (3/14/53) tells the story of Matt's suspicions being aroused when a ranch foreman tells him that the Cyclone Ranch has been sold—and the man who built up that ranch had suddenly left town.

Antony Ellis only wrote 8 episodes of *Gunsmoke* and all of them during the shows first season, but some of them are among the best produced. Ellis, at the time, was married to Georgia Ellis, who played

Kitty, and it is only natural that a couple of his scripts would better explore her character than some of the other early episodes did (though later on a female writer for the show, Marion Clark, would write scripts that gave the female perspective better than anybody and many of them were centered around Kitty).

The first script that Ellis contributed was titled **"The Ride Back"** (6/28/52) which was a two-character play centered on Matt and the prisoner (Larry Dobkins) he is taking back to Dodge. It's a long ride and the prisoner tests Matt all along the way—eventually earning the lawman's grudging admiration. Conrad so liked this particular show that in 1957 he produced a film based on the radio script which was also written by Antony Ellis. **"Kitty"** (11/29/52) is one of the best early showcases for Miss Kitty and explores the relationship between Kitty and Matt. Matt invites Kitty to a town social and Kitty at first refuses because she doesn't want Matt's good name to be muddied because he is associating with her. Finally she relents and they attend together, but when some of the towns people insult her—Matt steps up to defend her. **"Christmas Story"** (12/20/52) tells the story of Matt's horse breaking its leg and having to be put down forty-miles outside of Dodge. It's a long walk, but along the way Matt meets up with a man whose horse has seen better days and offers Matt the opportunity to ride with him.

Herb Purdum contributed 5 *Gunsmoke* scripts in its first year. Purdum was another writer on Macdonnell's *Romance* series and also wrote for *Suspense*. Of *Gunsmoke* Purdum would recall, "We worked together and we all tried to contribute, to make the characters real and three-dimensional…so that those writers who followed us had no problems writing for it." A top Purdum script was **"Doc Holliday"** (7/19/52), in which Holliday comes to Dodge and everybody expects a climactic showdown between the gunman and Matt. **"The Kentucky Tolmans"** (8/9/52) may be the best episode that Purdum wrote with its story of a young mountain girl who asks Matt to arrest her father for his own protection—since it appears somebody is trying to kill him. **"The Juniper Tree"** (8/30/52) is the final Purdum script recorded and it's also first-rate. It tells the story of Matt having to arrest a simple rancher who is accused by a gambling house owner of trying to steal money and then attempted murder. Matt suspects that the rancher is being framed and has to discover why.

The writing chores on *Gunsmoke* were not left only to experienced writers. Bill Conrad wrote a script during the first season. Sound men Ray Kemper and Tom Hanley also submitted scripts over the years and on occasion their efforts were produced. "Both Tommy and I had written for radio before *Gunsmoke*. I don't recall what shows Tommy wrote for. After I was discharged from the army following WWII, I began writing in late 1947 for *The Count of Monte Cristo* program on KHJ (the Don Lee Broadcasting System). I wrote under the name of N. Clint Reynolds, and also used my own name. When *Gunsmoke* had been on for a few years, I asked Norm Macdonnell if I could submit a script or two for the show and he said "absolutely". Prior to my asking, Tommy had asked Norm the same thing and received a positive response."

Macdonnell even allowed his sound men acting chores on the show. "We were occasionally given acting credits for crowd background, which was called "walla-walla" at the time," Kemper recalled. "That was Norm's way of giving us extra money for our sound effects work. Norm was a very thoughtful and appreciative director."

The regular cast and members of the stock company knew each other well from years of working together on radio and had a camaraderie that was considered among the best in radio. They also had a sense of fun about their job. They usually taped two episodes of *Gunsmoke* on Saturdays and the rehearsals of those shows often evolved into a series of pranks, profanity and goofiness which Howard McNear ultimately termed as "Dirty Saturdays." "I never heard a cross word spoken on those Saturday's by anyone," Sound man Ray Kemper later recalled. "I recall one time when Vic Perrin, a regular on the show, was deep into a dramatic dying scene when Georgia sneaked up behind him and pulled his pants down. Vic almost tripped and fell but he continued on with the scene until finished. However, his face was very red. Bill, Parley, Howie and everyone else in the studio were choking with laughter. So you can begin to see the rapport that was within the *Gunsmoke* cast and crew."

Kemper also tells the story of the sound effect for Matt Dillon when he walked being a heavy step in which you can faintly hear the spurs jangling, but on one such rehearsal he used a bass drum beat to simulate Matt's walk which convulsed Conrad into laughter for several minutes. Conrad was often the easiest to break up. "Bill had a good sense of humor," Herb Ellis, recalls. "It could be very risqué, but that is just the way Bill was." Parley Baer recalls that, "Bill was marvelous to break up—like Edward Arnold when he broke up—like an earthquake." On an episode titled "**New Hotel**" (2/19/56) even musical director Rex Koury got into the action when the scene being depicted was of the new hotel being burned to the ground he had his band strike up "I Don't Want to Set the World on Fire."

One thing was clear after the first few airings of *Gunsmoke* is that CBS had a big hit on its hands. And almost from the first there was speculation about whether the show would be adapted to television. While Mcdonnell kept that idea in the back of his mind he was in no big rush to do so. He found the radio show in the end to be "more authentic." While Conrad became a huge star on radio thanks to *Gunsmoke* (ultimately commanding up to $5000 per week for only a few hours of work on the show) he still took outside jobs on radio and one job in particular he took on shortly after *Gunsmoke* began its successful run proved to Herb Ellis that Conrad valued friendship above anything else.

Ellis created and wrote a show titled *Jason and the Golden Fleece* about a man (Jason) who owns a bar in New Orleans—as well as a chartered boat named "The Golden Fleece"—and the adventures Jason and (sometimes) his friend and bar tender, Louis Dumont, get involved in. Conrad didn't hesitate when Ellis approached Conrad to play the part of Louis. The show lasted only a season (from October, 1952-July, 1953). "When *Jason* began *Gunsmoke* was already an established success, and Bill was making (at that time) $500 per week and here I come and offer him a part at the standard rate of $39.50 per week for a non-sustaining program. The fact that he accepted it with no hesitation when he could have commanded much more money elsewhere was a sign of how much he valued our friendship and I was very grateful to him."

As for the success of *Gunsmoke* Conrad wasn't being coy or being unduly modest when he said:

"The success of any series has to do with the charisma that the leading character has. You can give it the best stories and the best production in the world, and the best support in the world, and if the guy or gal does

not have it, it isn't going to make it...it's charisma...I can't define it. I stand back and look at it. I've been on the other side for so long that I can evaluate it quite clearly without being involved emotionally, or ego wise. There was great character development."

IV

The success of *Gunsmoke* didn't mean that Conrad wasn't going to continue to work on other projects—in films or radio. He was a working actor and to be a working actor meant he had to work—besides he was always interested in earning money. "Bill liked working," recalls Herb Ellis. "He liked working because he liked to make money—he burned thru cash like there was no tomorrow." His next film was at MGM—a nifty crime thriller titled *Cry of the Hunted*. Conrad was again cast as a police detective partnered with Barry Sullivan (just as they had been in Metro's *Tension* back in 1949). Of course Sullivan is the senior partner. Conrad offers fine support playing an underpaid cop who would like to be the lead detective instead of the partner. It's the story of a prisoner who escapes from police custody and is on the run to the Louisiana bayou with Sullivan and Conrad in hot pursuit. The prisoner is played by Vittorio Gassman. Also in the cast are Polly Bergen, as Sullivan's picture perfect 1950's stereotypical wife, and Harry Shannon (perhaps best known for playing Charles Foster Kane's alcoholic father in *Citizen Kane*) as a hapless local sheriff. The director is Joseph H. Lewis, who specialized in B pictures and directed some genuine minor classics of film noir including *My Name is Julie Ross*, *So Dark the Night* and *Gun Crazy*. He would follow this film with another minor classic, *The Big Combo*. Lewis certainly looked out for Bill Conrad in this film. He and screen writer Jack Leonard gave Conrad some good wry and cynical lines and Lewis proved to be a Conrad fan telling Peter Bogdanovich years later, "I went out and got Bill Conrad, who I think is a fascinating actor. He certainly proved himself to be a very fine director, a fine producer, fine everything. He has great talent (a) magnificent actor."

That same month (May, 1953) Conrad was seen again on the nations movie screens, cast as a strong man Arab in Warner Brothers' lavish, but ultimately disappointing, version of operetta *The Desert*

Song which starred Gordon MacRae and (on loan out from MGM) Kathryn Grayson. The film was directed by H. Bruce Humberstone, who was long under contract to Twentieth Century-Fox directing several outstanding "Charlie Chan" vehicles and some of the better Fox musicals including *Sun Valley Serenade* and *Pin Up Girl*. The *New York Times* panned the film (with the exception of the score) with its critic writing, "Instead of settling for plain lubrication, Bruce Humberstone's bumbling direction merely underlines the pedantic dialogue, as does the generally indifferent emoting." Fortunately Conrad's part is small and not especially showy and he doesn't even warrant a mention in the review.

Conrad also continued to be heard on other radio shows—especially on *Escape* and *Suspense*. Among the outstanding episodes of *Escape* include **"A Study in Wax"** (2/1/53) about two men stranded in the arctic wilderness of Canada for several months on a government job—they will see nobody until the next spring and only have one another for companionship. Things take a drastic turn when their ability to communicate with the outside world, their radio transmitter, breaks down. Conrad plays Jack and Stacy Harris plays his partner, Kobel, who slowly begins to mad due to the isolation.

Initially they try to make do listening to music (Kobal prefers classical while Jack wishes there was some Benny Goodman) and playing games. But tension slowly mounts such as in this exchange between the two characters:

KOBEL: All right. All right, if you feel that way about it. How 'bout a game?

JACK: Ah, no, not right now, thanks. I want to finish reading this article.

KOBEL: What are you reading? Oh yeah, I read that. That's not much. Y'know, that guy never could write.

JACK: Oh? I think it's pretty good.

KOBEL: Depends on what you're used to reading, I guess.

JACK: What kind of a crack is that?

KOBEL: Nothing. Nothing it just depends on what you're used to reading, that's all.

JACK: Does that make me a lowbrow?

KOBEL: Oh, you said it, I didn't.

At one point in the story Kobel wants to listen to Shostakovich, and Jack has had enough—Kobel has played that album endlessly and he threatens to break the record. Kobel takes out his gun and tells him, "Put it down, Jack. I mean it. I mean it put it down. Put it down or I'll — I'll shoot. I'll do it if you don't put that record down!" At this point Kobel forces Jack outside in the freezing cold:

JACK NARRATING: And inside I thought I hear the music again. He was crazy. Crazy drunk. I went around the back trying to get away from the wind, but it wasn't any good, there wasn't anywhere to get away from it. I'd seen what happened to men caught in the open this way and I knew how quickly it could happen. So I ran and I jumped. Anything to keep moving. And all the time I couldn't believe it was happening. I don't know how much time went by. Maybe it was a minute. Maybe it was ten.

The tension continues to mount until the climax when tragedy strikes. The show was written and directed by Antony Ellis with Conrad and Harris giving superb performances.

While Conrad appeared on several more episodes of *Escape* in the final year (1953-1954) of its run two other episodes—besides **A Study in Wax**—especially standout. "**North of Polaris**" (5/17/53) Written by Charles Smith starred Conrad, Hy Averback, Vivi Janiss, Ralph Moody, Eddie Firestone and Frank Gerstle, it tells the story of a group of astronauts who travel twenty million miles to visit a post Atomic Warfare planet (which resembles Earth) and spend forty-eight hours there gathering data. What they encounter is truly chilling—rats have taken over the planet with humans have to fight to survive. Could this story have influenced the later *Planet of the Apes?* "**The Abominable Snowman**" (9/13/53), also written and directed by Antony Ellis, tells the story of three American who are determined to capture the Yeti (or the Abominable Snowman) in the Himalayas—with Conrad in the cast are Anthony Berrett, Hy Averback, Jack Kruschen and Edgar Barrier.

On *Suspense* Conrad appeared in one of his best episodes "**The Mystery of the Mary Celeste**" (6/8/53) written by Gil Doud and directed by Elliott Lewis and tells the story of the Ghost ship "Mary Celeste" which in December, 1872 was found abandoned off the coast of North Africa. The ship had left its New York port only a month earlier and had supplies for up to six months. When found the ship still had its cargo intact. This episode sought one possible explanation for what happened. The star of the episode was Van Heflin with Conrad, Joseph Kearns, Paul Frees, Jeanette Nolan and Dan O'Herlihy adding able support.

In September of 1953 *Gunsmoke* returned for its second season with John Meston firmly established as its principal writer. In fact, Meston would write forty-seven episodes of *Gunsmoke*'s second season episodes while producer/director Norman Macdonnell would pen the other four.

Among the stand out episodes include "**Fawn**" (9/26/53) About a woman (played by Helen Kleeb), who was held captive by the Cheyenne for ten years, and wins her release—with her eight year old daughter (Fawn, who she bore while in captivity)—they travel to Dodge, where they face prejudice from having been captives of Indians for so long. As usual we see the best in Marshal Matt Dillon, who is kind to the woman and the daughter she bore while with the Cheyenne—Chief Black Horne is the father—Matt doesn't judge her. For all his brusqueness, Matt Dillon is continually an open minded man.

"**Yorky**" (10/17/53) is another episode about a child raised by Indians and in this case a twelve year old Indian boy who is captured by raiders and (as it turns out) is a white boy who wants to continue to live among the Indians—much to the consternation of many in Dodge. "**Nina**" (1/23/54) turns from Indian prejudice to Mexican in its story of an Army Scout and his Mexican wife who are passing through Dodge City. Of course there is the element in town that makes them feel unwelcome. Matt Dillon, while not prejudiced and fully welcoming of the couple still has to keep the peace of Dodge City and understands that the bigoted element will try to create trouble so he advises the couple to stay in the outskirts of town, but when the wife needs medical help she needs to come to town for Doc to see to her needs. **The Queue** (7/19/54) focuses its story on a Chinese immigrant whose pigtail is cut off and according to the custom of his land he either has to get the pigtail back or kill the men who cut it off to restore his dignity and honor. Meston continued to explore prejudice with "**The Blacksmith**" (6/5/54) about an immigrant couple whose house is burned down.

"**How to Kill a Friend**" (10/3/53) demonstrates that Dillon is a man of integrity who will not give into the gambling interests even when he is offered a percentage of the money they plan to make if they are allowed to set up shop in Dodge. Matt Dillon is not a lawman on the make. "**Hack Prine**" (7/5/54) is an intriguing story about an old friend of Matt's, Hack Prine, who arrives in Dodge and they enjoy a happy reunion—however, Matt is unaware that Hack is now a hired killer and has been brought to Dodge to kill a man (but doesn't know that he is hired to kill Matt). Ever the lawman will Matt be forced to kill an old friend? In "**Texas Cowboys**" (7/5/54) Dillon has to take extreme measures when a cowhand is murdered, and the town won't come forward to tell Matt who did it, so what action is he forced to do to try and get somebody to some forward? Close all the saloons and shops in Dodge. Working for the government apparently Matt has the authority to do this. **Matt for Murder** (7/26/54) has Dillon being suspended when he is framed for the shooting of an unarmed man in cold blood. The War Department sends Marshal Wild Bill Hickok (played by John Dehner) to Dodge to escort Matt to his trial, but Hickok knows Matt Dillon and is willing to give him a chance to clear himself and bring the real culprits to justice. "**Young Man with a Gun**" (8/23/54) involves Matt killing a man in a gunfight—and then the problem he faces when the man's sixteen year old brother comes to town and tells Matt that once he learns how to use a gun he will avenge his brothers killing. All in all, the 1953-1954 season continues the high quality of scripts that made *Gunsmoke* a banner series.

The cast and crew of the show continued to enjoy making *Gunsmoke* and with it continued to play the pranks which made their 'Dirty Saturday' tapings among the most enjoyable in radio. "All I can say," Georgia Ellis once said, "is that it was ten years of having a ball every Saturday morning, not only of enjoying the drama of it, but of laughing, of humor and of having your wits exercised a little bit."

In the book *Gunsmoke: A Complete History*, Soundman Ray Kemper tells the following story regarding Bill Conrad:

"Bill Conrad came in one Saturday morning with a terrible hangover or the flu bug or something. He was feeling awful and during a break decided to go over to Stearns' Drug Store to get something to help him. Now the drug store was owned by a gentle person we all affectionately called Ma Stearns. Her hands were gnarled, she always wore like a funny looking apron and green sun visor...She whomped up a concoction for Conrad and gave it to him. Tommy (Tom Hanley, his co-soundman) found out about all this and watched closely until Bill had swallowed a good slug of Ma Stearns' snake oil. Hanley then signaled a page who came bursting into the studio with a note presumably from Ma Stearns but which in reality had been written with shaky hand by Tom Hanley. The note said, 'Mr. Conrad, do not take the medicine I gave you. I made a mistake. Call me immediately!' and it was signed Mrs. Stearns. Bill's face turned a little white and he headed for the phone, but we could contain ourselves no longer and broke out laughing. Bill did a slow take, then looked at Tommy and said, 'You son-of-a-bitch, I'll get you for that!' Later, he came over to us and said, 'Damn, if I'd had my wits about me I'd have faked a heart attack—that woulda gotcha.' Obviously, we were all very fond of one another or we could never have done all those silly things."

It was during the second season of *Gunsmoke* that Conrad's next film *The Naked Jungle* (1954) with Charlton Heston and Eleanor Parker was released by Paramount. Heston plays a man who has spent the prime years of his life in South America building a levee for a chocolate plantation. He is now thirty-four years old and wants to settle down with a wife and settles on a beautiful mail-order bride from New Orleans (Parker). Parker is tempestuous and willful—a woman with her own mind and Heston won't have her. As she awaits a boat back to the United States they learn that throngs of deadly army ants will strike within days, and she joins in the fight to save the plantation—naturally her spunk earns Heston's admiration. Conrad plays the local government official, known as the commissioner,—who has a great knowledge of the jungle—and who worries about Heston's emotional state and also about why suddenly birds and monkeys are fleeing the jungle. Together Heston, the commissioner, and the willful bride investigate and overlook a valley that is blackened with billions of soldier ants making their way. Sound familiar? The material wasn't new to Conrad who had performed this story back in 1949 on radio, "Lienigan vs. the Ants" (which was the working title of the film) on *Escape*. In that case he actually played the role that Heston plays in the movie.

Originally Joseph H. Lewis, Conrad's big supporter from the film *Cry of the Hunted* was to direct, and he had been the one responsible for Conrad's casting in the film, but a month before the film was to go before the cameras Lewis was replaced by producer George Pal by Byron Haskin who had previously directed *War of the Worlds* (1953) for Pal. As for the ants thousands of them were shipped to Hollywood from the Rocky and High Sierra Mountains.

The film got a good review from Bosley Crowther in the *New York Times*:

"Credit Philip Yordan and Ranald MacDougall for the script, which is literate as well as dramatic—a comparatively uncommon thing. And credit Byron Haskin for directing in a slow rhythm and a mordant style. But credit, too, Mr. Heston for performing with a fine, intense restraint and Miss Parker for playing the lady with spirit and dignity. William Conrad as a government official and Abraham... as a native right-hand-man, plus John Dierkes as a neighboring planter, give decent performances, too."

During the summer of 1954, just prior to the launch of the third season of *Gunsmoke*, Conrad filmed *The Conqueror* in which he joined a very strong cast (John Wayne, Susan Hayward, Agnes Moorehead, Pedro Armendariz, Lee Van Cleef) in one of the silliest films ever made. Set in the 12th Century it tells the story of a Mongol war lord (later to be known as Genghis Khan) who falls in love with the daughter of the man he conquers. Conrad plays Kasar, one of Khan's loyalists who, in his climactic scene, when imprisoned uses his super human strength to bend iron bars wide enough to allow another man to escape before coming to his own doom.

The film was produced by Howard Hughes who hired Dick Powell to direct. It was actually shot in the summer of 1954 at a cost of $4.5 million, but Hughes held back the release until early in 1956. The film has a terrible legend connected with it. It was shot on location in Utah near a site of a nuclear testing ground. When the film returned to Hollywood the studio had shipped in a lot of the sand and dirt from the location and over the next couple of decades many members of the cast and crew, including director Dick Powell, John Wayne, Susan Hayward, Pedro Armendariz and Agnes Moorehead developed cancer and ultimately died of the disease. Did the location shooting have something to do with it? Perhaps, but while a large percentage did develop cancer an even larger number didn't—including Conrad. But still the questions linger.

The film is routinely considered one of the worse ever made with the outlandish casting of Wayne as a Mongol warrior. The *New York Times* review was scathing, "John Wayne's portrayal of Genghis is elementary. Although his appearance in wispy mustaches and Mongol make-up is a mite startling at first, he is soon recognizable. Once in the saddle, he is the rough-riding John Wayne of yore. It's just that he is constantly being unhorsed by such lines as, "you are beautiful in your wrath." That's too much to expect even of a "Conqueror.'" Yet not all the reviews were bad including that from the 'bible' of show business *Variety*, "Just so there will be no misunderstanding about *The Conqueror*, a foreword baldly states that it is fiction, although with some basis in fact. With that warning out of the way, the viewer can sit back and thoroughly enjoy a huge, brawling, sex-and-sand actioner purporting to show how a 12th Century Mongol leader became known as Genghis Khan."

V

The third season of *Gunsmoke* began in the fall of 1954—again with John Meston as principal writer. One of the most interesting of the season is **Matt Gets It (10/2/54)** in which Matt Dillon goes up against a gunman who is quicker on the draw than he is and gets severely shot. Matt recovers, but his gun arm is useless for a while and Matt has to teach himself to shoot using his other hand. The gunman who shot him is still in Dodge causing trouble, and Matt challenges him to another gunfight. The gunman thinks it will be easy pickings going up against a man who can't shoot with his good hand. This episode has a couple of interesting distinctions. It is the first episode to air on the shows new Saturday time slot and it would be the first script adapted for the later television series. Another outstanding outing for Conrad is **Bloody Hands (4/2/55)** which involves Matt killing several men when he is attacked but having a kind of breakdown afterwards when he thinks of all the 'blood on his hands' from the many men he's killed over the years.

The third season began making the supporting characters more the focus of the show than in previous seasons. Howard McNear's 'Doc' had some nice showcases including **Love of a Good Woman (10/9/54)** in which Doc is smitten with the lady doctor who arrives in town and **Cow Doctor (5/28/55)** in which Doc Addams is called out to minister to a sick man who has always mistrusted doctors. **Doc Quits (8/27/55)** offers the dramatic story of Doc quitting when a flashy new doctor arrives in Dodge with new ideas and Doc begins to feel he is a relic of the past.

Georgia Ellis' Kitty is also front and center in some superb episodes including **Kitty Caught (10/16/54)** in which our gal is taken hostage during a bank robbery; **Kitty Lost (12/25/54)** has Kitty taking a moonlight carriage ride out into the country with a handsome stranger and after an argument being left in the middle of nowhere to freeze to death. **Tap Day for Kitty (7/30/55)** has Marshal Dillon wondering if Kitty actually shot and wounded a man who had been badgering her into marrying him.

Parley Baer's 'Chester' may have had the most show surrounding him of all the supporting cast. **Magnus (12/18/54)** tells the story of Chester's uncivilized cousin arriving in Dodge and Chester's attempts to reform him—a seriocomic episode. **Chester's Murder (1/15/55)** has Chester getting framed for murder. **Chester's Hanging (2/12/55)** has Chester the pawn in trying to get Matt to release his prisoner. **The Gypsum Hills (4/16/55)** has Matt and Chester investigating a feud between two mountain families. **Potato Road (5/7/55)** finds both Matt and Chester lured out of town so the coast is clear for a bank robbery and **The Army Trial (6/25/55)** finds Matt and Chester finding a wagon with an army deserter and his wife.

In the summer of 1955 another film featuring Conrad in a supporting role was released. Phil Karlson's *5 Against the House* shot at Columbia and starring Guy Madison, the fast-rising Kim Novak and Brian Keith. The film tells the story of four former college friends and a girl who are enjoying a reunion in Reno, Nevada with a night of gambling who decide (after hearing a cop say it cannot be done) to rob the casino! The mastermind of the friends plans it and they think it is no more than a hoax, but one of the group takes it very seriously. Conrad is cast as Eric Berg, a roving cashier, who is cohered into retrieving cash from the casino's money room. (This is actually one of the films weak points, in my opinion. Conrad is somehow convinced that there is a man with a gun inside his money wagon ready to shoot him unless he gets the money from the cashier's office! This is done by using a tape recorder—one would think that the person inside the cart would have to be a midget).

Originally United Artists was going to produce the film and Frank Tashlin was going to direct with his wife, Mary Costa, in the role Novak ultimately played. However, when UA backed out and Columbia acquired the rights the director chosen was Phil Karlson, who had specialized in crime-dramas in the past such as *99 River Street, Kansas City Confidential* and the gritty *The Phenix City Story*. Tashlin, a former cartoonist who up to that time had specialized in comedy films as both a writer and director, would have been an unusual choice for this material (and he would specialize in comedy for the rest of his career), but for Karlson this was right up his ally. The film was based on a novel by Jack Finney, who also wrote *Invasion of the Body Snatchers*.

There was a bidding war between Reno and Las Vegas as to which city would be used for location shots for this film. Las Vegas even put up $50,000. In the end Columbia utilized both cities but the major location of filming was Reno. When the film was released the *New York Times* generally liked it with its critic writing, "Although their motivations would appear to be somewhat fragile, director Phil Karlson has given his melodrama mounting tension as the holdup plan is unfolded and suddenly builds from a theoretical challenge to frightening reality."

VI

Gunsmoke continued to be a ratings winner even as radio was beginning to take a back seat to television. Almost from the beginning there had been talk about adapting *Gunsmoke* to television, but MacDonnell had fought against it feeling that the show and especially the characters would be more pure on radio than on television. But by early 1955, while *Gunsmoke* was in its third season, CBS approached Macdonnell again about doing a television version, and this time, Macdonnell didn't automatically turn them down, but decided to give the issue some thought. Macdonnell (and Meston) were coming to the undeniable conclusion that radio drama was on the way out and if they were to keep their characters alive they might have no choice but to make the plunge into television.

In the meanwhile since Macdonnell had been so ambivalent about television and had not given a straight answer CBS decided to go headstrong into a television series of *Gunsmoke* and hired film producer and director Charles Marquis Warren to adapt the television series, ultimately, Macdonnell would be named Associate Producer of the television series. To get the TV show off to a tremendous start they had to look no further than John Meston's radio scripts, which were adapted for television and were the foundation of the stories used on televisions *Gunsmoke* during its first few seasons.

Did William Conrad want to continue his role of Matt Dillon on television? "I don't look like Matt Dillon, god dammit!" Conrad told Leonard Maltin in denying that he had any interest in the job. Yet Conrad's friend Herb Ellis says, "Sure, he wanted to play Matt Dillon on TV and did try to get the job." The evidence tends to support Ellis's view that Conrad did want the opportunity to play Matt Dillon on television. *Gunsmoke* soundman Ray Kemper, when asked if Conrad was disappointed in not being cast as Dillon, replied,

"Absolutely. Bill Conrad trimmed down to a slender 170 or so, hoping that would make him look physically okay for the TV role of Matt."

Anticipating an opportunity to audition for the role of Dillon and understanding that one of the chief roadblocks to his getting the part would be his girth, Conrad went on a strict diet and managed to shed about twenty-five pounds in a matter of weeks, hardly trim, but still a big improvement. The main cast of Conrad, Parley Baer, Georgia Ellis and Howard McNear then rented some authentic looking western wear that they felt matched how their characters would look and went on an outing to Knott's Berry Farm in Buena Park, California. Knott's had an old fashioned western street façade and they decided that they would try and entice the network in giving them a shot at auditioning by having some pictures taken of them in character. Harry Bartell, one of the key members of the Gunsmoke stock company, was also a talented photographer and he agreed to take several pictures of the cast in character at Knott's Berry Farm. Vic Perrin recalled that the cast, "posed in front of a saloon and they looked like authentic tin-types of the West."

CBS was not interested in transferring the radio cast to the television show. They felt that the radio show was still a valuable commodity and wanted to continue with Gunsmoke on radio with the same cast that the public had grown to know and love for the past three years, while introducing an entirely new batch of actors on the television series. The head of CBS radio, Della Cioppa, felt this was unfair to the radio cast and complained to Harry Ackerman. Cioppa felt that the radio cast could handle doing both the radio show and the television show. After all, Jack Benny and his supporting cast were still doing a radio show while appearing on television—as was Marie Wilson in her *My Friend Irma* series.

Cioppa and the radio cast got additional help from Hollywood columnist Hal Humphrey who wrote several columns urging CBS to audition Conrad and the other radio cast members. Finally Harry Ackerman raised the white flag and decided (perhaps half-heartedly?) to appease the radio cast and agreed that they would be auditioned. The audition would take place in February of 1955 at Studio 43 at the CBS Television City complex on Beverly Boulevard in Hollywood.

Several other actors had already auditioned for the parts when the radio cast had their shot at it. After filming their tests, but before any announcements were made as to who would play the roles on television, Hal Humphrey would write in his column, "Last week they finally got around to making a test of William Conrad...If CBS will just let Macdonnell and John Meston do for TV what they've done for radio, it will have another hit. And Bill Conrad and Parley Baer will be hailed as 'discoveries' in their new TV roles."

Of his test for Matt Dillon Conrad told Leonard Maltin, "I got into making a test; it's pitiful. I was so bad; I was scared to death, the only time in my life that I really was ever scared to death. I was afraid I was gonna get it, which I didn't want, I really didn't, but I was committed to at least, for the sake of CBS, for them to look at me and say yes or no. But I was delighted not to have done it (the series)."

The producer of the TV show, Charles Marquis Warren, was asked by CBS to listen to a recording of the radio show and didn't particularly care for it. "I didn't like Bill Conrad's voice," he later said, "It was too Shakespeare, not Dodge City." Among the other actors who auditioned for Dillon were Raymond Burr, who had the same problem as Bill Conrad—his hefty frame—and Richard Boone—who Warren thought was "too ugly." In the end Warren showed the tests of the radio cast to the big wigs at CBS and got the word—they felt he could do better. While their voices seemed right—they were not visually what the network had in mind. Certainly not Bill Conrad—who was balding, average height and was inclined to be overweight.

In the end a call to Ackerman from John Wayne probably was what made the final decision as to who ultimately was selected to play Matt Dillon on TV. Wayne had an actor who had been under contract to him named James Arness. Arness had worked in some films in mostly supporting parts. His biggest claim of fame was probably playing alien in the 1951 Sci-fi classic *The Thing*. Wayne urged Ackerman to take a look at Arness because he felt that he processed everything he could want in the role of the classic lawman. A test was scheduled, the final test as it turned out, according to Arness, and the CBS suits liked what they saw in the rugged 6'7" thirty-two year old Arness—and hired him.

As an added incentive Wayne offered the network his services in introducing the first episode of *Gunsmoke* starring James Arness as Matt Dillon. While ultimately the selection of Arness to play Dillon worked out and was enthusiastically accepted by TV viewers for twenty-years, not all the old guard agreed. "I don't think there ever really was a six-foot-seven marshal in the west," Vic Perrin later said. "They were fat and kind of rough like Bill Conrad." And while Norman Macdonnell came to ultimately appreciate and accept Arness as Dillon he at first found it very difficult to even watch the actor. "I had my own private Matt Dillon, my own sexy particular Kitty, my own bumbling Doc, and my own nutty Chester and they all did things and looked exactly the way I wanted them to look."

Intellectually Conrad came to accept the decision that CBS ultimately made. He understood that listeners of the radio show probably saw Dillon differently in their minds than what Bill Conrad actually looked like, but he still took the rejection hard—and probably a bit personally. In the years after he stopped playing Matt Dillon he rarely would speak of the show or the character of Matt Dillon that he made famous. He would continue to keenly feel the hurt. When he did speak of the missed opportunity to play Dillon he would try to laugh it off by saying that had he gotten the role he would have had to take a pay cut ("The best they could come up with was $750 a week. At the time I was getting $1000 a week for the radio show and it took two hours a week to do. Needless to say, I wasn't interested in TV."). In 1971, just prior to his own successful television series (*Cannon*) debuting he said that *Gunsmoke* was still on the air, "maybe it's because James Arness is so much different, but now I can see only Jim in the part."

CHAPTER FOUR: THE RIDE BACK 1956-1961

While disappointed in not getting the TV version of *Gunsmoke*, Conrad didn't spend a lot of time crying into his coffee. He still had the radio version—which continued to be quite popular—and more invitations to make movies. *Johnny Concho* (1956) starred Frank Sinatra as the braggart younger brother of a gunfighter who bullies the citizens of the small town where he is the self-appointed boss. Enter Bill Conrad as a gunman named Tallman who challenges Sinatra's Concho when Concho cheats at cards. The cowardly Concho begs the town's sheriff and the towns people themselves for help, but they won't stand by him. Tallman tells Concho to either draw his gun or leave town by sundown. The cowardly Concho leaves town, while Tallman appoints himself sheriff and demands twenty-cents on every dollar that comes into the town for his protection. The town's people really are no better off than they were when they were bullied by Concho. Meanwhile the chastised Concho, labeled a coward, attempts to redeem himself and go up against Tallman—who isn't above shooting a man in the back if he attempts to thwart his goals.

Johnny Concho was produced by Sinatra and directed by Don McGuire, a former actor and screen writing buddy of Sinatra's (who had written the story and screenplay of the Sinatra film *Meet Danny Wilson* in 1952). More recently McGuire had written the screenplay to the acclaimed film *Bad Day at Black Rock* as well as two Martin and Lewis films, *3 Ring Circus* and *Artists and Models*. (Conrad had also previously worked in a McGuire adapted story when he made the movie *Dial 1119*).

When the film opened in New York (at the Paramount) Sinatra was on hand along with Tommy and Jimmy Dorsey to help pack the theaters by performing songs and wise cracks between showings. The *New York Times* was generous to Sinatra who they felt did "a pretty good job of making the chicken-livered tin-horn fairly credible," But felt that McGuire's direction and the story itself was not up to par. Furthermore the other actors are "either stiff or exaggerated" except for Conrad and Wallace Ford who are "a little better than the others."

By this time changes were brewing in Conrad's personal life. Conrad had found a new woman in his life—Susan Randall, a beautiful blonde fashion model in her mid-twenties, who also happened to be married. He had been married to June for over thirteen years and as each year passed they grew further apart. "June was a very nice lady but not in the theatrical field," recalled Herb Ellis. "She was not flamboyant and I don't really think she liked a lot of Bill's friends even though we tried very hard to get along with her because of our love for Bill. She wasn't overly gracious about Bill's friends coming over to their house and playing cards and getting together. She was unhappy and, I think, after a while he got unhappy with her which led to his looking elsewhere." With no children to consider they separated and eventually divorced—as did Susan and her husband.

As soon as possible Conrad and Susan got married. "Susan was more out-going," recalled Ellis, "though I wasn't crazy about her. She wasn't somebody like Virginia Gregg that you could hug. But at least early on Bill was crazy about her and that was what mattered." On March 3, 1957 Susan gave birth to a son, whom they named Christopher.

II

Even though *Gunsmoke* was a success on television (using mostly earlier radio scripts) the radio show continued to be superbly and compactly written and performed. By the fall of 1956, John Meston had become the script editor and while he continued to contribute a few scripts per season, the writing was by and large taken over by Les Crutchfield, who had contributed several scripts during the show's first season. Among the top scripts for the season are **Crowbait Bob** (11/10/56) in which an old prospector leaves everything to Kitty. **Speak to Me Fair** (12/2/56) tells the story of an Indian boy who has his tongue cut out. **Beeker's Barn (12/23/56)** in which a rancher wants Matt to evict his estranged son and his pregnant daughter from his barn. **Colleen so Green (3/3/57)** is about a conniving southern belle who charms the men of Dodge—but not Kitty. **Saludos (4/14/57)** finds Matt escorting three men back to Dodge, but having to wait for an unconscious and wounded Indian woman to identify which one of the men killed her husband and attempted to kill her. **Medicine Man (4/28/57)** is the story of a man who sells a tonic that could put saloon owners out of business. This episode is also significant as the fifth anniversary episode of *Gunsmoke* and, at the end of it, Bill Conrad addresses the audience to thank them for hanging in with them for the last five years—going on to tell them that *Gunsmoke* has, "tried for as much truth as good drama will allow." There is also a plug for the new film that was out in theaters with Bill Conrad.

Conrad produced and co-starred in an underrated gem of a western film released in April, 1957 titled *The Ride Back*. It was based on a script (with the same title) that Antony Ellis had written during the first season of *Gunsmoke* that Conrad believed was a particularly interesting story that showed potential for a motion picture. In it a slimmed down (but still beefy) Conrad plays a deputy sheriff who reluctantly, but with tenacity, rides after an escaped outlaw (played by Academy Award winner Anthony Quinn), a character that Conrad's deputy comes to envy (for example Conrad is in a loveless marriage while Quinn is in a happy one) and respect. The Conrad character ultimately captures Quinn and begins a dangerous ride back so the outlaw can face trial. Along the way they face many difficulties as the Quinn character continually tests him by trying to escape, but then the two must work together when they face Apaches along the way. The film is an intriguing character study of two contrasting men who ultimately have to depend on each other for survival.

The 1950's was a golden age for the westerns. They were popular on radio, television and in motion pictures. 1957 saw a number of outstanding little westerns produced including *Decision at Sundown* (Budd Boetticher), *Forty Guns* (Samuel Fuller), *Gun for a Coward* (Abner Biberman), *Night Passage* (James Neilson), *The Tall T* (Boetticher), *3:10 to Yuma* (Delmer Daves), *Three Violent People* (Rudolph Mate), and *The Tin Star* (Anthony Mann). *The Ride Back* can hold its head high among any of them.

It's a taut, compact film which logs in at 79 minutes, yet not one minute is wasted. The film is tightly directed by Allen H. Miner, who would work most consistently in television—including such westerns as *The Lawless Years* and *Wagon Train* (Miner would later be given another opportunity at directing on the big screen by Bill Conrad when he produced the film *Chubasco* in 1967).

Conrad co-produced the film with Robert Aldrich, who had already produced and/or directed such interesting films as *Vera Cruz, Kiss Me Deadly, The Big Knife, Autumn Leaves* and *Attack*. It's kind of a mystery as to why Aldrich didn't handle the directorial reins of *The Ride Back*—perhaps because of its limited budget? Of *The Ride Back* Aldrich would later say, "I produced a film, *The Ride Back*, with a young director, Allen Miner, whose documentary on tuna fishing I had admired. The Ride Back is a good western, with psychological overtones, dealing with a bitter deputy who has failed at everything in life…and has to bring in a man accused of murder on a long trek from Mexico to Texas. The accused turns out to be the better human being on all accounts." Aldrich also credits second unit director Oscar Rudolph with having to direct large portions of the film—not because Miner was not up to it, but because as the film was running out of money—it was on a shoe string—Rudolph had to help out.

Quinn is quite superb as the outlaw—a man who makes no apologies for his way of life, yet has a personal code which makes him an admirable figure—one who commands respect and even affection. Conrad is very good as the deputy sheriff—a man who is not happy with his lot in life and envies the respect that Quinn, the outlaw, has. He believes that capturing the outlaw will help him gain respect in the eyes of his wife and the town he serves—yet he is full of apprehensions and fear of what awaits him. The black and white photography by Joe Biroc captures the bleak beauty of the landscape (much of it filmed on location in Mexico). Biroc would later be nominated for an Oscar for his cinematography of the Aldrich film *Hush…Hush Sweet Charlotte* and win the Oscar (with Fred J. Koenekamp) for *The Towering Inferno*. In addition he was the director of photography on the classic film *It's a Wonderful Life* and had previously photographed Conrad in the 1951 film noir *Cry Danger*.

The music was by Frank Devol, who was best known for his television themes for shows like *My Three Sons, Gidget, Family Affair* and *The Brady Bunch*. Aldrich, however, had used Devol in earlier films such as *Kiss Me Deadly, The Big Knife* and *Attack*. The theme song "The Ride Back" tells the story from Conrad's perspective— a dark and tense anthem—it was later well recorded by Eddie Albert and an especially fine rendition by Vaughn Monroe.

The film, released by United Artists, got some respectful reviews, but was not a financial success. It pretty much came and went. "Actor William Conrad has given himself a juicy role in his own independently made western *The Ride Back*," wrote film critic Bosley Crowther in The *New York Times* on April 30, 1957. "He plays a lonely law officer who has the unenviable job of capturing and bringing back to Texas a suspected murderer who has escaped to Mexico. And he does it with grim and grand authority, even though the fugitive is played by Anthony Quinn, a highly respectable villain whom very few actors would dare take on." Crowther went on to write that "Mr. Conrad has plenty of problems which he handles manfully, even the problem of matching the angular acting of Mr. Quinn." But ultimately Crowther thought "The conclusion is much more sentimental than the picture's nature would lead us to suppose. Allen H. Miner has directed in a lean and leathery style which calls for cold steel at the climax." *Harrison Reports* in its review (April 20, 1957) wrote, "Theaters that play outdoor melodramas undoubtedly will find this one satisfactory, for its considerably different from the average film of its type...there is considerable rugged action all the way through...the photography is very good and the outdoor scenery different..."

Bill Conrad was quite proud of *The Ride Back*. According to his son, Christopher, he considered it to be one of his all-time favorite films. Certainly of all the films he either produced or directed *The Ride Back* (along with 1965's *Brainstorm*) has stood the test of time.

III

Radio's classic era had passed and television was becoming more and more the way that most households got their entertainment. There was still an audience for radio, but it was diminishing and the network radio divisions tried to come up with innovative ways to keep their audiences. One of the most unusual and acclaimed of these was *The CBS Radio Workshop* which was a dramatic anthology series that called itself "radio's distinguished series to man's imagination." Its hallmark was dramatizing the works of distinguished writers such as Aldous Huxley, Sinclair Lewis, Edgar Allan Poe, James Thurber, Mark Twain and Thomas Wolfe. The show ran from January, 1956 until September of 1957 and was produced by William Froug and William Robson and used as directors Elliott Lewis, Jack Johnstone, William N. Robson and Antony Ellis—among others. Its opening and closing score was written by Bernard Herrmann, who had a long and successful career in radio but was now working increasingly in motion pictures—including *The Man Who Knew Too Much, Vertigo, North by Northwest* and *Psycho*.

William Conrad would appear on several installments along with many other distinguished radio performers. Its premiere was a two-part presentation of Aldous Huxley's **Brave New World** which was introduced by Huxley himself. Conrad was the announcer for the first two episodes, as well as a performer. The story takes place in London, 632 years in the future, and explores how machines now dominate man. Time reviewed the opener in its February 6, 1956 issue, "It took three radio sound men, a control-room engineer and five hours of hard work to create the sound that was heard for less than 30 seconds on the air. The sound consisted of a ticking metronome, tom-tom beats, bubbling water, air hose, cow moo, boing! (two types), oscillator, dripping water (two types) and three kinds of wine glasses clicking against each other. Judiciously blended and recorded on tape, the effect was still not quite right. Then the tape was played backward with a little echo added. That did it. The sound depicted the manufacturing of babies in the radio version of Aldous Huxley's *Brave New World*."

Among the other episodes that Conrad appeared on is **Storm** (2/10/56) based on a novel by Professor George R. Stewart, which explores the life cycle of a killer storm which is passing over the Pacific Ocean. It's picturesquely and passionately narrated by Conrad. **Jacob's Hands** (4/13/56) also based on a story by Aldous Huxley about a farmer who discovers he has the power to heal. The cast, in addition to Conrad, included such *Gunsmoke* stock players as Harry

Bartell, Parley Baer, Vic Perrin, Virginia Gregg, Larry Dobkin and John Dehner. **A Matter of Logic: A Study in Semantics (6/1/56)** features Conrad in the leading role and is interesting in that the program is about a group of radio performers trying to understand the script and their characters during a rehearsal. The program also features Parley Baer and Stacy Harris. **Five at Malibu (1/20/57)** again features stirring narration by Conrad as it relates the events caused by weather which led to the devastating Malibu fires of December, 1956. Conrad had one of his best outings with **1489 Words (2/10/57)** which refers to four selections that Conrad reads over twenty-five minutes (*The Highwayman, The Portuguese, Of Time in the River,* and *Silence*—a poem of only seven words). Conrad's son, Chris, says that this is one of his favorites of the radio shows that his father did. "Every time I listen to that I smile, I cry…just a powerful piece." **The Ballad of the Iron Horse (3/3/57)** which deals with a Civil War era locomotive that ends up in an amusement park. Richard Crenna joins Conrad in this outing. There would be 86 episodes of *The CBS Radio Workshop*—ending its distinguished, but not overly popular, run on September 22, 1957.

In addition to his duties on *Gunsmoke* and *The CBS Radio Workshop*, Conrad continued to turn up from time to time on *Suspense* in episodes which include **A Matter of Timing (6/12/56)** produced and directed by Antony Ellis and features Parley Baer, Virginia Gregg and Sam Edwards. It tells the story of a man who hires a hit man to kill his business partner. **Speed Trap (12/8/57)** which features Conrad with Mercury Theater/Orson Welles alumni Everett Sloan in a story about two police officers who chase a speeding car down a mountain road and hope to prevent an inevitable crash because its believed that inside the car is the wife of one of the officers. **The Whole Town's Sleeping (8/31/58)** casts Conrad opposite radio great Agnes Moorehead and was based on a Ray Bradbury short story about a town that has been the focus of a series of bizarre murders and the woman who isn't going to be afraid to walk alone at night.

By the late fifties Conrad had conquered the dying art of radio drama and emerged as one of its great stars. He had established himself as a reliable character actor in films. In 1955 he made a futile attempt to at television when he auditioned for television's

Gunsmoke. And while that didn't succeed he knew that he had to eventually make the leap towards television in some way to continue to be a viable working actor.

By the late fifties Ziv Television Productions, founded by Frederick Ziv in 1948, was one of the leading producers of quality first-run syndicated television programming of the 1950's. Among the most popular were *Highway Patrol*, a police series starring Broderick Crawford, *Bat Masterson* with Gene Berry as the western dandy and *Sea Hunt*, which starred Lloyd Bridges as an ex-Navy seal who faces weekly nautical adventures. Ziv proved popular in local markets which needed programming to fill its time slots outside of 'prime time.' Conrad appeared on the Ziv television program *The Rough Riders*, which was set in the American west after the Civil War about three ex-soldiers (two Union & one Confederate) who ride together fighting outlaws along the way. His episode, titled "The Governor," aired on November 6, 1958—with Conrad playing the lead heavy who kidnaps the governor of a territory and holds him ransom in return for the release of a fellow gang member. Conrad liked the efficient way that Ziv cranked out their shows and approached them with a proposal to work for them—not so much as an actor—but as a producer and director.

Ziv gave him the opportunity to produce a pilot for a new series for them called *This Man Dawson*. The show starred Keith Andes as a former Marine Colonel hired to clean up police corruption in an unnamed American city. In addition to producing the pilot, Conrad also narrated many of the episodes (For his narration Conrad was paid an additional $400 per episode—at a time when the industry standard was $87.50). In a letter (dated February 27, 1959) Ziv executive Maurice Unger wrote, "I discussed with Bill the fact that we would like an option on his services to produce a series for us, and he said he would be glad to cooperate."

The deal that Unger worked out with Conrad called for him to earn $3,000 per month, "which is to cover two directorial assignments at $1000 each plus $1000 for anything and everything else that he might do on the lot in any manner in which we wish to use his services…We will also guarantee that his salary as a producer will not be less than $3000 per month and will be augmented by any directorial jobs that he does on pictures in addition to his producing."

It's clear from the correspondence that the main person who was handling Conrad's negotiations was not his agents with the William Morris Company, but Conrad himself. "If you have the slightest indication of any trouble with Bill's agent, don't get into a hassle over this," Unger wrote. "Simply contact Bill immediately and tell him that you have reduced to writing the arrangement that he and I discussed and his agent is giving you trouble."

There was one stumbling block in the way, however, and that was from CBS Radio where Conrad was under contract to do *Gunsmoke*. Ziv needed to make sure that Conrad was available when they needed him to work on one of their 'movies' and sought assurance from CBS Radio that this wouldn't be a problem. On April 23, 1959, Anne Nelson, Director of Business Affairs of CBS Radio, wrote to Art Stolnitz of Ziv Television, "to confirm our telephone conversation concerning William Conrad—you know that under our 'Gunsmoke' radio contract with him we have the right to call for rehearsals and taping or for live broadcast at our discretion." She, however, went on to assure the Ziv executive that "as a practical matter, that we have been taping this show on Saturday for a matter of years. This is done not only for Mr. Conrad's convenience, but because Norman Macdonnell, the director of the programs is the producer of 'Gunsmoke' television and, therefore, is not generally available on week days." She went on to say that, "during a 7-year period in which 'Gunsmoke' has been on the air every single week, Mr. Conrad has never lost a motion picture or other desired employment because of our demands upon him."

With that roadblock out of the way Conrad began working in earnest at Ziv. Over the next two years he would produce the series *This Man Dawson* (as well as direct 9 episodes) and produce and direct several episodes of another series—*Klondike*. *Klondike* (which aired on NBC) was set during the Klondike Gold Rush of the late 1890's and starred Ralph Taeger and James Coburn—and their adventures in the town of Skagway, Alaska. Conrad produced five episodes of *Klondike* and directed two others.

In addition to this he directed episodes of several other Ziv series including *Highway Patrol, Bold Venture* (6 episodes), *Lock Up* (2 episodes), *Tombstone Territory* (6 episodes), *Men in Space* (2 episodes), *Bat Masterson* (6 episodes), *Ripcord* (2 episodes). In all Conrad wound up directing 42 episodic television series for Ziv Productions. His option was picked up in April of 1960 with a monthly guaranteed salary of $4400. In addition to his producing and directing chores for Ziv, Conrad also directed other shows including *The Rifleman* (Four Star Productions), *Route 66* (Screen Gems Television), *Naked City* (3 episodes—Screen Gems), and six episodes of *Have Gun Will Travel*. Conrad later came to the conclusion that directing for television wasn't all it was cracked up to be. "Directing in TV is at best constantly settling for something less than you would like."

During the time he was working with Ziv Television Productions they received an unusual request for Conrad's services that they had to give their Okay to. Ziv let Conrad's agent know in a letter dated May 25, 1959, that "we approve Bill Conrad narrating 104 five minute television cartoon films, entitled "Rocky the Flying Squirrel" providing that the services he is to render in connection therewith do not interfere with the services Bill is to render for us and, provided further, that he receives no credit nor any identification with the films in any way, nor in the advertising or publicity in connection therewith."

The cartoon series, produced by Jay Ward productions, featured the adventures of a flying squirrel named Rocky and his moose friend Bullwinkle. They were cartoons that children could enjoy but were also intended to be enjoyed by adults—especially with their satire on the Cold War featuring the Russian spies Boris and Natasha. Other segments included Dudley Do-Right (a parody of the woman in distress being saved by the handsome (but in this case thick headed) Mountie), Fractured Fairy Tales (classic fairy tales told with a comic twist) and one of the most popular segments—Mr. Peabody and Sherman—an intellectual, glasses wearing dog and the little boy who he has time-traveling adventures with. In addition to Conrad, several other top voice actors participated including June Foray, Paul Frees, Hans Conried, Bill Scott, Edward Everett Horton and Daws Butler. Conrad narrated the Rocky and Bullwinkle adventures and shared narration of Dudley Do-Right with Paul Frees.

In the book *The Mouse that Roared: The Story of Jay Ward, Bill Scott, a Flying Squirrel...*, Bill Scott recalls that, "the recording sessions were the happiest time of everybody involved. Conrad, Paul, Hans Conried thought it was the greatest. Bill Conrad used to come over from shooting, in makeup and girdle, and say it was great to work with people who were professional. He would break up laughing, and although he had this deep voice, he has a high, high laugh." Scott recalls that Paul Frees was, "the most infuriating yet talented show-off son of a bitch I've ever known, but we all loved him. You just didn't dare let him know." Inevitably, according to Scott, Frees would reduce Conrad to a "fit of giggles" and one of them (either Frees or Conrad) would have to leave the room because if they looked at each other they might very well break up. June Foray (who voiced Rocky the flying squirrel) recalls that when Conrad, "did the narration…he turned comedic. He lost all the great profound voice, and it became hysterical."

Meanwhile Jack Webb invited Conrad to play a hard bitten city editor in the newspaper drama *-30-*. (-30- means "The End" in newspaper lingo). The entire film takes place inside the offices of the fictional Los Angeles Banner newspaper, and was based on the real *Los Angeles Examiner* right down to having its newsroom so well copied that many *Examiner* employees thought it must have been filmed inside their offices. The film tells the story of a typical day in the life of a large metropolitan newspaper (3PM-midnight). Webb stars as the managing editor and the cast includes lots of familiar faces from television including Whitney Blake, David Nelson, Joe Flynn, Richard Deacon and Howard McNear (as the sports editor).

The film was shot by Warner Brothers (though for some reason it was filmed on the sound stages of Republic Studios) in a three week period from late July to Mid-August of 1959 on a relatively miniscule budget with Webb (naturally) producing and directing in the semi documentary style he was so well known for from *Dragnet*. Conrad's character is sarcastic and overbearing but has a love for the newspaper business which is especially emphasized when he gives two copy boys a Sgt. Friday like monologue on the importance of newspapers:

"It's got print on it that tells stories that hundreds of good men all over the world have broken their backs to get. It gives a lot of information to a lot of people who wouldn't have known about these things if we hadn't taken the time to tell 'em. It's the sum total of the work of a lot

of guys who don't quit. And it only costs ten cents, that's all. But if you read the comic section or want ads, it's still the best buy for your money in the world."

Despite its low cost the film failed to find an audience and became one of Warner's biggest flops of the year. The reviews didn't help. "Mr. Webb has used for his title the traditional newsman's sign-off symbol. But his picture, crammed with so much smart-alec nonsense is rarely as authentic," opined the *New York Times*.

IV

In the final years of *Gunsmoke* a new writer pretty much took over the reins—Marian Clark. Marian Clark was a former news writer on KNX radio, the CBS affiliate in Los Angeles. She was also confined to a wheel chair. Kathleen Hite (who wrote 8 radio episodes of *Gunsmoke* and would go on to write several more for television) became an acquaintance of Clark's. She felt it would be therapeutic for Clark to write scripts and encouraged her write one for *Gunsmoke*. Clark's initial script was approved by Macdonnell and Meston, and it became the first of 81 radio scripts that Clark would write for the show from 1957-1961. Many of her scripts focused on women—but she could write well for any gender and some of her scripts are among the best written for the show.

Jud's Woman (12/1/57) has Matt and Chester encountering an obviously scared and abused woman in a lonely cabin out on the prairie—so afraid that she is clutching a gun when they enter. **Kitty's Killing** (2/2/58) tells the story of a religious fanatic who kills the husband of his deceased sister—who had died in childbirth. **The Surgery** (2/23/58) is about a woman so deathly ill that she will surely die if she doesn't have a surgery—but her husband won't allow Doc to perform it. **Livvie's Loss** (4/13/58) deals with a no-good husband who returns to his wife (Livvie) and son—and her fears that he will corrupt the son. **Old Flame** (6/15/58) has an ex-girlfriend of Matt's arriving in Dodge—with Kitty suspicious of her intentions, and Matt thinking she is just jealous. **Miguel's Daughter** (8/3/58) is a young Mexican girl who is abused by two cowboys who her father vows revenge on. **The Piano** (8/17/58) is one of Clark's best scripts about an ex-Southern belle who's bitter from the war and reluctant to help Matt and Chester as she clings to her few dear processions—including the piano of the title. **Kitty's Rebellion (9/28/58)** deals with the brother of an old friend of Kitty's visiting from New Orleans and aghast at finding Kitty running a saloon. **Kitty's Injury (12/14/57)** has Kitty thrown from a horse miles away from any help and Matt trying to figure out how to get her help in time. **Scared Boy (5/17/59)** involves a mother and her young son witnessing a murder and then becoming targets to keep them from talking. Kitty is abducted in an attempt to get Matt to release a prisoner in **Kitty's Kidnap (6/14/59)**. **Emma's Departure (7/5/59)** deals with a farm couple who live with virtually no human contact and the wife who hungers for it. **Delia's Father (2/7/60)** is an old friend of Matt's whose death he is partially responsible for—unbeknownst to his daughter. **Prescribed Killing (2/28/60)** tells the story of an abused woman who plans her own murder with the expectation that her husband will be blamed for it. **Kitty Accused (6/12/60)** deals with Kitty being accused of stealing a valuable piece of jewelry by the wife of a man who is infatuated with Kitty. **Two Mothers (9/18/60)** is the poignant story of two women—mothers—the mother of the murder victim and the mother of the murderer. All of these episodes feature strong plots and roles involving women—something that many western series or films didn't explore at that time.

As strong as Clark's writing for women was she proved she could write strong scripts involving male characters including Matt Dillon, Doc and Chester. **Blue Horse (5/25/58)** has Matt's horse stumbling and seriously injuring Matt. Chester has to ride back to Dodge to get help-leaving Matt with a prisoner. **Doc's Showdown (10/12/58)** deals with Doc trying to save the life of a young man shot in the back. The man dies and Doc comes up with a plan to smoke out the killer by keeping the dying a secret. **Target: Chester (11/9/58)** has Matt tricked into shooting Chester. **Chester's Mistake (4/12/59)** has Chester becoming a laughing stock of the town when he blunders on a simple task that Matt assigned to him. **The Badge (4/26/59)** deals with a man who thinks he will get the same respect as Matt Dillon as long as he wears his badge—even if he has to kill Matt for it. **Matt's Decision (9/6/59)** has Matt contemplating life free of marshalling and Dodge. **Hangman's Mistake (4/9/61)** involves Matt forced to release a prisoner he believes is guilty.

The final original episode of *Gunsmoke* was titled **Doc's Visitor** (**6/11/61**) from yet another Marion Clark script. The show deals with an offer Doc gets to move his practice to Philadelphia where he could make some big money and learn all kinds of new medical techniques. Doc is tempted to take the offer, but also feels an obligation to Dodge—a town that really needs him. The following week the episode **Letter of the Law** was rerun and at the end a simple announcement was made: "This is the final episode of *Gunsmoke*." According to Parley Baer the cast and crew had no idea that the show was ending until the last minute. It was the end of an era for the actors and also for radio drama.

CHAPTER FIVE: WARNER BROTHERS 1962-1968

In 1962 Jack Warner hired Jack Webb to be the head of the Warner Brothers television division. Warner decided that his studio's television efforts needed some retooling and thought that the no-nonsense Webb was the man to do the job in a cost effective way.

The previous season Webb had produced and hosted a new anthology series produced by Warner Brothers called *GE True* (sponsored by General Electric). The scripts were adapted from stories which had been published in *True Magazine*. As on *Dragnet* Webb wanted to present stories that were based on real life incidents.

Webb directed the premiere episode which was titled "Circle of Death," which was written by Dale Wasserman and dealt with the efforts of a Dr. James Fallon to remove a live 40 millimeter shell from the abdomen of a wounded Marine brought to the deck of a hospital ship during the battle of Okinawa during World War II. To portray Fallon Webb hired Bill Conrad. As he did on *Dragnet* Webb handled the narration of the story as well, "At 1830 hours exactly, the operation began on a human bomb dead center in the circle of death." Many critics liked the show and its premiere episode. *Variety* called "Circle of Death" a "slick, suspenseful half-hour. It's to the show's credit that the characters were credible and interesting. Production values were excellent."

In addition to starring in the premiere episode, Conrad was signed by Webb to direct several episodes of *GE True*. Out of thirty-three episodes produced during its single season on the air, Conrad directed twenty-one segments with most (but not all) of the remaining episodes directed by Webb himself. (The show lasted only a single season in part because it was up against the second half of the NBC ratings powerhouse *Bonanza*).

His acting job on the premier episode of *GE True* was virtually the last major acting job that Conrad would do for the next seven years. "I gave up acting… (Because) I felt then it was not honorable work for a grown man."

Webb was impressed with the efficient job that Conrad brought to his work on *GE True* and when he became the head of the Warner Brothers television division Webb decided to offer Conrad the post of his second in command. Conrad liked the challenge and accepted. Along with Conrad, Webb hired former actor Jimmy Lydon to be an associate producer working in tandem with Conrad. Lydon didn't know Conrad prior to meeting him through Jack Webb. "My first impression of Bill was this great big guy who had this commanding voice that made him a fortune and had a marvelous sense of humor and got along great with people."

Despite their long relationship there were often fireworks whenever Conrad and Webb got together. "Bill and I would go into Jack's office and Jack and Bill would pour themselves a drink—I didn't drink—and then they'd start fighting about this and that," Lydon recalls. "It was the way they were—the way the expressed themselves. I'd try to be the diplomat and tell them to cut it out and finally it would blow over. The truth of the matter is that despite the fighting they were really close friends and got along fine."

One of the first orders of business was to totally revamp *77 Sunset Strip* which had been a popular show for several seasons for Warner Brothers. The show had been on for five seasons and Warners thought the show needed a breath of fresh air to help bring in new viewers. "The show was successful but junk and Jack wanted us to revamp the show, and so, rightly or wrongly, we got rid of the rest of the cast except for Efrem Zimbalist, Jr., who became kind of a globe-trotting private eye," Lydon later recalled. For Conrad one of the joys of this decision was firing the actor who played the hair combing—valet parking 'Kookie' on the show, Edd Byrnes. "I had the pleasure of firing the little prick," Conrad later said. "He annoyed me no end." According to Conrad, who directed an episode of the series during its fifth season, he asked Byrnes to record a public affairs announcement for some charity and Byrnes flatly refused and then rubbed salt in the wound by asking, "What are you going to do—fire me?" Later, when he was fired, Byrnes went to Jack

Webb to appeal the decision and Webb told him, "Bill Conrad makes the decisions down there."

Efrem Zimbalist, Jr., recalls that with Jack Webb as head of the television division his character of Stu Bailey, "transformed into a civilian Sergeant Friday, even to the slacks and sport jacket identified with Webb in *Dragnet*." Still Zimbalist was impressed with the shows new producer, Conrad. "Despite such an enormous miscalculation on the front office's part, thanks to Bill Conrad's creativity we were able that year to turn out some memorable episodes."

Webb and Conrad devised an ambitious way to kick off the new season with a five-part story titled (simply) "Five." The shows took Zimbalist's private eye all over the world and featured a huge line up of guest stars including Richard Conte, Telly Savalas, Peter Lorre, Burgess Meredith, Walter Slezak, Victor Buono, Jacques Bergerac, Brian Keith, Herbert Marshall, William Shatner, Ed Wynn and Cesar Romero. The gambit didn't work. The show brought in no new viewers and the new concept (minus many old favorite cast members) alienated its loyal viewers. "We tried something new with an aging show and it didn't quite work," Lydon wistfully recalled years later.

One show that Conrad and Lydon developed that they were really proud of was a series called *Temple Houston* about a lawyer in the Wild West starring Jeffrey Hunter. Webb called Conrad and Lydon into his office and told them that he had sold *Temple Houston* as a series and they had four weeks to get the show on the air. Lydon recalls:

"We panicked because it was impossible to have scripts written and them shoot them, score them, dub them and deliver them to the network in four weeks! So we called in some very fast writers—they agreed and delivered us shootable scripts the following Friday. We put them into the mill right away and were shooting it Monday morning. We did all the pre-production work Saturday and Sunday. We shot two episodes together. We cut them, scored them and I got the print of the first one out of the lab on a Friday night about 8:30…We worked day and night…with preproduction, production, cutting scoring looping—everything! The composer wrote a whole score for it in two days (a variation of 'Yellow Rose of Texas')…It was just incredible…Bill Conrad directed

two scripts simultaneously on two different soundstages at Warners. We bicycled Jeff and (co-star Jack) Elam between two companies and Bill shot 'em both in four and a half days. Two complete one hour shows!"

Lydon recalls Hunter as "a lovely man" who, he thinks, may have had an affair with Conrad's wife, whom he was a particular favorite of. Conrad's son, Christopher, recalls Hunter being a welcome guest at the Conrad home and as "a dear friend of my mom." (Christopher does confirm that Susan Conrad did have a relationship with Hunter, but because of the Conrad's open marriage it didn't alienate Conrad's relationship with Hunter. Conrad would go on to use Hunter not only on this TV series but also in the 1965 film *Brainstorm*). Unfortunately *Temple Houston*, which aired on NBC, was not a ratings success—and neither was another Conrad-Lydon series, *Mister Roberts*, based on the famous Broadway play and 1955 Warner Brothers film. Both were cancelled after only one season.

It was while he was working at Warner Brothers as a TV producer and director that Conrad began working on *The Fugitive* for a producer that he would have his biggest TV hit with—Quinn Martin.

The Fugitive ran on ABC from 1963-1967 and tells the story of Dr. Richard Kimble (played by David Janssen), a man, we are told from the very beginning, was innocent of murdering his wife—even though he was convicted of the crime. While he was being transported to prison there was an accident and Kimble takes it on the lam—in hopes of clearing his name by finding the man that he knows killed his wife—known as "the one-armed man." Throughout the entire run Lt. Gerard (Barry Morse) relentlessly pursues Kimble. Each week finds Kimble incognito in some town or city trying to keep a low profile while earning some money so he can keep going and hoping nobody will recognize him. *The Fugitive* is loosely based on the case of Dr. Sam Sheppard who, in 1954, was convicted of murdering his wife in a controversial trial that garnered national headlines.

Lt. Gerard and the one-armed man were not used in every episode, but the voice of William Conrad was featured each week introducing the episode and explaining Kimble's predicament. "William Conrad had this voice that shook the world," recalled

Fugitive associate producer George Eckstein. "In the pilot, Bill tells you Kimble's innocent. You can't deny anything Bill Conrad says, he's so authoritative." The producer of *The Fugitive*, Alan Armer, who wrote most of Conrad's narration each week, later stated that he could "hear Conrad's voice" in his head as he wrote. Conrad's booming voice was mostly heard at the start of the first act and then again in the epilog. Conrad's opening narration did much to sell the show and create sympathy for Kimble:

"The name: Dr. Richard Kimble. Destination: Death Row State Prison. The irony: Richard Kimble is innocent. Proved guilty when Richard Kimble could not prove that moment before discovering his murdered wife's body, he saw a one-armed man running from the vicinity of his home. Richard Kimble ponders his fate as he looks at the world for the last time and sees only darkness. But in that darkness, fate moves its huge hand..."

On the night of Tuesday, August 29, 1967, Conrad declared, "the running stopped" and ABC broadcast the final episode of *The Fugitive* which was viewed by an audience estimated at 78 million (45.9 percent of American households with a television set) to see if Kimble is vindicated or not. This was a record which held out until the *Dallas* "Who Shot J.R.?" episode of November 21, 1980.

Despite being a part of this landmark series—Conrad wasn't overly impressed. "It's the same story over and over again," he proclaimed years later. "I'll say to you today it's a lousy idea. But that's what is nice about TV and why I am no longer a producer."

II

What of Bill Conrad, the private man during this period? Christopher Conrad later described his home life—growing up in the San Fernando Valley in Sherman Oaks:

"It was comfortable. We lived on the corner of Longridge and Valley Vista. The house, which had previously been owned by John Wayne, had a large front and back yard with lots of trees. We had oranges, lemons, grapefruits and mom made great preserves from all the plums.

We had walnut trees, one of which I built a tree house fort in and a big olive tree that mom hung one of those 'basket chairs' on. I guess you'd describe it as a sort of rambler, mom's large bedroom and my smaller room (both with their own bathrooms) were on one end, the garage, kitchen and dining room on the other. In the middle was the large sun room off the patio and a long living room with a piano on one side and a fireplace on the other, though in the center there was both a basement and one upstairs bedroom—that was dad's lair. We used to have a beautiful vine covered patio where mom and dad held great Fourth of July parties, but this was torn down when I was around ten and replaced with this ugly aluminum patio. When I was maybe six the kitchen got a big remodel, a 'maid's room' was added on top of the garage and a second dining/family/bar (complete with stain glass windows and two sided fireplace) was added. And somewhere between all that we had a big bomb shelter installed in the back yard. I remember going into it only once right after it was built, but it was quickly completely covered under a bunch of bushes to the point you couldn't get into it if you had wanted! In the backyard there was a big rectangular pool and a pool house, a kinda barn shaped building that had a small bathroom off the back side (off the pool, near the slab that housed the pool pump works and near my tree fort) and another entrance off a path leading from the patio. The room was large enough to house a full pool table, with alcoves holding a sit down card table (with windows looking out over the yard between the pool and the house), a single bed and a small wet bar/kitchen, as well as bathroom with a shower (which I turned into a darkroom when I lived in the poolroom in the summertime between my 15th and 18th years.")

They had some notable neighbors, though not all were in the entertainment business. There were dentists, doctors and lawyers along with some entertainment elites. Among them was the composer-musician David Rose (who was once married to Judy Garland) and who was best known for his composition of "The Stripper" and the theme to *Bonanza*. "His two daughters were five or six years older (than me)," Christopher Conrad recalls, "but David's hobby was miniature trains (some like you have around a Christmas tree, but mostly larger miniatures that pulled box cars big enough for a couple of kids to sit in), and he had one that went around his entire property that he'd invite the neighborhood kids over to ride." Other notables included Barbara Eden and her husband Michael Ansara—and down the street lived the great Dodger pitcher Sandy Koufax.

Among the celebrities who occasionally came over for social events included Jack Webb and his wife Jackie, Jimmy Lydon and his wife, Virginia Gregg (who Christopher would recall as a "very dear family friend" who he called Aunt Virginia) and Jeffrey Hunter. Old friends like Parley Baer, Larry Dobkin and Hans Conried were always welcome. Christopher recalls other 'industry' friends who his parents would socialize with but rather than being big star names they were mostly composers, writers, directors and other "behind the scenes" people. "You have to realize I grew up around all this so have a 'someone' over to our home wasn't really noteworthy," recalls Christopher. "Add to that I was a kid and not all that interested in most of these adults. By the time I was a teenager, it just wasn't cool to hang around too much with my parents. And even when I did go on sets with my dad or they'd have a party, seeing actors and other celebrities just wasn't a big deal nor particularly memorable."

Unsurprisingly there were servants in the Conrad residence. "I know we had a black maid by the name of Mary when I was really young," Christopher recalls. "But I remember Lynne Shanahan; she was a lithe young dark haired British lady who I'll always remember as my own Mary Poppins. After she left Manuel Ota came to work for us. Manny and I are very close. Both Lynne and Manny (as well as a couple of folks who worked for my parents in later years) were never really considered 'servants', they were part of our family—and with Manny that was particularly true."

Christopher came to realize that his parents were not conventional Ward and June Cleaver types. "Mom had boyfriends and dad had girlfriends. They loved each other deeply, but they had separate bedrooms and lived in the same house and led separate social lives…I grew up a perfectly adjusted and happy human being and I bless my mom and dad for that."

Jimmy Lydon offers a somewhat different perspective on the Conrad's marriage to Susan than what his son witnessed. "He was in love, but as time went on she made him miserable," Lydon recalls. "She was always cheating on him with another man. She would take some guy to Palm Springs—it caused him a great deal of pain. I recall once late at night at Warner Brothers his just breaking down and explaining to me that she was with some guy in Palm Springs. But he wouldn't divorce her—he loved her. Bill wanted to have a roving eye of his own, but he was too big and fat to really attract the women."

III

It was while working in the Warner Brother's television division that Jack Warner called on Conrad to make a feature film. It would be a relatively low budget horror film titled *Two on a Guillotine*. Conrad would produce and direct the picture. When Warner asked Conrad if he needed anything else, Conrad replied, "I need Jim" meaning, of course, his right hand Jimmy Lydon. Warner told Conrad to "Go and get him." Thus the Conrad-Lydon movie production team was born. In the next few years this team would produce ten efficiently made and low-cost pictures.

Two on a Guillotine was akin to the type of film that producer William Castle routinely produced—competent and inexpensive horror films on a 'B' picture budget that had plenty of shocks and were often promoted with in theater gimmicks to bring in audiences (films such as *House on Haunted Hill, The Tingler, 13 Ghosts*, and *Strait-Jacket*, which cast movie legend Joan Crawford and, as an additional gimmick, the theaters handed out cardboard axes to patrons). Conrad would not go in for the gimmicks but he did like the quick and efficient way that Castle produced his films—most of which made a healthy profit.

Two on a Guillotine begins with a magician who, while attempting an illusion, using a guillotine and accidentally (or was it?) beheads (nothing like the sight of a decapitated head to shock audiences straight away) his wife. The story then jumps ahead some twenty years or so with the death of the magician and the seemingly weird clause in his will that the only way his daughter can inherit his estate is to spend seven full nights in his supposedly haunted mansion. Her father also promises that during that week his spirit will appear. Well, this is too much for a reporter, who offers his services to stay with the daughter during this week so that he can write up any story of spooky happenings. The script was written by John Kneubuhl and Henry Slesar (based on Slesar's story). Slesar had written several stories for "Alfred Hitchcock Magazine" that Hitchcock himself had read and liked. He hired Slesar to write for his series *Alfred Hitchcock Presents* and *The Alfred Hitchcock Hour*. Slesar wrote over fifty TV scripts for the Hitchcock series. Later he became head writer of the TV crime/mystery soap, *The Edge of Night*. Kneubuhl was a veteran TV writer as well with several writing assignments on the Boris Karloff anthology *Thriller*. He later invented the character of Dr. Loveless for the TV series *The Wild Wild West* and wrote several episodes featuring Loveless as James West's arch enemy.

The cast assembled is first-rate. Cesar Romero is cast as the magician. The suave and handsome Romero had a long career in films including appearances in such classics as *The Thin Man, Wee Willie Winkie, Frontier Marshal, Captain from Castile, Vera Cruz*, and *Ocean's 11*. At the time he was making this film he was only a year away from Television immortality for playing 'The Joker' on the campy 60's series *Batman*. The daughter is played by pretty Connie Stevens, a Warner Brother contract actress, who played 'Cricket' on the detective series *Hawaiian Eye* and made several appearances on *77 Sunset Strip* (she recorded the song based on the character 'Kookie' on that series titled, 'Kookie, Kookie, Lend Me Your Comb'—which actually reached #4 on the pop charts). In addition she appeared in such Warner films as *Parrish, Susan Slade* and *Palm Springs Weekend*. For the part of the reporter Conrad hired Dean Jones, who had been a MGM contract player (he appeared with Elvis Presley in *Jail House Rock*) and TV actor (*Ensign O'Toole*) and around the time he was making this film he would also begin a career as the house leading man of the Walt Disney Studios, appearing in a dozen films (*Blackbeard's Ghost, The Love Bug, The Shaggy D.A.*, etc) over the next decade or so. The cast also includes old friends like Virginia Gregg and Parley Baer.

The cinematographer on *Two on a Guillotine* was the veteran Sam Leavitt, who had been in films since the early thirties and photographed such films as *A Star is Born* (the 1954 version with Judy Garland), *The Man with the Golden Arm, The Defiant Ones* and *Anatomy of a Murder*. Along the way he would be nominated for three Oscars for his photography (and win for *The Defiant Ones*). He would photograph all three of Conrad's directorial efforts in 1965. The music in the film was by Max Steiner, the Austrian-born composer who was nominated 24 times for an Oscar and ultimately won three: *The Informer, Now Voyager, Since You Went Away.* His most famous score was for *Gone with the Wind.* He would ultimately score some 140 films at Warner Brothers—with his assignment on *Two on a Guillotine* being his last for the studio.

Of the talent co-producer Lydon recalls Romero as "a thorough professional" with "a good sense of humor, always on time and always knew what to do. He's a snap, an easy guy to direct, and he knew the business upside down and back and he's what we call a professional." The younger leads—Stevens and Jones are recalled as "very pleasant, very nice." Lydon recalls that his job was to keep Conrad "on schedule and on budget." He goes on to say about director Conrad, "(Bill) growled a lot, but his growling was just good, competent growling, it wasn't meanness or anything like that."

Lydon later recalled a good directorial flourish by Conrad, as related to writer Tom Weaver:

"The kid from Disney, Dean Jones, is walking up the stairs in this dark, creepy house and all of a sudden there's a scream and this woman (the housekeeper played by Virginia Gregg) *stands up in front of him. You're not expecting it and suddenly here's this woman screaming and popping into the frame. It was wonderful."*

In another scene Gregg falls down stairs to her death. Conrad had the idea of putting the camera inside of a wheel. "After she falls, she'll disappear, and then the camera is going to be her, and I'm gonna roll it down the stairs so it goes upside down, right side up, upside down," Conrad told Lydon. It turned out to be a very effective scene.

Lydon was also asked about the scene where the magician's will is read. Rather than staging it (as would be usual) in an attorney's office or the drawing room of some mansion—Conrad filmed it on stage at the Hollywood Bowl. "That's what Bill would call a 'plot scene,' and Bill always had a way to get around those things," Lydon recalled to Weaver. "He once said to me, 'Jim, you know the secret of plot scenes? When you get the cast all ready and rehearsed and now you're gonna do the first take, when the camera gets up to speed, you say, 'Okay, fellas, now play it ten percent faster than you just did. ACTION!' Before they can even think about it they're doing it, and they're gonna cue-bite and everything else. And when they talk fast, all of a sudden, the audience is gonna start to really listen, and you're gonna get away with the plot scene.'"

When *Two on a Guillotine* was released in January of 1965 it was to mostly indifferent or poor reviews. Howard Thompson (the poor man's Bosley Crowther) wrote in the *New York Times* that *Two on a Guillotine* is a "dull, silly, tedious clinker." The only praise he gave to the picture was to supporting actresses Virginia Gregg and Connie Gilchrist. The film is better than that—it's as good as most William Castle pictures and maybe even a bit more entertaining— and Conrad adds some nice directorial touches. It's a fun popcorn movie—not to be taken seriously, but to be enjoyed on a nice rainy night—preferably with some thunder rolling. The film did end up making a profit for Warner Brothers.

Conrad had a real liking for *Two on a Guillotine*. Christopher Conrad recalls that it was one of his dad's five favorite films. He recalls that his dad often showed the film in the projection room of the Sherman Oak's house.

The next Conrad directed film is *My Blood Runs Cold* which starred Warner Brothers' blonde haired and blue eyed Troy Donahue. He had been making films since 1957, but his break came in 1959 when he was cast opposite Sandra Dee as the young lovers of *A Summer Place*. The film became a popular box office hit for the year (and the *Theme from A Summer Place* composed by Max Steiner became even more popular reaching #1 on the Billboard charts for nine straight weeks). The film catapulted Donahue to teen heartthrob status and Warner's believed (rightly so for a while) that they had a new box office star. Donahue then starred on the popular Warner Brothers TV series *Surfside 6* and appeared in such films as *Parrish, Susan Slade, Rome Adventure* and *A Distant Trumpet*—the last two with his then wife Suzanne Pleshette. But Donahue was tired of the roles that Warner's was offering him and went on suspension until a better role came up. Five months later Conrad and Warner's offered him *My Blood Runs Cold* and he took it. His part would at least be different than the others he had been playing.

My Blood Runs Cold tells the story of a young woman who accidentally runs a young man on a motorcycle off the road. She turns out to be the beautiful daughter of a wealthy businessman. The young man insists that he and she were lovers in a past life. She doesn't believe him, but then he convinces her when he gives her a locket that belonged to her great-great grandmother (and look-a-like). His charm seduces her and she falls in love with him, much to the annoyance of her father. This charm masks another side of him that he manages to keep out of sight as he appears to suffer from headaches which lead to what seems to be seizures. The film wants to make the audience guess if the young man is sincere or some kind of psychopath out for her daddy's money.

Donahue, of course, is cast as the young man. For the part of the young woman the studio at first thought about their contract star Connie Stevens who had just worked with Conrad on *Two on a Guillotine*. Then it was announced that Carol Lynley would play the young woman— but she soon backed out. Instead Conrad cast sexy Joey Heatherton, who had worked previously on Broadway in *The Sound of Music* and a straight dramatic play *There was a Little Girl* opposite Jane Fonda and Dean Jones. She had just played the nympho daughter of Susan Hayward in Warner's soaper *Where Love Has Gone*. An excellent supporting cast was assembled including Barry Sullivan (as the industrialist father), Jeanette Nolan, Nicolas Coster and Russell Thorson.

Donahue expressed his excitement about the picture to columnist Louella Parsons, "I love this picture! I've never done a chiller before. In fact, until now I seldom did anything other than smoke cigarettes and drive off in a car." Conrad also expressed happiness with his star, "The kid's an actor, and a good one."

Co-producer Jimmy Lydon told Tom Weaver that what he remembered most about the film was its two young leads—and he wasn't overly impressed. At one point at the climax of the picture Troy Donahue has to climb up a four story high structure where he has a fight scene and Donahue took liberty with his safety— seemingly close to falling several times which scared Lydon, who, as usual, was on the scene. Afterward Donahue came down and just seemed to laugh about it. "So, to me, he was a very strange man," Lydon says. "I don't want to accuse anybody of anything, but...his cigarettes looked kinda funny."

As for Joey Heaterton—Lydon told the following anecdote:

"Bill was doing a very sentimental scene with her, and she was not 'getting' it, and he finally blew his top, and he hollered. And after his outburst, she looked at him and said, 'Ya don't like dat? Okay, lemme try somethin' else!' Well, Bill just started to fall apart! He thought that the least she would do was cry or something! At that point, he just threw up his hands and walked away!"

Of the three films directed by Conrad *My Blood Runs Cold* is probably the least effective. It has plusses such as beautiful location work (in black and white photography) on the Monterey Peninsula in Northern California and the breathtaking physical presence of Joey Heatherton—at times Conrad's camera longingly stays focused on her sexy body. The supporting cast, particularly Jeanette Nolan, is uniformly good. But the story is rather bland and boring. There are long periods of tedious line readings (especially by the leads) without much emotion behind them. Despite their good looks the chemistry between Donahue and Heatherton is almost non-existent. The script by John Mantley who later wrote and produced hundreds of episodes of TV's *Gunsmoke*, lacks suspense.

The *New York Times* review (March 25, 1965) pretty accurately called the film a "wordy, bloodless, little Warner chiller." The review went on to pan Donahue ("Mr. Donahue has two expressions: stunned and pained") and Heatherton while throwing bouquets at the more experienced veteran supporting cast. The film didn't do well at the box office and Donahue's Warner's contract was not picked up.

Of all the films that William Conrad either produced or directed during the 1960's the one with the best reputation today is his 1965 film noir *Brainstorm*.

The plot is interesting. A woman's car is stalled on a railroad track, and a passing motorist stops to investigate, he finds the woman unconscious in the car. A train is fast approaching and he has to break into the car just in a nick of time to save her from certain death. Later he finds out that 1) she is the wife of the owner of the company he works for and 2) She parked on the tracks on purpose and took some medication to put herself out and meant to commit suicide. The two soon begin an affair and fall in love. The man wants her to leave her husband and marry him—but her husband tells her if she does she will lose custody of their child. Her lover comes up with a plan to kill her husband so they can be together and not worry about losing her child. The twist is that he immerses himself into studying how to appear that he murdered the husband not intentionally but due to temporary insanity. This way he would avoid the gas chamber and be released from a mental hospital in due course—once he is 'normal' again. The plan goes according to plan and he kills the woman's husband and is sentenced to a sanitarium, however, later on he is visited by the woman he committed the murder for and believed loved him only to find that she has another man in her life. As usual in film noir the man is played a sucker by a woman who is only using him.

The cast is one of the best that Conrad ever assembled for a film. The sucker is played by Jeffrey Hunter, who had recently played Jesus Christ in Nicholas Ray's underappreciated *King of King*, but whose best film was John Ford's classic *The Searchers*. More recently he had starred in the Conrad produced Warner television series *Temple Houston*. The femme fatale is played by beautiful Anne Francis, who gave scores of wonderful performances in movies (*Bad Day at Black Rock, Forbidden Planet, Blackboard Jungle*) and television (including that sexy cult series *Honey West*) without really becoming a big star—the mores the pity. The doomed husband is played by the always reliable Dana Andrews, who emerged as a strong leading man in the late forties and early fifties in films like *Laura* and *The Best Years of Our Lives*. Andrews was no stranger to the dark crevices of film noir having appeared in such films as *Edge of Doom, Where the Sidewalk Ends, While the City Sleeps* and *Beyond a Reasonable Doubt*. Lovely Viveca Lindfors plays a psychiatrist at the facility that the Hunter character is sentenced and he believes that she is to be trusted, but in actuality she believes he is dangerously unbalanced (and she may be correct). A strong cast is supplemented by nice turns by Stacy Harris, Strother Martin, John Mitchum (brother of Robert), and Richard Kiel. Conrad even takes on a cameo as a patient at the psychiatric hospital.

The screenplay was by Mann Rubin, who was mostly a television writer (*Climax!*, *The Alfred Hitchcock Hour*, *Checkmate*) and had written the screenplay for one film (The 1959 Hope Lange-Joan Crawford soap opera *The Best of Everything*). *Brainstorm* was his second feature film—Conrad would use him a year later for adapting the screenplay of Norman Mailer's novel *An American Dream*. The best film that Rubin wrote would probably be the gritty 1967 crime drama *Warning Shot*. Later he would do some writing for Quinn Martin Production including several episodes of *Barnaby Jones*.

As usual Conrad's co-producer was Jimmy Lydon. He recalled to writer Tom Weaver that "Dana Andrews was a pro. The bigger they are, the nicer they were to work with." Lydon recalls Jeffrey Hunter as a "nice guy, good actor (and) no problem whatsoever." He recalls that Conrad "enjoyed directing" and that he (Lydon) was his right hand man. "I arranged to get a lot of the things that we needed," he told Weaver. "I was supposed to find an auditorium where we could shoot a scene where Jeffrey Hunter marches down the center aisle, through the crowd, and shoots Dana Andrews in the middle of his speech. I went to TRW out in the San Fernando Valley, a big supplier of NASA stuff, and I went into their executive offices and I met with the vice-president and I explained what I wanted. And I figured he was going to throw me out when I said the scene involved Jeffrey Hunter walking down the main exhibit hall and shooting and killing the man on the stage. But the vice-president laughed and he said, 'Yeah! Okay.' Of course, in the movie we didn't identify the place as TRW, we made up a phony name for the place."

Anne Francis considered Conrad "one of the brightest directors I've ever worked with in my life—he is absolutely incredible." That is high praise considering that among the directors Francis worked with were John Sturges, Raoul Walsh, Richard Brooks, Charles Walters, William Wyler, George Marshall and Jean Negulesco. She told *Filmfax* that Conrad had "a great eye for the camera, and he would walk in on the set and see something that would suddenly set it all off in his mind, and away we'd go. We go on a wonderful trip, both visually with (a) camera, and with the scene as well. He was brilliant."

The film was released in the early summer of 1965. Howard Thompson in the *New York Times* felt that the "outcome was predictable from the start." He praised both Anne Francis and Dana Andrews, but thought that Jeffrey Hunter was "hopelessly miscast...He simply looks too intelligent and decent, which says a lot for Mr. Hunter. But it sabotages Brainstorm." Au Contraire, Mr. Thompson. The fact that Hunter seems so decent and intelligent is an asset for the film for it keeps the audience guessing—is this guy really acting like he is insane or IS HE REALLY INSANE. Other reviews were equally dismissive of the film including Judith Crist's comment that the film was "a sub-B potboiler for those who find comic books too intellectual." Film historian and critic Leslie Halliwell thought it started off well but hit the skids around the mid-way mark.

Over time *Brainstorm's* reputation has built. The book *Film Noir: An Encyclopedic Reference to the American Style* called *Brainstorm* "a minor masterpiece of the 1960's." One of the strongest proponents of the film is author Nicholas Christopher who in his book *Somewhere in the Night* writes:

"Just as Kiss Me Deadly is a very late entry in the classic noir cycle, Brainstorm, released in 1965, is a straggler to those black and white films noirs of the early part of the decade. While Party Girl (1958-MGM) marks the onset of the color film noir era, Brainstorm is undoubtedly the last of the truly great black and white films noirs...It is unquestionably the most nihilistic film noir of either the classic or present-day cycle; it serves as a precursor to the neo-noirs of the present day, which both draws on the earliest films noirs and anticipates unerringly the obsessions that will inform all subsequent ones."

Christopher goes on to write that the film was 'brilliantly directed by William Conrad.'

In the book *Film Noir* author Bruce Crowther calls *Brainstorm* "An interesting psychological movie of the paranoid post-noir period" and goes on to write, "Sharp direction and editing help make *Brainstorm* a better movie than its consignment to late-night television suggests." Finally Film critic Jack Stevenson (author of *Land of a Thousand Balconies*) included *Brainstorm* among his choices of the top ten films of all-time in the 2002 *Sight and Sound* poll of film critics and directors. Not bad for a little film that cost under a million dollars to produce.

IV

It was while he was employed at Warner Brothers that Conrad's son Christopher became more aware of what his father did for a living. He knew little of his dad's acting career. He became vaguely aware that he was a businessman and worked at a movie studio and on Halloween he could come to the studio's make up department to get made up in any kind of costume imaginable.

While Conrad was generally a workaholic and had little time for family life he did have many hobbies. Christopher Conrad later recalled:

"He collected pipes, shot guns, high end precision air rifles, he fly fished and flew gliders. He built radios and other electronic gadgets, and early hobby had been photography, he sailed, he deep sea fished, he traveled and he loved food as well as drink. I remember an early bit of advice, he said, 'Son, in all things moderation…especially moderation.'"

Conrad enjoyed playing games with Susan. "My mom and dad had this wonderful repartee and loved to play word games together," Christopher recalls. "He would get upset at her because she did the *New York Times* crossword puzzle in pen. She had a friend in New York who worked on the puzzles who would give her the answers."

Conrad's career kept him from truly bonding with his son during these years. "For reasons I still don't fully understand our relationship for him wasn't easy. I remember only going on one camping trip together (which he also brought our house boy along on to take care of me)…that said, I do have deeply fond memories of hours just sitting in the pool listening to this short wave radio he had, spinning the dial and hearing all sorts of snippets of conversations, odd trills and electronic beeps and buzzing. When the reception was poor or we became board we'd play 'clam' where he'd lean with his back against the side of the pool, stretch out his legs at an angle and I'd swim underwater between his legs and the wall trying not to touch his legs. With each pass he'd bring his legs closer to the wall till the point that I wasn't able to pass without brushing his leg, where upon he'd snap his legs tight against the wall trapping me like in a clam's shell. Sounds weird I know, but it truly is one of my fondest memories and probably the most time I ever spent with just him and me."

When Christopher was thirteen he walked by a dumpster by the side of their house and made a striking discovery—a bunch of reel-to-reel tapes that had been tossed out. He had a tape player and he thought he could salvage these tapes and record over them. "When I threaded them up to check what might be on them, that was when I first discovered my father's radio years," Christopher recalled years later. It was just something that father and son didn't talk about. Christopher had no idea that he had been a major star on radio—at thirteen he had little idea what radio was since he grew up in the television age. "That (radio) is the work that still sends chills down my neck, finds me choking back tears or has me rolling on the floor laughing. You see dad was never one to reminisce; he tossed out the past and moved on. He would occasionally talk to old friends, but rarely of old times."

V

Jack Warner was impressed by the fact that in a little more than six months Conrad had produced and directed three films that all came in on schedule and on budget. This was Warner's kind of producer, and so he made Conrad an offer of running his own production unit. Conrad wouldn't be responsible for directing these pictures, but he would be executive producer with (once again) his friend and partner Jimmy Lydon acting as co-producer.

Conrad would make seven pictures budgeted at $1 million each. That was considered an 'A' picture budget back in the 1930's, but distinctly a lower budget for the 1960's. The films were made with the kind of speed that the studios used to be famous for during the late, lamented studio era. "At one point, we were seeing three sets of rushes every day: We had one picture that was almost finished and two new ones shooting, so I would see two and a half hours of rushes!," Lydon recalled.

The first of the Conrad-Lydon films was *An American Dream* based on a novel by Norman Mailer, but adapted for the screen by Mann Rubin. As Lydon remembers they never had to deal with or see Mailer. As director Conrad hired a TV veteran and former actor named Robert Gist, who was once, briefly, married to the superb character actress Agnes Moorehead. Gist was a fairly active television director who by the time of making his feature film debut with *An American Dream* had already directed twenty episodes of *Peter Gunn* as well as multiple episodes of *Naked City, Route 66, Dr. Kildare, The Richard Boone Show, Slattery's People* and individual episodes of many other TV shows. Gist came cheap and was eager to direct a feature film and was soon signed on.

An American Dream tells the story an ex-congressman who is now a popular TV talk-show host—kind of a David Susskind in that he dealt with contemporary issues and problems. His latest target is a powerful mobster and the Los Angeles Police Department which may be helping to shield him. The talk-show host encounters police problems when his estranged wife commits suicide from a high rise apartment building following a fight with her husband. However, there is lack of proof to hold the talk show host and he is released by police and then gets involved with an old girlfriend who is now the girlfriend of the mobster he has been targeting on his show. Now he has not only to contend with the Los Angeles Police Department watching his every move but also gangsters—some dream!

The leads were Stuart Whitman (as the talk show host), Eleanor Parker (as his estranged wife) and Janet Leigh (as the gangster's mistress). "Whitman was sort of a second level leading man," says Lydon, "while Leigh and particularly Parker were stars, they were past their prime. But they were good and so were the supporting cast (which included Barry Sullivan, Lloyd Nolan, J.D. Cannon and Murray Hamilton) and they were affordable. We certainly couldn't afford big name stars, but we certainly wanted the best talent we could get according to our budgetary restraints—and we did." Sullivan worked previously with Conrad in *Tension* (and would later appear on *Cannon*), while Leigh worked with Conrad on a 1953 *Lux Radio Theater* adaptation of *The People Against O'Hara*.

Filming went relatively smoothly at first until Conrad and Lydon got some "troubling reports from the set." Lydon went down to investigate and found out that Gist had a bunch of film students following him around and watching his every move while he was explaining the intricacies of making a motion picture. "This was on our time," Lydon recalls. "I set him straight on his priorities." Gist got rid of the students and the film finished shooting on time and budget. Despite this Lydon has little good to say about his director, "Gist talked a great game but he didn't really deliver. He wasn't a bad director but he wasn't too good either—and his lack of imagination probably hurt the picture."

The reviews were nothing to brag about. The *New York Times* lambasted it, "With four months to go, the years worst movie may be *An American Dream*." Pauline Kael dismissed it as "being written and directed by some fellows from television." She also thought it was pretty "tawdry" junk—like the same years *The Oscar* but not nearly as good. *Monthly Film Bulletin* wrote in its review, "There is little to be said in favour of this relentlessly sordid and over-heated melodrama."

Despite this *An American Dream* is not a boring film. It holds interest and could be seen today as high camp—a kind of bizarre example of what a major establishment studio of the mid-to-late sixties would see as adult and contemporary. Furthermore Eleanor Parker's over-the-top performance is a treat to watch. Several of the reviewers (even those who condemned the film) found praise for Parker (one of our under-appreciated actresses). "An acid, shrewish performance by Eleanor Parker as a rich, alcoholic wife gets (the film) away to a tough, crackling start," wrote *The London Daily Mirror* in its review, "...but the moment...Parker regrettably exits, the film trails off into a soggy blend of police procedure, turgid romance and mild gangsterdom."

An American Dream was Norman Mailer's favorite novel but he contends he never saw the film, though he thought it was the only novel he ever wrote that would make a "transcendently splendid movie." It was probably for the best. He heard from friends who did see the movie and he thought that moving the setting from New York to Los Angeles was a huge mistake. "I mean—a guy wouldn't push his wife out a window in Los Angeles—For one thing, there aren't that many high windows!" (Really?)

The film may have not been a critical success but it did earn itself an Oscar nomination for Best Original Song, "A Time for Love", by Jimmy Mandel and Paul Francis Webster (and sung by a dubbed Janet Leigh in the film). The film was also photographed by three time Oscar nominee Sam Leavitt, who had also photographed all three of Conrad's previous directorial efforts.

Next on the Conrad-Lydon slate was a war picture titled *First to Fight*. Young actor Chad Everett was loaned out from MGM to play the sole survivor of a Japanese attack during World War II at Guadalcanal. He wins the Medal of Honor and is brought home to train new recruits. Despite finding love and marrying he finds he feels emptiness in his life and wants to return to the front lines. Along with Chad Everett the cast included Dean Jagger, Bobby Troup (the jazz singer wrote and performed the song "Daddy"in the film), Claude Akins, James Best, and, in only his second film, Gene Hackman.

The film was directed by Christian Nyby, whose first directorial effort was the sci-fi classic *The Thing From Another World*, but since that film was produced by Howard Hawks—most people have assumed that Hawks was the actual director of the picture. Nyby himself said, "Nobody believed a first-time director could have such a big hit. They gave all the credit to Howard." In the end Nyby became a solid journeyman director with more than one hundred credits to his name when Conrad hired him for *First to Fight*. "Nyby had a lot of experience," Lydon later recalled. "He knew how to work quickly—thanks to his years on television—and efficiently. Those were plusses. Another plus was that he came cheap." Also of interest is the man who wrote the film, Gene L. Coons, who was also a TV veteran including scribing several episodes of *Star Trek*.

Jimmy Lydon recalls, "We thought we had done a very good war picture with *First to Fight*. It starred a good looking young actor who seemed to be on his way up in Chad Everett (true enough, but Everett would find his biggest success on television not movies—he starred for several seasons on the medical drama *Medical Center*). But Bill had cast another actor, average looking, who had not yet made a big break in pictures named Gene Hackman. We would use Hackman in two of our films. He was a superb actor even then and we were always proud that we used him early in his career in our pictures. Shortly after than he got *Bonnie and Clyde* which really put him on the map."

Next up was *A Covenant with Death* which starred former *Route 66* star George Maharis, as a young Mexican judge who presides over the trial of a man who was convicted of the death of his wife in 1920's New Mexico. He is sentenced to hang. On the gallows he pushes the hangman off and kills him. Shortly thereafter another man confesses to the murder. But he now faces another murder trial due to killing the man who was going to put him to death for a crime he didn't commit. As usual a strong supporting cast of veteran players were hired ("Bill always had the last word on hiring," according to Lydon) including Katy Jurado, Earl Holliman (as the wronged man), Arthur O'Connell, John Anderson and Kent Smith. This is the second film by the Conrad-Lydon team to utilize Gene Hackman.

The director is Lamont Johnson, another television veteran, who would go on to win two Emmy Awards for his work (out of twelve nominations). During the 1970's he would direct several acclaimed TV-movies including *My Sweet Charlie, That Certain Summer, The Execution of Private Slovik, Wallenberg: A Hero's Story* and *Lincoln*. He (along with Robert Altman) is the most talented of the directors hired by Conrad. He also wanted a shot at directing a feature film, which Conrad gave him.

Jimmy Lydon recalls, "Lamont Johnson came from radio and was a very good director, but we had a problem with something one day and I went down to the set to speak with Johnson and he didn't want the producer on the set and didn't want to discuss the issue and bluntly told me to 'get off the set.' I went back to the office and told Bill what happened and he flew down to the set and tore Johnson a new ass hole and let him know in no uncertain terms that if Johnson didn't like it he (Bill) would take over the direction of the film. Johnson got the message."

A Covenant with Death almost made the grade with *New York Times* critic Bosley Crowther, who called the first half of the film "original" and "provocative" but that the second half of the picture "slackens disappointingly."

Conrad and Lydon next attempted to bring in the youth market with *The Cool Ones* which cast Roddy McDowall as a ruthless young millionaire promoter who tries to put together the next great rock and roll act. Originally Conrad offered the leading female role to Nancy Sinatra, who was at the peak of her "These Boots are made for Walking" fame. In the end Sinatra turned it down—to make *Speedway* with Elvis Presley. Instead Conrad hired a young beauty named Debbie Watson. She is paired Gil Peterson, who plays a former teenage singing idol who has fallen on hard times, but believes that Watson is his ticket back to the top. The film has some interesting things to say about greed and opportunism in the record industry. However, as a film whose aim was to appeal to the youth market, it is almost as embarrassing (but not quite) as Otto Preminger's *Skidoo*, despite a typically good performance by McDowall.

"Bill and I thought *The Cool Ones* had great potential, but it just didn't jell" Jimmy Lydon recalled. "Roddy did the best he could as did our director, Gene Nelson (best known as a dancer in several Warner Brothers films of the early fifties including *Tea for Two*, *Lullaby of Broadway* and *Starlift* before turning to TV directing). We wanted to make a modern type of film that we thought the younger generation could relate to—and we put all kinds of trendy singing acts but the picture didn't go anywhere. The kids didn't come—nobody came." In his review *New York Times* critic Bosley Crowther called the film a "so-called rock and roll comedy" and "I venture to guess this will even disgust the kids."

Chubasco starred real-life married Christopher Jones and Susan Strasberg. Jones plays Chubasco, a rebellious and wild kid who is taken under the wing of a tuna boat captain (played by Preston Foster) and given a job. Strasberg plays his equally rebellious daughter who Chubasco elopes with much to the chagrin of her irate father (played by Richard Egan). Also included in this excellent cast are Ann Sothern, Audrey Totter and Simon Oakland.

At the time Christopher Jones was a fast rising young actor who would have a brief period in the late sixties and early seventies of true stardom with films like *Wild in the Streets* and *Ryan's Daughter*. Susan Strasberg was the daughter of legendary Actor's Studio teacher Lee Strasberg. Conrad gave the directorial reins to Allen H. Meiner (who also wrote the script), who had directed Conrad's excellent and underappreciated western *The Ride Back*.

"*Chubasco* is probably the worst picture we made," contends Jimmy Lydon. "It was another one aimed at the youth market. It had Christopher Jones, who at that time was a very hot young actor, and Susan Strasberg. It was ridiculous and just plain horrible—the whole thing was a disaster. Jones took himself too seriously and was a pain in the ass and surprisingly, since they were married, Jones and Strasberg had no chemistry together." (Yet, apparently Conrad disagreed with Lydon's contention about *Chubasco* being there 'worst picture.' According to Christopher Conrad his dad included this film as one of the five best he ever made).

Surprisingly Howard Thompson in the *New York Times* was only mildly negative about the film. He called *Chubasco* "a curious little drama that might have gone places with more care." But ultimately the plot, according to Thompson, had too many "banal…contrivances."

Next up was *Assignment to Kill*, which had another top-notch cast with Patrick O'Neal, Joan Hackett, John Gielgud, Eric Portman and Herbert Lom in a story about a private eye who investigates shipping tycoon who may have arranged for the sinking of his own boats in an attempt to get insurance money. Parts of the film were shot on location in Switzerland. "We liked the idea of using real locations," Lydon recalls, "and the story was good, but again despite a very talented cast, it didn't have the kind of box office names that were needed to sell a film of this type." Howard Thompson in the *New York Times* called *Assignment to Kill*, "very scenic but off-target." He went on to call the film "tedious and flat."

Jimmy Lydon is most enthused about what turned out to be the final film that he and Conrad would produce for Warner Brothers, *Countdown*. Conrad got a first-rate writer, Loring Mandel, to write the script. Mandel was an Emmy-nominated writer (he would eventually win two Emmy Awards for his writing during the course of his career) of television drama and would be making his feature film debut with *Countdown*.

Countdown was based on a 1965 novel by Hank Searls titled "The Pilgrim Project." The story concerns a one-man, one-way trip to the moon. It was a contemporary story in that the space race between the Russians and the United States was heating up and it would be a big boost to the prestige of whatever country was the first to land a man on the moon. In *Countdown* it turns out that the Russians already have a Russian team circling the moon and may be landing soon, so it is imperative that the Americans get a man to the moon—ASAP. The only problem is that he would have to set up a shelter on the moon for approximately a year before a more advanced Apollo rocket could go to the moon to take him home. It was an intriguing premise.

With a credible writer at work on the screenplay the team next focused on who they could get to direct. They wanted a step up from their usual run of mediocre directors who had been churning their pictures out. But they certainly knew they couldn't afford an established feature director such as John Frankenheimer, who would have been ideal for such a project. One day they found out that one of the people who had been interested in optioning Searls' novel had been a TV director named Robert Altman, who was best known prior to this for his work on documentaries and such TV-shows as *Alfred Hitchcock Presents*, *Bonanza* and *Combat*. Conrad knew that Altman had a good reputation as a director, but also was increasingly seen within the industry as somebody who could not get the job done on time and on budget. If any production company needed a director who could get a film made timely and within a budget it was the Conrad-Lydon Unit of Warner Brothers.

One day Conrad and Lydon were discussing possible directors for *Countdown* when Conrad asked Lydon what he thought of the idea of Robert Altman directing. "I told Bill that the guy never was on budget in his life," Lydon later recalled. "Bill replied that he didn't ask me about that—he asked me what I thought of him as a director and I told him that he was a very talented director, but that he still had this reputation for not getting the job done on time or on budget. Bill just looked at me and said, 'let's talk to him.'" So they called Altman in for a meeting. They already knew he was interested in the story since he had tried to option it, but Warner Brothers had won the bid. Conrad told Altman that he knew he was a very fine director and wanted him to do the film but he had to adhere to the schedule and the budget. Altman agreed, and was signed to do the picture but not before he received one more warning from Conrad, "Remember, if you go a nickel over the budget—you're fired." Altman would later recall that Conrad stood his ground against Jack Warner as well. According to Altman, Warner had told Conrad, "You can't hire that person," but Conrad simply told Warner that he was going to hire him. End of story.

Next they put together a very good cast. James Caan, who had previously worked on two Howard Hawks films, *Red Line 7000* and *El Dorado* was cast as the astronaut launched into space. Robert Duval, who was building a strong reputation over the years beginning with his small but pivotal role as "Boo Radley" in *To Kill a Mockingbird* (1962) was cast as another astronaut who wants to be the one who goes to the moon, but loses the assignment to Caan's character. In addition to the two leads the cast includes Joanna Moore, Barbara Baxley, Charles Aidman, Michael Murphy and Ted Knight. Years later Lydon was still proud that he and Conrad had helped launch the starring careers of James Caan and Robert Duval.

When the picture began shooting problems began almost from the beginning with Altman. "A couple of weeks into the picture he (Altman) was a full day behind schedule," Lydon recalled. "Bill told me to go down to the set and lay the law down to Altman. I did just that. I told him that it was now Tuesday and that by Saturday (we worked six day weeks then) he'd had better be back on schedule or he'd be fired. I told him we would do everything to help him—to accommodate him to get back on schedule. But if he wasn't on schedule by that Saturday, Bill would step in and complete the film." As Lydon recalls it the threat worked and Altman got back on schedule and didn't deviate from the budget or the schedule for the remainder of the picture and completed it on time.

The ending of the picture turned out to be a major problem. Michael Murphy, who played another astronaut later recalled:

"So in the movie we have a way we figure we can get Jimmy (Caan) to the moon, but we haven't got a way to get him back. So they shoot a shelter up on the lunar surface, they send Jim up, and he has to find the shelter and stay in it until we can get him down. That was the idea of the movie. So Bob (Altman) shoots all this, and at the end of the movie you see James Caan arrive on the face of the moon and he's walking around and he finds the three Russians and they're dead...And there's a Russian flag there. So Jimmy takes out the American flag, he's got it in his pack. Jimmy put the American flag under it or beneath it or to the side of it. And you see him start to walk off, and the camera pulls back, and you see the shelter, and he's walking in the wrong direction, and that's the end of the movie. Well, Jack Warner thought it was a Communist plot."

Warner wasn't happy about this first cut at all. Warner not only didn't like the ending but also had a problem with the overlapping dialogue. "That fool has actors talking at the same time," Altman would recall Warner saying about him. Warner decided to fire Altman and instructed Conrad to film a new ending. "So Bob was off the picture and Bill Conrad came on," Loring Mandel recalled. "Conrad did a little rewriting of the last part of the movie and reshot a little of it, and that's the movie that came out. Before the movie was released I was brought to Hollywood to see a screening of it. I was really appalled at what happened at the end. I wanted to take my name off of it but my agent convinced me that was a disastrous thing to do on a first solo-credit screenplay."

The new ending satisfied Jack Warner. Now it was the American flag positioned above the Russian flag—not beside it or under it—and instead of Caan walking off away from the shelter he is walking back to the shelter where we are given a hopeful ending that Caan will survive in his American-built shelter until a rocket comes to pick him up. Caan was pissed off by what he thought was a cop-out of an ending and was still bitter years later—but his bitterness was not with the man who wanted the changes—Jack Warner—but with the man who delivered the news—Bill Conrad:

"Bill Conrad took the picture away from him at the end. It was so comic book, so corny, and Bob is anything but corny. The original ending, you don't know if he sees the beacon or if he's going off the wrong way. Conrad said, 'No we can't do that.' There was this whole bullshit with this toy mouse in my pocket. I spin the mouse and I head off in the direction of its ass or nose or whatever it shows—obviously towards the beacon. I think they called us back without Bob, and that fat bastard Conrad called us back to do a day of shooting, with that spinning mouse thing."

Jimmy Lydon recalls that *Countdown* was released on a Tuesday in New York and Los Angeles and got "terrific reviews," but that wasn't exactly the case. The *New York Times* tore the film to shreds calling it a "limp spaceflight drama" whose direction was "listless" and acting was "dreary." Film critic Roger Ebert later reviewed the film when it was shown at a Robert Altman film festival in 1977. He called *Countdown* "a movie that's fitfully interesting, often boring, and gives no hint at all of such riches to come as *MASH*, *Nashville* and *Three Women*." Yet he went on to praise the final scene in the movie—the one (unbeknownst to Ebert) that Conrad had directed.

"There's a lovely scene involving American and Russian flags and a little toy mouse." But he blames Conrad for the films defects. "His producer was William Conrad, who does not seem, in hindsight, to be the ideal person to produce for Altman. Perhaps it was Conrad, or somebody else at Warner Brothers, who dictated such un-Altman like touches as the painfully obvious sound track music, or the unbelievably false scene at a party where everybody gathers round to listen to an amateur folk singer."

Lydon recalls that the day after the film opened in New York and Los Angeles that it was pulled out and, "put out in second run markets in small towns and rural areas but even so it managed to break even and even get a small profit."

Conrad wanted to make another film, and had the idea of filming a screenplay by author Anthony Burgess (best known for his novel *A Clockwork Orange* which was later made into a famous film by director Stanley Kubrich). Burgess had written a fictional biography of William Shakespeare ("Nothing like the Sun") and the screenplay was to be the life of Shakespeare as a musical! (Perhaps titled "Will!" or "The Bawdy Bard"). Conrad and Burgess became good friends in the process. Burgess later called Conrad, "a true actor, in that he knew Shakespeare." Conrad went so far as to improvise a song for the movie that began, "To be or not to be in love with you/ to spend my life hand in glove with you." In the end nothing came of this planned film. But the friendship between Burgess and Conrad endured. In fact, Conrad had told Burgess that he had the idea of making a black *Oedipus* and calling it "Mother Fucker." Later Burgess published a novel titled *MF* which he said was actually a "homage" to that idea "except that the initials stood for the name of the hero of the book 'Miles Faber.' (According to Burgess, they did more than discuss movie or stage ideas. In his autobiography, *You've Had Your Time*, Burgess writes that "In… (a) Lavish (clip joint) Bill paid a hundred pounds to a large-breasted strumpet he favored: this was the fee for getting me laid as he had been laid. I declined the gift, rightly: Bill was later to complain that she gave him a dose").

By this time Jack Warner had left Warner Brothers and the studio was taken over by Kenneth Hyman and Seven Arts. Eventually the Conrad-Lydon unit closed down and Conrad wanted to take some time off and just relax and enjoy his boat—which is what he did for a time before the acting bug caught up with him again. Lydon stayed on for a bit at Warner Brothers and produced an interesting little racial drama, *The Learning Tree* which became the first major studio film to be directed by an African-American, Gordon Parks.

In the end Lydon would recall that the years he spent with Bill Conrad at Warner Brothers were "a wonderful time. I really loved Bill." He maintains that they made "a couple" of good films and that "every one of our pictures made the negative cost back, but that was all. The reason is we just didn't have any star power. Don't get me wrong we had very good actors—superb actors—wonderful character people, but we really didn't have a single star in one of our pictures. One actor went on to be a star—Gene Hackman—but he wasn't one then."

PHOTO GALLERY

William Conrad at the height on his TV fame as Cannon, 1974.

Conrad enjoying a poster of himself as Cannon, 1975.

Conrad in a publicity photo from the late 1940's.

The cast of radio's *Gunsmoke*—Bottom: Georgia Ellis & Parley Baer Top: Conrad & Howard McNear.

Conrad from the 1957 film *The Ride Back*—a gritty western he also produced.

Conrad with Anthony Quinn in *The Ride Back* (1957).

Conrad, Whitney Blake and Jack Webb from the newspaper drama *-30-* (1959).

After a decade as a movie producer and director at Warner Brothers Conrad returned to acting and landed his iconic TV role as Frank Cannon in *Cannon* (1971).

Conrad with Joan Fontaine in the *Cannon* episode "The Star" (1975)

Conrad with Buddy Ebsen in the *Cannon/Barnaby Jones* cross-over episode "The Deadly Conspiracy" (1975).

Conrad with David Hedison in the *Cannon* episode "Night Flight to Murder" (1973).

Conrad signing autographs for fans on location in Colorado.

In his personal life there were few things that Conrad loved more than the ocean and his boat.

Conrad hosted the wildlife documentary series *The Wild Wild World of Animals* from 1973-1978.

Conrad loved to get away from his Cannon persona—here he is with Ruth Buzzi on *Laugh-In* (1972).

Conrad's favorite of his TV series—*Nero Wolfe* which ran for half a season in 1981.

Conrad with Lee Horsley, who played Archie Goodwin to Conrad's Nero Wolfe.

Conrad with his second successful TV-series *Jake and the Fatman* which ran from 1987-1992.

The cast of *Jake and the Fatman*: Joe Penny, Alan Campbell and Conrad (along with Max the Bulldog).

CHAPTER SIX: CANNON
1969-1976

After leaving Warner Brothers Conrad needed to recharge his batteries. The long hours had left him mentally and physically exhausted. "I had a little money, so I decided to take a year off," Conrad later recalled. "I just got on my boat and stayed away a year and a half. I hadn't had a vacation since I was 16, and I paid no attention to the theatrical business." He recalls that when he got back there was "nothing doing in town, so I loafed." Christopher Conrad recalls this period as a darker time for his dad than Conrad would confess because he "was worried because he was getting no work." Conrad decided not to go back to producing or directing, but would give acting another try.

In December of 1969 he appeared in an episode of the NBC wheel series *The Name of the Game*. The show was similar to the later and more successful *NBC Mystery Movie* which rotated such shows as *McCloud*, *Columbo* and *McMillan and Wife*. In the case of *The Name of the Game* the show rotated episodes starring Tony Franciosa, Gene Berry and Robert Stack. The episode that Conrad appeared in starred Stack as a crusading ex-FBI agent turned magazine editor who, in an episode titled "The Power", is investigating corruption on the waterfront and casts Conrad as a longshoreman. Conrad's performance got him noticed and led to an invitation to appear as a sadistic talk show host in the TV-movie *The Brotherhood of the Bell*, which aired on September 17, 1970 on CBS.

Conrad is surrounded by a top-notch cast headed by Glenn Ford and Rosemary Forsyth and including such distinguished actors as Dean Jagger, Maurice Evans, Will Geer and two newer names—Dabney Coleman and Robert Pine. David Karp wrote the teleplay which was based on his own novel. The program was directed by Paul Wendkos. The hero, Dr. Andrew Patterson (Ford), is an economics professor who discovers that the elite fraternity he belonged to at University, the so-called 'Brotherhood of the Bell,' is a dangerous cabal that obtains wealth, influence and power through nefarious means. Eventually Patterson works to destroy the Brotherhood, which in turn seeks to destroy him. He eventually proposes to guest star on a local television talk show hosted by a super patriot named Bart Harris (Conrad).

Harris has a great deal of influence. He concedes that his program is a "side show" but points out that many influential people have appeared on his show and that this is a golden opportunity for the professor to get the word out about 'The Brotherhood,' but cautions that, "Nothing shows up a phony" like television. The Professor agrees to appear but in the end Harris and his audience humiliates and denounces Patterson on the air as a lunatic conspiracy theorist with no proof to back his story up. In a violent tirade Harris tells Patterson, "Somebody is going to pull a net over you—you creep... you make me sick." Patterson accuses Harris of being paid off by the brotherhood (which may or may not be true). With pent up rage Patterson attacks Harris on the air and lands in jail. The talk show that Harris hosts with its live, frenzied, and participatory studio audience foreshadowed such later talk shows as *Jerry Springer* and *Geraldo*. This TV-movie would be Chris Conrad's first time seeing his father as an actor because prior to that he had worked behind the scenes as a producer and director.

Conrad's performance as the gonzo talk show host is superb and caught the eye of CBS head of programming Fred Silverman, who was a fan of Conrad's to begin with going back to his radio days. "Fred Silverman," Conrad later recalled, "flipped over my role in *The Brotherhood of the Bell* and thought that he saw a great potential for a series lead in me. How he figured that out I don't know."

TV producer Quinn Martin also admired Conrad (after all he had spent all those years narrating *The Fugitive* for Martin) and was working on a TV-movie (that would serve as a pilot for a potential series) about a private eye who carries a lot of bulk—as much as 100 pounds in excess bulk to be exact—named Frank Cannon. As for it being Fred Silverman who saw potential for a

Bill Conrad TV-series, *Cannon* producer Anthony Spinner tells another story:

"Quinn had called Fred Silverman, who ran CBS, and told him, 'I want to do a show with Bill Conrad.' 'Oh, great, great great,' says Silverman. 'Put him in.' So I go in to the first day's dailies. Silverman's driven over from CBS to go in and see the dailies, and I hear this asthmatic breathing next to me, like somebody's gonna have a heart attack and it's Silverman. I said, 'What's the matter with him?' because he's panting so heavily. Finally the dailies are over. Silverman turns to Quinn. He says, 'Who the hell is that big fat guy in the striped shirt?' Quinn says, 'That's Bill Conrad.' Silverman says, 'Bill Conrad! I thought we were hiring Bob Conrad!' He stormed out of the projection room saying, 'This show will never air!' Well, he was wrong because Bill Paley (Silverman's boss at CBS) loved Bill Conrad from the days of Gunsmoke when Bill was playing Matt Dillon on the radio. So Paley said, 'We're gonna do the show.' Then Bill Conrad is a big hit, and suddenly there's a big article in Variety from Fred Silverman on 'How he picked Bill Conrad because he's changing the face of television.' I called Quinn. He said, 'Leave it alone. The man's got an ego. I've got the money. You've got the talent. He's got the ego.'"

Frank Cannon is a former Los Angeles detective Lieutenant who left the force because (as he concedes in one of the early episodes) "because I like working for myself." Not only that but as a top private eye he certainly gets paid more than when he worked for the LAPD. He certainly seems to be doing well because in the pilot film he has a penthouse apartment and comfortable sailing boat. (Interestingly enough in the early episodes of the series we rarely see Cannon at home—he is too busy traveling and solving cases). The character of Cannon is one that William Conrad certainly could relate to. He's a man's man, confident in his own shoes, un-phased by what people may think of him and takes no bull from anybody.

Cannon is also open about his weight. He knows he's fat and understand that other people will notice it too. In the pilot he notices a kid looking in wonder at his gut and, with a smile, Cannon tells him, "It wasn't easy." For such a large man Cannon is incredibly active. He often ends up running after (or away from) the bad guy or in a physical altercation with them (where he often uses a well-placed karate chop to bring the bad guy down). The bottom line is that there is a lot of action in *Cannon* and William Conrad, unlike on his later shows *Nero Wolfe* and *Jake and the Fatman*, is the one who takes on the bad guys—mentally and physically. "To begin with," Conrad said, "I was never very athletically inclined, and sometimes after we finish a *Cannon* episode, I wish I were back in that air-conditioned radio studio where I could do my best work sitting down."

CBS authorized the two-hour made for TV movie to serve as a pilot. The movie was titled (simply) *Cannon*. The film went into production in the late fall of 1970 and was completed in January of 1971. CBS scheduled it to air on March 26, 1971. As usual Quinn Martin surrounded Conrad with terrific actors as guest-stars: Vera Miles, Murray Hamilton, Barry Sullivan, Keenan Wynn, Lynda Day-George, Earl Holliman and Ellen Corby.

Terrific guest stars was a Quinn Martin tradition—not only on *Cannon* but on all of his shows. Martin not only paid his guest stars well but he made sure they felt appreciated. Many would appear on one or more Quinn Martin show every year. This inspired great loyalty from cast and crews. Actor David Hedison, who appeared in several episodes of *Cannon* was a regular guest-star on Quinn Martin shows recalled the producer:

"Quinn Martin was a classy guy. He always hired good people. You were there to work and work we did. Quinn had a great set up at the Goldwyn Studios. I always enjoyed working there. Quinn always liked me...I enjoyed their company and I really liked working for him...Quinn was old school-a real gentleman and one of the nicest men ever to grace this business. I miss working for him. Quinn would make a point to send me all the fan mail he got for me at Goldwyn, after my appearances aired. He didn't have to do that, but he seemed to get a kick out of the fact that I got it. So he'd send it to me, usually with a note about how popular I was. They don't make shows like he did any more. A good man—a smart producer and a dear friend."

Robert Pine, who appeared three times on *Cannon* backs up Hedison. "One thing about Quinn Martin Productions is if you proved yourself on one show they usually had you back to do more of their shows without having to audition or anything like that," the affable actor recalled. "It was a good place to work especially since they had so many shows on the air the same time and lots of parts to cast—and they treated us very well—and paid us well, too."

Veteran character actor Richard Anderson (Oscar in *The Six Million Dollar Man* and *Bionic Woman* franchises) is another Quinn Martin fan (having worked with him initially in several episodes of *The Fugitive*). Anderson probably made more guest appearances on episodic television during the 60's and 70's than nearly any other actor including two episodes of *Cannon*. "Quinn Martin was a writer primarily—starting out—and then he went into production. He was very good and the stuff I worked with him on was always interesting and he always used good, reliable actors."

Julie Adams, who was the young beauty the *Creature from the Black Lagoon* is infatuated with, appeared on several Quinn Martin series including two episodes of *Cannon*. "Quinn Martin was on the set a lot," she recalls. "I always thought his shows were very professionally and smoothly run—well produced and always a joy to work on. I always thought his shows were done at a very high level, and very classy. Everyone who worked on his shows were very good at their jobs. All the departments were well run. It was always a pleasure to work on his shows, and I was always pleased when I got the opportunity."

Lynda Day George, who would appear on the *Cannon* pilot and in several of his other series, states that "Quinn was a very shy man who felt uncomfortable around actors because often when an actor befriends a producer, he does it so he can get something. Quinn felt comfortable with me because I never tried to take advantage of anybody. I never tried to use anybody for anything. I didn't require anything from Quinn. I never asked him for anything…"

Efrem Zimbalist, Jr., who starred on Martin's *The FBI* for eight years recalls, "The production team was like a family, and of course, that family moved from show to show as Quinn did different shows. The crews liked Quinn. Quinn was very loyal to them. He was extremely loyal to actors and directors unless they did something he didn't like—then he just didn't have them back."

After such successes during the sixties as *The Untouchables* and *The Fugitive*, *Cannon* would become Martin's first hit of the new decade.

In a nutshell the pilot movie to *Cannon* concerns Diana Langston (Vera Miles) who is the police suspect in the murder of her husband. She insists she is innocent and calls her husband's old friend Frank Cannon to come to Gallitin, New Mexico to clear her and find the real murderer. The script was written by Edward Hume, who developed the show for television, and was directed by George McCowan who would direct twenty-three episodes of *Cannon*—more than any other director.

McCowan, a native of Canada, soon found that he worked easily with the sometimes cantankerous Bill Conrad. "George was the only director who wasn't there when I started everything rolling," Assistant Director David Whorf later recalled. "He didn't say 'Action!' He was a very quiet, unassuming guy. He was a dear man, loved by everybody, and he was perfect for Bill Conrad. George understated so much. He didn't over-manipulate people. He'd learned very early on that you choose certain places in the script to spend time. The rest, you just go in and out like a son of a bitch. He was totally prepared. There wasn't a mark or a note in his script about the camera angles. He had all that in his head."

This was the right way to handle a star like Conrad, who was in practically every scene, and didn't want to obsess over every scene. Whorf added that both Conrad and McCowan had a liking for alcohol and strong senses of humor in common. "We were up in Durango, Colorado, and it so happened (that) it was my birthday," Whorf recalled. "George McCowan comes into my room in the hotel and says, 'You better get down to the bar. (Director of Photography) Jack Swain and Bill are fighting.' I said, 'Oh shit, I'll be slaughtered in that. I'll be dead in the crossfire.' He says, 'You better do something.' He had me eating it all the way down to the bar, and there were Jack and Bill. They turned around; they started singing, 'Happy Birthday.' I said to George, 'you son of a bitch. You scared the shit out of me.'"

Guest star Lynda Day George had fond memories of working with Conrad on the pilot. "Bill Conrad was probably the most gentlemanly person, the most kindly person that I ever worked with as an actor, and he was my hero from then on," Day-George later recalled. "He and Burl Ives were my all-time heroes. They were the only serious competition Chris (her husband actor Christopher George) ever faced. I was pleased to be in Bill's company. I tried to spend as much time with him as I possibly could. We liked each other very much. Bill and Chris spent a good bit of time together too. They had a good time. They both hit the bottle. They were weaned on it. I remember Bill's wife calling me one time. She says, 'You know Lynda, the two of us need to keep our husbands apart.'"

Among the reviews for the *Cannon* TV-movie pilot is this from *Movies on TV*, "Playing for realism, producer Quinn Martin often uses hand-held cameras while filming near Las Cruces, New Mexico… When the plot complications tend to wear the viewer down, Martin shores it up with fine location work, Conrad's imposing presence, a supporting cast featuring Vera Miles, Barry Sullivan, J.D. Cannon, Keenan Wynn and Earl Holliman." Judith Crist in *TV Guide* was a bit less enthusiastic, "too many subplots make for confusion after halfway mark," but still thought it 'above average.'

Conrad summed up his feeling for 'Cannon' when he said, "Cannon is the type of role I enjoy. Especially since he's the kind of guy who, like me, saviors the finer things of life. He drives an expensive automobile, relishes gourmet cooking, appreciates good wine and lives in well-appointed, tasteful surroundings."

It wasn't only on *Cannon* that Conrad's authoritative and resonant voice could be heard. One of the most iconic television commercials of all-time began airing on Earth Day, 1971. It featured an Indian (Iron Eyes Cody) paddling his canoe up a polluted river. He passes smokestacks and finally comes ashore on a river bank which was full of liter and trash. He walks towards a highway where a passing motorist throws a bag of trash out the window. The camera comes in for a close-up of the Indian and the viewer finds a single tear running down the Indians face. Then the Conrad voice in tones one of the most famous advertising catch phrases of its time, "People Start Pollution, people can stop it."

II

It was around this time that Conrad and Susan decided that their fourteen-year old son needed a little discipline. "He (Conrad) was strict, but he never raised a hand to me," Christopher Conrad later recalled. "It was my mother who could pull out the belt when I was bad (and I was bad a lot), though honestly I preferred getting spanked by that belt to having him yell at me. While my mom and I were exceptionally close, we fought constantly. I think we were very alike and very adept at verbal repartee."

Conrad and Susan decided to send Christopher to a boarding school, so that some discipline could be instilled. In retrospect, Christopher feels this was a wise decision that his parents made. "I truly came into my own (at the boarding school, which was on picturesque Catalina Island), I was admittedly a pretty spoiled rotten brat, and so all those beltings were probably richly deserved." Conrad became a trustee of his son's boarding school. "It's a great school," Conrad said in an interview at the time. "Catalina is nice and rural—the kids have to chase buffalos off the soccer field—it's a small school (and) Chris is really thriving there." In his spare time Conrad enjoyed taking his son out on his boat, Moonraker. Bill also let the press know that Christopher was "an accomplished Scuba diver."

Despite the spankings that he received, Christopher Conrad is quick to add, "I don't feel I was 'beaten' by my mom (no Mommy Dearest issues here), spanking your kid was just what parents did back then and I honestly feel I carry no scars or was 'damaged' by the experience. While my upbringing was anything but normal—I have nothing but good memories, love, and respect for both (my) mom and dad."

While Christopher has good memories of both of his parents, Conrad thought he was a deficient father. "Bill didn't think he was a good father," according to Herb Ellis. "He thought he put his work first before his family and in doing so he was giving them the material things, but he felt he could have been a better father and should have spent more time with his son, but that wasn't in his constitution and he knew it."

III

As he began the first season of filming Conrad offered this perception of himself and his alter-ego, Frank Cannon which is worth quoting in detail:

"Part of the pleasure I get from my role of private investigator on the new 'Cannon' series is the fact the character of Frank Cannon is essentially William Conrad's. In other words, Cannon's likes and dislikes are my own, even to the point of being in love with boats and the ocean. Recently an episode of the series had Cannon puttering around his yacht when he is interrupted by a female client. Not coincidentally, the boat viewers will see on their screens is my own 47-foot ketch, 'The Moonraker,' which I keep at Marina del Rey harbor in Southern California. I think it's ideal to play a private eye who enjoys one of the greater pleasures of life—sailing an ocean-going craft. But I think it would be even more ideal if Frank Cannon made his investigative headquarters aboard his boat. So far I have failed to convince the producers of the efficiency of this plan. However, it is most convenient to be the possessor of such a craft when location shooting takes us somewhere along the harbor-dotted coastline of Southern California...Sailing is no new-found enthusiasm for me. I discovered it more than 20 years ago. But I resisted joining the ranks of boat owners until recently because I felt anyone was foolish to tackle the expense and responsibility of owner ship. Why not become the friend of a yacht owner? I finally lost my head and bought the 'Moonraker'. And, I have never regretted that decision."

Eating was another pleasure, of course. He loved gourmet cooking, but he contended that he didn't eat as much as people thought. "Believe me, I consume very little," he said in an interview. "It may be hard to believe when you look at me, but it's true. I have a wife who eats twice as much as I do and she stays thin as a rail. It's really disgusting! (but) Susan used to be a model and she's also a magnificent cook. Therefore, I don't do much cooking around the house."

Since he was the only real series regular, Conrad did participate in many stunts during the run of *Cannon*. Frank Cannon ran, had fist fights, gun fights, car chases and in the season one episode **"Stone Cold Dead"** he donned a wet suit for some action scenes in the ocean—an experience which led to a near catastrophe for the actor. "I was in a wet suit most of the day—no doubles mind you," Conrad recalled, "I jumped off the boat, for a scene, and suddenly a tidal surge pushed me 30 feet from the boat. I was scared! I ripped off my snorkel and yelled 'Help!' The captain stopped the boat and personally dived in. It was a real experience. I lost eight pounds that day, not that I couldn't afford to."

Conrad recalled that on another show he had to drive a bulldozer through a fire, "but that was easy, I only had my hair singed." As the filming on the first season continued, Conrad grew more and more fatigued. "We often film six days out of seven on diverse locations and when the week is over, I don't even have the time or energy to sail my boat, 'Moonraker,'" Yet Conrad also thought that the part was an easy one to play. "Now I can't think of an easier way to make money," Conrad said. "I could phone in my part. Face it, it's a part written for me. It's so comfortable I don't know when the camera's on," refuting his earlier statement about the weekly fatigue. Conrad acknowledged that it was all worth it in the long run. "This is the only way I know of taking a chance that will make me a fortune—if we last that long," Conrad told a reporter. "Actually I don't care what I do as long as I make money. I think I'm a pretty good actor, but I'm aware that if I'd come along two years ago, I'd be just another old face."

Among the highlights of the first season is the very first episode of the regular season titled **The Salinas Jackpot (9/14/1971)**. It is the story of an insurance company that hires Cannon to track down the thief's who stole $100,000 from a rodeo. He befriends a fatherless boy (Vincent Van Patten) and his mother (Susan Acker), the widow of a former rodeo clown—who at first wants nothing to do with Cannon—and must protect them from murderers (Tom Skerritt & John Perak) There are tender scenes between Conrad and Van Patten who comes to see Cannon as a father figure.

Call Unicorn (9/28/1971) has Cannon going undercover as a truck driver. **Scream of Silence (10/12/1971)** tells the story of a millionaire's (who is also a candidate for Governor) son who is kidnapped but manages to escape, but the trauma of the event causes him to become mute. Not wanting to involve the police, the family hires Cannon (for the price of a few bottles of rare wine) to find out who was behind the kidnapping. Again Cannon forges a close and trusting relationship with a child.

Stone Cold Dead (11/30/1971) has a young salesgirl drowning mysteriously. At the marina where her body is found, Cannon dons scuba diving gear for an underwater search for a missing bicycle that could be an important clue—besides the bike he runs into a surprise diver. Guest star Richard (Oscar on *The Six Million Dollar Man*) Anderson recalls that "What most impressed me about Bill Conrad was his voice and intelligence—and the sense of getting interest from an audience. He was an imposing guy and most scenes he was in he certainly dominated."

Death is a Double-Cross (12/7/1971), has Conrad taking on a routine bodyguard assignment that eventually finds him chasing down a gang of counterfeiters. He agrees to escort a wealthy stockholder's daughter and her three children by train from Chicago to Los Angeles. The assignment turns dangerous when Cannon discovers the woman's estranged husband is involved with the counterfeiting. The episode was directed by Richard Donner and featured real life siblings Leif Garrett and Dawn Lyn as brother and sister.

Vera Miles returned for **To Kill a Guinea Pig (02/01/1972)**, about a prison medical researcher (Miles) being harassed by thugs and prisoners and Cannon being brought in to find out why they want to scare her off. Parts of this episode were filmed on location at the Terminal Island Prison. Producer Harold Gast recalls, "It was a very chilling atmosphere. We had to be very careful where we went, what we did. Sometimes the inmates would howl and make noise when we were filming."

Other prominent guest stars during the first season include: Martin Sheen, Tab Hunter, Kim Hunter, Roy Scheider, Theodore Bikel, Keenan Wynn, Rose Hobart, Ed Nelson, Barbara Luna, Bradford Dillman, John Rubenstein and Harold Gould.

Since the show was a moderate success (#29 overall and usually winning its time slot), Conrad became an authentic recognizable TV star. "The other day someone asked me how it feels to be a star," Conrad said. "I laughed at him. Just to get up in the morning and kiss the ground and be grateful. In this age, to have work is a miracle. A lot of it was in the timing. The show hit just right when the audience was willing to accept a fat old man (Conrad was hardly old—51) as a lead." Women were a big part of his fan club. "Bill was an incredible guy," *Cannon* producer Alan Armer later recalled. "He had great charm. Great authority as an actor. He was one of the great voices in the industry. For a guy who was overweight, he was incredibly charming. Women because of his voice, and because of his charm, liked him. He had some successful relationships with women."

Over the years one of the things that stood out with Conrad's co-workers was the fact that he used cue-cards on nearly every project he worked on after 1971. However, this was not the case on the first season of *Cannon*. "The first season," assistant director David Whorf recalled, "Bill was a dream-boat. He was a consummate artist. The first season he memorized his lines. The second season, he posted his lines on other actor's foreheads and chests, he put them on the camera, he used cue cards. With his heavy, fleshy face, you really didn't see a lot of his eyes, so you couldn't see that he was looking someplace other than directly at the other actor."

So why was this? "To Bill," *Cannon* director William Hale recalled, "This was filmed radio. He was used to reading his lines, and I remember we had this bald-headed assistant cameraman on the show. So with a marker pen they would write Conrad's dialogue on this guy's bald head, so when it came time, the guy would tip his head toward Conrad and Conrad would read his lines right off the guy's bald head!" Conrad's old friend Jimmy Lydon recalls that, "I would visit him when he was doing *Cannon* and he was using idiot cards and had them set up all over the place. I asked him, 'Bill, why do they put up with you?' meaning the producers. He replied, 'This is garbage. I'm not going to spend half the night memorizing this shit.' And he meant it."

Robert Pine, who guest-starred in the season two episode "The Predators", was more understanding of Conrad's use of cue cards. "Many actors used cards—Lucy used them, so did Raymond Burr and Glenn Ford when he did television. He (Conrad) was the star of the show and in almost every scene and that's a lot of responsibility. If you look closely at Bill—in many episodes you'll see his eyeball going back and forth—but that takes nothing away from him." Richard Anderson who appeared in two episodes of *Cannon*, and numerous other Quinn Martin shows recalls, "Sure Bill used cue cards, but I worked with several series stars that did. Raymond Burr was another. For the first year Bill did learn everything and that is a tough game. It drove him crazy. It was difficult for him. To his credit he wasn't just sitting around smoking cigs—standing up reading the script. He wanted to tell the story. Yet with his great voice even if he was reading he was telling a story."

Pine also encountered the Conrad humor—in Pine's case Conrad's dark humor. "I was never close to him, but I liked Bill a lot," the actor recalled. "He was a very easy actor to work with and he was always very nice to me. A lot of times he would retreat to his trailer between scenes. He had a good sense of humor, but I found it could sometimes be sadistic. I recall once he kind of played a cruel prank on an assistant director—I forget exactly what it was—but the AD was made to think that he screwed something up and his job was at jeopardy. This went on for a while and I could tell that the AD was pretty stressed out before Bill finally let him off the hook. Of course the dynamic between the series regulars and the crew is different than that between a guest star and the crew—and the guy may have been used to the ribbing but he sure did seem stressed to me."

Another change in season two was the producer. During the first season the main producer was Alan Armer, a long time Quinn Martin employee having previously produced *The Fugitive* for which he won an Emmy Award. "I had a tough time on that series (*Cannon*)," Armer later said. "I'd gone over to Universal, and I wasn't happy there. Then Quinn asked me if I wanted to do *Cannon*. I said, 'Sure.' But the network was looking for violence, and I was having trouble giving them that. It was not the kind of show that I had a good feel for. I'd never done a private-eye show before. So, about half-way thru the year, I told Quinn I was not comfortable with the series. He says, 'Okay, I know another guy who can take over.'"

The other guy was Harold Gast, who had formerly produced the critically acclaimed legal series *Judd for the Defense*. Gast maintains that "the show hadn't been doing well," despite it consistently winning its time slot during the first season. "Bill Conrad the actor, and Cannon the private eye are basically the same men," Gast said at the time. "Both have strong appetites for all kinds of living. Our hero is not inconsistent with what our actor is. My point is only that Cannon is a very special person. He's not Mike Connors or a Jack Lord, and shouldn't be treated as such."

Gast later said that after he took over the show began to do very well. "Then someone published an article to that effect," Gast later recalled, "and when William Conrad saw that, he was furious. He didn't like the idea that he'd been doing a show that hadn't been doing well until I'd gotten on it." Yet in an article just as the second season was launching Conrad said, "The ridiculous thing was we got to be a hit in spite of those early shows, which were pretty bad. The formula is simple—laughing at one's self."

Gast recalls that Quinn Martin "liked to propose expensive things. Once he suggested to me that we go and shoot a couple of *Cannons* in Colorado, on location in the mountains. He said it would work out economically if we did two shows back to back. So we developed a couple of scripts that could be shot there." The two shows were both season two episodes, "Sky Above, Death Below" and "The Predators."

Among the best episodes of the second season include **Sky Above, Death Below (9/20/1972)** and **The Predators (10/18/1972)**, both filmed among the majestic mountains of Colorado—giving the shows some breathtaking photography. They were filmed successively but not shown in order. Of "The Predators" guest-star Robert Pine recalled:

"I remember it was a Monday morning and all of us gathered early, around 6am—cast, crew and Bill, of course, to fly to Colorado to do location work for the episode. We went to a place called Purgatory, Colorado—it was then a small ski resort—now it's considered a big one. We all stayed in the same motel. We shot the next day from something like 8 in the morning until about 6 at night. Now we were something like 8-9000 feet above sea level and Bill was a large man and he was doing all of this running around and I could tell it was taking a big toll on him. I was thinking 'this is a heart attack waiting to happen.' The next day I come on the set and Bill apologizes to me and says that he was so exhausted from the previous days filming that he didn't have time to learn his lines. I certainly understood—I was pretty tired myself. So Bill explains that because he didn't have time to learn his lines he was going to read his lines off of cards—which he did. Now cut

to the next time I'm on the show and now he was using cue cards all the time—he had it down to a science."

Child of Fear (11/15/1972) with guest star Julie Adams was another good offering from the second season. The episode told the story of Cannon being hired by the wife (Julie Adams) of a rancher, who it turns out is being held prisoner on the ranch by the security chief (Clu Gulager) and his men. The use of cue cards by the star didn't throw off the versatile Adams, "I thought Bill Conrad was very professional, a very good actor, and I enjoyed working with him a great deal. Yes, he used cue cards, but it didn't bother me or hinder my performance."

Moving Target (1/31/1973), with Susan Oliver, offered a good script based on current headlines (involving the author Clifford Irving claiming he ghost wrote Howard Hughes' autobiography and Hughes coming out (in his way) from hiding to rebuke this book as a hoax). The *Cannon* story followed this outline fairly closely. **The Seventh Grave** (2/28/1973) featuring Shelly Duvall in an early showcase offered a good story of a serial killer in a small town. **Deadly Heritage** (3/21/1973) featuring Beverly Garland concerned a step mother who hires Cannon to find her missing stepson. Naturally there is more to it than that. Among the other guest stars during season two are: Dana Wynter, Geraldine Brooks, Dick Van Patten, Richard Carlson, Paul Michael Glaser, Carl Betz, Lois Nettleton, Stephanie Powers, George Maharis, Patrick O'Neal, and Rosemary Murphy—the usual assortment of Quinn Martin veteran actors working with talented newcomers.

For the season, *Cannon* moved up 15 positions and ranked #14 in the ratings with an average 14.5 million weekly viewers. The show was right between *Marcus Welby, M.D.* (#13 with 14.8 million viewers) on ABC and *Here's Lucy* (#15 with 14.2 million viewers) on CBS.

Conrad was given the distinction of being named the "Honorary Mayor" of Sherman Oaks, California, where he lived for many years, at around this time. "I am most grateful and appreciative of the honor," Conrad said at a dinner held by the Sherman Oaks Chamber of Commerce. "I was a little disappointed, however when I learned the dictionary definition of 'honorary.' It is: 'designating a title or place which is held without rendering service or without receiving the emoluments or privileges to it.' Or carrying it a little further, 'gratuitous, fee or for love. Since I am doing this for love, I guess that rules out higher political ambitions."

IV

Bill Conrad was in a cantankerous mood as he was interviewed just as the third season was to begin. "I was meant to be heavy," the 268 pound star said. "It's ridiculous for me to try and get down to a normal weight. It'd be hell for me dieting all the time. I do everything everybody else does." He soon moved on to discuss the show. "We expect to have better scripts this year. Real stories with a beginning, middle, and end." When asked why he thought *Cannon* was successful he said, "There's a fella in the lead who looks like the guy next door or maybe the guy in the house." Conrad summed up by saying, "My doctor tells me I'm going to die very soon because I'm overweight. But the last doctor I went to who told me that was skinny; and the next time I went to see him I was told he had just died of a heart attack. I'd rather enjoy life and be fat." As for the work, he lambasted that the show was on location more than any other series on TV, "We're out of the studio 5 shooting days in 7."

In another interview he conceded that with *Cannon* being the only weekly show with just one star and no regular supporting players was a burden on him. "I have seen too many shows ruined by having the hero's image divided too many ways," he said. "There's not enough of the hero in any one man. But it's rough on me. I'm in practically every shot. I worked from the first of last June to the middle of February without a day off. When we were on location I worked Saturdays, too. Our days were long—13 hours." However, he quickly added, "If I worked an eight hour day, I'd feel I'd hardly worked."

One thing that Conrad felt was a positive was the idea that the leading man on a TV series was changing thanks to his fat and balding *Cannon*, Buddy Ebsen's elderly *Barnaby Jones*, Telly Savalas' bald *Kojak* and Peter Falk's rumpled *Columbo*. "You no longer have to be seven feet tall and handsome...the whole concept of the leading man has changed. I think it's wrong to bring up a generation believing that only beautiful people can do things. It doesn't happen that way."

The third season began strongly with a two-hour season premiere **He Who Digs His Grave (9/12/1973)** with an excellent guest cast consisting of veterans like David Janssen, Anne Baxter, Barry Sullivan, and Murray Hamilton. This episode tells the story of an old war buddy of Cannon's being arrested on two counts of murder in a small cattle town and it's up to Cannon to get him off. The episode had location scenes filmed in Grass Valley, California. In one incident just as Conrad was about to start a scene with Anne Baxter a cloud of some 300 pigeons came down out of the sky. This was actually part of the script! According to one contemporary news report of the scene being shot, "After six abortive scene takes, much wing flapping, and several beak passes perilously close to the actor's eyes, (director Richard) Donner settled for a raven landing on Conrad's arm. When asked later if he ever wanted to work with ravens again, Conrad replied, 'Never more.'" Director Richard Donner would within just a few years go on to direct such big blockbuster films as *The Omen* and *Superman*.

Michael Caffey directed the first of four episodes during season three—the first being an excellent episode titled **Night Flight to Murder (10/17/1973)**. "He was a hard-nosed tough individual who'd been head of Warner's television, so he knew everything," Caffey recalls of Bill Conrad. "He knew exactly what he was doing, why he was doing it. He didn't want to be on camera for anybody, didn't care, wasn't gonna do it. He had a temper. He'd bite at you, and then it was gone. There was no rancor. There was no carrying on or anything." Caffey also attests to Conrad's sense of humor. "Bill…loved to put people on; He'd do it with a straight face." This was guest star David Hedison's second of three guest shots on *Cannon* and his favorite, "I liked the one where I played the FAA inspector. It was a large part, it fit me well—plus we got to go out on location to this airplane graveyard."

The Perfect Alibi (10/31/1973) is another stand-out episode involving Cannon getting involved with a gang of crooks and a redneck sheriff in a small Southern town. Guest star Richard Anderson recalls that "Bill Conrad was pretty much to himself and knew who he was and just went and did it. He didn't seem to do a lot of visiting with people and between scenes spent most of his time in his dressing room." **Photo Finish (01/02/1974)** with guest-star Jack

Cassidy has great claim to being the best single episode of the entire run of the series with its story of a General hiring Cannon to find out details of the death of his brother who has been deceased for many years. The episode takes several intriguing turns—and, as usual; Cassidy (as he proved on *Columbo*) is the perfect villain. **The Stalker (3/20/1974)**, the final episode of the season has Cannon trying to enjoy a fishing vacation—but instead being stalked by an escaped murderer. Cindy (*Laverne and Shirley*) Williams has an early career guest shot in this episode.

During the third season Conrad was asked to guest star on the first episode of a new private eye series produced by Quinn Martin about an elderly private eye named *Barnaby Jones* which starred Buddy Ebsen. "Quinn who produces both shows asked me if I would do Buddy's first program and I said I'd be delighted," Conrad told *TV Guide*. "If I hadn't wanted to do it, I wouldn't have. Besides, since I'm doing a commercial television show, it means I'm already a product that's being sold. It's part of the reality of this business—so why not take advantage of it."

The third season found the show moving up a half-hour, "We'll get bigger ratings," Conrad said at the time, "but less share." Conrad was half right—the show got a bigger rating AND share—and moved into the top ten—ranked #10 with 15.3 million viewers. Right above him at #9 was *The Mary Tyler Moore Show*, which had roughly the same number of viewers, and right below at #11 was *The Six Million Dollar Man*. It must have given Conrad a twinge of delight when he saw that his show outranked the aging (now in its 18th season) *Gunsmoke* which still performed well ranked at #15. As for other Quinn Martin show—*Barnaby Jones* ranked a solid #18 (14.1 million viewers) and *The Streets of San Francisco* clocked in with 13.7 million viewers to rank #22 overall.

It was while in the middle of *Cannon*'s third season that Conrad began a hosting chore he truly enjoyed for the next eight years. From 1973 thru 1981 William Conrad hosted *The CBS All American Thanksgiving Day Parade*. He was a natural host since he made no bones of his love for parades. "I'm a sucker for parades," he told a reporter in 1978. "Always have been. Always will be. As a matter of fact, there are two public events that I love more than any others—parades and circuses." His love of parades included his hosting duties. "Thanksgiving Day, Christmas Day, and New Year's Day are family days. I enjoy the feeling that I am reaching people I like and who, I feel, like me. When I host the parades, I am not 'Cannon,' I am Bill."

The CBS broadcast didn't focus on one single parade (such as The Macy's Thanksgiving Day Parade) but would telecast from several locations where Thanksgiving Day parades were being held from New York, Philadelphia, Toronto, Detroit, Hollywood and all the way to Hawaii. Among co-hosts and guest performers who would appear with him over the years included (usually stars from other CBS TV shows, but not always) Rob Reiner, Sebastian Cabot, Lucie Arnaz, Jack Lord, Michael Learned, Loretta Swit, Valerie Bertinelli, Victoria Principal, Linda Lavin and Jamie Farr.

Kevin Butler has been researching a book about the history of children's television, and had an opportunity to meet and speak to Conrad in 1978 when he was preparing that year's Thanksgiving Day telecast:

"I first met Mr. Conrad in Manhattan around 1978…I walked up to him and I asked him 'Excuse me, but aren't you William Conrad, that actor, singer and radio and TV broadcaster?' and he laughed and said, 'Yes, I am son.' We talked a bit about his career in TV before he had to go to an appointment, but he was a sweet, charming and caring gentleman—nothing like the tough, no nonsense character of 'Frank Cannon' or 'The Judge' in Jake and the Fatman—his personality never changed—he remained a sweet and kindly man.

He told me that it took two weeks for him to review the research on the information about the history and culture of the cities that held their parades that were broadcast on the network. He told me that he arrived at the studio two hours before the broadcast…(I recall) Mr. Conrad…rehearsing the songs that he would perform with the pianist at the end of the telecast (This was when his hosting segments were still being aired from the recreation of a living room set of a private home in Hollywood, CA)…

I did get a sense that he really enjoyed hosting those parade telecasts and he told me that he enjoyed introducing the parades from Philly, Detroit,

Toronto (When CBS still aired the pre-taped Eaton's Santa Claus Parades), The Hawaiian Floral Parades and the New York City Macy's Parade. He also enjoyed presenting info about the cities that hosted the parades and he enjoyed spending time with the viewers. I felt that I was spending my Thanksgiving morning with a kindly uncle or grandfather."

When Butler met Conrad again, after his final Thanksgiving Day parade hosting duties, he asked him if he was 'upset about no longer being the main host/moderator of the parade broadcasts,' and Conrad replied, "No Kevin, My stint with the parade would have to end sooner or later, so I'm not the least bit upset." While he was (as usual) stoic when his hosting duties ended on a gig he so enjoyed—scores of parade fans would come to miss his enthusiasm, knowledge, and sense of history. In 1982 Dallas star Larry Hagman would begin a six-year hosting stint. (His love of parades didn't just pertain to Thanksgiving, for several years he also hosted the Lone Star State Annual Cotton Bowl Festival Parade from Dallas, Texas on New Year's Day).

V

While Bill Conrad could be a cantankerous curmudgeon—he did have a good sense of humor and did appreciate the staff of *Cannon*. Production Manager Bob Jeffords recalls that Conrad "had a great sense of humor" and pointed out that one Christmas he gave every member of the *Cannon* crew a dart-board with his picture on it. He had printed on the dart board the following message, "For all you bastards who've wanted to all year long. Have a ball."

Speaking of Christmas the *Cannon* Christmas parties became legendary. The highlight was a profanity filled gag reel put together by Conrad that often poked fun at himself. The profanity was just an extension of Conrad and nobody really thought much about it. "Bill swore like a seaman," the script supervisor Kenneth Gilbert once said, "which never made any sense. The guy had such command of the language, but the words would come out. The women on the set never took offense. It was just the way he expressed himself. He was rough and hard, and because he had such an over-powering presence, you'd shake in your boots sometimes. But he was really a pussycat."

Often in the Christmas gag reel, Conrad made fun of his weight and compared and contrasted it with his stunt-man, a gentleman named Jimmy Casino. "Jimmy had to look like Bill in profile," Bob Jeffords later recalled. "But the minute Bill started running, Bill would bend over from the waist, the top of his body would be almost parallel with the ground. Well, the minute Jimmy started running, he'd straighten up more. So you could immediately tell whether it was Bill or Jimmy doing the stunt."

Speaking of look-a-likes for Conrad there was a press story about a man named Gene Kempfer who the writer said, "looks more like Conrad than himself." Apparently an attorney and his family took a trip to an amusement park and the entire family knows Kempfer. Bill Conrad happened to be staying at their hotel. One day Conrad got on the elevator with the attorney and his family already on board. The Attorney's twelve year old daughter took a look at Conrad and said, "Why, Mr. Kempfer, whatever in the world are you doing here."

Season four includes some outstanding episodes including **Voice from the Grave (9/25/1974)** which is a murder in retrospect episode as Cannon looks into and tries to solve a fourteen year old homicide. **The Prisoner (12/11/1974)** involves Cannon going undercover as a hit man (given many of Conrad's 1940's and 50's films a pretty easy and convincing transformation). **Missing at FL307 (2/5/75)** offers an intriguing episode about an ex-con who goes missing while a plane is in-air. **Lady on the Run (3/5/1975)** features Barbara Rush as a woman who seeks sanctuary at a sanitarium after witnessing a murder and Cannon trying to find her before the killers do.

Among the other fourth season guest stars include: Alex Rocco, Monte Markham, Barbara Luna, Hari Rhodes, Cameron Mitchell, Bradford Dillman, Patty McCormack, Mitch Ryan, Leif Erickson, Leslie Nielsen, Ruth Roman, Robert Loggia and Richard Kiley.

During the fourth season, *Cannon* slipped a bit in the ratings. It still ranked a quite solid #21 with 14.8 million viewers. It was ranked right below *Mannix* (#20 in its final season) and *Cher* (#22). The only other Quinn Martin series in the top 30 was *The Streets of San Francisco* which was ranked at #23. By the way, *Gunsmoke* finally ended its twenty-season television run that season ranked at #28.

It was while working on episodes for the fourth season of *Cannon* that a fire broke out at the Samuel Goldwyn Studios where both *Cannon* and *Barnaby Jones* were filmed. The fire broke out on the soundstages of a children's series *Sigmund and the Sea Monsters* and quickly traveled to the *Cannon* and *Jones* sets. Luckily both shows were filming on location and nobody was hurt, but there was more than $2 million in damages.

VI

The *Cannon* years made Bill Conrad a star beyond anything he had ever been before. He had, of course, been a successful and much sought after radio performer, voice actor and character man in films. But being the star of a successful television series made William Conrad a house hold name. And he enjoyed it. Throughout those years Conrad enjoyed appearing as a guest star on TV variety shows. He loved singing and these shows often gave him an opportunity to show case his wonderful, deep baritone singing voice as well as his comedic ability when appearing in sketches. He did so many side jobs that *Cannon* producers thought it would hurt him and the show in the long run. "The Cannon people would be happy if I didn't do anything else—they're worried I might collapse," Conrad said at the time. "I do all these things because I like to do them. It's relaxation for me, a kick in the butt; it gives me a wonderful opportunity to be stupid and silly and do all the crazy things I never got a chance to do before."

He was a frequent guest on *The Dean Martin Show* as well as the *Dean Martin Celebrity Roasts*—he himself was roasted by Martin in 1973—naturally there was an abundance of fat jokes. Among those roasting Conrad included Phyllis Diller, Nipsey Russell, Bob Newhart and, most surprisingly, British singer Petula Clark who is introduced as Conrad's mistress! Stand-up comic Jackie Gayle jokes about Conrad's "illustrious" career as a movie director—*My Blood Runs Cold, Two on a Guillotine, Brainstorm*. Conrad takes the ribbing well and seems to be enjoying himself as he chomps on a cigar. Earlier that year Conrad appeared on Martin's variety show and had the chance to perform an Anthony Newley medley and then joined Dean and fellow guest stars Nancy Sinatra and Dom Deluise in singing "Easter Parade" in the finale.

Among the other variety shows he appeared on were *Tony Orlando and Dawn, Laugh-In* (in which he portrays Hollywood's finest dancer of yesteryear & dons a Captain America—but in his case a Captain Amazing outfit), *The Flip Wilson Special* (joining Helen Reddy and Sammy Davis, Jr.), and *Sonny and Cher* in which he joins Jean Stapleton and Chad Everett in receiving the "Third Annual Bono Television Awards"—naturally played for laughs (he would join Sonny and Cher on their show three times—twice during the third season and once during the fourth season). He also appeared on two episodes of *The Carol Burnett Show*. If this wasn't enough he also became the host and narrator of a syndicated wildlife/nature show called *Wild, Wild World of Animals* of which 129 episodes were produced between 1973 and 1978. A dedicated outdoorsman and conservationist he truly enjoyed this venture.

As they say "all good things have to come to an end." The fifth season of *Cannon* proved to be its last. The previous season had seen the show's ratings fall from #10 to #21—still strong, but a precipitous fall nonetheless. In the fifth season the show dropped out of the top 30 altogether. In fact, the only Quinn Martin show still in the top 30 was *The Streets of San Francisco*, but just barely at #28. Conrad was, after five years, exhausted and not overly disappointed by the shows cancellation.

Among the highlights of the season include **The Deadly Conspiracy (9/17/1975)** with guest-star Buddy Ebsen as Barnaby Jones. It was typical stunt programming. The two-parter begins on *Cannon* and gets solved on *Barnaby Jones* two nights later. **The Man Who Died Twice (10/15/1975)** with guest star Leslie Nielsen is an intriguing episode about a man who has been dead for many years suddenly becoming the main suspect in a murder. **The Melted Man (11/12/1975)** casts Diana Hyland as a woman who panics when she spots a snowman with a hatchet imbedded in its head on her estate—in the desert!—it's a nifty mystery. **The Wedding March (11/19/1975)** about a psychopath who beats a series of women to the strains of "The Wedding March." The episode was directed by Leo Penn and features Julie Adams who recalls, "I loved working with Leo Penn, he was a very good director, and a charming man. Also, Leo was good friends with my late husband Ray Danton, who also directed a lot of television during that time, so I knew Leo pretty well. He took the work very seriously and got excellent performances from the actors." **The Hero (11/26/1975)** features veteran character actor Philip Pine as Police Lt. Gold. Pine wasn't one of the fans of Conrad's use of cue cards and recalls that in one scene Conrad's dialogue was written on a blackboard. "We started to shoot this scene going into a police station," recalled Pine, "and there's this guy with a big blackboard with Conrad's lines on it. We're doing this dolly shot, going along walking and talking and here he is—every shot that he did—he had the guy holding this big blackboard with his name on it, with his lines on it. God Almighty! That's very distracting for the other actor, but apparently Conrad just didn't want to bother." **The Star (12/10/1975)** has Joan Fontaine as (what else) a legendary film star with a problem child. **Revenge (1/21/1976)** is another nifty outing with Cannon getting framed for murder. **Snapshot (2/11/1976)** has a former hit man hiring Cannon to find out who it is and why he is being stalked by somebody.

However the most intriguing episode of the fifth and final season is **Nightmare (9/10/75)** which was the season premiere. Conrad was impressed with the episode and even did some interviews to promote it. "It's rather painful for the character I play," he told reporters. "As Cannon, I hear the deathbed confession of a hit man who says he murdered my wife and child 14 years earlier. This confession shakes me up to begin with but then the hit man claims that my wife was a lady of loose morals. Now I start on a trail that has many unexpected angles, but I don't want to telegraph any of the moves. It would ruin a good story."

Among the other prominent guest stars during season five include: Scott Hyland, Andrew Duggan, Robert Hays, Ralph Bellamy, Gary Merrill, Pernell Roberts, Vera Miles, Dean Stockwell, Sondra Locke, Donna Mills, Charles During, and Barry Sullivan.

"Television is a business, and I'm not ashamed of it," he said shortly after the show was given its pink slip. "You try to do the best job you can within the limitations. If you have to make shoes that sell for $12 a pair, you make the best possible pair you can for $9. If you spend $12 to make the shoes, you're a fool because you won't make any profit. But if you spend, $6, you're cheating the public." He went on to call much of television "crap" including *Cannon*. "I don't mean to demean *Cannon* by calling it crap. It's as good as anything else on television. It's what the audience wants. If they wanted something better, they wouldn't be watching it." Despite this caviler attitude towards television and his show Conrad was deeply affected when the show was cancelled. "There never was a man who was as wedded to anything as Bill Conrad was to that show," Producer Anthony Spinner recalls. "I think he wanted that show to go on forever. That show was his whole life."

CHAPTER SEVEN: NERO WOLFE 1977-1986

After *Cannon* left the air Conrad kept busy on a variety of shows—either as an actor or narrator. He narrated several episodes of the TV-miniseries *How the West Was Won* (which, ironically, starred television's Matt Dillon, James Arness). He was narrator for a horror anthology series *Tales of the Unexpected* and for the TV-series *Buck Rogers in the 25th Century.* As usual his voice work was highly lucrative. He also made a trio of made for television movies: *Night Cries* (1/29/78) cast him as a psychoanalyst; *Keefer* (3/16/78) has him leading a group of secret agents behind enemy lines during WWII and *Turnover Smith* (6/8/80) found Conrad playing a private detective investigating series of serial killings.

But more exciting and certainly more challenging was making his stage debut in a summer tour of Jason Miller's 1973 Pulitzer Prize winning play, *That Championship Season.* "I'd wanted to do a play for a long time because my fellow actors kept telling me how gratifying it is. The offer came through. It hit me at the time so I jumped in with both feet with everything to lose and nothing to gain," Conrad remarked.

Conrad was front and center of an ensemble piece about the twentieth anniversary of a Catholic High School winning a State Championship Game in Pennsylvania. Conrad plays the dying coach who meets up with four members of that championship team to reminisce about their glory days and also to discover some profound truths about each other in the process. It was a play that Conrad greatly admired.

Among the cities that *That Championship Season* appeared in was Miami. Jon Marlowe, the entertainment critic for the *Miami News,* wrote, "Conrad's portrayal is a living advertisement that you can be a weekly TV character (as he was with Frank Cannon) and still be able to leave it all behind you and turn in a most convincing job IF YOU HAVE THE TALENT. Conrad fuses both his physical attributes, along with his credible acting ability, to portray the Coach who refuses to let the past go. Conrad brings both domineering and fatherly qualities to the role of a man who will settle for nothing less than success. Conrad walks the tightrope nicely; drifting off into the past and then snapping back into the present—knowing but refusing to believe that both he and his former players are losers." However N.L. Sheffield the critic for the *Boca Raton News* was less enthusiastic. "William Conrad put forth a great effort as the coach but there was a certain credibility lacking in his character."

When the play moved on to its final run in Chicago (at the then new Arlington Park Theater) the show got decent if not enthusiastic notices, "Conrad's substantial stage debut still has folds to fill out, but the five man evening remains a solid piece of naturalistic theater," wrote Linda Winer in the *Chicago Tribune*. Despite generally favorable notices and packed houses Conrad was strangely unhappy. He growled to one reporter in Chicago that "I'll never do it again. I can't wait for the last performance."

One of his co-stars was the actor Danny Aiello (later nominated for an Oscar for his role in Spike Lee's *Do the Right Thing*), who played one of the former teammates. Aiello had worked in more than one production of *That Championship Season* and was happy to be working with Conrad. Yet by the end of the run it was clear even to Aiello that Conrad had had it. "None of us in the company were aware of his dissatisfaction until the last stop of the tour, in Chicago," Aiello later recalled. "Conrad took us all out for dinner and presented each cast member with a gold watch. Mine was inscribed, "To Danny, a champion of all seasons. Love, Bill." We were all stunned by Conrad's generosity, thanking him profusely. 'Now I want you all to go fuck yourselves,' Conrad said calmly. 'This has been the worst experience of my life.' He walked out. We were left speechless."

Soon afterward he returned to the big screen in a low budget (about $700,000) action movie produced by Roger Corman that would go on to gross millions—*Moonshine County Express*. A moonshiner is killed by a rival (Conrad, once again cast as the heavy on the big screen), and so his three daughters (played by Susan Howard, Claudia Jennings and Maureen McCormick) take over the business and together with a local stock car driver (John Saxon) they seek their revenge.

Saxon is too old for his role and the three female leads don't seem believable as southern hillbillies (with the exception of former *Playboy* playmate Claudia Jennings), but the supporting cast of reliable character actors like Conrad, Dub Taylor, Albert Salmi, Morgan Woodward and Jeff Corey seem to be having a great deal of fun with their colorful roles. This was just one of several films of this type released in the late seventies including *Cannonball, Eat My Dust, Grand Theft Auto* and *Smokey and the Bandit*—a genre that led to the popular television series The Dukes of Hazzard.

II

Around 1974-1975 Conrad's wife, Susan, was diagnosed with breast cancer. She made the decision to have a double mastectomy. This was a difficult decision for her to make. "She could be a very vain, socially conscious and very proud woman," her son Christopher later recalled, "but after the mastectomy she showed great character and accepted what happened and was just happy to be alive—she said, 'I'm going to live!'"

Sadly her victory over cancer was short-lived and within four years she had a recurrence. By the Christmas and New Year season of 1978-1979 Conrad was told that the cancer had spread to Susan's brain. Christopher, who was exceptionally close to his mother, was a daily caregiver to her. "My mother's illness was very hard on my dad," Christopher recalled. "I was a caregiver to my mother...my dad helped but due to his career not on a day to day basis."

Susan's doctor told Conrad that they could try to treat her with aggressive chemotherapy which would give her at least some more time. Conrad and Christopher discussed it and concluded that they should not go the aggressive route and prolong her suffering. However, the next morning Christopher was surprised that Conrad changed his mind and told the doctor to continue to do whatever could be done to prolong her life. "My dad came to the conclusion that he wanted to do everything he could for her—and today I understand," Christopher recalls.

The time it bought her was minimal and Susan Randall Conrad died on April 13, 1979. They had been married for over twenty-years and even though they maintained an open marriage for much of that time—they never ceased to love each other. "My mom was an incredible force," Christopher Conrad says. "She could stand up to my dad—which is one of the reasons why he loved her."

About a year or so after her passing Conrad and Christopher were driving to Forest Lawn to visit Susan's grave. It had been a particularly painful period for Christopher. As close as they were he and his mother never discussed life and death issues. At one point they pulled over to the side of the road and Christopher asked his father if he ever spoke with her about dying. Conrad replied, "Yes, she was frightened and didn't want to die." This no doubt influenced his decision to try and prolong her life by taking aggressive measures.

III

Tippy Stringer was born in Chicago in 1930, the daughter of a newsman who worked for the *Chicago Tribune.* Later her father moved to Washington D.C. and Tippy attended the University of Maryland. After graduation she decided to pursue a career in television. A petite, blue-eyed blonde her effervescent personality got her places—she soon was hosting a cooking and homemaking show on WRC-TV out of Washington, D.C., and by 1953 became the popular new weather girl. If that wasn't enough between delivering the weather on the evening and late night news she ran over to the Shoreham Hotel where she sang in a nightly floor show at the hotel's nightclub. "Her long suit is fashion, beauty and the undeniable fact that she's about the cutest thing seen on TV in these parts," wrote the TV critic for the *Washington Post* about Stringer. No doubt about it Tippy Stringer was a go-getter.

By 1959 what she got was the attention of the NBC News anchorman Chet Huntley, half of the famed *Huntley-Brinkley Report.* In fact it was Huntley's partner, the avuncular David Brinkley, who introduced Tippy to Huntley. "She sat in my lap or something corny like that," Brinkley later recalled, "and I told her who Chet was while she looked on in the monitor. The next thing I knew he was taking her out." They married the same year and in 1960 they moved into a fashionable Manhattan townhouse between First and Second Avenues on Sixty-Ninth Street. Tippy took an active interest in her husband's career and often accompanied him on overseas trips on behalf of NBC News. By all reports she and Huntley had a happy marriage. When Huntley decided to retire in 1970 he and Tippy returned to his native Montana where he built and operated a ski resort near the town of Bozeman. But his retirement was cut short after just a few years when he died of lung cancer in March of 1974.

Conrad, during the course of his career, knew many prominent people and he got to know the Huntley's in the 1960's and considered them friends—not close—but socially. He certainly had an appreciation for the impeccably dressed and coiffured Tippy. Peggy Webber, still a good friend of Conrad's, recalls that after Huntley died, "Bill was at her door the next day with a bouquet of roses and said whenever she decided to marry again he would like to be first in line. Tippy told me this story herself." (While this is undoubtedly what Miss Webber recalls being told it is unlikely that Conrad would have been right at her door with a bouquet of roses asking for her hand in marriage before Huntley was even buried. For one thing Bill was married to Susan—but it is not inconceivable that within a more respectable time frame that Conrad did make his feelings clear to Tippy given that he and Susan did have an open marriage).

Meanwhile Tippy, perhaps to the surprise of many, stayed in Montana after Huntley's death. She later sold the resort and ran for congress as a Republican in 1978—losing the election. In 1979, after Susan's death, she and Conrad became reacquainted and in 1980 they married. Apparently Conrad wasn't interested in having Tippy merely as a stay-at-home wife. "He called me after he married Tippy and told me what I never expected to hear from Bill," recalls Peggy Webber. "He was not overly sentimental with fellow actors. But he told me that of all the actresses he had worked with in his life…and he had worked with any number of famous actresses, he said that he always thought I was the best he ever worked with, and he asked me as a favor, if I would teach Tippy to act. He wanted to go on the road in plays with her. I did and I found her to be a fine, natural actress."

Webber recalls that the union between Conrad and Tippy appeared to be a happy one—an assessment backed up by Conrad's friend Jimmy Lydon who feels that after two tries Conrad had finally succeeded in matrimony. "It was a very happy marriage," states Lydon.

Christopher Conrad had a more strained relationship with Tippy. Christopher confirms that his dad and Tippy were involved prior to his mother's passing. "Tippy was a very large woman—I don't mean physically, but in personality," Christopher says. "She was a tough lady—intellectually and spiritually she was his equal. That is what drew her to him. That said she was also quite insecure about being appreciated or liked. She once overheard me saying to somebody that I thought she was weird. I didn't really mean it badly, but she took it that I didn't like her and my dad came to me about it because she was upset over it and I tried to explain to him what I meant. Overall we had a strained, but cordial relationship. I think there was a jealousy between us for my father's affection. She was far wealthier than dad, but she grew up during the depression and so money was always important to her—she could never have enough."

The same year that he married Tippy, Conrad returned to his most famous TV role—in the TV-movie *The Return of Frank Cannon*. Cannon had been enjoying retirement when he is called to investigate the death of an old friend who worked for the CIA. The death had been ruled a suicide, but Cannon has his doubts and is soon on the trail of his friend's murderer. The TV-movie, which co-starred Arthur Hill, Diana Muldaur, Ed Nelson and Joanna Pettet, aired on November 30, 1980 to mediocre ratings. Conrad always insisted that this was a one-shot TV-movie, but indications are that if it had been more successful it might have led to more *Cannon* TV-movies or even a new series. This turned out to be a temporary set-back for Conrad. Within a couple of months he would be back on network television not as Frank Cannon but as another well-known heavyweight sleuth—Nero Wolfe.

IV

"William Conrad's a rough, gruff man who chewed up people and spit them out," maintains actor Lee Horsley, who co-starred with Conrad in his third major television series—Nero Wolfe—but luckily for Horsley, "he took me under his wing."

Nero Wolfe was based on the popular series of mystery novels written by the prolific Rex Stout, who penned 33 novels and 39 short stories featuring the obese, arm-chair crime solving detective who lives in a New York City brownstone and whose great passions (besides solving complex mysteries) are his roof top orchid garden, beer, and gourmet cooking. The character rarely ventured from his brown stone and so much of his leg work is supplied by his associate (and the stories narrator) Archie Goodwin. Archie is a street smart ladies man. Other characters who populate Wolfe's world are his chef, Fritz; live-in orchid nurse, Theodore; a free-lance detective, Saul—and the often exasperated Inspector Cramer, who Wolfe time and again frustrates.

Nero Wolfe had been a character in some Columbia 'B' pictures of the 1930's and was a very popular character on radio before making some sporadic TV appearances over the years. The most recent, before the Conrad series, was a TV pilot filmed in 1977 by Paramount and telecast on ABC in 1979—but which fell by the way-side when it's leading actor (Thayer David) died.

By 1980 NBC was trying to resurrect its moribund prime-time TV schedule and Brandon Tartikoff and Fred Silverman thought "Nero Wolfe" might make an interesting mystery series—and one which would involve little physical activity for Orson Welles—but Welles balked at the idea of doing a weekly series. Instead he wanted to make it a series of ninety-minute TV-movies. The network disagreed and Welles was out of the picture. Enter William Conrad. "We didn't even make a pilot," Conrad later said. "Everybody was faced with the problem of not being able to get anything ready. We didn't expect to go on as soon as we did; suddenly, they said, 'we don't want you on in six weeks…now, we want you on NEXT week.'"

Luckily Conrad was a Wolfe fan and didn't need a lot of convincing to do the series. "I have been reading Nero Wolfe books ever since I was a kid, and I've always thought they were the most fun of any detective fiction I had ever read. I never thought I would ever play the role, and all of a sudden, somebody offered me the job and I said 'yes' without thinking."

Being a TV-veteran with a successful prior series under his belt allowed Conrad to arrange a fee of $50,000 per episode. The show was a traditional mystery in which the culprit is usually revealed to the television audience near the end when all the suspects are gathered in Wolfe's brownstone. "When Nero says so-and-so did it, that's the joy of these shows," Conrad said in an interview in early 1981. Another appeal that the character had for Conrad is that Wolfe is the "brightest and rudest" of sleuths in all of detective fiction.

Unlike Frank Cannon, Conrad was mainly sedentary on this show. "I could never stand doing another series like that (*Cannon*)," Conrad maintained. "This is a whole 'nother thing. All those car chases, that action, running around and jumping in and out of cars—and hitting my head every time… On *Nero Wolfe*, "I never get outside of my brownstone house. My leg man is Archie. He does all the footwork. I stay at home, grow orchids, and piece all the information he's gathered into a solution."

Ironically, Conrad in real life was no lover of orchids, "I despise orchids. I just don't like exotic flowers. I like daisies and pansies and things like that." He quickly added, "Don't quote that out of context." Another reason for Conrad's happiness with doing this particular series, "It takes seven days to shoot an episode, so I only have to work about half the week. This is much better."

Conrad was surrounded by a highly competent supporting cast including the handsome twenty-five year old Horsley, who began his career in musical theater and whose first major television role as Wolfe's leg man, Archie Goodwin, this would be. Rounding out the regular cast are George Voskovec, as Fritz the Chef, George Wyner as Saul, Allan Miller as Inspector Cramer and the delightful British actor Robert Coote as Theodore Horstman.

Veteran actor Allan Miller would recall that he had never met Conrad prior to working with him on *Nero Wolfe*. However they quickly discovered that they lived within four blocks of one another in Sherman Oaks. "We never got to know each other intimately," recalls Miller, "but we were friendly and we would socialize. My wife and I would visit with Bill and his wife. We would go out to dinner and discuss all kinds of things such as our mutual experiences as actors and the little theatre that my wife and I ran. He loved his sound studio at his home and we would visit him there and listen to music."

Miller also discovered that Conrad had a good sense of humor. "He loved self-mockery," recalls Miller. "I remember one time on the set when we were filming that something dropped off the desk he was standing next to—and he didn't pick it up. The guy comes out of the control room and asked Bill if he was going to pick it up? Bill with an incredulous look on his face replied, 'What! Me bend over!?' It broke everybody up."

Conrad thought that the show also would highlight the humor between these characters that live in the brownstone. "Nero is constantly telling Fritz how to prepare a dish. He tries to tell Horstman how to raise the orchids, but he won't listen. They bicker like three old maids which gives us an opportunity for some humor." Allan Miller maintains that Conrad, "enjoyed the fact that the show included a good deal of humor and it allowed him to play comedy from time to time. We had a fun piece of business that was put in the script of having my character raise himself out of his chair without using his hands to do so, and Nero was always so astonished that he could do that and his character would even attempt to do it himself—without success. Bill got a kick out of that kind of thing."

Conrad also hoped to show a warmer side of the character. "I think Nero Wolfe is one of the best drawn detectives in fiction. He is the brightest detective ever. And he's the rudest detective ever. He would never let anyone think he had any nicety at all. He never showed any warmth toward the people around him. But the audience is allowed to see that he has warmth and a sense of humor." Of his relationship with Archie and the others in the 'Wolfe' household, Conrad said, "I have grown into being the father figure; age has been good to me. In the scripts, he's the papa of them all! He has a whole house full of people he lords over."

Conrad felt he had a great deal in common with his TV counterpart. "Obesity—obviously. I am a very brusque man, as he was. I love good food. Good wine. Beer. Unfortunately in the IQ department we are not alike. They say about Nero that he is definitely over 250 and you never know if they are talking about his weight or IQ."

Horsley, who later became a more famous television detective, *Matt Houston* (1982-1985), recalls that he first read for the part of Conrad's TV side kick in New York and they liked his looks and reading enough that he was then sent to Los Angeles for further tests. "I got all excited because, it being so early in my career, anything with a first class plane ride on it, I thought was heaven. I thought it was definitely the big time." The role of Archie eventually came down to Horsley and Edward Albert, Jr.—who had an extensive resume and pedigree as the son of actor Eddie Albert. In the end the executives decided to go with the newcomer, Horsley, who was thought to have more sex appeal.

Horsley recalled that he "had a lot of fun with it. Archie was good at a wisecrack now and then. I think we played it a little more tongue in cheek but that is really what made it so much fun. We had to update the dialogue but the feeling of the whole show captured the era when the books were written."

As for Conrad, Horsely recalls that, "I couldn't have asked him to be any nicer. We would get together off-set. We both loved to fish, so we had lots of talks about other than show business." Yet, on the set, Horsley recalls that Conrad, typical to form, could be "brusque and demanding at times." When he did work Conrad's schedule was sweet—between 9 a.m. and 4 p.m. "I remember the days when he would shoot the final scene when Wolfe called all the suspects together," recalled Horsley. "Bill had (it) in his contract that he would only work so many hours a day. If the clock struck whatever, and it was time for him to go, he'd put on his bedroom slippers and he was gone. It didn't matter if we were in the middle of a scene or not. He loved the work but he was that way. When he decided he didn't want to play anymore, that was it. We'd have to figure it out how to shoot the rest of the scene just to get it done."

And yes, he still used cue-cards. But Allan Miller offers a strong defense for Conrad on how he used them:

Bill was a very professional guy—he didn't like unprofessionalism of any kind. He did use cue cards. When we first met and he was using the cards he apologized to me, but explained that he used the cards to rehearse at home and he felt more comfortable using them on the set—it may be because of his radio training. But he practiced with those cards at home and it gave him more freedom to rally think about the character and the words he was saying. It's not that he didn't know his lines—he would often say his lines and just glance now and then at the cards. He was always perfectly credible. The way he used the cards was very different from how other people I worked with used them—there was a real thought process with Bill.

NBC thought the show would be good counter programming against the *The Dukes of Hazzard*, a then popular CBS series with strong rural appeal. "Listen, we're all gambling," Conrad said at the time. "We're taking a chance. But in comparison with some of those other shows which are 90 per-cent car chases it's a welcome relief."

Maybe so, but audiences didn't rally to Conrad's new series. Debuting as a mid-season replacement on Friday, January 16, 1981, *Nero Wolfe* lasted only fourteen episodes. While the show garnered generally lackluster reviews and some Stout purists didn't particularly care for the updating of the show to contemporary times (not to mention the fact that Archie didn't narrate the shows as he did in the books) the show did receive some favorable notices. "I know, I know, the show pales next to *The Rockford Files*, but I've tried it a couple of times and I think there's a good TV series there," wrote Peter Boyer, TV-writer for the Associated Press, "They did have the good sense to hire William Conrad, who is perfectly suited to the part." The *Los Angeles Times* TV critic wrote, "Not quite Rex Stout's Nero Wolfe but head and shoulders above most crime series."

Yet some Wolfe purists pan the series (especially when compared to the excellent A&E series from 2001-2002 which had starred Timothy Hutton and Maury Chaykin). An example would be this comment on the website "The Wolfe Pack": "The William Conrad series was poorly received by fans of the books due to its lack of adherence to the book's plots (even in those few instances when the episode name corresponded to a book title) and Mr. Conrad's lack of similarity to Mr. Wolfe in appearance and personality." An example of this can be that the book's Wolfe didn't wear a mustache and beard where Conrad did sport both (and if Orson Welles had done the series he would have too).

Years later Conrad commented to writer James Bawden of the *Toronto Star* about the demise of the series. "How the hell should I know what makes a hit TV series? I was really excited about doing a show called *Nero Wolfe*. I thought it couldn't fail. Here we had one of the most popular characters in mystery fiction; everybody has read a Rex Stout novel. The books still sell, although they were written fifty years ago. But you know how long we lasted? Just 13 weeks. Try to figure that one out." Christopher Conrad maintains that his dad put more effort into *Nero Wolfe* than he did for either *Cannon* or *Jake and the Fatman*, "he just loved that character."

V

Conrad enjoyed singing—he sang on variety show guest appearances and he sang in the privacy of his own home. Christopher Conrad recalls that singing became one of the joys of his life. "My dad rarely spoke of his movies or TV roles—he just didn't like looking back," Christopher says. "He would say some of it was just a 'load of shit.' He really started to sing in the mid 70's and I recall he did a show at some place like the Hyatt in Los Angeles and he was doing stuff like 'Send in the Clowns' which really made me and my mom roll our eyes. But he didn't care—he just had fun and, of course, he got so much better."

In 1982 Conrad got a major singing opportunity when he was offered the starring role in a television version of the Gilbert and Sullivan operetta *The Mikado*. It was one of a series of Gilbert and Sullivan shows that were being filmed by one time boxer George Walker at Twickenham Studios outside of London. Walker had made a lot of loot producing the film *The Stud* in the late seventies—the soft porn film had starred a middle aged—but still luscious looking Joan Collins. But Walker was a big Gilbert and Sullivan fan and so now he decided to put some of that money towards this project.

According to Conrad he was vacationing in Hawaii when his agent called him with the offer to do *The Mikado*. "I thought he was kidding," Conrad later recalled. "I'd never sung professionally before in my life. But he said, 'Think about it.' At first I laughed. The next day I laughed a little less and the next day I didn't laugh at all and called my agent to say, 'Yes.'" Conrad recalled that many years earlier he had gone to singing teachers. "They told me I had a terrific voice. But I couldn't afford to stop working long enough in those days to take lessons. The only singing I've done since then has been in the shower." (Not exactly true, as mentioned he sang several times on variety shows and even on his Parade telecasts).

Christopher Conrad recalls that his dad was passionate about this production. "Two whole summers I would be home and listen to him practice for hours at a time—Gilbert and Sullivan." Christopher recalls that for *The Mikado* he had "many happy memories hanging out in the pool with him as he practiced 'See how the Fates Their Gifts Allot' ('Yet A happy! Oh, so happy! Laughing Ha! Ha! Chaffing Ha! Ha!...")

This was the second in a series of television projects. The first, *The Pirates of Penzance*, had already been filmed starring Linda Ronstadt, Kevin Kline and Angela Lansbury. To play the part of the Japanese ruler, Conrad packed on twenty pounds on his already expansive 260-pound frame. Joining him in the project were Clive Revill as the Lord High Executioner, John Stewart as Nanki-Poo and Kate Flower as Yum-Yum. The program was first shown in Europe and then was presented on PBS in the United States on June 6, 1984. The *New York Times* review called the program "flawed but enjoyable... but it's well worth seeing for some delectable solo performances." Conrad was called a "genial Mikado" who "makes his singing debut in this production, and comes through unscathed." Having done this musical, Conrad seemed interested at the time in doing more. He told the London reporters, "I'll take more singing lessons when I get back to Los Angeles and see what comes my way."

In the summer of 1983 Conrad had the opportunity to play the part of Tevye in *Fiddler on the Roof* produced by the prestigious Kenley circuit of Ohio. Actor-Director Kevin Moore (now Producing Artistic Director of the Human Race Theatre Company of Dayton, Ohio) played the part of Motel, the Tailor, recalls Conrad as "an amazing actor." Moore went on to say that "playing scenes with him was like being paid to take acting lessons. His choices were honest and emotional." Mr. Moore went on to say:

"Kenley audiences loved to see television stars in roles on stage, but Bill's tough-guy image made him an unlikely candidate for the role of "Tevye." But that was so far from the case. He was ideally suited. His powerful, resonant speaking voice was equally as effective singing. And his range of emotions matched the happy, frustrated, tear-your-heart-out roller-coaster-role of "Tevye." Playing scenes on stage with him was a master class in acting. He was 100% engaged—playing WITH you—allowing for give and take. He was one of the sweetest and most generous scene partners I have ever had. And one of the finest "Tevye's" I have ever seen. I do remember there was a bit of shock on the first day of

rehearsal. Everyone remembered the larger-then-life image of Bill from his days as Cannon and Nero Wolfe. What we did not know is that he had been on a major diet, and he showed up looking half the size of his TV persona. The costume shop quickly started taking in all his costumes that day."

Christopher went with his dad on tour with stops in Dayton, Ohio and Flint, Michigan. He recalls, "Audiences were sold out and they just loved him and dad gave an amazing performance." In addition to these musical opportunities Conrad also appeared in productions of *Our Town* and *The Man Who Came to Dinner*.

The theater critic for the *Dayton Daily News* began his review with these words, "There has been concern among certain theatergoers that this week's Kenley Players production might be mutated into *Cannon on the Roof*." The critic, Hal Lipper, however, went on to write, "Fears about Conrad's casting…are unfounded…What Conrad, and much of the cast, lacks is movement. Too much is stated without physical expression. However, Conrad's vocal capabilities more than compensate for his inertia…*Fiddler on the Roof* is Kenley Players summer stock approaching its best."

An intriguing offer came Conrad's way in the mid-80's that would bring him to the stage to star in a one-man play about Orson Welles. Certainly Conrad was an interesting choice to play Welles. Both had their initial success in old-time radio. Both had worked in all realms of show business: acting, voice work, producing and directing. Both had experienced career set-backs that they didn't allow to get them down—they came bouncing back time and again. And, of course, both were corpulent. The Welles play was written by Michael B. Druxman who later related:

"I decided I wanted William Conrad to star in my one-man play about Orson Welles. He might have been shorter than Welles, but otherwise he was perfect casting. He had the same kind of voice, similar facial features and a like general body mass. His agent, who I knew, wouldn't even present my script to him unless there was a cash offer on the table (something I could not do), so I sent the actor a letter c/o the agent, but marked it "Personal/Confidential—Please Forward".

Sometimes, in this business, you just have to ignore agents. The letter was forwarded unopened, and a few days later, Conrad called personally to request the script. I sent it out that same day. About a week later, he called again and asked me to come over to his home in Sherman Oaks. When I got there, he took me out to his pool house, which he'd converted into a recording studio, and played me a recording he had made of the play. It was brilliant! Letter perfect! It was as if Welles was reading my workd himself.

I asked Conrad if he would be willing to do a production of the play, either on the stage or on television. 'I'd prefer television,' he said. 'That way I wouldn't have to learn all the lines.' I called my producer friend, Stanley Rubin, and told him that Conrad was interested. Would Stanley like to put the project together? 'Absolutely,' he said. 'Send me the script.'

I sent Stanley the script and he also started to get excited about the project. He said that he would put his agent right on it. I called Conrad to tell him that Stanley was getting involved, and that's when the actor told me…He'd just been signed to do a new television series, entitled Jake and the Fatman, and that would be taking up all his time in the foreseeable future."

CHAPTER EIGHT: JAKE AND THE FATMAN 1987-1994

The success of the Angela Lansbury series *Murder, She Wrote* in the mid-80's brought forth other series which networks hoped would appeal to seniors and aging baby boomers. For instance, *Matlock* which starred Andy Griffith as a wily southern lawyer, had proved to be a big hit for producers Fred Silverman and Dean Hargrove. The show ranked #15 in its first season on the air during the 1986-1987 TV season. (The show would go on to be a top 20 hit for the first five of its nine seasons and reasonably rated afterward until its final season.) Interestingly, during the first season of *Matlock*, Conrad guest-starred on a two-parter titled "The Don" in which he plays a prosecuting attorney named James McShane who does battle with Matlock in court. Also in a prominent role in this two-parter is actor Joe Penny (then best known for his role on the TV series *Riptide*).

It was while making this episode that Silverman had the idea of bringing Conrad back to series television. The *Matlock* episode isn't really a spin-off, since Conrad wouldn't be playing the character he portrayed in the episode. Silverman greatly admired Conrad as an actor, ("I loved his voice—going all the way back to listening to him as Matt Dillon the radio version of *Gunsmoke*,") and wanted to develop a series for the actor. "People accepted him as the gruff, rough curmudgeon," Silverman later said. "Underneath he was just a nice man."

Dean Hargrove (who would win an Emmy for his work as a producer of *Columbo* in 1974) worked with the TV writers Joel Steiger (who was also working on many of the *Perry Mason* TV-movies which were also produced by Silverman and Hargrove) and Douglas

Stefen Borgi to create and develop the series which evolved into *Jake and the Fatman*.

Jake and the Fatman is the story of J.L. McCabe, who was born in and served as a cop in Hawaii. He later moves to Los Angeles with his pet bull dog, Max, where he is employed as a Los Angeles District Attorney. McCabe is profane (the show utilized bleeps to cover up some of the words) and has a tough gruff and ornery exterior but, as usual, has a heart of gold and deep commitment to the justice and the rule of law. Given McCabe's girth, he is nick-named "Fatman." Conrad liked the character but made it clear that he didn't want to embark on any *Cannon* like car chases and fist fights, so the character of detective Jake Styles, McCabe's personal investigator, was created.

Jake was a good twenty-five years younger—eye candy for the ladies—and possessed a more easy-going, cocky personality than McCabe. He would do a lot (if not most) of the leg work. They didn't have to go farther than look at the cast list of the episode of *Matlock* that Conrad had guest-starred on. As it turned out *Riptide* was cancelled and Joe Penny was available to play Jake. Director Michael Lange, who would helm 8 episodes of the series, knew Penny from *Riptide* and contends that he, "loved Joe. I thought he was an excellent actor. Joe was great to work with most of the time. But he was a bit temperamental and went to a dark place every once in a while. I think he was very fond of Bill but he got frustrated by the cue cards because Joe is more of a method actor, needing the feedback from the other actors in the scene. So there was a bit of stress sometimes, but overall they got along well." The actor did develop a good relationship with Conrad, later remarking, "Everybody had the impression he was a gruff guy, but in realty he was like your lovable granddad. He was like my granddad, that's the kind of relationship we had."

Added to the mix is a young Assistant District Attorney named Derek Mitchell played by thirty-year old blonde actor Alan Campbell (who also had a role on the *Matlock* two-parter). At the time, Campbell was best known as Jack Tripper's (John Ritter) nemesis on the *Three's Company* spin-off *Three's a Crowd*. Campbell describes the character of Mitchell as "the 'fatman's young and green assistant…This gave Bill a lot of teachable moments and put me in charge of a lot of the exposition and research." Campbell had, of course, met Conrad at the final audition for the *Matlock* episode, "He was relaxed, irreverent and always gracious in his trademark gruff way." Campbell was also a fan of the actor. "I loved *Cannon* and was a fan of *The Killers* and some of his early film noir work. I was also aware of his successful voice over career for Quinn Martin and in commercials."

When it came to working with Conrad, Campbell was exposed to his gruffer side. "He had his 'buttons— things that would set him off and he had little patience with the indulgent side of the business. Be it actors, directors or production staff. However, he used his gruff persona to keep us laughing on a lot of the very long days and nights shooting. He loved a bawdy joke!—bawdy is an understatement."

Of the relationship between Conrad and Joe Penny, Campbell recalls they had a good relationship but "were a bit competitive. Joe could also be unpredictable and more method, which Bill at times had little patience. Bill, however, respected Joe as an actor, a great deal. Because of Bill's physical limitations the show and story lines begin to shift more towards Joe's character. This, I think, was frustrating to Bill at times."

Campbell learned a good deal working so intimately with Conrad. "Once Bill said he was going to show me the use of star power," Campbell recalls. "He gruffly called for the line producer to come immediately to the set. When he nervously showed up he shook our hands and complimented Bill on the daily's, and left without ever asking Bill why he wanted to see him. Bill looked at me, smiled, and said, 'Sometimes you have to keep them a little nervous.'"

When they weren't working, Campbell didn't spend a lot of time with Conrad. "He and Tippy kept to themselves outside of work. Bill and I spent SO much time sitting next to each other and talking in the courtroom and his TV office that I think we covered almost everything. I felt especially honored to have his attention and experience and we talked and laughed and mused about a lot."

In an interview prior to the show's September, 1987 premiere, Conrad said that the bulldog Max "is the real scene stealer." He went on to say, "I did some research on this mutt. He's actually a vigorous, two-year old English bulldog, who's had a career as a poster dog in beer commercials. And here he is playing a dog who's kin of a down-and-outer. W.C. Fields was right. An actor has to beware of kids and dogs."

The network, which scheduled the show Tuesdays opposite the very popular ABC series *Moonlighting*, was under no illusions about its success—in some ways it was considered a filler and only 13 initial episodes were ordered. Conrad, too, was under no illusions. "It's a gamble. All new series are. I'll give it my all. If it works—fine. If it doesn't, I'll have more time for hunting, fishing and flying." Of his newest TV character, Conrad would say, "He's an old curmudgeon with a heart of gold. The audience can love him because he loves people, although he desperately pretends not to. I think he is the most successful and likable type of character anyone can play." The courtroom scenes near the end of the show are played by Conrad with a great deal of bravado and one gets the idea that he really was in his element and his performance is like a combination of Raymond Burr's *Perry Mason* and Orson Welles' Darrow-inspired character from the film *Compulsion* (1959).

While initially 13-episodes were ordered, the show did well enough to get a full 22-episode network order. Some of the things that Conrad insisted upon in his contract was working only 3-days (sometimes four) and leaving for the day at five o'clock sharp—even if they were in the middle of a scene. This meant that Penny, like Lee Horsley, a few years earlier in *Nero Wolfe*, worked both more days and hours. Director Michael Lange explained the shooting schedule:

"The shooting schedule was 7-days. The days were usually 12 hours long and yes, we tried to get Bill off the clock as soon as possible. His energy waned a bit in the afternoon, so we would try to consolidate his scenes into the morning's work. We were very considerate of his time, and he was, while generally cooperative and enthusiastic, insistent that we were considerate of his time. I remember one shot I did which was a bit complicated and after 8 takes, he told me that the next take was his last. If the shot didn't work on take 9 he was going home. Sure enough, he exited the shot and I saw him through the window, walking to his motor home and getting in even before I said 'Cut.' Then the next day, he called me into his trailer and with love/hate, told me that I was not considerate of him because I did an 'artsy-fartsy' shot and made him do 9 takes when he wasn't feeling well. He ended by saying he loved me,

though and that made it all better. Great guy."

Lange had been a long standing Conrad fan. "When I was a young boy, I sued to pretend to be asleep with my head under the covers and my transistor radio and I'd listen to episodes of *Gunsmoke*. Of course, I didn't know who anyone was back then, but when I got my first episode of "Jake" I was most thrilled to be working with Matt Dillon. I was also a fan of his television work prior to *Jake and the Fatman* and loved *Cannon* and *Nero Wolfe*, especially *Nero Wolfe*. I thought he brought a lot of panache to the character." As an actor, Lange says that Conrad's "amazing voice was a big plus." Lange adds that, "He also had a presence in his performance that was always compelling. He was very professional and courteous to his fellow actors…He could be very powerful and also very sensitive…Also, his eyes were very probing…he knew his strengths and used them to their fullest." Lange recalls his first meeting with Conrad on the set of *Jake and the Fatman*:

"Of course he was 'The Fatman' and, knowing my sense of humor; the producer suggested I not make any fat jokes around Mr. Conrad. A note—I'm also a large guy, though I looked small next to him. So, of course, the first time I met him, I fired off a couple. He did his patented killer stare and then broke into a huge smile and said, I think I'm going to like you, Mike.' It was love from that moment onward."

Writer Paul Robert Coyle (who had written some *Barnaby Jones* and *Chips* episodes in the 70's and *Crazy Like a Fox* during the 80's and would find cult status as a writer of several episodes of *Hercules: The Legendary Journeys* and *Xena: Warrior Princess* during the 90's) would write five episodes of *Jake and the Fatman* during its first season (*Love Me or Leave Me, Smoke Gets in Your Eyes, After You've Gone, It Had to be You, I Guess I'll Have to Change My Plan*) plus one episode during the third season (*I Only Have Eyes for You*) and two (one unproduced) during the fourth season (*More than You Know, School Days*), offers his recollections of his experiences on *Jake and the Fatman*:

"The type of stories they wanted was set by the pilot. Generally open sto-

ries (as opposed to closed whodunits), with strong guest star roles...I would pitch story ideas and Phil (Philip Salzmann (1929-2009), the shows supervising producer) would run by Dean (Hargrove) and CBS for a green light. I was a freelancer, not on the staff. In those days staffs were small.

Because Bill Conrad's deal called for him to work only three or four days (per episode), I was required to limit McCabe's scenes to a certain number of sets or locations. Courtroom, McCabe's office, one or two exteriors. They had Jake for all seven, so that character could be used more.

First, let me say, I was a Conrad fan largely because I had been a big fan of The Fugative, which he narrated. That's why I was drawn to Quinn Martin shows in the first place (Streets of San Francisco and Barnaby Jones were my first shows.) I admired his voice and his presence, so I was excited to write for him.

Bill Conrad worked exclusively off cue cards. Every line of McCabe's from the script was written on cardboard signs, and held off-camera for him to read. This often annoyed the other actors, because Conrad wasn't looking at them, he was looking past them, at the cards.

As a writer I was thrilled because he never changed a word. He didn't ad-lib, or forget, or consciously change a comma, because he was simply reading back what was written. Let me make a small amendment...if a director called for a wide shot outdoors, maybe involving McCabe and another character walking and talking, and the cards couldn't be brought close enough to read, then yes, under those circumstances and given advance notice, then Bill would memorize the lines. He was always professional and cooperative in that respect.

When it came time for his closeups, Conrad simply read his lines in succession off the cards. He didn't even want the other actor delivering his or her lines, off-camera. Nor did the director or script supervisor read them. Bill simply read his lines one after the next, and the film editor pieced everything together later.

If Bill ever objected to a script or situation or dialog, he certainly never said anything to me. I suppose he would have brought that up with Dean Hargrove in advance of shooting. I was present on set for most or all of my first season episodes, and chatted with Bill often, but I don't remember him ever complaining, or even commenting one way or another about the scripts. I don't think he saw that as his role. He was there to star in the show, not to produce it. He'd done that before.

Joe Penny, on the other hand, was probably more interested in the scripts and his dialog. But he always had more to do onscreen, thanks to Conrad's limited schedule.

In those days Conrad was visibly overweight. (Fitting enough for 'The Fatman.') He had health issues, some eyesight problems. When he came on set, he tended to stay there for hours between setups. Other actors might vanish to their trailers, but not Conrad. Frankly it was too much physical effort to make that walk back and forth. So he was often present, and accessible. Friendly and easy to talk to, but it was mostly 'small talk,' never serious discussions about his character or the scripts.

This was a first-season show, so it wasn't like the set of a long-running hit where the crew had been together for years. I remember more than one time when, during a scene, crew members across the stage would be whispering (not all that quietly,) and at those times Conrad would break the scene and yell loudly at the talkers. Then things quieted down, and things would proceed. His style wasn't subtle, but it got the job done.

My lasting recollection of Conrad? That voice. His presence. And those cue cards!"

The pilot for the series was titled **Happy Days are Here Again** and aired on 9/26/1987. It had a good story about the mistress of a senate candidate (Robert Reed) who is killed when she threatens to go public about their affair. His speechwriter (John Rubinstein) is the actual killer, and threatens his boss to cooperate or he will frame him for the murder. The guest star roster was good with recognizable names and faces—which was very much in line with the Quinn Martin formula on *Cannon* but wasn't always the case on *Jake and the Fatman*. The television critic for *TV Guide*, Jeff Jarvis, wasn't impressed. He gave the show a below average D+ grade and then wrote acidly, "One thing impresses me about William (Cannon) Conrad's performance: He does a great imitation of Jabba the Hutt. The man is a cone of blubber held prisoner by inertia. That's why they save the chase scenes for his investigator, Joe (Riptide) Penny."

Three days later in its regular time slot would come the actual series premiere titled **Fatal Attraction.** One of the gimmicks of the series was that most episodes were titled after a song title, usually a standard that gives an idea of what the plot of that episode is. Among the other top episodes of the first season of the show are **The Man That Got Away (10/13/1987)** featuring guest star Robert Culp as a revengeful lawyer who murders his ex-wife's lover; **Brother, Can You Spare a Dime? (11/3/1987)**, a story about a serial killer, and included a featured role by soap actor Mark Drexler, who recalled that "I worked with both William Conrad and Joe Penny. I don't believe William Conrad ever picked up a script before coming to work, everything was off cue cards, but he was very good at hiding that he was basically reading."

Smoke Gets in Your Eyes (12/1/1987) features Amy Steele as a woman blinded in a robbery who plans the murder of her husband is the favorite of the writer, Paul Robert Coyle. "I took the cliché of the poor innocent blind girl everyone feels sorry for, and turned it inside-out. That one turned out really well." Another strong episode written that season by Coyle is **It Had to be You (1/12/1988)**. Coyle later recalled this episode:

"One particularly interesting thing happened that I have Bill Conrad to thank for. For my fourth script, I had written my first courtroom finale, a lengthy scene. James Olson was playing a serial rapist, and McCabe had him on the stand. I was pretty proud of the scene, in which McCabe uses subtle psychological methods to unhinge the guy, and bring about an incriminating admission. A day or so before that scene was to be shot; I received a revision of the whole scene that Dean Hargrove had written. It was a total rewrite, not just of the dialog, but all the material and clues. It had to do with proving the guy had lost a contact lens or something at a crime scene...physical evidence that incriminated him. Nothing clever or subtle about it. Now I respect Dean Hargrove immensely, but frankly this was recycled stuff he'd already

used on Columbo and Matlock. Still, Jake was ultimately Dean's show, so he had that right. But then something funny happened. On the day of shooting, Bill Conrad and the director, Ron Satlof, decided they preferred the original version of the scene to Dean's. So they overruled the Executive Producer, and went with my pages instead! Nothing was said to me, and I wasn't there that day. But I think the scene played beautifully, and Conrad and Olson were excellent in it. So I'm grateful to Mr. Conrad for sticking up for a freelance writer."

But Not for Me (1/19/1988) directed by Michael Lange is another top-notch episode of the freshman season. It tells the story of a mobster who is murdered at the home of a star reporter, played by beautiful Barbara Parkins. Lange recalls the professionalism of William Conrad in the courtroom sequence:

"My second episode involves a young girl on the witness stand who was questioned by McCabe. Bill had trouble memorizing lines, so he used cue cards. That's a whole other story but let me say that he was amazing at the cards. He didn't have the off camera actor there because the eye line wouldn't be as good. The funny part was the other actor's lines were on the cards, but in tiny print. Just the cue line was in big print. Anyway, he wasn't feeling too well that day, so he went home when we shot the young girl's testimony. The next day, after he viewed the dailies, he came to me and asked if he could redo his close up. He had been so moved by the girl's performance that he felt his needed to be adjusted. It wasn't out of ego, I don't think he had a big ego even though he certainly could have gotten away with it, it was out of professionalism and concern for his fellow actors. Also, it was amazing that he watched the dailies. That was his level of professionalism and dedication to the art. Obviously, thirty years later, this impression still sticks with me."

Perhaps the best episode of the first season and one of the most memorable for writer Coyle and director Lange is **I Guess I'll Have to Change My Plans (3/30/1988)**, which featured guest star Anthony Franciosa as an ex-cop turned author who resorts to murder to get that elusive best seller. "Once when Tony Franciosa was guest starring in one of my shows he was having trouble remembering his lines," Coyle recalls. "He saw that Bill used cue cards, so he requested them too. With two card holders per actor (for different eye lines), the set was filled with sign holders those days. There was even a card inside a refrigerator when Tony opened it to get some food in the scene."

Michael Lange continues, "We had Anthony Franciosa in an episode I directed. I had heard that he was a bit of a nightmare on the set sometimes, so I took him to lunch in the commissary one day during prep. I asked him outright and he confessed that he had trouble learning his lines and got stressed out and that's what caused his outbursts. I told him no problem. We had the best cue card guys in the business and they'd be happy to have his lines on cue cards. He was thrilled and, by the way, was a joy to work with. The funny part was that since he wasn't as adept as Mr. Conrad with the cards, he still needed the off camera actor there to deliver the lines. So poor Joe Penny, who was in the scene with Tony and Bill had to stand behind the cue cards while Tony did his close up. The cue card guys reused the cards and on the back, the side Joe had to look at, was a routine from the latest George Burns comedy special. Joe took it in stride."

Coyle recalls that he wrote a nice bit of action for Conrad during this episode—different from what was usually expected of him during "The Fatman" years:

"There was much more physical action required from Conrad on that one (Cannon),—running, fighting, ext. There was a stunt double, of course, but I think Conrad at that time enjoyed doing much of it himself. By the time Jake started in 1987, it was over 10 years past Cannon, so he obviously wasn't up for that kind of thing anymore. I did have McCabe shoot the bad guy once, though. Because it was unexpected. His character was supposed to be an ex-cop, so it figured he'd know how to handle a gun. He didn't carry one, but I had him borrow one from a uniformed cop. He shot Tony Franciosa and saved Jake. I think Bill appreciated that small gesture of still being an action hero."

The first season of *Jake and the Fatman* ranked an unimpressive #59 in the ratings, However, It did well enough in its time slot to just miss cancellation.

One element that had CBS's censors up in arms in the first season was profanity that Conrad used as "The Fatman." Naturally you don't hear it as it's bleeped out but still the networks department of Standards and Practices in New York had concerns. Conrad thought the whole thing rather silly. "It's a shame we cannot use words that are used every day by virtually everybody. If you protect the audience by bleeping them, they can imagine what I said. Unfortunately, there are a few people who lip read."

Change was in store for *Fatman* fans in the second season. *Magnum P.I.* had ended its run on CBS at the end of the previous year. Between *Hawaii Five-O* in the 70's and *Magnum* in the 80's CBS had found ratings gold having a crime series located on the 'ceded lands.' Somebody had the bright idea that bringing *Jake and the Fatman* to Hawaii would help its ratings—besides the series had indicated in its first season that McCabe is a native Hawaiian—so rather than let its CBS Studios facilities gather dust— it made a certain amount of sense to move McCabe back.

"I can't tell you the reason behind the move except that Fred Silverman, whose idea it was, knows that I love Hawaii with a passion," Conrad told the press around the time the second season premiered. "I always have. I'm so much in love with Hawaii that it's ridiculous." So Conrad was happy and that was a good thing—not that he really got into his own series. "I never watch it. I can't stand to watch myself. I swear to God it's the truth. I don't like looking at what I do."

Joe Penny stated publicly that he would like to see, "more character development and interplay between Jake and Fatman. People want to see characters react to one another. Successful shows like *Mary Tyler Moore* and *Hill Street Blues* are based on characters. I mean, how many cocaine smugglers and bank robbers can you chase? Success is based on good writing—always." Penny went on to tell columnist Marilyn Beck, "I want the show to get a little more realistic and I'd like the love scenes to be a little hotter. I'm not saying anything out of school, because the producers all agree."

Alan Campbell recalls that, "CBS had always been successful with shows originating from Hawaii. With the cancelation of *Magnum*, the Diamond Head studios opened up and CBS thought it would help the ratings and bring another dimension to the show. Bill was also a huge fan of the islands and had many friends there. He lived like a king in the penthouse of an exclusive hotel in Waikiki. He Ate in his favorite restaurants. Shooting was also more centralized than it was in LA and locations were closer to the studios." As for Campbell, he was "thrilled" about the move to Hawaii. "I had never been there and thought it was a real adventure. It was also nice to be the only game (TV show) in town. We were very appreciated due to the attention and revenue we brought to the islands. I did feel that I was missing out a bit on being a part of my industry back in LA, but the good always outweighs the downside in my mind."

The season began late and included only ten episodes. This was due to two industry strikes: A Writers Strike and then a Teamsters Strike. The first episode of the season introduced the move to Hawaii—**Wish You Were Here (3/15/1989)**, The two-hour season premiere takes Jake to Hawaii to visit a friend, and winds up being accused of the friend's murder. He calls on Hawaii native McCabe's help. Naturally now that they are in Hawaii—they might as well stay. Possibly the best episode of the season was titled **They Can't Take That Away From Me (5/10/1989)**, the episode was written by Catherine Bacos Clinch with a story about Two colleagues who help Jake with a drug bust and are later found dead—Jake needs to find the killers before he is the next victim. Other stand outs include **Bewitched, Bothered and Bewildered** in which McCabe and Jake track down those who robbed a shipping company and **It Ain't Necessarily So**, which involves murder inside a the headquarters of a *Playboy* type magazine.

The move to Hawaii seemed to do the trick. *Fatman*, while not a powerhouse in the ratings, improved all the way up to #33 (from #59 in its first season) with a 15.2 rating and tied with the CBS sitcom *Designing Women*.

Season three finds a thinner William Conrad. "I was down to 242 from 290 pounds, Conrad told reporters. "This year I was way down to 235. But after I worked a couple of weeks, I was really tired. And I needed to eat, so I know I've put back couple of pounds. But I want to get down to 220." But Island living hadn't made the weight loss easy for Conrad. "I do love that island food. But the killer is the mal tais and the chi chis—Gosh! I can drink those all day long." It was also Conrad's goal to do more than he had in the previous two seasons on the show during season three, "I simply didn't have enough to do. I'd show up at the end of the show and say something like, 'Well, is everything OK, Jake?' Now I look forward to going to work, not only because I have more to do, but because the scripts have been absolutely great. We're rolling." Joe Penny backed up this sentiment. "We're trying to put together another group of guys who are really hungry and want to work their hinnies off," Penny told columnist Marilyn Beck. "I want the show to get a little more realistic and I'd like the love scenes to be a little hotter. I'm not saying anything out of school because the producers all agree," with his assessment that the previous season's shows had been 'too cops and robbers' and formulistic.

Among the stand-out episodes of the third season are **I Only Have Eyes for You (9/20/1989)**, written by Paul Robert Coyle with a story of a convict is released from prison he starts seeking revenge against the woman who helped lock him up and she seeks help from McCabe, who prosecuted him. **Who's Sorry Now? (1/31/1990)** was written by J. Michael Straczynski, and tells the story of McCabe being abducted by the brother of a cop killer that he had convicted years earlier and who now is about to be executed for his crime. Staczynski wasn't particularly a fan of the show when he was invited to pitch some story ideas. "I pitched, like, 5 stories—none of them really worked. I thought, 'Oh good, I'm getting to get of here with my skin intact.' I mentioned one last thing, just in passing…I said, 'William Conrad is a big guy, and big guys don't like to walk around a lot. What if we did an episode where he is taken hostage and tied to a chair for the whole episode?' They said, 'Great idea! He doesn't like to walk around much.' I'm thinking 'I'm going to hell for this.'" So instead of talking himself out of a job he was hired and ended up writing four episodes.

In the ratings for Season Three, "The Fatman" fell seven places, from #33 to # 40 (tied with the ABC sitcom *Family Matters*) but still performing well enough in its timeslot to warrant a fourth season.

After directing four episodes of *Jake and the Fatman* during season one, Michael Lange returned for one during season three and did his final three directing jobs during season four. His warm feelings for Conrad continued, though at times Lange could have his hands full. "He was tricky to direct because by this time he was pretty tired of the whole thing. He didn't like doing extra takes so I had to blame other elements if I wanted another one. Sometimes I'd hold something in my hand and drop it during the take so I could say there was a noise and the take was no good. Also because of his memory issue he didn't like a lot of movement in scenes. He'd do it if you really asked, okay begged. He rarely had concerns but when he did he'd voice them." The other actors, on the whole, accepted Conrad's continued use of cue cards, "the only rough part for the other actors was the master shot of the scene with Bill looking at the cards, not at them. I never had a problem though." Lange summed up his feelings regarding Conrad this way:

"Bill was an Amazing, talented man. He knew every aspect of the business because he had done it all. I learned a lot from Bill, and since it was very early in my career, use the skills I learned working with Mr. Conrad to this day."

In other changes, Season four found the show returning to Los Angeles, after two seasons in Hawaii. The stated reason being to cut costs—especially for a show that had performed solidly in its timeslot but wasn't exactly a ratings powerhouse. According to a story in the *Los Angeles Times*, Conrad favored leaving the series in Hawaii—while Penny favored the return to LA. Michael Lange seems to give support to this theory, "I believe the main reason the show moved back from Hawaii to Los Angeles was that Joe Penny was very unhappy there after a few years." Alan Campbell recalls that the move back to L.A. "may have been about money and also I think Joe influenced this a bit. It was extremely expensive to film in Hawaii and at some point I think they just decided to make the change."

That Conrad wasn't happy about the series move is evident in an interview the actor did with *TV Guide* (October 20, 1990 issue). Conrad took on producer Dean Hargrove. "He loves shows that I don't," Conrad candidly said. "I look for human emotions, human involvement. I don't like car chases. I don't like gunfights. I don't like fights that are unnecessary." Conrad predicted that Hargrove's decision to move the show from Hawaii to Los Angeles would result in more violent shows. "I would have quit a year and a half ago if I'd had the chance, but if you sign on for five years, you go on in production for five years." In the end the move could have been from a combination of things—an unhappy leading actor (Joe Penny) and a studio that decided that costs were too high for a show which had a mediocre rating. In any event Conrad was not pleased.

It was during season four that Fred Silverman used *Jake and the Fatman* to spin off a new series starring Dick Van Dyke. **It Never Entered My Mind (3/20/1991)** introduces McCabe's doctor, Mark Sloan (Van Dyke), who finds himself accused of the murder of the hospital's by the books administrator, so Sloan joins forces with McCabe to clear himself. This episode didn't lead right away to a series, instead there were three TV movies which featured Sloan as the crime solving doctor and then the series *Diagnosis: Murder* premiered which ran from 1993-2001 and produced 178 episodes (20 more than Van Dyke's classic 1960's sitcom!).

In terms of ratings, "Fatman" ranked #44 overall during its fourth season (falling four notches from the previous season) but beating its time slot opposition on NBC, *Seinfeld*, which that year ranked # 45. As usual Jerry Seinfeld found humor in having *Jake and the Fatman* opposite his show. He joked that more people were watching "The Fatman" in hopes of seeing him run.

In its fifth season the show ranked #50 overall, just ahead of *Beverly Hills 90210* on Fox, and even out-performing the Silverman-Hargrove *Matlock* (which was an older show, then in its ninth season) which ranked #56. But CBS decided it was time to pull the plug on the Fatman. In retrospect, Conrad's health might have been an issue as well. "His health made him impatient and he would get angry with some of his limitations, especially toward the end of the run," Alan Campbell recalls. "He was, however, always supportive and gracious and appreciative to our (TV) family and we in turn protected him whenever we could. It was always fragile in retrospect. He was hypoglycemic and depending on what he ate his energy could fluctuate. He was also his own worst enemy as he would sneak snacks which would cause him to get very tired. I also think his girth and diabetes limited his movement as he told me he had little feeling in his feet that made walking difficult at times."

Joe Penny recalled that he would occasionally suggest that Conrad needed to lose weight. "Does a guy like me need a 32-inch waist? No! Look at this face! I feel sorry for a poor bastard like you," he told Penny. "You're six foot tall. You got size 44 shoulders. Great-lookin'. You can't afford to have a cookie."

He was by this time (and for some time before this) unable to stay on the set and do lines off camera. "I would often, on occasion, stay to do Bill's off camera lines with guest stars," Campbell recalled. "Not great for the other actors because they had to play off my voice and readings but everyone knew his energies were limited. He used to joke he did not stand up on Fridays! It was a running joke." Among the best episodes of the season are **I Could Write a Book** (11/13/1991), in which yet another friend of McCabe's is found dead in what appears to be a suicide, but McCabe is sure it's murder (during the course of the series several friends of McCabe's seem to have been murdered!). The friend was an author who apparently hadn't written anything new in ten years but has been working on a new book that McCabe is sure led to his murder. Another good episode is **Just Me and You Kid** (1/22/1992) which features Christopher Templeton as a wheelchair bound shopkeeper who heads a battle against a local gang after she refuses to comply with the gang's order to closer her store.

How did the cast find out about the cancelation? One member, Alan Campbell, recalls, "I read it in the trades. That's Hollywood, sadly."

Overall *Jake and the Fatman* was a solid detective/legal series which never scaled the heights in the ratings, but had a loyal (and older) audience demographic. The chemistry between the actors is good and given the state of his health it was probably the best type of vehicle that Conrad could have at this point in his career (aside of the return of radio drama). When the show ended its run on September 12, 1992, William Conrad had only about a year and a half to live.

III

Conrad lived about a year-and-a-half following the cancellation of *Jake and the Fatman*. He did little professionally during that period of time. He would occasionally lend his authoritative voice to a television commercial, but not much else. His health was a constant concern. His doctors were always on him to lose weight. "He was perpetually on a diet—he had diabetes and problems with his feet," Christopher Conrad would recall. Christopher, understanding that his father was in ill health, decided he would reach out to his dad and talk to him about some deeply felt issues—something he hadn't done with his mom before she passed away. About six months before Bill's death he and Christopher met and "we talked about everything—and some very personal stuff." Christopher sensed that Bill thought that he was embarrassed by him. "I was against being identified as Bill Conrad's kid," Christopher later recalled. Christopher assured Bill he wasn't embarrassed by him—"I wanted to be known as me—not as your kid."

In his attempt to be his own person, Christopher knew from a very early age that he didn't want to live in Southern California. He eventually moved to the Seattle, Washington area to live and pursue his career. He, like Bill, had a great interest in photography and Christopher opened a studio. It was while living in Washington that he met the woman who would ultimately become his wife, Janet. "I was in school studying photography and was in my last couple of months," Janet Conrad later recalled. "Christopher called the school's placement office for someone to fill the studio manager position and I along with two other students were recommended to him. For someone just getting out of school it was an amazing opportunity. Christopher was very well known in the photography community and it was exciting to be able to potentially work for him."

Janet recalls that she and Christopher hit it off right away and he hired her on the spot. They would remain friends, not romantic partners, for several years. In fact, they wouldn't "get together" as a couple and ultimately marry until after Bill's death. But she did get a chance to meet Bill when he visited Christopher and came to his photography studio. "He was gracious, kind, easy to talk to," Janet recalls. She also got a first-hand opportunity to witness Bill's sometimes obstinate nature. "We were photographing a product of which I forget what," Janet recalled. "Christopher was being meticulous in getting it right the first time, was taking his time getting it just right. Bill (was) getting a bit impatient, loudly said, 'Will you shoot the ******* thing already?!' Wow, to the CORE it was felt."

Janet really didn't get to know Bill well despite his coming to the studio two or three times. She did accompany Christopher a few months before Conrad's passing when he went to visit his dad and buy one of his cars. They stayed at Bill's house. "Again, I was just accompanying Christopher as a friend. Still I remember he (Bill) was always kind, gracious, friendly...Sadly I never had an opportunity to develop a relationship."

While he was in declining health, Conrad wasn't (unlike Susan) in and out of hospitals and didn't require around the clock nursing. According to Christopher Conrad in his last months he did make compensations for his ever worsening feet problems (brought on by diabetes) by moving his bedroom to the maid's quarters downstairs so he wouldn't have to climb up and down stairs. He also had kidney problems in which Conrad did self-dialysis at home. At one point Conrad fell and Tippy was unable to help him back up and had to get help. He was also depressed during his last months and told his son that he felt that his life had been a failure.

Conrad's friend and cast mate Alan Campbell kept in touch with Bill for a time after *Jake and the Fatman* was cancelled. He recalls that Tippy came to see him at the Shubert on Sunset Blvd, in Los Angeles. "Bill loved singing and always loved the fact that I had started my career as a musician," Campbell recalled. "Sadly, Tippy said he wasn't well enough to attend. He died just a few months later."

Herb Ellis, his old radio pal since the 1940's, recalled that the last time he saw Conrad was a few months prior to his passing. "We stayed up and talked until 3 in the morning," Ellis recalled. "We talked about all kinds of things—about our dreams, desires and regrets— Bill despite his bluster was a decent, loving, funny irascible man and one of the best friends anybody could ever have."

Another old friend, Jimmy Lydon, called over to Bill's house to see if he could stop in for a visit. "Tippy told me, 'Please don't come over—you wouldn't like what you see.' Meaning that Bill had really gone to pieces and he wouldn't want me to see him that way. About a week later he died."

The last time that Christopher saw his father was during New Year's holiday of 1993-1994. "We hung out and watched movies— and we would watch movies and to his way of thinking a movie wasn't about art—what mattered he said was, 'at the end of the day did it make money!'" During this period Christopher took his final photograph of his dad. It was taken on the back patio and it is one of Christopher's favorite photos as it shows a clear (blue) eyed and more slender Bill Conrad (who lost about 70 pounds) but not looking in any way gaunt.

On February 11, 1994, Conrad woke up in great spirits and had a lot of energy and was feeling great when out of the blue he was felled by cardiac arrest. He was rushed to the Medical Center of North Hollywood where he was pronounced dead.

Dean Hargrove, the executive producer of *Jake and the Fatman*, recalled Conrad as a man who, "loved music, he loved travel, he loved food. He had many appetites." His widow, Tippy, would say, "you get a guy like Bill, he simply wasn't concerned about whether he was successful or not. He just had a strong notion about what he wanted, and he went ahead and did it." Joe Penny, Jake to his fatman, recalled Bill as "a very good friend and (I) was very honored to work with him for the years that we had together. I will miss him very much."

A private memorial service was held, and more than one old friend would comment that they didn't feel it captured the spirit of Bill Conrad. "I went to his funeral—it was not what I expected," Herb Ellis later recalled. "It just didn't seem like the right kind of send-off for a guy like Bill. It didn't have a good feel to it. It was too sad—too depressing. To me, Bill's funeral should have been more like an Irish wake—had more fun and humor to it—more like the man." It was a sentiment echoed by Jimmy Lydon.

Christopher Conrad concurs that he thought the funeral was "too sad—morose." But on this he doesn't find fault with Tippy. "I'm not sure she had anybody there to advise her—and she was grieving... I'm sure that if dad had made the arrangements or one of his friends had—it would have been much different."

Not long before Bill died he told Christopher that he was not going to leave him anything—Tippy was going to get it all. He explained to his son that "you'll be a happier man if you make it on your own." At first Christopher was hurt, but as time went by he now agrees that his father was right and holds no grudges. It should be noted that Tippy did allow Christopher to have a number of personal items after his dad died such as his hair brush, robe and walking sticks. "She did, however, request I return a shotgun and two fishing rods he had given me—which I did." There was a strain in the relationship when a few months later Christopher asked

Tippy for several of his dad's pipes—which she refused to do. Later on, he found out that the Maltese Falcon statue which Jack Warner had given Conrad at Warner Brothers in the 60's and which had been promised to Christopher was being sold by Tippy. "When she heard my response to that—which was only my surprise and incredulity when told that she 'needed' to sell it for money—I was told I was never welcome in 'her' home…we spoke a few times after that, but never met again. While my father had told me I could have the falcon, there was no will and I had no desire to fight Tippy for it. For me it wasn't about money, what was important were memories… Ultimately it is all just stuff and I wasn't willing to sour memories."

Bill Conrad lived his life on his own terms. He wasn't a classic leading man, but he achieved a stardom that few professional radio people ever did. He wasn't classically handsome and yet he fascinated women. That great voice of his mesmerized many and he had a charisma that attracted people like honey attracts bees. His son Christopher recalls that he once said, "If I died tomorrow I've done everything I've ever wanted to do—I am happy—I am satisfied." What more could anybody want?

EPILOGUE

When William Conrad died in 1994 most people recalled him best for his television work—two successful detective series: *Cannon* during the 1970's and *Jake and the Fat Man* during the late 80's and early 90's. Unless you were an old time radio aficionado few people realized that Bill Conrad was also one of the great voices of the golden years of radio drama on shows like *The Whistler, Suspense, Escape!*, and most memorably as the voice of Marshal Matt Dillon on the acclaimed radio version of Gunsmoke (1952-1961). Conrad would later estimate that he appeared on some 7500 radio shows during his career.

Conrad once related why he was he was such a successful radio/voice actor. "There was always a danger thing in my voice," Conrad said. "Now, I don't know how that got there, but I covered everything with a black drape. I never took a drama lesson in my life. I never even thought about what it is to be an actor." He would go on to add in his typical sardonic and profane way, "All I thought about was the money that it was possible to make, maybe. And it turned out to be possible. I was just fucking lucky to have a voice that fascinated people."

In 1997 the medium of radio finally got around to honoring Bill Conrad for his contributions. He was inducted, posthumously, into the Radio Hall of Fame. The proceedings were hosted by Kasey Kasem who introduced actress June Lockhart—who really had nothing to do with William Conrad or his career—the question is why they didn't get an old friend like Parley Baer (who would play Chester to his Matt on *Gunsmoke*) or Jimmy Lydon (who was his partner in producing low budget films at Warner Brothers in the

1960's and remained a close and valued friend since). But Miss Lockhart was up to the challenge and proceeded with the induction:

"How many of you remember the time when you could turn on your radio at night and hear drama? If you can recall that age, then certainly you remember the voice of William Conrad and his marvelous characterization of Marshal Matt Dillon on radio's "Gunsmoke." It was the last of the great network radio dramas. And "Gunsmoke", and William Conrad, and CBS, the network that carried the show for nine years, closed out, in a very graceful way, radio's 'golden age.'

When Gunsmoke went on the air in 1952, the number of prime-time radio listeners was still greater than the number of prime-time television viewers. When "Gunsmoke" went off the air in 1961, a new day had long since dawned—and there would be no turning back the clock. On radio, "Gunsmoke would have no sequel.

Because 'Gunsmoke' ran as long as it did, and because it came at the end of an era, William Conrad will be remembered best for his portrayal of Matt Dillon. But from the end of World War II until the end of radio drama, William Conrad took on countless other roles in some of radio's most memorable dramatic programs...William Conrad was a big man with a big voice, and a dramatic talent that was bigger still—and so big that radio alone couldn't contain it...William Conrad was seventy-three when he died of a heart attack. Fortunately, hundreds of his performances have been preserved—and they remain a monument to what radio drama was at its best. Listen..."

At this point the audience was treated to a montage of the best of William Conrad on radio and when the montage ended Miss Lockhart introduced Conrad's third wife and widow, Tippy, who accepted the award on behalf of her late husband. As Tippy walked up to accept the award the music playing was "Memories of You"— "Waking skies at sunrise, every sunset too/Seems to be bring me memories of you."

SELECTED RADIO CREDITS OF WILLIAM CONRAD

Adventures of Sam Spade

The Adventures of Sam Spade is best known for its 1946-1950 radio run (on ABC, CBS & NBC) starring movie tough guy Howard Duff (1946-50) and later Steve Dunne (1950-51) as Dashiell Hammett's Los Angeles private eye Sam Spade and Lurene Tuttle (one of OTR's all-time great actresses) as his efficient and loyal secretary Effie. In addition to Conrad such top-notch radio actors as Alan Reed, Cathy Lewis, Jerry Hausner, and Paul Frees also worked on this show.
6/27/48—"The Bail-Bond Caper" (radio & television actress Sandra Gould (*Bewitched* 1966-1972) voices Effie in this episode when Lurene Tuttle took ill).

7/18/48—"The Missing Newshawk Caper"
5/18/50—"The Red Amapola Caper"
5/23/50—"The Honest Thief Caper"
11/24/50—"The Terrified Turkey Caper"
12/15/50—"The 25-1235679 Caper"
12/29/50—"The Prodigal Panda Caper"
1/5/51—"The Biddle Riddle Caper"
1/26/51—"The Chateau McLeod Caper"
2/2/51—"The String of Death Caper" (John Michael Hayes, who wrote four Alfred Hitchcock films, *Rear Window, To Catch a Thief, The Trouble with Harry, The Man Who Knew Too Much*, wrote this & other episodes of the series)
4/6/51—"The Denny Shane Caper"

Crime Classics

Crime Classics was created and directed by Elliott Lewis and profiled true-life crimes from the past—often including stories about true life historical figures. The show ran on CBS for just over a year (1953-1954) and Conrad was a frequent performer along with Jay Novello, Mary Jane Croft, Harry Bartell, Hans Conried, Jack Kruschen, Irene Tedrow, Joseph Kearns, Sam Edwards and Betty Lou Gerson. Bernard Herrmann did the musical score for all but one episode. The show was hosted by Lou Merrill, "a connoisseur of crime, student of violence, and teller of murders." Merrill's introductions were often in the tongue-in-cheek manner that would later characterize Alfred Hitchcock's intros and closing to his long-running suspense anthology series *Alfred Hitchcock Presents.*

8/31/53—"Your Loving Son, Nero"—Bill Conrad plays Nero with Betty Lou Gerson as Agrippina.
10/14/53—"The Seven Layered Cake of Madame LaFarge"
10/21/53—"Billy Bonney, Bloodletter: Also Known as 'The Kid'"—Conrad plays Sheriff Pat Garrett with Sam Edwards as Billy the Kid.
11/11/53—"Blackbeard's Fourteenth: Why She Was No Good For Him"—Conrad plays the notorious pirate Blackbeard.
11/18/53—"The Triangle of the Round Table"—Conrad plays King Arthur.
12/9/53—"The Assassination of Abraham Lincoln"—Conrad portrays Gen. U.S. Grant.
1/27/54—"The Bourne Brothers and The Hangman—A Study in Nip and Tuck"
4/21/54—"Caesare Borgia—His Most Difficult Murder"—Conrad has the title role.
4/28/54—"Widow Magee and The Three Gypsies"

Escape

Escape was one of the leading radio anthology series and ran from 1947-1954 on CBS. It had a well-known opening that was often introduced by Paul Frees and William Conrad, "Tired of the everyday grind? Ever dream of a life of romantic adventure? Want to get away from it all? We offer you…ESCAPE!" The show often dealt with suspense tales, science fiction and ghost stories and many of the episodes were adapted from novels and short stories. For instance, *Escape* did the first adaptation of Daphne du Maurier's *The Birds* years before the Alfred Hitchcock film. Many fine radio actors (in addition to Conrad) appeared on the show including Parley Baer, harry Bartell, John Dehner, Jeanette Nolan, Jack Webb, Peggy Webber, Vic Perrin, Sandra Gould, Alan reed and Marvin Miller.

"Pollack and The Porrah Man" (10/28/47) A story about a man haunted by the severed head of a jungle savage. The snakes don't help much! H. G. Wells (author), Barton Yarborough, William Conrad, Luis Van Rooten, John Dunkel adapted the story.

"Chilling Primrose" (11/5/47) based on the short story by John Collier with Conrad as a man who resides in a department store. He sleeps by day and attempts to keep out of the sight of the night watchman after hours. He makes a startling discovery, however, that the store mannequins come to life at night when seemingly nobody is watching. (This was also made into a *Twilight Zone* episode in 1960).

"The Young Man with the Cream Tarts" (11/12/47) based on a famous trilogy of stories written by Robert Louis Stevenson titled *The Suicide Club*. Paul Frees and William Johnstone star with Conrad cast as the president of the Suicide Club.

"Casting the Runes" (11/19/47) based on a short story by Montague R. James. John Dunning (John McIntire) a scientist believes he is under a curse that will kill him within three months. It seems this curse may have been cast after he gave a negative review to a manuscript written by a man named Karswell (Conrad).

"The Country of the Blind" (11/26/47) A mountain guide finds a hidden valley where no-one has eyes. However, the blind think that he is deformed.

"An Occurrence at Owl Creek Bridge" (12/10/47) An adaptation of the Ambrose Bierce short story classic of the Civil War. William Johnstone also appears.

"Wild Oranges" (12/17/47) A man and woman are trapped on an island by a murderer. Paul Frees and Jeanette Nolan star. Conrad plays the part of Halverd, the heroes best friend and first mate on his boat. Jack Kruschen also appears.

"Confession" (12/31/47) A soldier suffering post-traumatic stress walks the streets of London—finding all along the way murder. Peggy Webber also appears. (A great performance by Conrad as the shell shocked veteran).

"The Second Class Passenger" (1/7/48) A man on a cruise stops for a day in Mozambique. He goes to town with a fellow passenger. His fellow passenger leaves a souvenir behind in a restaurant and the man goes back to retrieve it—and finds himself in one adventure after another. Harry Bartell stars with Conrad cast as "The Fat Thug."

"Leinengen vs. the Ants" (1/17/48) A classic from *Escape*—about a man who battles killer insects while trying to save his marriage.

"Snake Doctor" (2/14/48) Cast also features Paul Frees—and direction by Norman McDonnell.

"Ancient Sorceries" (2/21/48) A story involving witchcraft in a small Welsh village. Paul Frees stars with William Conrad as the doctor.

"The Grove of Ashtaroff" (2/29/48) Supernatural goings-on connected to the temple of a goddess fond in an African jungle.

"Misfortune's Isle" (3/21/48) The cast includes Paul Frees and Virginia Gregg, with a script by Les Crutchfield, who later wrote several episodes of *Gunsmoke*.

"The Man Who Would be King" (8/1/48) Excellent adaptation of the Kipling story—Conrad is the announcer and the stars are Peggy Webber, John Dehner, Ben Wright and Jack Kruschen.

"S.S. San Pedro" (8/22/48) Conrad functions as the show's announcer rather than an actor.

"The Diamonds are as Big as the Ritz" (8/29/49) Conrad functions as the show's announcer rather than an actor.

"Evening Primrose" (9/12/48) Interesting story of a group of people who live in various New York department stores. The cast includes Jeff Corey and Irene Tedrow.

"He Who Rides the Tiger" (3/12/49) A man (Conrad) can't remember anything about his life during the last years of the Chinese-Japanese war.

"The General Died at Dawn" (4/16/49) Based on the famous 1936 film with Gary Cooper and also featuring Lawrence Dobkin, Jack Kruschen and John Dehner. Conrad plays O'Hara, the mercenary that Gary Cooper played in the film.

"The Sure Thing" (10/15/49) A triple murder occurs during a cruise thru the Bahamas. John Hoyt stars with Conrad cast as Felix.

"Night in Havana" (10/22/49) Lots of action in this story of gun-runners in Cuba. The cast includes Jack Webb, Alan Reed and Jeff Corey.

Maracas" (11/22/49) Three bandits try and get away with stolen guns. Conrad stars as Doyle.

"Border Town" (12/13/49) Evan (Jack Webb) is an aspiring actor on a bus making its way to Hollywood. The bus stops off in Texas, where the man sitting next to him is arrested for counterfeiting. Afterward Evan decides to stay the night in El Paso, where he finds that the counterfeiter has stashed money into his coat pocket. Conrad appears as Jake. The cast also includes such radio stalwarts as Bea Benaderet, Harry Bartell, Paul Frees and Jeanette Nolan.

"Seeds of Greed" (12/27/49) Two men are on a boat in the South

Pacific greedily in search of a treasure in pearls and letting their greed get the best of them. Gary Merrill also appears.

"Two If By Sea" (2/14/50) A journalist tries to save his Russian wife who is being held captive in Moscow.

"Port Royal" (3/10/50) A shop recovers over a $1 million while the crew comes down with incurable greed. Conrad's *The Killers* sidekick Charles McGraw also appears.

"Green Splotches" (3/31/50) Alien plants which arrived on a space saucer captures a scientific expedition in South America!

"The Ambassador of Poker" (4/7/50) A southern card shark does battle with a band of Chinese war lords. John Dehner and Elliott Reid also appear.

"The Shanghai Document" (4/21/50) Story set in aboard a river streamer in China and stars John Dehner as an American reporter. Conrad appears as Rattigan.

"Something for Nothing" (4/28/50) An ex-movie actor witnesses a murder and decides to try his hand at extortion. Cast also includes Will (Grandpa Walton) Geer.

"A Shipment of Mute Fate" (7/7/50) A deadly snake is loose aboard an Ocean liner.

"Shark Bait" (7/14/50) A story of gun-runners during a Central American revolution. Will Geer, Mary Shipp, Paul Frees and John Dehner are also in the cast.

"Yellow Wake" (7/21/50) Conrad stars as Jonas Love in a story of hidden treasure in the Panama jungle also featuring John Dehner, Stacy Harris and Will Geer.

"Poison" (7/28/50) Classic story of a man (Conrad) trapped in a bed with a deadly snake quietly sleeping next to him. Jack Webb also appears.

"Two Came Back" (8/4/50) A love triangle set in a New Guinea jungle with head hunter savages to boot. Conrad serves basically as the announcer.

"The Red Forest" (8/11/50) A group of people are trapped during a forest fire. The cast includes Georgia Ellis, who went on to play Kitty on *Gunsmoke* with a script by her husband, writer Antony Ellis.

"The Footprint" (8/18/50) rubies and adventure set in the desert.

"Crossing Paris" (8/25/50) A story of the black market set during German occupied Paris during World War II. The cast also includes Howard McNear, who would go on to play Doc on radio's *Gunsmoke*.

"This Side of Nowhere" (12/3/50) A couple crash their plane which has over $250,000 in a Mexican village in the middle of nowhere. Virginia Gregg also appears.

"Conquest" (1/7/51) Well...The first man who is said to conquer Mt. Everest finds a man's cigarette lighter on the top of the mountain!

"The Follower" (2/18/51) A man (Conrad) tries to find his missing wife in Mexico. Virginia Gregg and Georgia Ellis also appear.

"The Island" (7/11/51) Two Marines on Okinawa are split up by a beautiful woman. Harry Bartell also appears.

"The Gladiator" (8/1/51) A boxing champ things he's retired until his promoter pits him against the biggest, strongest man he's ever seen before.

"Gringo" (10/12/52) A story of lost treasure and romance set in South America. Conrad stars as Jim Canovan and also features Parley Baer, who, by this time, was Chester to Conrad's Matt on *Gunsmoke*.

"Robert of Huntingdon" (10/26/52) Another take on the Robin Hood legend with a cast featuring Herb Ellis and Harry Bartell. Conrad plays Robin Hood.

"The Running Man" (11/2/52) Conrad handles the announcing chores on this episode.

"The Return" (11/9/52) An explorer in Northern Africa seeks the 'perfect place' to settle down. Kathleen Hite who would later write several episodes of *Gunsmoke* wrote this script.

"The Loup-Garou" (11/16/52) The swamps of Louisiana feature in this story of a spirit that can change into an animal. John Dehner, Georgia Ellis and Tom Tully also are part of the cast.

"Incident in Quinto" (12/7/52) A man trades in his wife to a group of headhunters. Conrad acts as the episodes announcer.

"A Study in Wax" (2/1/53) One of Conrad's best episodes of *Escape* deals with two men stuck in an arctic cabin for six months. Stacy Harris also appears.

"Pressure" (3/22/53) Set during WWII with an American sub trapped underwater by a Japanese destroyer. Herb Ellis and Jerry Hausner also appear.

"Classified Secret" (4/12/53) Story of spies on a cross-country bus trip. Conrad is joined by his *Gunsmoke* co-stars Georgia Ellis and Parley Baer in a script by Antony Ellis.

"North of Polaris" (5/17/53) Another standout episode about three astronauts who arrive on a barren planet.

"Clear for Action" (6/14/53) Exciting episode set at sea. Also in the cast are Vivi Janis, John Dehner and Ben Wright.

"The Out-Station" (7/12/53) Based on the W. Somerset Maugham story.

"Open Boat" (7/19/53) Four men in a small boat awash at sea try to find land, based on the Stephen Crane story with Conrad lending his great voice as narrator.

"The Abominable Snowman" (9/13/53) Set in the Himalayas as a group seek out the yeti.

"Zero Hour" (10/4/53) based on the Ray Bradbury sci-fi story.

"Elementals" (10/11/53) A loving couple are manipulated into a fierce fight with deadly consequences. Georgia Ellis also appears.

"The Adversary" (5/6/54) Conrad works as announcer on this episode.

"The Coward" (8/14/54) A pilot tries to safely land his disabled plane which is also loaded with money.

Family Theater

Family Theater was an anthology series that aired from 1947-1957 and aired on the Mutual Broadcasting System. Produced by Family Theater Productions, which was associated with the Family Rosary Crusade the show mixed religious stories with adaptations of major literary works.

"Moby Dick" (7/13/1949) an adaptation of Herman Melville's classic story hosted by Celeste Holm and featuring, along with Conrad, Dane Clark, Henry Hull, Joseph Kearns and James Nusser.

"Robin Hood" (7/27/1949) Another literary adaptation featuring Conrad, Edmond O'Brien, Ed Begley, and Jeff Corey.

"Ivanhoe" (10/19/1949) MacDonald Carey hosts this episode based on Walter Scott's famous story. The cast also includes Hans Conried and Jeanne Bates.

"A Tale of Two Cities" (1/11/1950) Robert Ryan hosts this adaptation with a cast that also includes Jay Novello, Virginia Gregg, Hans Conried, and Francis X. Bushman with Henry Mancini conducting the orchestra.

"The Black Arrow" (2/1/1950) Director Leo McCarey hosts this episode based on Robert Louis Stevenson's story and also featuring in the cast Betty Lynn and Junius Matthews.

"The Short Career of Dexter Coles" (2/8/1950) John Charles Thomas hosts a program this episode about a corrupt politician which teams Conrad with Jack Webb.

"The Valiant Lady" (4/26/1950) The cast includes, in addition to Conrad, Gale Storm, Dan O'Herlihy and Hy Averback.

"Twenty Thousand Leagues under the Sea" (8/23/1950) Maureen O'Sullivan hosts this adaptation of the Jules Verne classic with performances by Conrad and LeRoy Leonard.

Favorite Story

Favorite Story was a syndicated series, produced by Ziv Productions (a company that Conrad would work for extensively on television in the late 50's and early 60's). The program was hosted by Ronald Coleman and as Ziv said in its advertising for the series, "here are the greatest stories of all-time, masterfully adapted by writers pre-eminent in their field; a superb cast of radio's finest actors; a 15-piece orchestra, 52 half-hours available for local and regional sponsorship." How does it come by its title? well, each week some well-known figure chooses his or her 'favorite story.'

7/2/46 "The Diamond Lens" by Fitzjames O'Brien (The favorite story of composer George Antheil).

8/6/46 "Jane Eyre" by Charlotte Bronte (The favorite story of theater producer and director Brock Pemberton).

10/15/46 "The 1001 Arabian Nights" (The favorite story of newsman and commentator Lowell Thomas).

12/3/46 "Wuthering Heights" by Emily Bronte (The favorite story of Random House publisher Bennett Cerf).

12/17/46 "Journey to Bethlehem" (Christmas broadcast sponsored by Phillip Corin, of Bullock's Department Store).

0/0/47 "The Strange Mr. Bartleby" by Rudyard Kipling (The favorite story of actor Robert Montgomery).

0/0/47 "Pride and Prejudice" by Jane Austen (The favorite story of stage designer Oliver Smith).

2/4/47 "Moby Dick" by Henry Melville (The favorite story of playwright Howard Lindsey).

0/0/47 "Mr. Shakespeare" by Robert E. Lee & Jerome Lawrence (The favorite story of actor Spencer Tracy)—The story of the great bard being brought back to life and getting a job at a Hollywood studio.

0/0/47 "Dr. Jekyll and Mr. Hyde" by Robert Louis Stevenson (The favorite story of director Alfred Hitchcock)—Conrad plays both Jekyll & Hyde.

0/0/47 "The Tell-Tale Heart" by Edgar Allan Poe (The favorite story of actor Cary Grant)

3/25/47 "Lodging for the Night" by Robert Louis Stevenson (The Favorite story of writer and humorist Frank Sullivan).

4/22/47 "Mayerling" by Claude Anet (The favorite story of actor Gregory Peck).

6/14/47 "Joan of Arc" (The favorite story of actress Jennifer Jones).

11/11/47 "Mutiny on the Bounty" by James Morrison (The favorite story of Producer Walter Wanger).

12/16/47 "The Man from Yesterday" by Maurice Level (The favorite story of actor and singer Frank Sinatra).

12/30/47 "The Suicide Club" by Robert Louis Stevenson (The favorite story of writer S. J. Perelman).

2/10/48 "The Brownings" by Garson Kanin (This is also the favorite story of playwright and director Garson Kanin).

2/24/48 "The Young Years" by Jerome Lawrence and Robert E. Lee (The favorite story of actress Ethel Barrymore).

3/16/48 "The Doll's House" by Henrik Isben (The favorite story of cellist and conductor Alfred Wallenstein).

5/18/48 "The Bet" by Anton Chekhov (The favorite story of actor Charles Boyer).

9/28/48 "The Monkey's Paw" by W.W. Jacobs (The favorite story of composer Oscar Hammerstein II).

10/5/48 "The Valiant" by Halworthy Hall (The favorite story of comedian Bob Hope).

Let George Do It

Broadcast over Mutual from 1946-1955 this radio drama starred Bob Bailey as detective George Valentine who gets his clients thanks to a newspaper ad which reads, "Danger's my stock in trade. If the job's too tough for you to handle, you've got a job for me. George Valentine. Write full details!" Other regulars included Joseph Kearns as Caleb, the elevator man and George's secretary, Brooksie, played over the years by Frances Robinson, Virginia Gregg and Lillian Buyeff.

7/26/1948 "The Seven Murder" also features John Dehner, Georgia Ellis Herb Butterfield and Frances Robinson.

9/12/1949 "Valley Sunset" also features Jane Webb and Tony Barrett.

9/28/1949 "No Riders" also features Virginia Eiler, Jospeh Du Val and Walter Burke.

1/2/1950 "Needle in the Haystack" also features Ben Wright and Stanley Farrar.

2/13/1950 "Go Jump in the Lake" also features Dan O'Herlihy, Michael Ann Barrett and Walter Burke.

4/24/1950 "Death Begins at .45" also features Doris Singleton, Lawrence Dobkin and Robert Griffin.

12/11/1950 "The Bookworm Turns" also features Jack Kruschen, Robert Griffin and Ken Christy.

1/15/1951 "Tune On a Triangle" also features Tony Barrett, Ken Christy, and Jack Kruschen.

3/12/1951 "The Prairie Dog" also features Don Diamond, Ken Christy and Bob Jellison.

4/2/1951 "The Eight Ball" also features Stanley Farrar, Will Wright, and Herb Butterfield.

6/21/1951 "The Man from Fench Guiana" also features Ken Christy and Bill Bouchey.

Lux Radio Theatre

Conrad appeared more than 40 times on this landmark radio anthology series which began in 1934 on NBC, but then spent most of its run (35-54) on CBS before returning to NBC for a final year. From 1936-1945 Cecil B. DeMille hosted the program. After he left and for the appearances that Conrad made on the show the hosts were William Keighley (47-52) and then Irving Cummings (52-55). What distinguished the *Lux Radio Theatre* is that many (but not all) of its stories had been famous motion pictures and in many instances major stars from those films recreated their roles on the radio broadcast. While major stars were often the leads, many of the supporting players came from the best of radio drama including Conrad, Hans Conried, Virginia Gregg, Parley Baer, Howard McNear and Paul Frees—among many others.

"Nobody Lives Forever" (11/17/47) William Keighley (host) starring Jane Wyman and Ronald Reagan.

"Body and Soul" (11/15/48) William Keighley (host) Conrad recreates his movie role. John Garfield, Jane Wyman and Marie Windsor star.

"The Big Clock" (11/22/48) William Keighley (host) Ray Milland and Maureen O'Sullivan star (as they did in the 1948 film).

"Luck of the Irish" (12/27/48) William Keighley (host) with Anne Baxter, Dana Andrews and a special appearance by Jack Benny.

"When My Baby Smiles at Me" (4/25/49) William Keighley (host) with Betty Grable and Dan Dailey, who also starred in the film.

"Sorry, Wrong Number" (1/9/50) William Keighley (host) with Barbara Stanwyck and Burt Lancaster recreating their film roles.

"Double Indemnity" (10/30/50) William Keighley (host) Barbara Stanwyck and Fred MacMurray recreate their film roles.

"Broken Arrow" (1/22/51) William Keighley (host) with a cast featuring Burt Lancaster, Jeff Chandler and Debra Paget (the last two recreating their film roles).

"Treasure Island" (1/29/51) William Keighley (host) with stars James Mason, Bobby Driscoll and Nigel Bruce.

"Down to the Sea in Ships" (4/30/51) William Keighley (host) with stars Richard Widmark and Lionel Barrymore.

"Sunset Boulevard" (9/17/51) William Keighley (host) with William Holden and Gloria Swanson recreating their film roles.

"Winchester '73" (11/12/51) William Keighley (host) with James Stewart, Stephen McNally and Julie Adams recreating their film roles.

"Strangers on a Train" (12/3/51) William Keighley (host) adaptation of the Hitchcock film with Ray Milland, Ruth Roman and Frank Lovejoy.

"The Lemon Drop Kid" (12/10/51) William Keighley (host) adaptation of the film with Bob Hope and Marilyn Maxwell recreating their roles.

"Come to the Stable" (3/24/52) William Keighley (host) Loretta Young and Hugh Marlowe star. (Scatman Crothers has a part as well).

"Viva Zapata!" (11/3/52) Irving Cummings (host) Charlton Heston takes on the Marlon Brando part also with Jean Peters. Paul Frees narrates.

"The Blue Veil" (11/24/52) Jane Wyman stars in this adaptation of her 1951 film.

"King Solomon's Mines" (12/1/52) Stewart Granger and Deborah Kerr recreate on radio this adaptation of their 1950 MGM film.

"Appointment with Danger" (1/19/53) Irving Cummings hosts with William Holden starring.

"The People Against O'Hara" (3/9/53) Irving Cummings hosts with Walter Pidgeon taking on the role played by Spencer Tracy in the 1951 MGM film.

"Deadline U.S.A." (4/20/53) Irving Cummings hosts with Dan Dailey and Debra Paget starring.

"High Tor" (6/1/53) William Holden stars with *Gunsmoke* director Norman Macdonnell producing and directing and roles played by Conrad, Howard McNear, Georgia Ellis, Parley Baer, Lawrence Dobkin, Vic Perrin and Harry Bartell.

"The Fall of Maggie Phillips" (6/22/53) Ken Carpenter announces and hosts with Dorothy McGuire starring. Parley Baer narrates.

"Taxi!" (10/19/53) Irving Cummings hosts with Dan Dailey and Coleen Gray starring.

"Man on a Tightrope" (12/7/53) Irving Cummings hosts with Edward G. Robinson starring in the role played by Fredric March in the film of the same title.

"The Day the Earth Stood Still" (1/4/54) Irving Cummings hosts with Michael Rennie and Jean Peters starring in the adaptation of the Sci-fi classic.

"Carbine Williams" (3/22/54) Irving Cummings hosts with Ronald Reagan, Wendell Corey and Jean Hagen starring.

"A Blueprint For Murder" (3/29/54) Irving Cummings hosts with Dan Dailey and Dorothy McGuire starring.

"Detective Story" (4/26/54) Irving Cummings hosts this adaptation of the 1951 film with Kirk Douglas and Eleanor Parker recreating their roles.

"How Green Was My Valley" (9/28/54) Irving Cummings hosts with Michael Rennie, Alexis Smith and Donald Crisp. Hans Conried narrates.

"David and Bathsheba" (10/19/54) Irving Cummings hosts with Michael Rennie and Arlene Dahl starring.

"The Song of Bernadette" (10/26/54) Irving Cummings hosts with Ann Blyth taking on the part played by Jennifer Jones in the 1943 film.

"The Big Trees" (11/2/54) Irving Cummings hosts with Van Heflin starring.

"All About Eve" (11/23/54) Irving Cummings hosts with Claire Trevor and Ann Blyth playing the roles played by Bette Davis and Anne Baxter in the 1950 film.

"The Blue Gardenia" (11/30/54) Irving Cummings hosts with Dana Andrews and Ruth Roman starring.

"Battleground" (12/7/54) Irving Cummings hosts with Van Johnson recreating his role from the 1949 MGM film.

"Secret of the Incas" (12/14/54) Irving Cummings hosts with Charlton Heston and Conrad recreating their roles from the 1954 Paramount film.

"Miracle on 34th Street" (12/21/54) Irving Cummings hosts with Edmund Gwenn recreating his classic role as "Kris Kringle". In addition to Conrad and Gwenn, Virginia Gregg, Parley Baer, Herb Butterfield, Howard McNear and Mary Jane Croft also appear.

"The Iron Mistress" (12/28/54) Irving Cummings hosts with John Lund and Virginia Mayo starring.

"Island in the Sky" (1/11/55) Irving Cummings hosts with Dick Powell playing the part played by John Wayne in the film version. Conrad narrates the story.

"The Awful Truth" (1/18/55) Irving Cummings hosts with Irene Dunne and Cary Grant recreating their roles from the classic 1937 film.

"Sangaree" (1/25/55) Irving Cummings hosts with Arlene Dahl and Caesar Romero starring.

"Five Finger" (2/1/55) Irving Cummings hosts with James Mason starring. Conrad narrates the story.

"War of the Worlds" (2/8/55) Another radio adaptation of the famous H.G. Wells story—told differently from the famous 1938 Halloween prank pulled by Orson Welles. Dana Andrews and Pat Crowley star. Paul Frees narrates.

"Treasure of the Sierra Madre" (2/15/55) Irving Cummings hosts with Edmond O'Brien and Walter Brennan starring in the parts played by Humphrey Bogart and Walter Huston in the 1949 film.

"The Walls of Jericho" (3/8/55) Irving Cummings hosts with stars Cornel Wilde and Terry Moore.

"Gentleman's Agreement" (3/15/55) Irving Cummings hosts with Ray Milland taking on the role played by Gregory Peck in the film. Dorothy McGuire recreates her movie role.

"Rawhide" (3/22/55) Irving Cummings host with Donna Reed and Jeffrey Hunter starring.

"Trouble Along the Way" (3/29/55) Irving Cummings hosts with Van Johnson taking on the role played by John Wayne in the 1953 film.

"Rope of Sand" (5/31/55) This episode also features Barry Sullivan and Joseph Kearns.

Mr. President

Mr. President aired on ABC, June 26, 1947-Sept 23, 1953, with Edward Arnold as a different president each week with Betty Lou Gerson as Miss Sarah, the president's generic secretary. Conrad appeared in several segments both as an announcer and a performer in several roles. Others who appeared include Jeff Chandler, Howard Duff, Joe Kearns, Irene Tedrow, Parley Baer, Barney Phillips and John Brown.

7/24/47 "Ulysses S. Grant"
7/31/47 "James Monroe"
9/21/47 "James Garfield"
11/6/47 "Woodrow Wilson"
1/28/48 "William McKinley"
2/8/48 "Woodrow Wilson"
2/15/48 "Andrew Jackson"
2/22/48 "John Tyler"
3/14/48 "Theodore Roosevelt"

4/4/48 "Grover Cleveland"
4/11/48 "James K. Polk"
5/2/48 "Theodore Roosevelt"
5/16/48 "John Tyler"
5/23/48 "Grover Cleveland"
6/6/48 "John Quincy Adams"
6/20/48 "Andrew Jackson"
7/25/48 "Abraham Lincoln"
8/8/48 "John Adams"
8/15/48 "Zachary Taylor"
8/23/48 "Thomas Jefferson"
8/30/48 "Grover Cleveland"
9/6/48 "Ulysses S. Grant"
9/13/48 "Grover Cleveland"
9/20/48 "Abraham Lincoln"
10/24/48 "John Tyler"
10/31/48 "Abraham Lincoln"
11/14/48 "Woodrow Wilson"
11/21/48 "James K. Polk
7/4/49—A special July 4 show which departs from the usual format with a story about an army lieutenant who was never allowed to hear about America titled "The Man Without A Country."

Night Beat

Night Beat was a newspaper drama that starred Frank Lovejoy as reporter Randy (Lucky) Stone who covered, as the title would indicate, the night beat for a Chicago newspaper. Among the top flight talent to voice the show include Joan Banks (Mrs. Frank Lovejoy), Lurene Tuttle, Parley Baer, Jeff Corey, Paul Frees, Howard McNear, Lawrence Dobkin, Herb Ellis, Georgia Ellis, Bea Benaderet, Sheldon Leonard, Jeanette Nolan—and Conrad, of course. The show ran from February, 1950-September of 1952 on NBC.

2/20/50—"A World All His Own" (replayed 4/16/50)
4/30/50—"Am I My Brother's Keeper?"
5/8/50—"Elevator Caper"
6/12/50—"Football Player and the Syndicate"

6/26/50—"The Juvenile Gangster"
10/13/50—"Einar Pierce and Family" (Lamont Johnson, who Conrad would later hire to direct the film *A Covenant with Death* has a part on this episode).
5/4/51—"Big John McMasters"
5/18/51—"Juke Box Romance"
7/13/51—"Antonio's Return"
12/21/51—"Five Days Off for Christmas"
12/28/51—"Expectant Father"
5/8/52—"Long Live the Clown"
6/19/52—"Railroaded"
6/26/52—"Reformer"
7/31/52—"Flight from Fear"
9/11/52—"Larry, the Understudy"

Richard Diamond, Private Detective

Singer Dick Powell created a new screen persona for himself in the mid-forties as a movie tough guy in films like *Murder My Sweet* (as Raymond Chandler's private dick, Philip Marlowe), *Cornered* and *Pitfall*. In 1949 Powell took this new persona to radio as the star of *Richard Diamond*. Diamond was an ex-OSS operator turned New York City gumshoe. The tough guy however did have a musical side to his personality as the show often ended with Diamond crooning a song to his girlfriend Helen (played by Virginia Gregg). The show was often written by Blake Edwards. Later *Richard Diamond* became a popular TV series starring a pre-*Fugitive* David Janssen. The following episodes feature Conrad.

7/16/49—Diamond seeks to capture a serial killer. Along with Conrad the cast includes Ed Begley and Jack Kruschen. This script was also used on 4/12/50.

8/27/49—Diamond seeks to help a teenager from following his older brother's footsteps into serious crime. The cast also includes Sheldon Leonard and Mary Shipp.

11/12/49—Diamond is framed as a diamond thief.

8/30/50—A body is found in the river and a ladies' softball player is missing. The cast also includes John Dehner.

1/12/51—A woman hires Diamond to protect her when her husband gets out on parole.

2/2/51—A woman who hires Diamond to protect her is killed.

2/8/52—Diamond investigates counterfeit plates. Jeanette Nolan and John Dehner also appear.

8/9/53—A man dies in Diamond's office after being ice picked in his back. Jay Novello and Dan O'Herlihy also appear.

The Railroad Hour

The Railroad Hour sponsored by the Association of American Railroads presented various variety shows and musical-comedy (and occasional dramatic) plays each week and was hosted by singer Gordon MacRae with scripts by the noted team of Jerome Lawrence and Robert E. Lee, who would go on to write *Inherit the Wind* and the book to *Mame* (based on *Auntie Mame*). 299 episodes were produced between 1948 and 1954.

11/12/51—"The Bohemian Girl"
1/28/52—"The Three Musketeers" (the cast also includes silent screen star Francis X. Bushman)
4/21/52—"Erminie"
7/28/52—"The Pirate of New Orleans"
11/3/52—"Seventh Heaven"
3/23/53—"Lute Song"
6/15/53—"Love Story"

Romance

Romance was an anthology series which ran over 12 years and was often used as a filler for such radio shows as *Lux Radio Theater* and *Gunsmoke* when they were on hiatus. The series presented, as the title would indicate, stories of a romantic nature but not without action, suspense and sometimes humor. When Conrad began appearing on *Romance* the show was directed by Norman Macdonnell, who would go on to direct *Gunsmoke* and many of the scripts were written by Les Crutchfield and John Meston—two of *Gunsmoke's* most frequent writers.

7/2/51—"To Live Again"

8/6/51—"Pagosa" Written by John Meston, this episode is considered an inspiration for "Gunsmoke". Conrad plays the lead character of Sheriff Jeff Splain. Also in the cast is Georgia Ellis, who would go on to play Miss Kitty.

8/21/51—"Paris Encounter"—Conrad plays the leading role of a bored American seeking romance in Paris.

7/28/52—"Paradise Package"

8/25/52—"The Barrier Reef"

8/27/53—"Captain Huckaby's Beard"

6/5/54—"Lost Horizon"—based on the story by James Hilton and also featuring Howard McNear and Parley Baer.

7/10/54—"Cordoba"—set in old Mexico, Conrad plays a bullfighter who falls for an American girl.

5/5/56—"The Prelude"—Also featuring Cathy Lewis and Joseph Kearns.

The Six-Shooter

The Six-Shooter was a radio western which lasted a single season (1953-1954) on NBC and starred James Stewart as Britt Ponset, a drifter who finds adventure on the frontier in the final days of the Wild West. Even though Conrad was the star of one of the most successful westerns on radio, *Gunsmoke*, he made three guest spots on *The Six-Shooter*—often credited as Julius Krelboyne—so that viewers would not easily realize that the star of CBS's *Gunsmoke* was also appearing on this NBC series. Conrad wasn't the only *Gunsmoke* veteran to appear on this series—Parley Baer, Harry Bartell, Howard McNear and Virginia Gregg also did several guest spots. This series was later adapted for television (1957-1959) starring John Payne.

7/15/53—Audition show
11/1/53—"Ben Scofield"
1/17/53—"The Silver Buckle"
4/15/54—"Crisis at Easter Creek"

Strange Wills

Produced by Teleways, a syndicated company, *Strange Wills*, starred Warren William was an anthology series in which William played an either a lawyer or an investigator who looks into "strange stories from strange wills under strange circumstances."

5/19/47—"Crosswinds" The cast also includes Peggy Webber.
5/30/47—"The killer and the Saint"
6/6/1947—"Portsmouth Square" The cast also includes Hans Conried.

Suspense

William Conrad appeared as a voice actor on several episodes of *Suspense*. *Suspense* was one of the premier dramatic radio programs of the era. As was said in the introduction, *Suspense* told tales that were "calculated to intrigue you, to stir your nerves, to offer you a precarious situation and then withhold the solution... until the last possible moment...We hope to keep you in (Dramatic music)... Suspense!" So prestigious was *Suspense* that the show often used major film stars along with the very best of radio actors—Conrad, Jeanette Nolan, Joseph Kearns, Paul Frees, Alan Reed, Parley Baer, June Foray, John Dehner, Elliott Lewis, Cathy Lewis.

"The Black Curtain" (1/3/48) A man finds himself accused of

murder. This episode also features Robert Montgomery, Cathy Lewis, Jerry Hausner, Jeanette Nolan, Paul Frees with Joseph Kearns as the announcer.

"Nightmare" (3/13/48) A man dreams he has committed murder—then finds out a murder actually occurred. Also starring Robert Montgomery, Eddie Bracken, Ben Wright, and William Johnstone (announcer).

"Beware the Quiet Man" (8/12/48) A wife who commits adultery finds out her supposedly meek husband is planning to murder her. Ann Sothern stars.

"Night Cry" (10/7/48) What will a detective do when his girlfriend is accused of a murder? Ray Milland stars.

"To Find Help" (1/6/49) A handyman terrorizes the elderly woman who hired him. Gene Kelly and Ethel Barrymore star.

"The Copper Tea Strainer" (4/21/49) A woman poisons her mother. Betty Grable and Raymond Burr also appear.

"Death has a Shadow" (5/5/49) A fast-talking lawyer is threatened by a killer in an empty office building. Bob Hope stars (very dramatic performance by Hope with Conrad as 'Joe' his cop friend).

"Search for Isabell" (11/3/49) A man keeps getting phone calls asking for a woman named 'Isabell' he decides to find her. Red Skelton stars.

"The Bullet" (12/29/49) A jealous husband suspects his wife of cheating and decides to scare her with an 'unloaded' gun. Ida Lupino stars.

"Salvage" (4/6/50) A love triangle during a treasure hunt. Van Johnson stars.

"The Chain" (4/27/50) A nagging, vindictive woman sends a chain letter with disastrous results. Agnes Moorehead ("The First Lady of Suspense") stars.

"Statement of Mary Blake" (5/4/50) A scientist kills his wife and blames his assistant. Joan Bennett stars.

"The Man in the Room" (5/11/50) A writer hires a typist in a building which has an elevator operator who is overly fond of Edgar Allan Poe. John Lund stars.

"Over the Bounding Main" (9/14/50) The captain of a charter boat tries to kill a man while out at sea. Dan Dailey stars.

"After the Movies" (12/7/50) A juror receives a $10,000 bribe meets a tragic and unexpected end. Ray Milland stars.

"The Case Study of a Murder" (10/1/51) A wife is worried about her husband who loses his job and then confesses to a series of murders. Jeanne Crain stars.

"The Hunting of Bob Lee" (10/29/51) The story of a Texas feud based on a true 1868 case. Richard Widmark stars.

"The Case Against Loo Doc" (1/7/52) Story of the San Francisco Tong Wars set in Chinatown between the 1880's & the 1920's. (Bill Conrad plays his role with a Chinese dialect). Jeff Chandler stars.

"The Perfectionist" (1/21/52) A perfectionist killer sends a trunk containing a body to the wrong address—he needs to fix this wrong. Richard Basehart stars.

"The Shooting of Billy the Kid" (4/28/52) The life and death of the notorious baby-faced outlaw. Interestingly this episode was broadcast only two days after the first episode of *Gunsmoke* whose debut episode was titled "Billy the Kid". Parley Baer (Chester in *Gunsmoke*) also appears in this episode with Conrad.

"The Death of Me" (5/26/52) A lumberjack witnesses a murder—which was co-planned by his own wife. George Murphy stars.

"The Death of Barbara Allen" (10/20/52) Story based on an Irish folk song. Anne Baxter stars.

"Man Alive" (11/24/52) Thriller set aboard the ferry between San Francisco and Oakland. Paul Douglas stars.

"The Spencer Brothers (1/26/53) Story of three bank robbing/killer brothers who escape by horseback across Kansas. Richard Widmark stars.

"Plan X" (2/2/53) Earth sends its first rocket to land on Mars, where a martian named "Zeno" (played by Jack Benny) meets it.

"The Love and Death of Joaquin Murietta" (2/16/53) Conrad narrates this story about the Mexican bandit. (The show features several *Gunsmoke* stock players including Parley Baer, Harry Bartell and Virginia Gregg and stars Victor Mature).

"St. James Infirmary Blues" (2/23/53) Story of how the famous song was inspired. Rosemary Clooney stars.

"Tom Dooley" (3/30/53) Another story of how a hit song (in this case by the Kingston Trio) was inspired. Joseph Cotton stars.

"Othello" Part one (5/4/53) Radio adaptation of the famous Shakespeare play (adapted by Antony Ellis). Richard Widmark stars with a cast including Cathy Lewis, Joseph Kearns, Conrad, Herb Butterfield and William Johnstone.

"Othello" Part two (5/11/53) Conclusion (see above).

"The Mystery of the Marie Celeste" (6/8/53) Excellent story of what might have caused the abandonment of the famous ghost ship. Van Heflin stars.

"The Girl in Car Thirty-Two" (3/15/54) A detective undercover tries to forge a relationship with a gangster's moll aboard a train. Victor Mature stars.

"The Guilty Always Run" (3/22/54) A man is accused of murder and a 'friend' blackmails him. Tyrone Power stars.

"Lost" (10/14/54) A woman with amnesia is found in New York and accused of murder. Paula Winslowe stars.

"The Shot" (12/2/54) Set in the Confederacy during the Civil War as a man attempts to right a wrong to his honor.

"The Case Study of a Murderer" (1/20/55) previously told on "Suspense" on 10/1/51.

"The Whole Town's Sleeping" (6/14/55) A killer nick-named "The Lonely One" is on the prow strangling women after dark. Based on a Ray Bradbury story.

"Kaleidoscope" (7/12/55) Based on another Ray Bradbury story about a space ship which explodes leaving the crew members having a final conversation as they await certain death.

"Love, Honor or Murder" (8/9/55) A cab driver who found $12,000 in his cab commits murder.

"A Study in Wax" (8/16/55) William Conrad and Stacy Harris deliver superb performances in this classic story of two men trapped in an arctic blizzard driven insane.

"The Waxwork" (5/1/56) Tour-de-force by Bill Conrad who plays all the roles in this story of a reporter who spends a night in a spooky wax museum.

"A Matter of Timing" (6/12/56) A man hires a professional killer to bump off his business partner.

"Double Identity" (8/8/56) A man steals $50,000 from his workplaces safe and jumps on a train to Paris, only to find his boss onboard!

"Leinengen vs. The Ants" (8/25/57) Conrad reprises a story he starred in on *Escape* on 1/14/48.

"Speed Trap" (12/8/57) The drunk wife of a cop is driving at break-neck speed down a mountain road.

"An Occurrence at Owl Creek Bridge" (12/15/57) Ambrose Bierce's story of a spy captured during the Civil War.

"Never Steal a Butcher's Wife" (12/29/57) What happens when a seemingly meek clerk fools around with a big and burly butcher's wife.

"Rub Down and Out" (7/6/58) A man who runs a gym is having an affair with the wife of a gangster. Lloyd Bridges stars.

"Command" (9/14/58) Richard Anderson who appeared several times with Conrad on television stars in this radio program.

"Two for the Road" (9/9/58) the bad men of *The Killers* (William Conrad & Charles McGraw) are reunited in this story of two TV actors accused of murder while driving across country. Radio's revenge on television?

"Misfire" (11/30/58) An Atomic bomb test that goes wrong. Conrad narrates.

This Is Your FBI

This Is Your FBI was a highly successful radio crime drama which aired on ABC from 1945-1953 about the exploits of FBI agent Jim Taylor, played by radio actor Stacy Harris. J. Edgar Hoover once endorsed the program as "the finest dramatic program on the air."
4/1/49—"The Comeback Kid"

6/24/49—"The Rocking Chair Shakedown"
8/5/49—"Out of the Storm"
8/18/50—"The Vanishing Witness"
9/8/50—"The Swing-Shift Racketeers"

11/24/50—"Quartet for Crime"
2/16/51—"The Penny Lender"
3/23/51—"Success Story"
8/17/51—"The Bogus Highjacking"
10/26/51—"Citizen Caldwell"
11/2/51—"The Million Dollar Question"
12/14/51—"Crime For Sale"
1/18/52—"Knockout"
3/14/52—"The Cross Country Fugitive"
6/6/52—"Jackpot"
1/2/53—"Mr. Big-Shot"

THE VOYAGE OF THE SCARLET QUEEN

Adventure series set on the high seas which aired on the Mutual Radio network. Each episode opened with an entry from the ships log and then the story is unfolded. In the pilot (broadcast on 2/2/47) Howard Duff played the show's lead character, Captain Carney. For the remainder of its run the part was played by radio veteran Elliott Lewis. The secondary lead was a first mate named Red Gallagher (played by Ed Max). Conrad would play several different roles during the run.

2/2/47—audition program
7/3/47—"The Shanghai Secret"
7/10/47—"The Report from the White Jade Buddha"
7/17/47—"The Spaniard and the Lascar Pirates"
8/7/47—"The White Cargo Act and Ah Sin"
10/16/47—"Ah Sin and the Balinese Beaux Arts Ball"
11/13/47—"Kang's Treasure and the Ghost of Tangolin"
12/10/47—"The Wandering Master and the Warlord at Rest"
12/24/47—"The Fifteenth Lama and the Wise Guy From the East"
2/11/48—"Rocky III and the Dead Man's Chest"
2/25/48—"The Winchester Rifle and the Ambitious Groom"

Per the Digital Deli too: "The *Doud and Tallman* scripts were innovative, well-paced, taut and more than a little reminiscent of *Bold Venture*, which succeeded *The Voyage of The Scarlet Queen* by almost five years. The effort to maintain fairly tight continuity was highly successful up through Episode No. 20. The first twenty scripts had Captain Karney announcing his 'miles traveled since departing San Francisco' at the close of each episode. The announcer would also occasionally tease the following 'port of call.'"

The Whistler

The Whistler was an anthology series in which each week somebody plans what they think will be the perfect murder, only to be undone by the end of each play. This is one of radio's top anthology suspense series.

6/11/44 "The Doctor Prescribes Death" (Host Peter Lorre)

3/25/46 "Trigger man" (What happens when a crook's lawyer is the only man who can convict him)

7/8/46 "Confession" (A dying man confesses to a murder to get $10,000 to support his wife)

7/15/46 "Custom Built Blonde"

7/29/46 "My Love Comes Home"

8/5/46 "Bullet Proof" (Conrad plays a detective named "Conrad"—the cast also includes Mary Jane Croft and Gerald Mohr).

8/12/46 "Stolen Murder" (a man steals his friend's novel because the man has only a short time to live. Paul Frees also appears).

9/9/46 "Witness at the Fountain" (Conrad plays two roles and Virginia Gregg is the commercial spokeswoman).

9/16/46 "The Brass Ring"

10/7/46 "Present for Ricky (an aging dancer is dumped by his younger partner—Joseph Kearns also appears)

2/3/47 "Seven Steps to Murder" (Howard Duff, William Johnstone and John Brown appear).

7/28/48 "Lady of the Sea"

9/22/48 "Still Death" (A woman hires an artist to paint her picture, and soon after her husband is paralyzed by a stroke).

12/12/48 "Stormy Weather" (The wife of a doctor has a past she wants kept secret—but a down and out reporter knows the truth and soon has an accident).

1/2/49 "Man on the Roof" (A man who works on a rooftop witnesses a murder below him and instead of calling the police he attempts blackmail).

1/9/49 "The Tell Tale Brand" (A small town has a "Frontier Week" and the man who is promoting it has a romance with the fiancée of the town's leading citizen. Mercedes McCambridge also appears).

8/14/49 "Best Friend" (A man kills his girlfriend, who happens to be married to his business partner, and best friend, and if that isn't enough he frames his "best friend" for the murder!).

9/4/49 "Smart Girl" (Also appearing is Jeff Chandler, still going by the name Ira Grossell).

9/11/49 "Brief Pause for Murder" (A radio announcer plots the murder of his wife—Mary Lansing also appears).

10/2/49 "Woman's Privilege"

1/15/50 "Escape to Skull Island"

3/12/50 "Strange Meeting"

4/9/50 "Dark Voyage" (Two divers who love the same woman, dive for sunken treasure—also featuring Dorothy Singleton).

4/16/50 "Murder in the Mind"

5/14/50 "Blue Alibi" (The wife of a crooked city official tries to get him to break off with the racketeers—also featuring Mary Lansing).

10/8/50 "Fatal Action" (A crooked sea captain gets a taste of his own medicine—also featuring Betty Lou Gerson).

11/12/50 "Friendly Case of Blackmail" (cast includes Joseph Kearns)

12/31/50 "Evening Stroll" (While on a nice evening stroll, a man meets up with a man from his past who knows why he moved away and changed his identity).

2/18/51 "Man in the Storm"

4/29/51 "The Clayton Affair" (A woman's husband is killed and it seems like the wife may be getting away with murder—or is she?).

12/23/51 "Christmas Gift" (A woman attempts to flee gangsters)

5/11/52 "A Matter of Odds"

6/15/52 "The Last Message" (A retired criminal wants to go straight but will a member of his old gang let him?)

3/7/54 "Hudson Bay Incident" (John Dehner also appears)

Yours Truly, Johnny Dollar

Your Truly, Johnny Dollar was a long-running radio action/crime/adventure series about a freelance insurance investigator, Johnny Dollar. The stories required Dollar to travel to different, often exotic, locales to investigate some unusual or suspect claim. Dick Powell starred in the audition series and then Johnny was played over its initial run by radio actor Charles Russell and then movie actors Edmond O'Brien and John Lund. Conrad did guest voices on two-dozen episodes. The stock company included several outstanding radio voices including such members of the *Gunsmoke* stock company as Parley Baer, Howard McNear, Virginia Gregg, Harry Bartell, Vic Perrin and Larry Dobkin.

12/7/48 "Milford Brooks III" (Pilot with Dick Powell)
4/15/49—"The Case of the $100,000 legs" (Charles Russell plays role of Dollar)
10/8/49—"The Racehorse Piledriver"
12/3/49—"Bodyguard to Ann Connelly"
12/10/49—"The Animal Show Unscheduled performances"
2/10/50—"The S.S. Malay Trader" (Edmond O'Brien plays Dollar)
4/4/50—"The Story of the Big Red Schoolhouse"
4/25/50—"The Search for Policy Holder Pearl Carassa"
7/20/50—"The Henry J. Unger Matter"
8/3/50—"The Blood River Matter"
8/17/50—"The Mickey McQueen Matter"
11/4/50—"The Queen Anne Pistols Matter"
11/25/50—"The Woodward Manila Matter"
1/20/51—"The David Rocky Matter"
2/24/51—"The Jarvis Wilder Matter"
3/10/51—"The Stanley Springs Matter"
4/14/51—"The Mickey McQueen Matter" (repeating the same script as 8/17/50)
9/26/51—"The Protection Matter" (writer/director Blake Edwards wrote this episode)
10/13/51—"The Millard Ward Matter"
1/5/52—"The Glenn English Matter"
8/4/53—"The Voodoo Matter" (John Lund plays Dollar)
8/25/53—"The Nelson Matter"
10/27/53—"The Howard Arnold Matter"
1/12/54—"The Celia Woodstock Matter"
5/24/56—"The Tears of Night Matter"

Gunsmoke Episode Log

Billy the Kid (4/26/1952) Written by: Walter B. Newman
The first introduction of Matt, Chester & Doc (Kitty would enter the scene a few episodes down the road). Chester tells Matt that he

has locked up a runaway—a twelve year old kid named Billy Bonny. Matt seems to take a shine to the kid (who he calls Bud) who seems to hero worship Dillon and at one point tells Matt that one day he will be a famous gunfighter who will get a "bunch of notches" on his gun. "When I'm famous you can tell people you helped to get me started," young Billy tells Matt. There is another story running as well. A man is killed (thought to be shot dead) and a mob wants to lynch the man they think murdered him. However, Doc tells Matt that the man didn't die of a gunshot wound, but actually from a stab wound caused from a barlow knife. Meanwhile the kid's mother arrives to pick him up, but the boy has run away again. "Truth is, he's a wild one," she tells Matt. She goes on to explain that he ran away because she wouldn't buy him a gun—instead she gave the boy a barlow knife.
Note: While Kitty doesn't appear in this episode, Georgia Ellis does—playing an old flame of Matt's.

Ben Thompson (5/3/52) Written by: Herb Purdum
A gunman is killed in a gunfight with Matt—a gunman who was once his friend. The man's widow promises to ruin Matt's reputation before having him killed. Guest stars include: Larry Dobkin, Harry Bartell, Sam Edwards and Don Diamond.

Jalisco (5/10/52) Written by: Les Crutchfield
A young man rides into Dodge and tells Dillon that his family has been killed and their house burnt down, but before he can reveal who committed this act he dies. It's up to Matt to find the culprits. This episode introduces Georgia Ellis as Saloon keeper/prostitute Kitty Russell. Guest stars Harry Bartell, Lou Krugman, Jack Kruschen, Vivi Janiss and Barney Phillips.

Dodge City Killer (5/17/52) Written by: Herb Purdum
Dillon finds justice for the daughter of a Comanche warrior chief who killed a man while he was trying to rape her (this is considered a lost episode and description came from the book "Radio Rides the Range: A Reference Guide to Western Drama on the Air, 1929-1967 by Jack French and David S. Siegel). Guest stars include Larry Bobkin, Ralph Moody, Lillian Buyeff, Ben Wright, Vici Raaf and Paul DuBov.

Ben Slade's Saloon (5/24/52) Written by: Norman MacDonnell
A man who was drinking and gambling in Ben Slade's saloon is found dead—and the money he won (about $3000) is missing. This is the third killing in as many months and it could very well be the same killer. Herb Ellis and Richard Morrison are among the guest stars.

Carmen (5/31/52) Written by: John Meston
An army payroll is stolen and two soldiers are killed and unless Matt can find the perpetrators within 48-hour the Army will put Dodge under martial law. Guest stars include Michael Ann Barrett, Jeanette Nolan, Harry Bartell and Don Diamond.

Buffalo Hunters (6/7/52) Written by: Joel Murcott
Buffalo hunters are coming to Dodge to cash in their load of hides—except for two men who were robbed and killed for their hides. Guest stars include John Dehner, Larry Dobkins, Sam Edwards and Stan Waxman.

Jailbait Janet (6/14/52) Written by: Les Crutchfield
A family takes revenge on a train line after a train sparks a fire that destroys their crops. The family—a man, wife, son and daughter rob another train of $50,000 and in the process a baggage clerk is killed. Guest stars include John Dehner, Harry Bartell and Sammie Hill.

Heat Spell (6/21/52) Written by: Lou Houston
There is a heat wave and high temperatures as well as revenge in Dodge as Matt has to try and keep a gunman accused of stealing a horse from being lynched. Guest stars include John Stephenson, John Dehner, Paul Frees and Jack Kruschen.

The Ride Back (6/28/52) Written by: Anthony Ellis
Matt travels to Texas to bring back a murderer—on the ride back—they are attacked by Indians and must unite against them if they are to live. Larry Dobkin is the guest star.
Note: Writer Anthony Ellis was the husband of Georgia (Kitty) Ellis. This script was a favorite of William Conrad's and later he produced (with Robert Aldrich) and starred (with Anthony Quinn) in a 1957 film based on this radio script.

Never Pester Chester (7/5/52) Written by: John Meston
Matt has revenge on his mind when two rowdy cowpokes that Matt sends Chester out to handle leave Chester near death. Guest stars include Paul DuBov, Lou Krugman, Jack Kruschen, and Don Diamond.

The Boughton Bride (7/12/52) Written by: John Meston
A young woman is kidnapped during a stage robbery. Herb Ellis, Jim Nusser, John Stephenson and Mary Lansing guest star.

Doc Holiday (7/19/52) Written by: Herb Purdum
A man starts a fight with another man who he thinks is a tenderfoot. The man, however, turns out to be Doc Holiday (played by Harry Bartell), an old friend of Matt's. The man who starts the fight winds up in jail, but his cattle baron father will try to use his influence to get him out. Also in the cast are Tom Tully and Lee Milar.

Gentleman's Disagreement (7/26/52) Written by: Les Crutchfield
A man has vowed to kill another man for marrying a certain girl they both love—but then the man who made the threats turns up dead. Guest stars include Larry Dobkin, Tom Tully, Lynn Allen and Barney Phillips.

Renegade White (8/2/52) Written by: John Meston
Matt suspects that a man who killed two men in a fair fight may actually be selling rifles to the Cheyenne. Harry Bartell, Jack Kruschen, Lawrence Dobkin and Herb Vigran guest star.

The Kentucky Tolmans (8/9/52) Written by: Herb Purdum
A Kentucky wildcat wants Matt to arrest her father, Jed Tolman, so that he can be safe in jail because she is convinced that somebody is trying to kill him. Guest cast includes Virginia Gregg, Joseph Kearns and Harry Bartell.

The Lynching (8/16/52) Written by: John Meston
A man is lynched by a mob for killing another man's brother—shot in the back—and Matt knows who the head of the lynching party is but has to gather evidence to lead to an arrest—and then a fair trial and hanging. Among the guest stars are John Dehner and Tom Tully.

Shakespeare (8/23/52) Written by: Antony Ellis.
Irving Henry, a Shakespearian actor, comes to Dodge to ply his trade, but finds trouble when a man is found dead in the back of his wagon. Hans Conried plays the thespian.

The Juniper Tree (8/30/52) Written by: Herb Purdum
Mingo (John Dehner), who runs a gambling house, has Matt arrest a rancher named Jim Stanley for allegedly stealing. The drunken Stanley doesn't understand what is happening and Matt is suspicious—it seems that Mingo's girl is paying too much attention to Stanley and Mingo may be trying to frame Stanley to get him out of the way. Paul DuBov, Bill Lally and Michael Ann Barrett make up the remaining guest cast.

The Brothers (9/6/52) Written by: Les Crutchfield
A man comes into Dodge to gun down another man—who happens to be a fast draw. Guest stars include Harry Bartell, Vic Perrin, Paul DuBov and Lou Krugman.

Home Surgery (9/13/52) Written by: John Meston
Matt and Chester come upon a homesteader in the wilds who is suffering from blood poisoning. To save his life, Matt must amputate his leg. John Dehner, Larry Dobkin and Sammie Hill guest star.

Drop Dead (9/20/52) Written by: Les Crutchfield
Trouble brews when a rancher puts a fence up around a water hold on his property. Guest stars include Harry Bartell, Lou Krugman, Joe DuVal and Barney Phillips.

The Railroad (9/27/52) Written by: David Ellis.
A woman won't sell her property to a railroad company—which needs the land to pass thru—and will take whatever means it can to get her to change her mind. Guest stars include Jeanette Nolan, John Dehner and Tom Tully.

Cain (10/3/52) Written by: John Meston
A man with only two months to live attempts to avenge the suicide of a young woman by killing the man he blames for her death. Guest stars include Harry Bartell and Larry Dobkin.

Hinka-Do (10/10/52) Written by: Les Crutchfield

Matt comes to believe that the new owner of a saloon killed the previous owner so that she can take over the establishment. Guest stars include Jeanette Nolan, John Dehner, Ralph Moody and Byron Kane.

Lichinvar (10/17/52) Written by Les Crutchfield.

Complications arise for a young couple planning to be married when an old flame of the bride arrives in Dodge and makes it clear that he won't allow a wedding. Guest stars include Herb Ellis, Vivi Janiss, Tom Tully and Barney Phillips.

The Mortgage (10/24/52) Written by: Les Crutchfield

A bank needs to foreclose on a family and Matt tries to convince him not to—even though he has the law on his side. Guest stars include Paula Winslow, Harry Bartell, Jim Nusser, Richard Beals and Larry Dobkin.

Overland Express (10/31/52) Written by: John Meston

Matt has to transport a suspected murderer back to Dodge by stage, but when the stage coach (the Overland Express) is held up by bandits, Matt has to trust his prisoner to help him fight them off. Guest stars include Larry Dobkin, Vic Perrin, Jim Nusser, Ralph Moody and Lou Krugman.

Tara (11/7/52) Written by: Norman MacDonnall

Kind of a follow up to "Home Surgery" as the young girl orphaned in that episode is taken in by a kindly couple who try to warn her to stay away from a dangerous man with deadly consequences. Sammie Hill, John Dehner, Vivi Janiss and Ralph Moody guest star.

The Square Triangle (11/14/52) Written by: Les Crutchfield

A married woman falls in love with a young cowboy—then her husband is knifed in the back while he sleeps. The town believes it was the love sick cowboy who did the deed. Guest stars include Lillian Buyeff, Harry Bartell, Larry Dobkin and Jack Kruschen.

Fingered (11/21/52) Written by: John Meston
A man's first wife disappeared and years later he marries again and shortly thereafter she also disappears—is there a connection? Guest stars include Jeanette Nolan, Harry Bartell, John McIntire, Jack Kruschen and Paul DuBov.
Note: John McIntire was the equally talented husband of Jeanette Nolan.

Kitty (11/29/52) Written by: Antony Ellis.
Matt shows a bit of his romantic side when he invites Kitty to be his date at a school social—Kitty, however, understands that some in town might look at this the wrong way. Guest stars include John Dehner, Vivi Janiss, Mary Lansing, Bob Sweeney and Larry Dobkin.
Note: One perk of being married to a writer is that he might write a good episode for your character—as Antony Ellis did here for Georgia Ellis.

I Don't Know (12/6/52) Written by: Antony Ellis
The Birch family comes to Dodge looking for their missing—and usually drunken—patriarch. Guest stars include John Dehner, Larry Dobkin, Lee Millar and Michael Ann Barrett.

Post Martin (12/13/52) Written by: Les Crutchfield
A Woman comes to Dodge looking for her brother. Guest stars include Sam Edwards, Jeanne Bates and Ralph Moody.

Christmas Story (12/20/52) Written by: Antony Ellis
An episode in flashback as Matt tells the story of the Christmas miracle of the previous year—in which on his way back from the Oklahoma territory his horse breaks his leg and Matt has to put him out of his misery and then begin a 40-mile long walk back to Dodge when he happens to meet a stranger along the way. Guest stars include Larry Dobkin, Harry Bartell and John Dehner.

The Cabin (12/27/52) Written by: John Meston
During the Christmas season, Matt finds refuge in a cabin with a group of strangers during a blizzard. John Dehner, Harry Bartell and Vivi Janiss are the guest stars.

Westbound (1/3/53) Written by: Les Crutchfield
Matt and Chester have their hands full trying to get a prisoner into Abilene. Guest stars include Sam Edwards, Barney Phillips, Jim Nusser, John Dehner, Tom Tully and Larry Dobkin.

Word of Honor (1/10/53) Written by: John Meston
Doc is brought to tend to the needs of an injured kidnapping victim—and Matt becomes concerned when he isn't seen around town for more than two days. Guest stars include John Dehner, Harry Bartell and Larry Dobkin.

Paid Killer (1/17/53) Written by: Les Crutchfield
A man is summoned by another man with a proposition. He knows that the man he is offering the proposition to has been trying to establish a gambling business in Dodge and Matt keeps getting in his way. The proposition: For $5000 he will kill Dillon. Harry Bartell, Jack Kruschen and Lawrence Dobkin guest.

The Old Lady (1/24/53) Written by: Kathleen Hite
Matt and Chester take pity on Ellen Henry (Jeanette Nolan) a widow woman with a good-for-nothing son. But Ellen Henry is hiding a secret from the law and she doesn't want Matt to discover what it is. Additional cast include Sam Edwards, Harry Bartell and John Dehner.

Cavalcade (1/31/53) Written by: Les Crutchfield.
A deputy from Richmond, VA makes his way to Dodge intent on arresting Doc—who he knows as a killer named Calvin Moore. This episode gives some interesting background information on "Doc Addams". Guest stars include Larry Dobkin, Lou Krugman, Paul Dubov and Vivi Janiss.

Cain (2/7/53) rebroadcast of 10/3/1952 episode.

The Round-Up (2/14/53) Written by: John Meston
Dodge merchants are certain that an upcoming weekend round-up will cause all kinds of problems in town and want Matt to deputize up to 20 men to help keep the peace. Guest stars include James

Nusser, Larry Dobkin, Lou Krugman, Harry Bartell and John Dehner.

Mascoutah (2/21/53) Written by: John Meston
Matt and Chester ride into a town that is deserted—despite signs that it had recently been occupied. What happened to and where are the towns people? Guest stars include Larry Dobkin, Lou Krugman, Vic Perrin, Bob Sweeney, and John Dehner.
Note: Actor Bob Sweeney eventually went into directing and he directed the first three seasons of *The Andy Griffith Show* where he was reunited at times with Howard McNear who played "Floyd the Barber."

Trojan War (2/28/53) Written by: Les Crutchfield
An old girlfriend of Matt's is killed in a robbery on a stage coach on its way to Dodge. Guest stars include Louise Fitch, John Dehner, Tom Tully, Larry Dobkin and Harry Bartell.

Absalom (3/7/53) Written by: Les Crutchfield
Trouble brews when a Texas cattle baron and his son are arrested and then just as quickly the Mayor of Dodge over rules Matt and releases them. Guest stars include Sam Edwards, John Dehner, Larry Dobkin and Harry Bartell.

Cyclone (3/14/53) Written by: Les Crutchfield
Matt is suspicious when the "Cyclone Ranch" suddenly changes hands—being 'sold' to a stranger from Texas. Guest stars include Vivi Janiss, Harry Bartell, Larry Dobkin and Jerry Hausner.

Pussy Cats (3/21/53) Written by: Antony Ellis
A seemingly ordinary man and woman wait in the Long Branch intent to ambush four men. Guest stars include John Dehner, Tom Tully, Michael Ann Barrett and Larry Dobkin.

Quarter-Horse (3/28/53) Written by: Norman McDonnell
A man makes fun of another mans "funny looking" quarter horse and challenges him to a race. Larry Dobkin, Joseph Kearns, Harry Bartell and Lou Krugman guest star.

Jayhawkers (4/4/53) Written by: John Meston.
Matt is sought to help capture a group of jayhawkers, a group of guerillas fighters, who are after a herd. Guest stars include Larry Dobkin, Harry Bartell, Jack Kruschen, Jim Nusser and Sam Edwards.

Gonif (4/11/53) Written by: Antony Ellis
Two men that Matt told to get out of Dodge and stay away return—surprising the Marshal.
Among the guest stars are John Dehner, Lawrence Dobkin and Jack Kruschen.

Bum's Rush (4/18/53) Written by: John Meston
Matt captures and escorts two men back to Dodge to stand trial for murder when another man enters the fray claiming that the two men couldn't possibly be guilty. Guest stars include John Dehner, Harry Bartell, Lou Krugman and Larry Dobkin.

The Soldier (4/25/53) Written by: John Meston
Two soldiers are arrested after starting a fight in the Long Branch. Lawrence Dobkin, Paul Frees, Vic Ferrin and Harry Bartell.

Tacetta (5/2/53) Written by: John Meston
Tacetta is a dance hall girl who gets the unwanted attention of Dorigan, a man used to getting what he wants. Tom Tully, Larry Dobkin, Paul DuBov and Lillian Buyeff guest star.

The Buffalo Hunter (5/9/53) Written by: John Meston
A buffalo hunter has a habit of killing the men who work for him rather than paying them. Guest stars include Larry Dobkin, John Dehner, Harry Bartell, Richard Beals and William Oiler.

The Big Con (5/16/53) Written by: John Meston
A man borrows $20,000 from a bank with a poker hand that seems like a sure winner—but loses. Guest stars include Harry Bartell, Larry Dobkin, Ralph Moody and James Nusser.

Print Asper (5/23/53) Written by: John Meston
A dishonest lawyer tries to cheat a man out of his ranch—when the

lawyer winds up dead a few days later the son of the man he was trying to cheat is suspected. Among the guest stars are Joseph Kearns (best known to TV audiences as the first 'Mr. Wilson' on *Dennis the Menace*), Sam Edwards and John Dehner.

Fall Semester (5/30/53) Written by: John Meston
A cattle man is convinced that he is being cheated by his foreman since his cattle are being stolen, but he needs to find out how. Among the guest stars are John McIntire, Harry Bartell and John Dehner.

Sundown (6/6/53) Written by: William Conrad
Matt and Chester investigate when they find an Indian squaw dying alone on the prairie—they are convinced that foul play is involved. The only Gunsmoke script scribed by star William Conrad, it's a top-notch episode. Among the guest stars are John McIntire and Lawrence Dobkin.

Spring Term (6/13/53) Written by: John Meston
When a man is shot on the streets of Dodge, Matt comes to the conclusion that the shot was meant for him. Guest stars include John Dehner, Harry Bartell, Vic Perrin and Lou Krugman.

Wind (6/20/53) Written by: John Meston
A saloon girl brings luck to whatever gambler she is standing next to—which leads to men fighting and killing for her attentions. Guest stars include Virginia Gregg, John Dehner and James Griffith.

Flashback (6/27/53) Written by: Les Crutchfield
A father and son bring in a herd in from Big Bend Country. The son warns Matt that there may be trouble because his father, an ex-military man, treated the cow hands as if they were under his military command while on the cattle drive and that some may be out to get the old man. Guest stars include Sam Edwards, Lou Krugman and Larry Dobkin.

Dirt (7/4/53) Written by: John Meston
A man marries a woman whose brother doesn't want him in the

family. The groom is then shot leaving the church with the brother-in-law (who wasn't present for the wedding he opposed) the chief suspect. Guest stars include Larry Dobkin, Sam Edwards, Joyce McCluskey, Joe Cranston and Elaine Williams.

Grass (7/11/53) Written by: John Meston
Some men pretending to be Indians attack a man at night and one of the attackers is killed—which causes the 'Indians' to want revenge. Guest stars include Larry Dobkin, Ralph Moody, and Harry Bartell.

Wild West (7/18/53) Written by: John Meston
While riding back to Dodge, Matt finds a young boy alone who tells him that the previous night some men tied up and abducted his father. Guest stars include Michael Ann Barrett, Joseph Kearns, John Dehner, and John McGovern.

Hickok (7/25/53) Written by: John Meston
Abilene Sheriff Hickock sends Matt a telegram telling him to keep two men in Dodge until he can arrive to arrest them for a murder, but without evidence Matt finds it difficult to keep the men until Hickok arrives. John Dehner, John McIntire, Larry Dobkin and Harry Bartell are among the guest stars.

Boy (8/1/53) Written by: Norman McDonnell
A man buys a saloon and imports lots of pretty girls from St. Louis, one of whom Chester is attracted to. Guest stars include John Dehner, Charlotte Lawrence and Larry Dobkin.

Sky (8/8/53) Written by: John Meston
A young man flees Dodge after he is suspected of killing a woman whose attentions he has spurned. Guest stars include Vivi Janiss, Jim Nusser. Helen Kleeb, Ralph Moody and Sam Edwards.

Moon (8/15/53) Written by: John Meston
A crooked card shark is being kept under surveillance by a gunman hired by another card player to make sure he doesn't cheat. Guest stars include Vic Perrin, John Dehner, Harry Bartell and Vivi Janiss.

Gone Straight (8/22/53) Written by: John Meston
A New Mexico Deputy asks Matt to accompany him to Tescosa to arrest a man. Helen Kleeb, Tom Tully, John McIntire and Harry Bartell are among the guest stars.

Jesse (8/29/53) Written by: John Meston
A young man is determined to learn how to handle a gun so he can take revenge on the man who killed his father—Matt. Guest stars include Sam Edwards, Harry Bartell and John Dehner.

The Sutler (9/5/53) Written by: John Meston
Chester is hired to unload a train (for .20 cents per hour!) into a wagon belonging to a man named Will Jonas—who has something to hide. Guest stars include Harry Bartell, John Dehner, Jospeh Kearns and James Nusser.

Prairie Happy(9/12/53) Written by: John Meston
Word arrives in Dodge that the Pawnee Indians will attack Dodge the next day—is it fact or rumor—Matt tries to find out all the while trying to calm the towns people. Guest stars include John Dehner, Larry Dobkin, Vic Perrin and James Nusser.

There Was Never a Horse (9/19/53) Written by: John Meston
A Gunfighter kills a pig farmer in self-defense—but his real target is Matt, who actually feels some vulnerability about this confrontation. Guest stars include Larry Dobkin, John Dehner, and Ralph Moody.

Fawn (9/26/53) Written by: John Meston
A woman who was held captive by the Cheyenne for ten years wins her release and with her eight year old daughter (that she bore while in captivity) she travels to Dodge, where they face prejudice from having been captives of Indians for so long. Guest stars include John Dehner and Helen Kleeb (best known to TV audiences as Mamie Baldwin on *The Waltons*).

How to Kill a Friend (10/3/53) Written by: John Meston
Two gamblers hire a man to kill Matt when Matt won't take a bribe. Guest stars include John Dehner, Harry Bartell and Larry Dobkin.

How to Die for Nothing (10/10/53) Written by: John Meston
A Texas cattle herder is killed when he pulls a gun on Matt—his brother comes to Dodge to seek revenge—and when the brother is arrested the entire trail herders come to Dodge to shoot up the town and get the younger brother out of jail. Vic Perrin, Harry Bartell, Larry Dobkin and John Dehner guest star.

Yorky (10/17/53) Written by: John Meston
A twelve year old Indian boy is captured by raiders and it turns out he is a white boy who wants to continue to live among the Indians. Guest stars include Richard Beals, Larry Dobkin and John Dehner.

The Buffalo Hunter (10/24/53) A rebroadcast of the 5/9/53 episode.

How to Kill a Woman (10/31/53) Written by: John Meston
A stagecoach is held up and the drive is convinced that the stage owner is behind it. Guest stars include John Dehner, Larry Dobkin and Jack Edwards.

Stolen Horses (11/7/53) Written by: Norman MacDonnell.
Matt goes to a ranch intending to buy a horse. When he gets to the ranch he finds it deserted—the rancher was murdered and his horses stolen. Guest stars include Helen Kleeb, Ralph Moody, James Nusser and Paul Frees.

Professor Lute Bone (11/14/53) Written by: John Meston
A medicine man comes to Dodge—and Doc wants him run out of town. Guest stars include John Dehner, Barney Phillips, and Larry Dobkins.

Custer (11/21/53) Written by: John Meston.
Matt and Chester are on a trail of a man who hung an innocent man. The killer is an army deserter and the army wants him too. Guest stars include Sam Edwards and John Dehner.

Kick Me (11/28/53) Written by: John Meston
A bank robber arrives in Dodge and pretends to be a respected citizen all the while planning to rob the bank. Guest stars include Larry

Dobkin, Ralph Moody, Byron Kaye and Harry Bartell.

The Lamb (12/5/53) Written by: John Meston
A seemingly nice, easy-going man arrives in Dodge and is quickly befriended—turns out he is a notorious gunfighter. Guest stars include Harry Bartell, Herb Ellis, Vic Perrin and Larry Dobkin.

The Cast (12/12/53) Written by: John Meston
A man is convinced that Doc deliberately killed his wife during an operation and seeks revenge.
Note: Howard McNear was absent from this episode and the role of Doc was assumed by Paul Frees.

Big Girl Lost (12/19/53) Written by: John Meston
When Matt interferes in a man trying to see his ex-fiancee (she doesn't want to see him), he hires a man to kill Dillon. Guest stars include Joyce mcDluskey, Harry Bartell, Larry Dobkin and Vic Perrin.

The Guitar (12/26/53) Written by: John Meston
A guitar player is bullied by another man—he can only take too much before he comes to his breaking point. Guest stars include John Dehner, Larry Dobkin, Harry Bartell and Vic Perrin.

Stage Holdup (01/02/54) Written by: John Meston
Matt is on a stage traveling from Hayes City to Dodge that is held up. A man is killed and later Matt is convinced that a man whose voice he recognizes at the Long Branch is one of the robbers. Guest Stars: Vic Parrin, John Dahner, Lawrence Dobkin.

Joke's On Us (1/9/54) Written by: John Meston
A man hangs another man for horse stealing—but was the hanged man really innocent? Guest stars include Helen Kleeb, John Dehner, Ted Bliss, Sam Edwards and Herb Ellis.

The Bear (1/16/54) Written by: John Meston
Things turn deadly when a man continually humiliates and pulls practical jokes on a big 'bear' of a man. Guest stars include John Dehner, Lou Krugman, James Nusser and Larry Dobkin.

Nina (1/23/54) Written by: Norman MacDonnell
An army scout encounters prejudice when he travels thru Dodge with his Mexican wife, Nina. Guest stars include Vic Perrin, Lillian Buyeff, James Eagle and Larry Dobkin.

Gun Smuggler (1/30/54) Written by: John Meston
The pawnee's are being armed with Rifles coming out of Dodge— Matt has to find out who is behind it. John Dehner, Larry Dobkin, Harry Bartell and Barney Phillips are among the guest stars.

Big Broad (2/6/54) Written by: John Meston
The "Big Broad" of the title refers to 200 plus pound Lena Wave who arrives in Dodge. Guest stars include Virginia Gregg, Vic Perrin and John Dehner.

The Killer (2/13/54) Written by John Meston
A man cold-bloodedly kills another man he just met. Guest stars include Larry Dobkin, Howard Culver, Richard Deacon and Vic Perrin. **Note:** Howard Culver played "Mark Dillon" in an early pilot program for "Gunsmoke", and later on the TV series he played Howie, the hotel clerk of the Dodge House.

Last Fling (2/20/54) Written by: John Meston
Two men come to town claiming that Kitty shot them. Guest stars include John Dehner, Helen Kleeb, Ralph Moody.

Bad Boy (2/27/54) Written by: John Meston
Two young cowboys with a chip on their shoulders shoot up the Dodge House. Guest stars include Sam Edwards, Paul DuBov, Charles Bastin and John Dehner.

The Gentleman (3/6/54) Written by: John Meston
A gambler from Philadelphia falls in love with one of the saloon girls—who is considered the girlfriend of another man in town with a notoriously bad temper. Guest stars include John Dehner, Eleanore Tanin and Harry Bartell.

Confederate Money (3/13/54) Written by: John Meston
A young man goes on a drunken spree in Dodge. Guest stars include Vic Perrin, James Ogg, Barney Phillips and Harry Bartell.

Old Friend (3/20/54) Written by: John Meston
Yet another episode about a man hiring another man (this time for $300) to kill Matt. (Same basic plot as the 10/3/53 episode "How to Kill a Friend"). Guest stars include John Dehner, Vic Perrin and Larry Dobkin.

Blood Money (3/27/54) Written by John Meston
A man kills another man who saved his life when he finds out there is a reward for him—dead or alive. Guest stars include Harry Bartell, Sam Edwards, John Dehner, and James Nusser.

Mr and Mrs Amber (4/3/54) Written by John Meston
A wealthy rancher accuses Mrs. Amber of trying to steal one of his calves—this coming after her husband was caught stealing seeds from the general store. Guest stars include Helen Kleeb, John Dehner, Frances Drew, James Moody, Lawrence Dobkin, Harry Bartell.

Greater Love (4/10/54) Written by: John Meston
A killer takes Doc hostage at gunpoint in an effort to help save his dying partner. Guest stars include Joyce McCluskey, John Dehner, and Ralph Moody.

What the Whiskey Drummer Heard (4/17/54) Written by: John Meston
A whiskey drummer (aka whiskey salesman) tells Matt that he overheard a man make an offer to kill Matt for a price. Shortly afterward an attempt is made on Matt's life. Guest stars include Edgar Barrier, Vic Perrin and John Dehner.

Murder Warrant (4/24/54) Written by: John Meston
Matt has to figure out a way to keep a man from being taken to a corrupt town where he faces certain hanging over a trumped up murder charge. Guest stars include Lawrence Dobkin, Joseph Du Val, and Sam Edwards.

Cara (5/1/54) Written by: John Meston.

An old flame of Matt's arrives in Dodge and it seems that the woman wants to pick up where things left off, but there is something about her that has hardened which makes Matt wary. There may be another motivation as well—a bank robber, known to send a woman ahead of him to scout the town, is on his way to Dodge. Harry Bartell, Vic Perrin and John Dehner are included in the cast.

The Constable (5/8/54) Written by John Meston

The town council of Dodge objects to Matt's methods in dealing with a bunch of rowdy cowboys, so they go over the Marshal's head and hire a constable to keep the peace. John Dehner, Joseph Kearns, Jack Kruschen and Vic Perrin are included in the cast.

The Indian Horse (5/15/54) Written by Norman MacDonnell

Lt. Flagg challenges an Indian chief to a foot race at Fort Dodge. Guest stars include John Dehner, Harry Bartell, Ralph Moody and Paul Savage.

Monopoly (5/22/54) Written by: John Meston

An Eastern businessman who wants to establish control of Dodge's freight shipment hires a vicious gunman to help him achieve his goal. Joseph Kearns, Herb Ellis, Vic Perrin and Jack Kruschen are among the guest stars.

The Blacksmith (6/5/54) Written by: John Meston

An immigrant couple see their house burned down on their wedding night. Vic Perrin, John Dehner, Jeanne Bates and Lou Krugman are the guest stars.

The Cover-Up (6/12/54) Written by John Meston.

A man is accused of murdering two squatters on his land and is locked up by Matt—but then a third squatter is killed while he is incarcerated. Guest stars include Joseph Kearns, Clayton Post, Helen Kleeb and Paul Savage.

Going Bad (6/19/54) Written by John Meston

While in the barber shop a young man threatens to kill Matt who is sitting in the barber's chair—Matt bluffs the kid telling him that under the towel around his neck he has a gun pointed straight at him. The kid backs off and Matt tells the barber it was all a bluff and not to tell anybody. The barber ignores this and the town takes to laughing at the young man. The cast includes Sam Edwards and Harry Bartell.

Claustrophobia (6/26/54) Written by John Meston
Matt and Chester come upon a man shot in the back and suspect that the culprit is the men who have been trying (without success) to get him to sell his land. Guest stars include Vic Perrin, Lawrence Dobkin, Jack Kruschen, and John Dehner.

Hack Prine (7/5/54) Written by: John Meston
An old friend of Matt's, Hack Prine, arrives in Dodge and enjoy a happy reunion—however, Matt is unaware that Hack is now a hired killer and has been brought to Dodge to kill a man (but doesn't know that he is hired to kill Matt). Guest stars: Lawrence Dobkin, Vic Perrin, John Dehner and Harry Bartell.

Texas Cowboys (7/12/54) Written by John Meston
When a cowhand is murdered the town won't come forward to tell Matt who did it, so he takes the extreme stand of closing all the saloons and shops in Dodge until somebody comes forward. Guest stars include Harry Bartell, John Dehner, and Lawrence Dobkin.

The Queue (7/19/54) Written by John Meston
Two men cut off the pigtail on a Chinese immigrant, who tells Matt that he can only go home with dignity if he either gets the pigtail back or kills the men who stole it. Guest stars include Edgar Barrier, Lawrence Dobkin and John Dehner.
Note: Bill Conrad does a closing commercial for sponsor Chesterfields.

Matt for Murder (7/26/54) Written by John Meston
Matt is suspended when he is accused of shooting an unarmed man in cold blood. Wild Bill Hickok (played by John Dehner) comes to Dodge to escort Matt to his trial. Other guest stars include Vic Perrin and James Nusser.

No Indians (8/2/54) Written by John Meston
Matt suspects that it isn't Indians who are responsible for a series of raids that are being blamed on them—but actually white men. Joseph Kearns, Harry Bartell, Vic Perrin and Larry Dobkin guest star.

Joe Phy (8/9/54) Written by: John Meston
Matt and Chester travel to a small town to arrest a killer, but first have to contend with a bogus U.S. Marshal. Guest stars include Ralph Moody, Vic Perrin and John Dehner.

Mavis McCloud (8/16/54) Written by: John Meston
Mavis McCloud is on her way to Dodge to get married—there is even some speculation that she is on her way to marry Matt. But Mavis is a woman who harbors many secrets. Guest stars include Eleanore Tanin, Harry Bartell, and Sam Edwards.

Young Man with a Gun (8/23/54) Written by: John Meston
Matt kills a man in a gunfight and then the man's teenage brother comes to town to tell Matt that he will learn how to use a gun and when he does he will come back and kill Matt. Guest Stars include Sam Edwards, Lawrence Dobkin, Vivi Janiss, and John Dehner.

Obie Tater (8/30/54) Written by John Meston
An old prospector gets married to a young saloon gal. The speculation is that she wants to know where his gold is hidden. Among the guest stars are Joseph Kearns, Virginia Gregg and Vic Perrin.

Handcuffs (AKA The Promise) (9/6/54) Written by John Meston
A man claims that a corrupt sheriff framed him for murder and escapes from the Dodge jail with the intention of killing the man he believes framed him. Guest stars include Lawrence Dobkin, Jack Kruschen, John Dehner and Irene Tedrow.

Dooley Surrenders (9/13/54) Written by John Meston
A man believes that he killed another man and wants Matt to lock him up; however, Matt doesn't believe the man is guilty and wants to lure the true killer out in the open. Guest stars include Vic Perrin, James Nusser and Harry Bartell.

The F.U. (9/20/54) Written by John Meston
Matt has to apprehend the man who shot another man in the back following an argument. John Dehner and Lawrence Dobkin are among the guest stars.

The Helping Hand (9/27/54) Written by John Meston
Matt and Chester arrive just in time to prevent a lynching of an 18 year old suspected cattle thief. Matt then tries to help the young man. Sam Edwards, Lawrence Dobkin, Joe Cranston and John Dehner guest.

Matt Gets It (10/2/54) Written by John Meston
A gunfighter critically injures Matt in a show down and then runs wild in Dodge while Matt recuperates. Later, Matt challenges the man to another showdown.
Note: The show moved to Saturday nights with the airing of this episode. **Trivia:** This story was utilized a year later as the first episode of the *Gunsmoke* television series. Vic Perrin, John Dehner and Harry Bartell are among the guest stars.

Love of a Good Woman (10/9/54) Written by: John Meston
An old female friend of Doc's who is a nurse visits and he is happy that she is in Dodge and hopes she will stick around. Guest stars include Vivi Janiss, John Dehner and James Nusser.

Kitty Caught (10/16/54) Written by: John Meston
A gang of bank robbers head to Dodge and Kitty is taken hostage during the bank robbery. John Dehner, Lawrence Dobkin and Joe De Val guest star.

Ma Tennis (10/23/54) Written by: John Meston
A mother wielding a shot gun helps her son escape from the Dodge jail. Guest stars include Virginia Gregg, Lee Millar, Sam Edwards and Harry Bartell.

The Patsy (10/30/54) Written by: John Meston
A woman kills a man in a back alley and then blames another man, her patsy. Vic Perrin, Lawrence Dobkin and James Kruschen guest star.

Smoking Out the Beedles (11/6/54) Written by: John Meston
A man will do whatever it takes to get a family of squatters off his land. Lawrence Dobkin, Harry Bartell and Jeanette Nolan guest star.

Wrong Man (11/13/54) Written by: John Meston
A man shoots and kills an outlaw for the $1000 reward, but when he brings the body back to town he discovers he killed the wrong man. Guest stars include John Dehner, Vivi Janiss, Vic Perrin and Lawrence Dobkin.

How to Kill a Woman (11/20/54) Written by: John Meston
(This is a repeat of the 10/31/53 episode).

Cooter (11/27/54) Written by: John Meston
Matt exposes a gambler at cheating and in retaliation the gambler gives slow-thinking Cooter Smith a gun and begins a rumor that Cooter plans to challenge Matt to a gunfight. Guest stars include Vic Perrin, John Dehner and Harry Bartell.

Cholera (12/4/54) Written by: John Meston
A father and son are determined to run a family which has a spring well off their land, so they can have the well on the land. Guest stars include Ralph Moody, Sam Edwards, Virginia Christine, Clayton Post and Vic Perrin.

Bone Hunters (12/11/54) Written by: John Meston
Two men are fighting over a woman—and one of them is killed. Guest stars include John Dehner, Herb Ellis and Frank Katie.

Magnus (12/18/54) Written by: John Meston
Magnus, Chester's uncivilized mountain man brother, arrives in Dodge, and Chester decides to try and reform him—but Magnus might be more on the ball than Chester thinks. Guest stars include Robert Easton.

Kitty Lost (12/25/54) Written by: John Meston
Kitty is missing after last being seen the previous night on a buggy ride with some mysterious man from the East. John Dehner, James Nusser and Vic Perrin guest star.

Bottle Man (1/1/55) Written by: John Meston
A drunk seeks revenge on the man who stole his wife thirteen years before—an event that shattered his life and made him into a drunk. Eleanore Tanin, Lawrence Dobkin, Vic Perrin and Ralph Moody guest star.

Robin Hood (1/8/55) Written by: John Meston
A holdup man robs from the rich and leaves the poor basically alone, so they will not testify against him. Matt has to find a way to get them to give evidence. Guest stars include Larry Dobkin, Harry Bartell, Frank Cady and Helen Kleeb.

Chester's Murder (1/15/55) Written by John Meston
A drunkard that Chester is escorting to jail is shot dead in an ally and Chester is suspected of the crime. Guest stars include Vic Perrin, Lawrence Dobkin, James Nusser and Joyce McCluskey.

Sins of Our Fathers (1/22/55) Written by John Meston
The manager of a Dodge hotel wants a man and his wife evicted from his hotel because she is a Kiowa Indian. Lawrence Dobkin and Harry Bartell are among the guest stars.

Young Love (1/29/55) Written by John Meston
A man murders an aging rancher and then tries to steal the cattle from his much younger widow. Among the guest stars are Sam Edwards, Eleanore Tanin, Vic Perrin, Don Diamond and Frank Katie.

Cheyennes (2/5/55) Written by John Meston
Matt tries to help an Indian Chief track down the men who are supplying Cheyenne braves with rifles which had been used to murder homesteaders. Guest stars include Harry Bartell, Ralph Moody, Lawrence Dobkin and Vic Perrin.

Chester's Hanging (2/12/55) Written by John Meston
Matt arrests a man for robbery and murder. He orders his partner to get him out by any means or else he will make sure he is implicated too. Guest stars include Paul Dubov, Clayton Post, James Nusser and Joe Cranston.

Poor Pearl (2/19/55) Written by John Meston
A saloon girl receives marriage proposals from two men and also threats—if she turns either of them down they will do her harm. Virginia Christine, Vic Perrin and Harry Bartell guest star.

Crack-Up (2/26/55) Written by John Meston
A steely gunfighter arrives in Dodge intending to kill somebody, but the man seems increasingly nervous about this assignment—why? John Dehner and Harry Bartell guest star.

Kite's Reward (3/5/55) Written by John Meston
Matt takes away the gun of a young man who killed another man in a gunfight under the (false?) belief that nobody will challenge an unarmed man to a gunfight. Vic Perrin, Harry Bartell and Virginia Christine guest star.

The Trial (3/12/55) Written by John Meston
A store keeper wants a man jailed for stealing potatoes, but then he is accused of murder. Guest stars include Lawrence Dobkin, Vic Perrin, John Dehner and Harry Bartell.

The Mistake (3/19/55) Written by John Meston
A man who is accused of murder escapes from the Dodge jail—Matt finds evidence that he didn't do the crime, but must stop the man before he actually does commit a crime. Guest stars include: Lou Krugman, James Nusser, John Dehner.
Note: Ray Kemper, one of the key sound effects men on the show, plays a small part in this episode.

Horse Deal (3/26/55) Written by John Meston
There are shenanigans in Dodge when a man sells unbranded horses to buyers only to have another man come in to claim the horse. Guest stars include Harry Bartell, Vic Perrin James Nusser, Joe Cranston and Sam Edwards.

Bloody Hands (4/2/55) Written by John Meston
After Matt kills several members of an outlaw gang in self-defense he has a breakdown of sorts, thinking of all 'the blood on his hands'

from all the men he has killed over the years. Lawrence Dobkin and John Dehner guest star.

Skid Row (4/9/55) Written by John Meston
It's Matt and the gang to the rescue when an Eastern woman arrives in Dodge to visit her brother—the town drunk. Harry Bartell, Eleanore Tanin and Barney Phillips guest star.

The Gypsum Hills (4/16/55) Written by John Meston
Matt is fired upon and he and Chester investigate and find a feud between two mountain families. Guest stars include Vivi Janiss, John Dehner and Vic Perrin.

Born to Hang (4/23/55) Written by John Meston
A man is nearly killed by two men who try to lynch him. He gives Matt 24-hours to find the men who did this or else he will track them down and kill them himself. Guest stars include Joseph Kearns, Lawrence Dobkin and James Nusser.

Reward for Matt (4/30/55) Written by John Meston
Matt kills a man and his widow put out a bounty of $1000 to anybody who kills Matt. Guest stars include Jeanette Nolan, Sam Edwards and Helen Kleeb.

Potato Road (5/7/55) Written by John Meston
A family lures Matt and Chester out of town so the coast is clear so they can rob the Dodge bank. Guest stars include Vic Perrin, Virginia Gregg and John McIntire.

Robber Bridegroom (5/14/55) Written by: John Meston
A man robs a stage coach and at the same time abducts a passenger on her way to Dodge to marry an unscrupulous businessman who threatened her into marriage. Guest stars include: Jeanne Bates, Harry Bartell, Lawrence Dobkin and Clayton Post.

Liar from Blackhawk (5/21/55) Written by John Meston
A newcomer to Dodge goes around bragging about his reputation

as a gunman, but Matt suspects the man is lying. Guest stars include Vic Perrin, Paul Dubov, and Barney Phillips.

Cow Doctor (5/28/55) Written by John Meston
Doc has to try and treat a sick farmer who has always mistrusted doctors. Guest stars include Vivi Janiss, John Dehner, Sam Edwards and Tom Hanley.

Jealousy (6/4/55) Written by John Meston
A friend of Matt's, who is newly married, is driven to jealousy and possibly murder when a gambler starts rumors that Matt is courting the man's new wife. Guest stars include Don Diamond, Harry Bartell, Vic Perrin and Virginia Gregg.

Trust (6/11/55) Written by John Meston
(This episode is a virtual remake of "Overland Express")

Reed Survives (6/18/55) Written by Les Crutchfield
The wife of a wealthy ranch owner uses a man who works for his husband so that he will kill her husband. Guest stars include Michael Ann Berret, Edgar Barrier, Sam Edwards and Ralph Moody.

The Army Trial (6/25/55) Written by: Norman MacDonnell
Matt and Chester find a wagon with its wheel off—and inside an army deserter and his woman. Guest stars include Lawrence Dobkin, Vivi Janiss, Harry Bartell and James Nusser.

General Parsley Smith (7/2/55) Written by John Meston
A man who is known around town as a liar is vehement in telling the towns people that the new banker is a swindler. Guest stars include John Dehner, Joe Deval and Vic Perrin.

Uncle Oliver (7/9/55) Written by John Meston
A man arrives in Dodge with the intention of making his simple minded nephew the new deputy to Matt. Guest stars include Vic Perrin and Harry Bartell.

20/20 (7/16/55) Written by John Meston
An ex-lawman with fading eye-sight is the target of revenge from a man whose brother was killed two years earlier. Guest stars include Vic Perrin, Joe Cranston and James Nusser.

Ben Tolliver's Stud (7/23/55) Written by Norman MacDonnell
Trouble begins when a cowboy is fired by a trail boss, and takes a horse as a way to recover a loss of wages. Guest stars include Sam Edwards, Eleanore Tanin and James Nusser.

Tap Day for Kitty (7/30/55) Written by John Meston
Matt wonders if Kitty shot and wounded a man who tried to abduct her in hopes that he could force her to marry him. Guest stars include John Dehner, Michael Ann Berret and Virginia Gregg.

Innocent Broad (8/6/55)
A man is waiting for the stage bringing in his new bride from St. Louis when a man steps off of the stage who clearly intimidates him but yet the man tells Matt he has no idea who he is. Guest stars include Eleanore Tanin, Vic Perrin, Lawrence Dobkin and Paul DuBov.

Johnny Reb (8/13/55) Written by John Meston
A criminal named Johnny Reb arrives in Dodge posing as the long lost son of a widow. Among the guest stars are Sam Edwards, Virigina Gregg, Vic Perrin and Larry Dobkin.

Indian Scout (8/20/55) Written by John Dukel
An Indian scout for the army is accused of deliberately leading troops to a massacre. Guest stars include Lawrence Dobkin, Harry Bartell, Barney Phillips, and Joseph Kearns.

Doc Quits (8/27/55) Written by John Meston
When a homesteader that Doc has been treating dies and then a flashy new doctor with lots of 'modern' ideas arrives in town—Doc decides that he isn't needed any longer. Guest stars include Lawrence Dobkin, James Nusser, Frank Katie, Anne Morrison.

Change of Heart (9/3/55) Written by John Meston
Why would a man's new bride be so insistent that he leave a ranch that he inherited just six-months earlier? Guest stars include Sam Edwards, Virginia Christine, Vic Perrin and Joe Deval.

Alarm at Pleasant Valley (9/10/55) Written by John Dunkel
While on their way back to Dodge, Matt and Chester help homesteaders who are under Indian attack. Guest stars include Vic Perrin, Helen Keeb, Eleanore Tanin, Sam Edwards and John Dehner.

Throughbreds (9/17/55) Written by John Meston
Matt and Chester, low on water, run into a man with two horses who will not help him, yet when they run into him back in Dodge he is a totally new man—friendly and trusting—the life of the town. Why the change? Guest stars include Lawrence Dobkin, Harry Bartell and John Dehner.

Indian White (9/24/55) Written by Tom Manley and John Meston
A 12-year old Cheyenne boy is brought to Dodge as a prisoner and a woman insists its her son who was kidnapped years before. Guest stars include Sammy Ogg, Virginia Gregg, Joseph Kearns, Harry Bartell, John Dehner and Ralph Moody.

Barton Boy (10/1/55) Written by Les Crutchfield
When a baggage clerk aboard a Dodge bound train is killed and $20,000 stolen suspicion falls on young Billy Barton, despite the fact that he has been shot, too. Guest stars include Virginia Christine, Dick Beals and Lawrence Dobkin.

Good Girl-Bad Company (10/8/55) Written by John Meston
When an army payload is stolen suspicion somehow falls on a new girl in town being involved. Guest stars include Virginia Christine and John Dehner.

The Coward (10/9/55) Written by John Meston
A man sitting in Matt's chair is shot in the back by somebody believing it to be the marshal. Guest stars include Vic Perrin, John Dehner, and Jack Edwards.

Trouble in Kansas (10/16/55) Written by John Meston
A man comes to town bragging about all the people he has killed. Guest stars include Lawrence Dobkin, Barney Phillips and Harry Bartell.

Brush at Elkader (10/23/55) Written by John Meston
Matt must figure out a way to get the people of a small town to identify a psychotic murderer who has the people intimidated and afraid for their lives if they do so. Guest stars include Harry Bartell, Vic Parrin, Paul Dubov, and Lawrence Dobkin.

The Choice (10/30/55) Written by John Meston
Matt tries to help a young gunman who is trying to go straight and succeeds in getting him a job riding shot gun on a stage. Part one of two. Guest stars include Sam Edwards, Barney Phillips, Harry Bartell and Lawrence Dobkin.

The Second Choice (11/6/55) Written by John Meston
Part two of above episode.

The Preacher (11/13/55) Written by John Meston
A stage coach arrives in Dodge with on board two men with distinct personalities who are bound to clash: a loud braggart who says he can kill a man with his fists and a peace loving (seemingly) meek man who detests violence. Guest stars include John Dehner, Lawrence Dobkin and Joe Cranston.

Dutch George (11/20/55) Written by John Dunkel
Dutch George is a man who runs a horse theft operation—who has never been caught until he attempts to personally steal a horse himself instead of using others. Guest stars include John Dehner, Vic Perrin and James Nusser.

Amy's Good Deed (11/27/55) Written by John Meston
Amy is a woman who comes to Dodge and tells Matt she is "going to die." Matt suggests he gets Doc, but Amy has something else in mind—she wants Matt to kill her. Guest stars include Virginia Christine, John Dehner, and Ralph Moody.

Sunny Afternoon (12/4/55) Written by Les Crutchfield
It's a hard winter in Dodge and a farmer wants to buy some hay from a man who has more than enough, but isn't allowed to. John Dehner, Ralph Moody and Virginia Christine guest star.

Land Deal (12/11/55) Written by John Meston
A man brings immigrants out west with the offer of land—but it's a swindle since the man doesn't own the land—it belongs to the railroad. Guest stars include Lawrence Dobkin, Vivi Janiss, Vic Perrin and John Perrin.

Scared Kid (12/18/55) Written by John Meston
When a man insults a saloon gal, another man rises to defend her honor and ends up killing the man. Guest stars include Sam Edwards, Eleanore Tanin, John Dehner and Anne Morrison.

Twelfth Night (12/25/55) Written by John Meston
Basically the same plot as the 5/29/1954 episode.

Puckett's New Year (1/1/56) Written by John Meston
A man lost and crippled by the cold is rescued by Matt and Chester and tries to make a new life in Dodge. Ralph Moody and James Nusser guest star.

Doc's Revenge (1/8/56) Written by John Meston
A stranger arrives in Dodge and is recognized by Doc—who to the surprise of Matt and Chester vows to kill the man. What is their past history and why does Doc hate him so much? Guest stars include Vic Perrin and John Dehner.

The Bureaucrat (1/29/56) Written by John Meston
The War Department has been getting some bad reports about the situation in Dodge and are sending out an investigator. Who is making these bad reports and is Matt's job on the line? Guest Stars include Vic Perrin, John Dehner and Harry Bartell.

Legal Revenge (2/5/56) Written by John Meston
Doc finds things suspicious when he goes out to greet some newcomers

farming the land on the outskirts of town. He wants them to know there is a doctor available—the wife greets him rudely and tells him that her husband is out farming the land—Doc discovers that he is lying in bed with an infected leg—why doesn't she want him to get medical care? Helen Kleeb, Lawrence Dobkin and Stacy Harris guest star.

Kitty's Outlaw (2/12/56) Written by: John Meston
An old beau of Kitty's comes to Dodge, and she is wondering why he is acting so suspicious. It turns out he is in Dodge to rob the bank. Guest stars include Vic Perrin and Barney Phillips.

The New Hotel (2/19/56) Written by John Meston
A new hotel is being constructed which would put it in direct competition with the venerable Dodge House. Guest stars include Larry Dobkin, Vic Perrin Harry Bartell and John Dehner.

Who Lives by the Sword (2/26/56) Written by John Meston
A young man being bullied by bullied in the Long Branch is shot dead. Guest stars include John Dehner, Sam Edwards and Clayton Post.

The Hunter (03/04/56) Written by John Dunkel
A Buffalo Hunter who once left Matt for dead comes to Dodge. Guest stars include Sam Edwrds, Harry Bartell and Nestor Paiva.
Note: This was a rarity in that this episode actually aired first on television and then was recycled for the radio show.

Bringing Down Father (3/11/56) Written by John Meston
A leisurely day in Dodge is interrupted when a cowhand arrives in town and tells Matt there has been a shooting out on the prairie. Doc joins Matt and Chester and ride out to see what can be done to help the injured man. Matt is suspicious of the stories being told and suspects a dysfunctional family. Guest stars include Larry Dobkin and Vic Perrin.

The Man Who Would be Marshal (3/18/56) Written by John Meston
A man who deposits $50,000 in the Dodge bank thinks he can

force his way into being the new Dodge Marshal. Guest stars include John Dehner, Harry Bartell and James Nusser.

Hanging Man (3/25/56) Written by John Meston
An old man is found hanging by a rope in his hide shop. It is initially considered suicide but Matt is suspicious when a lump is found on the old man's head and money is missing. Guest stars include Larry Dobkin, John Dehner and Virginia Gregg.

How to Sell a Ranch (4/1/56) Written by John Meston
Why would a man be willing to buy a ranch for $15,000 which is being offered for sale for $10,000? Guest stars include Harry Bartell, Ralph Moody and Kathy Marlowe.

Widow's Mite (4/8/56) Written by John Meston
A widow remarries and soon afterward disappears. Guest stars include Virginia Christine and John Dehner.

The Executioner (4/15/56) Written by John Meston
A gunman provokes another man to draw and kills him—the killed man's brother vows revenge. Guest stars include John Dehner, Vic Perrin and Sam Edwards.

Indian Crazy (4/22/56) Written by John Meston
A couple moves to a ranch near Dodge and are assured by a neighboring rancher and Matt that there are no Indians around—but when the wife is killed by a seemingly Indian attack—the husband vows revenge on the neighboring rancher and Matt. Guest stars include Larry Dobkin and Helen Kleeb.

Doc's Reward (4/29/56) Written by John Meston
On his way to render aid to a sick patient, Doc's horse is shot away under him. Guest stars include Vic Perrin and John Dehner.

The Photographer (5/6/56) Written by John Dunkel
A self-proclaimed 'Artist of the Camera' is in Dodge to take pictures—and experience—the 'real west.' Guest stars include Larry Dobkin, Harry Bartell and James Nusser.

Cows and Cribs (5/13/56) Written by John Meston
A family that lives out on the prairie contracts spotted fever and Matt and Doc ride out to bring them back to town for treatment. The father and mother die before they get treated, but their baby is still alive. There seems to be more to the reason for the parents dying than originally meets the eye. Guest stars include Vic Perrin, Virginia Christine, Frank Cady, Jeanette Nolan and John Dehner.

Buffalo Man (5/20/56) Written by John Meston
Doc finds the headless body of a buffalo hunter near the river and goes to retrieve Matt and Chester who go out to investigate. Guest stars include Vic Perrin, John Dehner, Helen Kleeb and Larry Dobkin.

Man Hunter (5/27/56) Written by John Meston
A bounty hunting deputy comes to Dodge in search of man who has made many friends in Dodge—while Matt is sure that the man has had problems in his past—he is suspicious of the deputy who has come to town. Guest stars include Larry Dobkin and John Dehner.

The Pacifist (6/3/56) Written by John Meston
A peace loving man comes to town who only wants to be left alone, but soon there are two men after him who want to settle an old Civil War score with him. Guest stars include James Nusser, Vic Perrin, Harry Bartell and Paul DuBov.

Daddy-O (6/10/56) Written by John Meston
Nice show case for Georgia Ellis when Kitty's father, who she has never met before, comes to Dodge. John McIntire plays Wayne Russell, Kitty's father.

Cheap Labor (6/17/56) Written by John Meston
A man encounters more trouble than he would have expected for doing a good deed—he helps a woman load her wagon of supplies—and her hot head brother wants to kill him for it. Guest stars include Larry Dobkin, Vic Perrin, Harry Bartell and Barney Phillips.

Sunday Supplement (6/24/56) Written by John Meston
Two New York writers visit Dodge hoping for a real story about the

violent wild west—and are disappointed when things are sedate. They may soon regret coming altogether. Guest stars include Joseph Kearns, Harry Bartell and John Dehner.

Gun for Chester (7/1/56) Written by John Meston
Chester tells Matt that he is sure that a stranger in town plans to kill him—but Matt remains unconvinced while Chester moves to arm himself for protection. Lawrence Dobkin guest stars.

Passive Resistance (7/8/56) Written by John Meston
A man is forced to stand by when all his sheep (24 of them) are shot dead in front of him by cow hands. Guest stars include Ralph Moody, John Dehner and Harry Bartell.

Letter of the Law (7/15/56) Written by John Meston
A landowner who wants more land for himself forces Matt by the 'letter of the law' to evict a small rancher from his homestead when he discovers that the rancher didn't file the proper paperwork. Guest stars include Joseph Kearns, Vic Perrin and Helen Kleeb.

Lynching Man (7/22/56) Written by John Meston
A man takes the law into his own hands when he hangs a man who he suspects is a horse thief. Guest stars include Vic Perrin, Harry Bartell, James Nusser and Larry Dobkin.

Lost Rifle (7/29/56) Written by John Meston
A friend of Matt's is accused of shooting another man (who he has been feuding with) in the back. Matt is dubious and won't arrest him until he has more concrete evidence. Guest stars include John Dehner, Jack Kruschen and Vic Perrin.

Sweet and Sour (8/5/56) Written by John Meston
Trouble brews when a man forces his attention on a woman in town. Guest stars include Lynn Allen, Harry Bartell and Larry Dobkin.

Snakebite (8/12/56) Written by John Meston
A man takes revenge on another man who shot his dog dead. Guest stars include Jospeh Kearns, Vic Perrin and Larry Dobkin.

Annie Oakley (8/19/56) Written by John Meston
Why are some men fighting for the attentions of a homely middle-aged ranchers wife? Jeanette Nolan and Harry Bartell are among the guest stars.

No Sale (8/26/56) Written by John Meston
Two men make an offer to Kitty to buy the Long Branch—when they are told 'no sale' they won't take no for an answer. Guest stars include John Dehner, Vic Perrin, Lawrence Dobkin and Harry Bartell.

Old Pal (9/2/56) Written by Les Crutchfield
A man is killed for his payroll and the killers are thought to have left town—but have they? Guest stars include Lynn Allen, Tim Graham , John Dehner and Larry Dobkin.
Note: John Meston who had written the vast majority of previous *Gunsmoke* scripts becomes the series' story editor from this point forward.

Belle's Back (9/9/56) Written by Les Crutchfield
Belle returns to Dodge after a three year's absence—and the town shunts her as a 'bad' woman—given the circumstances of her leaving, but she vows she won't leave again and will take up residence on the family ranch. Virginia Christine, Sammie Hill, and Ralph Moody guest star.

Thick 'N' Thin (9/16/56) Written by Les Crutchfield
Two men who share a farm both want to evict the other. Guest stars include Vic Perrin, Peggy Rea and Barney Phillips.

Box O' Rocks (9/23/56) Written by Les Crutchfield
Why is Packy Roundtree's coffin empty at his funeral? Guest stars include Jospeh Kearsn, Paul DuBov and Ralph Moody.

The Brothers (9/30/56) Written by William Leicester
A former lawman turned gunman arrives in Dodge. Guest stars include Vic Perrin and Sam Edwards.

The Gambler (10/7/56) Written by John Dunkel
A riverboat gambler arrives in Dodge looking for a man he wants to kill. Guest stars include Larry Dobkin and Ralph Moody.

Gunshot Wound (10/14/56) Written by Gil Doud
A doctor tells a man that the gunshot wound he was inflicted with cannot be removed. He seems healthy until the bullet begins to move around in his body, so the man goes to Dodge to avenge his impending death by killing the men who shot him. Guest stars include Harry Bartell, Vic Perrin and Larry Dobkin.

'Til Death Do Us Part (10/21/56) Written by Les Crutchfield
A gunman is hired to kill a miserly old man in Dodge. Guest stars include John Dehner, Virginia Gregg, Ralph Moody and Don Diamond.

Dirty Bill's Girl (10/28/56) Written by Les Crutchfield.
A lady gambler arrives in Dodge and gets employment at the Long Branch. Guest stars include Virginia Chrisine, John Dehner and Vic Perrin.

Crowbait Bob (11/10/56) Written by Les Crutchfield
An old prospector draws up a will which leaves everything to Kitty. Guest stars include Ralph Moody, Larry Dobkin, and Virginia Gregg. **Note:** This episode was preempted on 11/4/56 and instead telecast on 11/10/56.

Pretty Mama (11/11/56) Written by Les Crutchfield
Was a rancher killed by a man who was giving too much attention to the rancher's pretty wife? Guest cast includes Jeanne Bates and John Dehner.

Brother Whelp (11/18/56) Written by Les Crutchfield
A man returns to Dodge finding that after being away for six years that his brother married the girl he was in love with. Guest stars include Vic Perrin and Larry Perrin.

Tail to the Wind (11/25/56) Written by Les Crutchfield
A father and son will go to any length to get a farmer's land including arson and the burning down of the farmer's chicken coop—yet the farmer is reluctant to have Matt get involved. Guest stars include John Dehner, Helen Kleeb, Ralph Moody.

Speak to Me Fair (12/2/56) Written by Les Crutchfield
An Indian boy suffers injustice and violence when his tongue is cut out. Guest stars include John Dehner, Harry Bartell and Vic Perrin.

Braggart's Boy (12/9/56) Written by Les Crutchfield
A young man from Philadelphia arrives in Dodge to meet his father for the first time. Guest stars include Sam Edwards, Larry Dobkin and John Dehner.

Cherry Red (12/16/56) Written by Les Crutchfield
A widow of a stagecoach robber is being courted by the man who killed her husband, though she is unaware of this fact. Guest stars include Sammie Hill, Vic Perrin and Bill Lally.

Beeker's Barn (12/23/56) Written by Les Crutchfield
Christmas episode—A young couple take refuge in her estranged father's barn—she is pregnant—the father wants Matt to evict them. Joseph Kearns and Ralph Moody are among the guest stars.

Hound Dog (12/30/56) Written by Les Crutchfield
An old and blind dog is shot and killed and the owner (naturally) wants revenge. Guest stars include John Dehner and Vic Perrin.

Devil's Hindmost (1/6/57) Written by Les Crutchfield
Chester is reading Shakespeare and observes that human behavior hasn't changed all that much in the last 250 years. Guest stars include Virginia Christine, Harry Bartell and Vic Perrin.

Ozymandias (1/13/57) Written by Les Crutchfield
Krager wants another man off his land, even though that little patch of land means little or nothing to him. Vic Perrin, John Dehner and Larry Dobkin guest star.

Categorical Imperative (1/20/57) Written by Les Crutchfield
Matt and Chester ride in a blizzard to try and capture an escaped prisoner—the problem is that the prisoner was probably going to be turned loose anyway. Guest stars include John Dehner and Ben Wright.

Woman Called Mary (1/27/57) Written by Les Crutchfield
An older woman nicknamed "Buffalo Mary" is beat up and robbed by a man, and when he turns up at the Long Branch, Matt decides to give him some of his own medicine. Virginia Gregg and Vic Perrin guest star.

Cold Fire (2/3/57) Written by Les Crutchfield
A mother cannot believe that her son, a respected banker, actually would steal $2000 in gold and then resist arrest which leads to his death. Helen Kleeb, Sam Edwards and Harry Bartell guest star.

Hellbent Harriet (2/10/57) Written by Les Crutchfield
Matt has to deliver the sad news that Harriet's husband is dead—kicked by a horse—later he wonders if there is more to his death than meets the eye. Guest stars include John Dehner and Virginia Christine.

Doubtful Zone (2/17/57) Written by Les Crutchfield
A teenage girl runs away from her abusive home life and ends up making her way by committing robberies. Sammie Hill, Larry Dobkin and Ben Wright guest star.

Impact (2/24/57) Written by Les Crutchfield
An old woman who owns a ranch has a series of near life and death misses and Matt begins to wonder if the ranch foreman who is named in her will as next of kin may have something to do with it. Guest stars include Ben Wright and Sam Edwards.

Colleen so Green (3/3/57) Written by Les Crutchfield
A beautiful southern belle charms many of the men in Dodge, but she isn't fooling Kitty. Guest stars include Jeanne Bates, Ben Wright and John Dehner.

Grebb Hassle (3/10/57) Written by Les Crutchfield
A man named Grebb that Matt ran out of Dodge two years earlier telling him never to return—comes back and this time Matt is determined not to give him another chance. Guest stars include Sam Edweards, Vic Perrin and Vivi Janiss.

Spring Freshet (3/17/57) Written by Les Crutchfield
Two notorious outlaws wanted in over a half-dozen states for robbery and murder come to Dodge. John Dehner, Larry Dobkin and Ben Wright guest star.

Saddle Sore Sal (3/24/57) Written by Les Crutchfield
When Matt and Chester investigate gun fire they are surprised to find it coming from a woman who won't tell them who or what it was she was shooting at. Guest stars include Virginia Gregg and Vic Perrin.

Chicken Smith (3/31/57) Written by Les Crutchfield
"Chicken Smith" is accused of starting a fight, but Matt is dubious. While Chicken Smith is a chicken farmer—he is also known to be a notorious coward. Larry Dobkin, John Dehner and Virginia Christine guest star.

Rock Bottom (4/7/57) Written by Les Crutchfield
A gunfighter who gave up his guns two years earlier and settled in Dodge has been keeping his pledge to avoid gunfights until a man from his past who wants to kill him arrives in Dodge. Guest stars include Harry Bartell, Jeanne Bates and Barney Phillips.

Saludos (4/14/57) Written by Les Crutchfield
Matt is escorting three men back to Dodge where they have to wait for a wounded Indian woman to identify which one of them killed her husband and shot her. Guest stars include John Dehner, Larry Dobkin and Jim Nusser.

Bear Trap (4/21/57) Written by Les Crutchfield
A man who spent nearly two years in prison returns to Dodge where the man who identified him as a bank robber worries that he has returned to do him harm. Ralph Moody guest stars.

Medicine Man (4/28/57) Written by Les Crutchfield
A medicine man arrives in Dodge selling a tonic that is supposed to cure all sorts of ailments, but in actuality it is 100 proof alcohol and the saloon keeper doesn't take kindly to this competition. Guest stars include John Dehner, Vic Perrin and Virginia Gregg.
Note: This is the fifth anniversary show and William Conrad takes time off at the end to thank the audience for hanging in with them. "We tried for as much truth as good drama will allow," he tells the audience. There is also a plug for Conrad's new film with Anthony Quinn, *The Long Ride*.

How to Kill a Friend (5/5/57) Written by John Meston
This is a repeat of the 10/3/53 episode

Sheep Dog (5/12/57) Written by Les Crutchfield
Matt rides out to a ranch to arrest a man, but his bible thumping father refuses to give his son up.

One Night Stand (5/19/57) Written by Les Crutchfield
A man arrives in Dodge with $15,000 in gold and two men on his tracks.

Pal (5/26/57) Written by Tom Hanley
A stray dog who was poisoned is found and taken care of by Chester, however, Matt tells Chester he can't keep him as the dog belongs to a local rancher. Chester is too attached to the dog and believes the dog is being abused.
Note: The script writer, Tom Hanley, was, along with Ray Kemper, one of the key sound men on Gunsmoke.

Ben Tolliver's Stud (6/2/57) Written by Norman MacDonnell
Rebroadcast of 7/23/55 episode—for the first time in the series run much of the summer product will be rebroadcasts of past shows.

Dodge Podge (6/9/57) Written by Les Crutchfield
There is a feud between a cattle man and sheep herder, but the cattle man's son finds himself admiring the sheep herder causing family disharmony.

Summer Night (6/16/57) Written by Tom Hanley
A wagon train making its way thru Dodge leaves behind a small package: a baby girl.

Home Surgery (6/23/57) Written by John Meston
(See 9/13/52 episode)

The Buffalo Hunter (6/30/57) Written by John Meston
(See 5/9/53 episode)

Word of Honor (7/7/57) Written by John Meston
(See 7/3/54 episode)

Bloody Hands (7/14/57) Written by John Meston
(See 4/2/55 episode)

Kitty Caught (7/21/57) Written by John Meston
(See 10/16/54 episode)

Cow Doctor (7/28/57) Written by John Meston
(See 5/28/55 episode)

Big Hands (8/4/57) Written by Les Crutchfield
A woman brings her murdered husband's body into Dodge and is looking for a man with 'big shoulders' as the man who killed him. Vic Perrin is in the cast.

Jayhawkers (8/11/57) Written by John Meston
(See 4/4/53 episode)

Peace Officer (8/18/57) Written by Norman MacDonnell
Matt exposes a sheriff of another town as being crooked and the now ex-sheriff vows revenge.

Grass (8/25/57) Written by John Meston
(See 7/11/53 episode)

Jobe's Son (9/1/57) Written by Marian Clark
A young man returns to Dodge to help his sick father—in hopes that his presence will help him regain his health. Vic Perrin and John Dehner are among the guest stars.

Looney McCluny (9/8/57) Written by Les Crutchfield
An old prospector comes to Dodge sure he has found gold—but it turns out to be only fool's gold—well, that is what it is thought until the old man is found murdered. Guest stars include Virginia Gregg and Larry Dobkin.

Child Labor (9/15/57) Written by Robert Mitchell
Matt befriends two orphan boys who are hired at a ranch owned by a man who isn't above breaking the boys as well as horses.

Custer (9/22/57) Written by John Meston
(See 11/21/53 episode)

Another Man's Poison (9/29/57) Written by Les Crutchfield
A woman runs into her former husband—a man she thought had died at sea many years earlier—and she has remarried. Vic Perrin is among the guest stars.

The Rooks (10/6/57) Written by Marian Clark
Two brothers arrive in Dodge and start fights all over town—meanwhile a sick Matt must investigate when they shoot and kill a man. Vic Perrin, Harry Bartell, Larry Dobkin and Don Diamond are among the guest stars.

The Margin (10/13/57) Written by Les Crutchfield
A young man is accused by the daughter of a cattle rancher of rustling her father's cattle, but the girl won't testify against him. Vic Perrin and John Dehner are among the guests.

Professor Lute Bone (10/20/57) Written by John Meston
(See 11/14/53 episode)

Man and Boy (10/27/57) Written by Les Crutchfield
A deputy from California arrives in Dodge looking for an outlaw. Matt offers to help but the young lawman turns down his offer.

Bull (11/3/57) Written by Robert Mitchell
Bull is a buffalo hunter who comes to Dodge to let off a little steam and gets into a fight with another man. When the other man is found dead—suspicion is automatically set on Bull. John Dehner and Sam Edwards guest star.

Gun Shy (11/10/57) Written by Marian Clark
A young man is fired from a job on a ranch because he is incompetent as a cowhand.

The Queue (11/17/57) Written by John Meston
(See 7/19/54 episode)

Odd Man Out (11/24/57) Written by Les Crutchfield
An old man reports to Matt that his wife of nearly forty years has left him, but Matt smells a rat when a drifter is found selling the old woman's clothes. Guest stars include John Dehner, Harry Bartell and Larry Dobkin.

Jud's Woman (12/1/57) Written by Marion Clark
Matt and Chester are caught in a storm out on the prairie and seek refuge at a cabin by a gun-toting and obviously scared woman.

Long as I Live (12/8/57) Written by Les Crutchfield
Doc is shot and badly hurt but still conscious enough to talk Matt thru an operation to remove the bullet. John Dehner guest stars.

Ugly (12/15/57) Written by Robert Mitchell
A man who was deformed as a youth comes to Dodge and the citizens are repulsed by his appearance. When he saves a woman from a wolf attack she instead insists that he tried to attack her. John Dehner and Vic Perrin guest star.

Twelfth Night (12/22/57) Written by John Meston
(See 12/25/55 episode)

Where'd They Go (12/29/57) Written by Les Crutchfield
A man is accused of robbing the general store, even though he wasn't actually seen by a witness but the store owner is sure it was him because he recognized his voice. Guest stars include Joseph Kearns, Virginia Gregg and Ralph Moody.

Pucket's New Year (1/5/58)
Rerun of 1/1/1956 episode.

Second Son (1/12/58) Written by Marion Clark
An Englishman loses his horse in a poker game to a gambler and works hard to learn how to play effective poker to win the horse back. John Dehner, Vic Perrin and Ben Wright guest star.

Moo Moo Raid (1/19/58) Written by Les Crutchfield
There is a cow that has the ability to lead a herd of cattle through water safely and both cow and owner disappear. John Dehner and Vic Perrin guest star.

One for Lee (01/26/58) Written by Les Crutchfield
A Senator visiting Dodge is the target of an assassin. John Dehner guest stars.

Kitty's Killing (2/2/58) Written by Marian Clark
A religious fanatic (John Dehner) wants to kill the man who was married to his sister—who died in childbirth—when the man's new wife is expecting a baby.

Joke's On Us (2/9/58)
Rerun of 9/1/54 episode.

Bruger's Folly (2/16/58) Written by Les Krutchfield
A man named Bruger is released from prison after serving three years for a murder he didn't commit—and discovers that his wife has divorced him and is planning to marry another man.

The Surgery (2/23/58) Written by Marian Clark
A woman needs an operation but her husband (John Dehner) won't allow Doc to perform it—the woman is sure to die without it.

The Guitar (3/2/58)
Rerun of 12/23/53 episode.

Laughing Gas (3/9/58) Written by James Fonda and Norman Macdonnell
A former gunfighter now runs a medicine show—he vows to his wife to stay clear of gunfights, but three men who are harassing him make it a difficult promise to keep. Vic Perrin, John Dehner and Ralph Moody guest stars.

Real Sent Sonny (3/16/58) Written by Les Crutchfield
A young man tries to kill Matt and Matt wants to find out who put him up to the job.

Indian (3/23/53) Written by Les Crutchfield
While out in the prairie Matt and Chester find an Indian who has been murdered—it was such a brutal killing that when Matt recounts it at the Long Branch it is difficult for him to do so, and is not amused when a man overhearing the story finds it all so funny.

Why Not (3/30/58) Written by Les Crutchfield
A man (John Dehner) arrives in Dodge searching for his runaway daughter.

Yorky (4/6/58)
Rerun.

Livvie's Loss (4/13/58) Written by Marian Clark
A no-gooder returns to his long suffering wife (Jeanette Nolan) and has a bad influence on their son. John Dehner and Vic Perrin also guest.

The Partners (4/20/58) Written by John Dunkel.
Two men who run a "William Tell" show and depend on each other to stay safe during a performance have a falling out over a woman

(Virginia Christine). Other guest stars include James Nusser, John Dehner, Sam Edwards and Barney Phillips.

The Squaw (4/27/58) Written by John Dunkel.
A fight breaks out when one man calls another man who has married an Indian woman a 'Squaw man'. Guest stars include Vic Perrin, Richard Crenna, Ralph Moody, Lillian Buyeff and Frank Cady.

Little Bird (5/11/58) Written by Les Crutchfield
A big, ornery buffalo hunter arrives in Dodge with a beautiful young woman (Lillian Buyeff) who is plainly frightened, but unbeknownst is married to another man and was kidnapped by the buffalo hunter—who claims that she is his wife. John McIntire and Harry Bartell also guest.

The Stallion (5/18/58) Written by Marian Clark
A man borrows money from another man, but when the son takes over his father's business the son demands that the loan be paid back immediately. Unable to do so, the borrower's prized horse is taken for payment. Larry Dobkin, Ralph Moody and James Nusser guest star.

Blue Horse (5/25/58) Written by Marian Clark
Matt's horse stumbles and falls injuring itself and Matt. Chester has to put the horse down and then leave the injured Matt with a prisoner while he rides back to Dodge to get Doc. Harry Bartell, Richard Crenna and Vic Perrin guest star.

Quarter-Horse (6/1/58)
Rerun.

Hot Horse Hyatt (6/8/58) Written by Les Crutchfield
A group of men want to lynch another man they think is a horse thief—Matt stops it and and then has to figure out if the man is an actual horse thief or not. Guest stars include John Dehner, Jack Moyles and Richard Beals.

Old Flame (6/15/58) Written by Marian Clark
An old girlfriend (Jeanne Bates) of Matt's arrives in Dodge claiming that she is running away from her abusive husband. Kitty is dubious. Is she jealous or does she really see thru this 'old flame'? John Dehner and Joseph Kearns also guest.

Target (6/22/58) Written by Les Crutchfield
A group of gypsies camp on the land of a rancher who wants them off. Tommy Cook, Ralph Moody and John Dehner guest star.

What the Whiskey Drummer Heard (6/29/58)
Rerun.

Chester's Choice (7/6/58) Written by Marian Clark
Chester overhears two men plotting to rob the Dodge bank—they discover him and vow to kill Doc and Kitty unless he helps them carry out their plan. Larry Dobkin, Jess Kirkpatrick and Harry Bartell guest star.

The Proving Kid (7/13/58) Written by Les Crutchfield
A young man turns unwanted attention towards Kitty resulting in Matt humiliating him. The man seeks revenge against Matt. Virginia Christine, John Dehner and Vic Perrin guest star.

Marshal Proudfoot (7/20/58) Written by Tom Hanley
Chester's father visits Dodge and has the impression that Chester is the marshal and Matt works for him. John Dehner guest stars. **Note:** Another script written by sound man, Hanley.

The Cast (7/27/58)
Rerun

Miguel's Daughter (8/3/58) Written by Marian Clark
A young Mexican woman is harassed by two cowboys. Her father seeks revenge and it's up to Matt to get to the cowboy's first before the father does. The guest stars include Lynn Allen, Richard Crenna, Vic Perrin and Larry Dobkin.

A House Ain't A Home (8/10/58) Written by Les Crutchfield
An old man who generally keeps to himself is at the Long Branch with a gun and seems to be waiting for somebody. Guest stars include Vic Perrin, John Dehner, Ralph Moody and Sammie Hill.

The Piano (8/17/58) Written by Marian Clark
Matt and Chester are in pursuit of a killer who stole $20,000 from a stagecoach. They stop for help at the home of a bitter old southern woman (Virginia Gregg) who is reluctant to be of service. Why? Vic Perrin also guests.

The Blacksmith (8/24/58)
Rerun

I Thee Wed (8/31/58) Written by Les Crutchfield
The wife (Virginia Christine) of a wife beater testifies against her husband and then when he is locked up she bails him out. John Dehner and Harry Bartell also appear.

Tried It—Didn't Like It (9/7/58) Written by Les Crutchfield
A man seeks Matt's help to stop a 12-year old from taking shots at the man's prized turkeys. Jeanne Bates plays the kid's mother. Vic Perrin and Richard Beals also guest.

False Witness (9/14/58) Written by Marian Clark
A young man is found guilty of murder thanks to an eye witness who seems to enjoy the limelight. Matt finds out that this man has testified at several other trials that have winded up with somebody being convicted and hung for murder. Sam Edwards, Harry Bartell and James Nusser guest star.

Big Lost Girl (9/21/58)
Rerun

Kitty's Rebellion (9/28/58) Written by Marian Clark
The brother of a childhood friend of Kitty's comes to Dodge for a visit and is surprised to find Kitty, who he always thought proper and respectable, running a saloon and tries to rescue her—she tries

to keep him from being killed by some of the roughians who think he is too much of a dandy. Sam Edwards, John Dehner and Vic Perrin guest star.

Tag, You're It (10/5/58) Written by Les Crutchfield
A gunfighter rides into Dodge and citizens wonder who his intended victim might be. Virginia Christine, Vic Perrin and Richard Crenna guest star.

Doc's Showdown (10/12/58) Written by Marian Clark
Doc tries to save the life of a young man who was shot in the back—the boy doesn't reveal the shooter before he dies so Doc comes up with a plan to bring the culprit out in the open. Helen Kleeb, Sam Edwards, Irene Andres, Lawrence Dobkin and John Dehner guest star.

Kick Me (10/19/58)
Rerun

The Tragedian (10/26/58) Written by Les Crutchfield
A down on his luck Shakespearian actor arrives in Dodge who Matt takes a liking to—before he finds out that the man is also a card shark. John Dehner, James Nusser, James Westerfield and Vic Perrin guest star.

Old Man's Gold (11/2/58) Written by Marian Clark
A couple who are heading west to seek a cure for the wife stop in Dodge because the wife becomes deathly ill and needs a doctor. Meanwhile the husband entrusts a suitcase of all their 'valuables' to Matt. John Dehner and Harry Bartell are among the guest stars.

Target: Chester (11/9/58) Written by Marian Clark
Two cowboys decide to have some fun by bullying the town drunk. When Matt intervenes and one of the cowboys is injured his partner plots revenge by tricking Matt into shooting Chester. Larry Dobkin, Vic Perrin, John Dehner and Sam Edwards guest star.

Brush at Elkader (12/16/58)
Rerun

The Correspondent (11/23/58) Written by Marian Clark
A newspaper man from the big city of St. Louis arrives in Dodge to find out information about a recent stagecoach hold up. Harry Bartell, Larry Thor and Sam Edwards guest star.

Burning Wagon (11/30/58) Written by Marian Clark
Matt and Chester come upon a wagon which is on fire and then as they approach they find out that there are cartridges inside the wagon. Virginia Gregg, Larry Dobkin and Tom Hanley (one of the key sound men on *Gunsmoke*) guest star.

The Grass Asp (12/7/58) Written by Les Crutchfield
Some rowdy cowboys again invade Dodge, Matt is inclined to let them blow off some steam, but then a woman is found dead and one of the cowboy's is blamed. Vic Perrin, Harry Bartell and James Nusser guest star.

Kitty's Injury (12/14/57) Written by Marian Clark
Matt and Kitty are miles outside of Dodge when Kitty's horse throws her and she is badly injured and Matt has to figure out a way to get her the help she needs. John Dehner, Vic Perrin and Jeanne Bates guest star.

Where'd They Go? (12/21/58)
Rerun

The Choice (12/28/58)
Rerun

The Coward (1/4/59)
Rerun

The Wolfer (1/11/59) Written by John Dunkel
A rancher hires a man to do away with the pack of wolves on his land—the man hired, "A Wolfer" insists that there is no pack—just

one wolf. Guest stars include Larry Dobkin, Vic Perrin and Tom Hanley.

Kangaroo (1/18/59) Written by John Meston
Matt and Chester come upon two young men whipping another man. Chester unleashes the whipped man and religious fanatic vows revenge. Soon afterward Chester is arrested and put on trial in a kangaroo court. Guest stars include Joseph Kearns, Sam Edwards and Harry Bartell.

The Boots (1/25/59) Written by John Meston
A twelve year old boy hero worships the town drunk, but a gunman tells the drunken man that if he doesn't help rob the Dodge store he will tell the boy the true story of how the man became a down and out drunk. Larry Dobkin, Richard Beals and Vic Perrin guest star.

The Bobsy Twins (2/1/59) Written by John Meston
Two elderly, but deranged, brothers ride into Dodge looking for Indians to kill. Joseph Kearns, Jeanne Bates, James Nusser, Ralph Moody and Sam Edwards guest star.

Groat's Grudge (2/8/59) Written by Marian Clark
A former Confederate soldier arrives in Dodge with a mission—to kill a former Yankee he blames for his wife's death during the war. Harry Bartell, Frank Cady, Larry Dobkin and Jess Kirkpatrick guest star.

Body Snatch (2/15/59) Written by Marian Clark
A new doctor from the East arrives in town with new ideas of how to do things, and makes it clear that he thinks that Doc's methods are behind the times. Not only that, but to keep up on the times it appears the new doctor may be a body snatcher. Guest stars include Jack Moyles, James Musser, Howard Culver and Vic Perrin.

Sarah's Search (2/22/59) Written by Marian Clark
Matt and Chester find a buggy by the side of the road—containing a spinster who is looking for the man who spurned her. Vic Perrin and Anne Morrison guest star.

Big Town (3/1/59) Written by Marian Clark
A former prize fighter is challenged to a fight—but after a medical examination by Doc, the ex-fighter is told that a fight might kill him.

Maw Hawkins (3/8/59) Written by Tom Hanley.
Maw Hawkins (Jeanette Nolan) is a devoted mother who wants her son to follow the footsteps of his father and rob a stagecoach. Other guest stars include Sam Edwards and Vic Perrin.

Incident at Indian Ford (3/15/59) Written by John Dunkel
Troops 'rescue' a woman from the Arapahoes—the woman reveals that she was actually kidnapped by Cheyennes who sold her to the Arapahoes, but insists that in the time she was with them they never mistreated or laid a hand on her. Guest stars include Jeanne Bates, Vic Perrin and Jack Moyles.

The Trial (3/22/59)
Rerun

Laurie's Suitor (3/29/59) Written by Marian Clark
Two cowboys ride into Dodge for a night of fun—when one of the men discovers that his 'girl' is making time with an Eastern gambler. Eleanore Barry, Same Edwards, Larry Dobkin, and Vic Perrin guest star.

Trapper's Revenge (4/5/59) Written by John Dunkel
A man is left for dead by his partner after being attacked by a grizzly bear—he crawled for days on his hands and knees with only one thing on his mind—revenge. Vic Perrin, Ralph Moody and Larry Dobkin guest star.

Chester's Mistake (4/12/59) Written by Marian Clark
Chester fouls up on a simple assignment from Matt and becomes the laughing stock of the town—and intends to redeem himself.

Third Son (4/19/59) Written by Marian Clark
A young man who makes a ruckus in town is released into custody

of his father—who has lost two previous sons, and wants to make sure that this one stays alive. Sam Edwards, Ralph Moody and Barney Phillips guest star.

The Badge (4/26/59) Written by Marian Clark
A young man notices Matt's badge and believes that if he wears it he will get the respect that is denied him—he will do what he can to get the badge even shoot Matt.

Unwanted Deputy (5/3/59) Written by Marian Clark
A man whose brother was brought to justice by Matt offers Matt his assistance as a deputy which Matt turns down, so the man decides to act as a pseudo deputy and turn the town against Matt. Guest stars include Vic Perrin, Paul DuBov and Jeanne Bates.

Dowager's Visit (5/10/59) Written by Marian Clark
The widow of a former U.S. Senator arrives in Dodge to seek her grandson. Jeanette Nolan, Sam Edwards, Vic Perrin and Joseph Kearns guest star.

Scared Boy (5/17/59) Written by Marian Clark
A boy and his mother witness a murder and they are threatened by the culprit if they say anything. Guest stars include Larry Dobkin, Virginia Christine, Richard Beals and Ben Wright.

Wagon Show (5/24/59) Written by Tom Hanley
A circus arrives in Dodge which causes a great deal of excitement with the townspeople, but not so much with Matt who knows that in the last town the circus played in caused the death of two people. Ralph Moody, Jeanette Nolan, Vic Perrin and James Nusser guest star.

The Deserter (5/31/59) Written by Marian Clark
A soldier and another man steal from the army—The soldier is wounded in the robbery and they seek refuge at the home of his parents, who take on Chester and Matt in an attempt to help their son. Virginia Christine, Joseph Kearns, Vic Perrin and Ben Wright guest star.

Doc's Indian (6/7/59) Written by Marian Clark
Doc and Kitty are captured by Indians—whose chief wants Doc to try and save his sick son. Guest stars include Harry Bartell, Larry Dobkin, James Nusser and Howard Culver.

Kitty's Kidnap (6/14/59) Written by Marian Clark
Matt and Chester save a man from a lynching—a man whose wanted in three other states for murder. The man is wanted by others and Kitty is kidnapped in an attempt to get Matt to release the man. Harry Bartell, Vic Perrin, Ken Lynch and James Nusser guest star.

Carmen (6/21/59)
Rerun

Jailbait Janet (6/28/59)
Rerun

Emma's Departure (7/5/59) Written by Marian Clark
A couple farm out on the prairie with little human contact—which is just the way the husband likes it—but his wife relishes human contact and welcome Matt and Chester when they stop by along the way of picking up a prisoner. Later her husband is found murdered and their money is missing. Virginia Christine, Harry Bartell and Larry Dobkin guest star.

Friend's Payoff (7/12/59) Written by Marian Clark
A boy arrives for a message for Matt and he leaves immediately not even giving an explanation to Chester—it seems that an old friend was shot in the back. Joseph Kearns, Larry Dobkin, Barney Phillips and Richard Beals guest star.

Second Arrest (7/19/59) Written by Marian Clark
A man is on trial for stealing horses, when the man whose horses were stolen fails to show up for trial, the judge has to release the suspected horse thief. Frank Cady, Jeanette Nolan, Vic Perrin and Larry Dobkin guest star.

Old Beller (7/26/59) Written by Marian Clark
Doc is called out to aid what he thinks is a sick cowboy on a cattle drive, but the sick party turns out to be a prized steer. Guest stars include Harry Bartell, Ken Lynch and Ralph Moody.

Ball Nine, Take Your Base (8/2/59) Writen by Vic Perrin
Doc is umpire in a baseball game between the citizens of Dodge and a professional team from the East. Guest stars include Ralph Moody, Joseph Kearns, Sam Edwards, Harry Bartell and Vic Perrin.
Note: The long time stock company player, Vic Perrin, got a chance to write this episode.

Marvis McCloud (8/9/59)
Rerun

Pokey Pete (8/16/59) Written by Marian Clark
A simple minded, partly crippled old man is made fun of by the local children, but he never loses his temper with them. Chester tries to stop one boy from tormenting the old man by telling him that the man has buried gold and the boy believes him—and so do two thieves who happen to be listening. Guest stars include Vic Perrin, Barney Phillips, Jeanne Bates and Richard Beals.

The Reed Survives (8/23/59)
Rerun

Shooting Stopover (8/30/59) Written by Marian Clark
Matt and Chester are escorting a prisoner to Wichita by stage and at a station stop along the way they are attacked by bandits. Guest stars include Harry Bartell, Vic Perrin, Jeanne Bates, and Barney Phillips.

Matt's Decision (9/6/59) Written by Marian Clark
Matt has had enough! A lot of pity problems come his way and he begins to think about a life apart from being the Marshal of Dodge. A man comes forward with an opportunity that would take him away from being a lawman and away from Dodge. Guest stars include Vic Perrin, Ben Wright, Virginia Christine, Joseph Kearns and Larry Dobkin.

Johnny Reb (9/13/59)
Rerun

Gentleman's Disagreement (9/20/59)
Rerun

Personal Justice (9/27/59) Written by Marian Clark
Matt and Chester take a suspected woman killer to Wichita for trial, and are met by the man's brother who tells Matt that if his brother is hung the marshal will die. Jack Moyles, Harry Bartell and Vic Perrin guest star.

Hinka-Do (10/4/59)
Rerun

Kitty's Quandary (10/11/59) Written by Marian Clark
It seems to Matt that Kitty is being taken in by a no-gooder. Matt is right as the man and his partner rob the Dodge bank. Vic Perrin, Larry Dobkin and Harry Bartell guest star.

The Mortgage (10/18/59)
Rerun

Old Gunfighter (10/25/59) Written by Marian Clark
An old man who tells tall tales about a notorious gunfighter annoy a group of men who don't want to coddle the man and call the old man out—and the old man decides to take them on in a gunfight—is the old man the gunfighter that he was always telling these tall tales about? Guest stars include Ralph Moody, Sam Edwards, Vic Perrin, Jack Moyles and Dick Beals.

Westbound (11/1/59)
Rerun

Cavalcade (11/8/59)
Rerun

The Square Triangle (11/15/59)
Rerun

Paid Killer (11/22/59)
Rerun

Hard Lesson (11/29/59) Written by Marian Clark
A man returns to the family ranch with an injury that he feels only his mother's 'healing' touch can cure—only to be told that his mother died a year earlier. Larry Dobkin, Vic Perrin, Sam Edwards, and Harry Bartell guest star. Note: Georgia Ellis went by the name of Georgia Hawkins on this and a few other episodes for the next several months.

Big Chugg Wilson (11/6/59) Written by Ray Kemper
A saloon gal tries to make a young cowboy jealous enough to ask her to marry him by giving her attentions to a big, hardned buffalo hunter—who takes her attention seriously. Guest stars include Virginia Christine, Barney Phillips, Larry Dobkin and James Nusser. Note: yet another episode written by soundman Kemper.

Don Matteo (12/13/59) Written by Marian Clark
An old friend of Matt's comes to Dodge seeking his help tracking down a man who hurt his woman and now must be found and punished. Don Diamond, Vic Perrin, Barney Phillips and James Nusser guest star.

Beeker's Barn (12/20/59)
Rerun

Pucket's New Year (12/27/59)
Rerun

Trojan War (1/3/60)
Rerun

Luke's Law (1/10/60) Written by Marian Clark
An old man refuses Matt to intervene when he is savagely beaten by another man—instead he wants to handle it in his own way. Richard Crenna, Larry Dobkin and Ralph Moody guest star.

Fiery Arrest (1/17/60) Written by Marian Clark
Matt and Chester take refuge in a cabin during a storm—not knowing that the cabin is the hide-out of two bank robbers—one of whom think that his wife is the one who sent for the law. Guest stars include Jeanne Bates, Vic Perrin, Harry Bartell and Sam Edwards.

Bless Me Till I Die (1/24/60) Written by Ray Kemper
A married couple settles in Dodge, and soon run into trouble including a man who informs Matt that the husband is an escapee from an Arizona prison. Virginia Christine, Larry Dobkin, Harry Bartell and Ralph Moody guest star.

Chester's Dilemma (1/31/60) Written by Vic Perrin
Chester becomes infatuated with a young woman whose affections are not returned. John Dehner, Barbara Eiler, Joseph Kearns and Vic Perrin guest star.

Delia's Father (2/7/60) Written by Marian Clark
Chester and Matt capture a criminal while on their way to Hayes City and during a storm take refuge at the house of Delia, who welcomes Matt warmly because she recalls him as a good friend of her late father's—unaware that Matt was partly responsible for her father's death. Guest stars include Virginia Christine and Larry Dobkin.

Distant Drummer (2/14/60) Written by Marian Clark
Two men decide to terrorize an army drummer, who is feeble minded, who proudly walks around Dodge with his drum—proud of his earlier service to the army. Vic Perrin, Joseph Kearns, Harry Bartell and James Nusser guest star.

Mr. and Mrs. Amber (2/21/60)
Rerun

Prescribed Killing (2/28/60) Written by Marian Clark
A woman is put thru misery by her wandering husband and decides to get even by planning her own death and having her husband blamed for it. Guest stars include Virginia Christine, Jeanne Bates and Larry Dobkin.

Blood Money (3/6/60)
Rerun

Unloaded Gun (3/6/60) Written by Marian Clark
Matt tracks two brothers—kills one—but the other one escapes, Matt is not able to continue the search as he becomes very ill with fever and returns to Dodge—where the other brother plans to kill him for killing his brother. Guest stars include Vic Perrin, Sam Edwards, Harry Bartell Barney Phillips.

The Constable (3/20/60)
Rerun

Indian Baby (3/27/60) Written by Marian Clark
Doc and Kitty find a woman unconscious out in the prairie and the woman has with her an Indian baby. Guest stars include Jeanne Bates, Vic Perrin and Ralph Moody.

Greater Love (4/3/60)
Rerun

Dave's Lesson (4/10/60) Written by Marian Clark
Two of Matt's very best friends die of fever leaving behind their 16 year old son, Dave. Sam Edwards, Jospeh Kearns, Harry Bartell guest.

Solomon River (4/17/60) Written by Kathleen Hite
Matt and Chester come upon a woman digging a grave—her husband has died and though she is only 25, she has five other little graves for the babies she had who also have died. Virginia Christine and Vic Perrin guest star.

Stage Snatch (4/24/60) Written by Marian Clark
Matt is taking a prisoner to Hayes City by Stagecoach when two Indians stop the stage and ask Matt to hand over the prisoner to them. Guest stars include Larry Dobkin and Vic Perrin.

Nettie Sitton (5/1/60) Written by Kathleen Hite
Matt gets shot in the leg and Chester takes him to a cabin belonging

to a woman named Nettie Sitton who insists on being paid before she will allow Chester to bring Matt in and render him aid. Virginia Gregg plays Nettie.

Wrong Man (5/8/60) Written by Marian Clark
A sheriff gives Matt information about a wanted murderer and soon after a man, who seems very much a gentleman, arrives in Dodge and fits the description of the wanted man—Matt arrests him, against Kitty's wishes (he has charmed her). Harry Bartell, Sam Edwards, Vic Perrin and Larry Dobkin guest star.

Tall Trapper (5/15/60) Written by Marian Clark
A trapper is offered lodgings by a man and his wife, and he finds himself attracted to the wife, who is in a bad marriage. The wife is later found to be brutally beaten and the husband blames the trapper. Vic Perrin and Barney Phillips guest star.

Marryin' Bertha (5/22/60) Written by Tom Hanley
A widow from St. Louis (Virginia Gregg) arrives in Dodge to meet up with her fiancé—Chester. Kitty has a suspicion that the lady is actually a black widow who marries men and has them murdered. Joseph Kearns and Vic Perrin.

Bad Seed (5/29/60) Written by Norman Macdonnell
Matt finds a runaway out on the plains and returns her home only to find that her father is abusive. He is forced to kill the father and bring the girl back to Dodge where the girl thinks about becoming Mrs. Matt Dillon. Eve McVeigh, Sam Edwards and John Dehner guest star.

Fabulous Silver Extender (6/5/60) Written by Vic Perrin
While Matt is out of town, Chester is left in charge. Chester is approached by a Professor Cramston who claims that that he is the target of assassins and has a $10,000 bounty on head. Vic Perrin, Joseph Kearns, Harry Bartell and Jack Moyles guest star.

Kitty Accused (6/12/60) Written by Marian Clark
A husband has a crush on Kitty, who certainly does not reciprocate.

While traveling to visit friends Kitty is on a stage with the husband and wife and later the wife accuses Kitty of stealing her diamond pin. Virginia Christine, Barney Phillips, Vic Perrin and Richard Beals guest star.

Homely Girl (6/19/60) Written by Kathleen Hite
A lonely, homely woman arrives in Dodge expecting to find a husband among the desperate men who live there. Virginia Gregg, John Dehner and Vic Perrin guest star.

Line Trouble (6/26/60) Written by Marian Clark
Matt investigates a cut telegraph line out of town, and finds that the Army is involved—it seems Matt's friend Small Hawk, has confessed to being the culprit—Small Hawk feels the telegraph line is a bad omen for his people. Jospeh Kearns, Larry Dobkin, Ralph Moody and Harry Bartell guest star.

Little Girl (7/3/60) Written by Kathleen Hite
Matt and Chester find a little girl whose home burned down thanks to her drunken father who died in the fire. Matt takes the little girl back to Dodge to find a home, but the little girl would be happy just to stay with Matt. Anne Whitfield, Joseph Kearns and Larry Dobkin guest star.

Reluctant Violence (7/10/60) Written by Marian Clark
A man arrives in Dodge preaching about peace and giving up guns—and is beaten senseless for his trouble. John Dehner, Same Edwards, Joseph Kearns, Larry Dobkin and Barney Phillips guest star.

Busted-Up Guns (7/17/60) Written by Kathleen Hite
Matt and Chester ride out to the Sioux reservation and are confounded by what they find—the Indians are being forced by the Indian agents for the U.S. government of hunting, guns and their rations. Vic Perrin, Ralph Moody and Virginia Christine guest star.

The Imposter (7/24/60) Written by Kathleen Hite
A man arrives in town claiming to be a Texas sheriff on the lookout for a wanted outlaw—and Matt cooperates, but is this Sheriff actually

who he claims to be? Vic Perrin, Lawrence Dobkin and Jeanne Bates guest star.

Stage Smash (7/31/60) Written by Marian Clark
Matt arrests a killer, who tells the Marshal that it is all in vain—his brother will free him. Later the brother arranges a stage coach which is carrying Kitty to crash and several people die in the accident, with Kitty seriously injured. He kidnaps Kitty and uses her as a trade for his brother. John Dehner, James Nusser, Vic Perrin and Barney Phillips guest star.

Old Fool (8/7/60) Written by John Meston
A long married couple find complications when he finds himself attracted to a widow—who is only out to make sure he doesn't press charges against her son who he caught trying to steal one of his pigs. Joseph Kearns, Virginia Gregg, Peggy Webber and Sam Edwards guest star.

The Noose (8/14/60) Written by Marian Clark
A wild young man arrives in Dodge wearing a noose around his neck—he is on the look out for the man he feels is responsible for the death of the woman he loved. Vic Perrin, John Dehner, Harry Bartell, Larry Dobkin, Ben Wright and Barney Phillips guest star.

Dangerous Bath (8/21/60) Written by Marian Clark
Matt and Chester decide to cool off and clean up with a bath in a creek—meanwhile pair of outlaws make off with their horses, guns and shoes and they are forced to walk back to Dodge—where along the way Doc finds them and picks them up until Matt finds a cowboy wearing his boots! Sam Edwards, Jeanne Bates and Larry Dobkin guest star.

The Tumbleweed (8/28/60) Written by Tom Hanley
Chester finds himself having trouble getting a prisoner to leave jail—it turns out he likes being incarcerated. Vic Perrin, Jospeh Kearns, Virginia Christine and Barney Phillips guest star.

Peace Officer (9/4/60)
Rerun

About Chester (9/11/60) Written by Frank Paris
Doc has been missing for several days and Matt and Chester try to find him—they split up and Chester meets up with a horse thief who threatens to kill him. Bartlett Robinson, Harry Bartell, Vic Perrin John Dehner and Lynn Allen guest star.

Two Mothers (9/18/60) Written by Marian Clark
The story of two mothers—the mother of a murdered man and the mother of the man who will be hung for the murder. Jeanne Bates, Virginia Christie and John Dehner guest star.

Doc Judge (9/25/60) Written by John Meston & adapted for radio by Norman Macdonnell
A man who spent seven years in prison arrives in Dodge and mistakes Doc for the judge who sentenced him—and plans to kill Doc. Harry Bartell, James Nusser, and John Dehner guest star.
Note: This story actually appeared on the television series before it was adapted for radio.

Big Itch (10/2/60) Written by Marian Clark
A wife tells Matt that her husband has been missing for two days. He was supposed to come into Dodge to deliver the money that would have paid off their bank loan on their house. (The itch is caused by poison ivy which gives Matt a clue in solving the case). Guest stars include Sam Edwards and Lynn Allen.

Born to Hang (10/9/60)
Rerun

Crack-Up (10/16/60)
Rerun

Newsma'am (10/23/60) Written by Marian Clark
A female reporter from Philadelphia causes too much trouble on a cattle drive in trying to get 'the true picture' that the trail boss delivers

her to Matt—Matt locks her up for her own good. Jeanne Bates, Harry Bartell, Vic Perrin and Barney Phillips guest star.

Never Pester Chester (10/30/60)
Rerun

Jedro's Woman (11/6/60) Written by Marian Clark
Matt and Chester find a woman who has been beaten and half-starved and is just barely alive. They need to find out who the woman is and how she got into this condition. Virginia Christine, Larry Dobkin and James Nusser guest star.

The Big Con (11/13/60)
Rerun

The Professor (11/20/60) Written by Marian Clark
A Professor is on his way to Dodge and meets up with two robbers along the way. Vic Perrin, Larry Dobkin, Barney Phillips and Ralph Moody guest star.

Dirt (11/27/60)
Rerun

Kitty's Good Neighboring (12/4/60) Written by Marian Clark
Kitty is out of town helping a sick woman get well when her husband comes home with a stranger—who just happens to be the murderer that Matt is on the lookout for. Virginia Christine, Vic Perrin, John Dehner and Barney Phillips guest star.

The Cook (12/11/60) Written by John Meston & adapted for radio by Frank Paris
A man becomes a cook at Delmonico's in order to pay off a debt, later a buffalo hunter and the cook lock horns in the kitchen and the hunter is hit on the head with a skillet—the hunter dies and the panicked cook flees and is captured by Matt. The townspeople don't want him to go to trial because he's the best cook in town! Guest stars include Sam Edwards, Bart Robinson, John Dehner, Jeanne Bates, Harry Bartell and Larry Dobkin. Note: This script

aired on radio just days before it aired on Television.

Hero's Departure (12/18/60) Written by Marian Clark
A Civil War hero comes to live in Dodge much to the excitement of the townspeople, but he carries an awful secret about his past—he is actually a coward and there is a man after him looking for revenge. Guest stars include John Dehner, Vic Perrin and Sam Edwards.

Minnie (12/25/60) Written by John Meston
Doc treats a woman who becomes attached to him despite the fact that she is the wife of a buffalo hunter. Guest stars include Virginia Gregg, Vic Perrin and John Dehner.

Spring Term (1/1/61)
Rerun

Old Faces (1/8/61) Written by John Meston with radio adaptation by Frank Paris
Tilda (played by Jeanne Bates) is a new bride with a past she wants to keep hidden from her new husband. Harry Bartell, Vic Perrin, Larry Dobkin and John Dehner also guest star.

The Wake (1/15/61) Written by John Meston with radio adaptation by Norman Macdonnell
Why would a man bring into Dodge a coffin that he says contains the body of his best buddy? Matt wants to find out. John Dehner and Virginia Gregg guest star. Note: This script idea was first aired on television.

Hard Virtue (1/22/61) Written by John Meston with radio adaptation by Norman Macdonnell
A hot tempered man and his wife arrive in Dodge penniless and look to sell their wagon which is accidentally destroyed by another man—who to make amends gives the couple $20, but it turns out that the man is actually interested in the wife. Guest stars include Jeanne Bates, Vic Perrin, John Dehner and Harry Bartell.

Harriet (1/29/61) Written by John Meston with radio adaptation by Frank Paris
A woman witnesses her father being murdered by two men and she walks to Dodge where she gets a job at the Long Branch in hopes that the men who killed her father will turn up there, and she will get her revenge. Eve McVeigh, John Dehner, Barney Phillips and Ben Wright guest star.

Love of Money (2/5/61) Written by John Meston with radio adaptation by Norman Macdonnell
A former lawman and friend of Matt's turns up in Dodge and is soon found dead—shot in the back. A saloon girl is a witness but won't help unless there is money involved. Virginia Christine, John Dehner and Larry Dobkin guest star.

Daddy-O (2/12/61)
Rerun

Kitty Love (2/19/61) Written by Frank Paris
Kitty was excited because Matt was going to take her to a social in town, but he had to back out due to his job duties—having to pick up a bank robber. Meanwhile the disappointed Kitty finds herself attracted to a man she is helping Doc tend to, who happens to be the partner of the man that Matt had to give up the social for to pick up. John Dehner guest stars.

Joe Sleet (2/26/61) Written by Marian Clark
A gunfighter is in Dodge and gets into a fight with another man—Matt breaks up the fight, only to find that the gunfighter has been shot and is hovering between life and death. The man who was in the fight with the gunfighter says he is innocent even though it was his gun that was the weapon. Vic Perrin and Harry Bartell guest star.

Melinda Miles (3/5/61) Written by John Meston
A young couple plan to marry over the objections of her father and the father's ranch hand who has a thing for the bride—but soon he turns up dead and suspicion falls on the groom to be. Guest stars include Anne Whitfield, John Dehner, Sam Edwards and Vic Perrin.

Sweet and Sour (3/12/61)
Rerun

Joe Phy (3/19/61)
Rerun

No Indians (3/26/61)
Rerun

Chester's Inheritance (4/2/61) Written by Vic Perrin and Harry Bartell
Chester inherits the (then) large sum of $368.63—meanwhile a farmer is given with ten days to come up with the money he owes a man or else he will be evicted. These two stories intertwine. Writers Vic Perrin and Harry Bartell guest star along with Ralph Moody and Jack Moyles.

Hangman's Mistake (4/9/61) Written by Marian Clark
Matt is forced to release a man he believes is guilty when another man is arrested for the same crime in Abilene. Guest stars include Ken Lynch, Vic Perrin and Larry Dobkin.

Cooter (4/16/61)
Rerun

Father and Son (4/23/61) Written by Vic Perrin and Harry Bartell
A father has some strange ideas of how to teach his son to be a man: he beats a man to a pulp and rapes the man's Indian bride. The writing team of Perrin and Bartell also guest star along with Lillian Buyeff and Ralph Moody.

Ex-Urbanites (4/30/61) Written by John Meston with radio adaptation by Frank Paris
Doc and Chester try to aid a wounded man but things get complicated when the man's two partners return and try and kill him because they are afraid he will reveal information. To make sure that Doc can't help the man they shoot him. John Dehner, Vic Perrin and Harry Bartell guest star.

Ma's Justice (5/7/61) Written by Marian Clark

Two young men bring two wild colts back to their ranch, but another rancher wants the horses for himself and shoots the two young men to try and attain them—which bring about their ma's (Virginia Christine) brand of justice. Sam Edwards, Richard Crenna, John Dehner and Vic Perrin guest star.

The Lady Killer (5/14/61) Written by John Meston with radio adaptation by Frank Paris

A man arrives in Dodge to testify at a trial and soon is invited to come to the room of a new saloon girl who shoots him claiming that he was trying to steal some valuable jewelry from her. Lynn Allen, Harry Bartell, Larry Dobkin and John Dehner guest star.

Chester's Rendezvous (5/21/61) Written by Marian Clark

A hard wind blows a lady's bonnet Chester's way and when he returns it to the lady he is smitten. Meanwhile the young ladies brother is a wanted man. Jeanne Bates, James Nusser and John Dehner guest star.

The Sod Buster (5/28/61) Written by Ray Kemper

Matt is out of town on the trail of a murderer and Chester is in charge in town where he is mistaken for the marshal by a man who wants to fix his less than beautiful daughter up with him. Jeanne Bates, John Dehner, Ralph Moody and John Dehner guest star.

Cows and Cribs (6/4/61)
Rerun

Doc's Visitor (6/11/61) Written by Marian Clark

A doctor arrives in Dodge with a tantalizing offer for Doc—an old friend of Doc's has passed away and Doc has the opportunity to take over the man's prosperous clinic in Philadelphia. Doc must decide whether to go East and learn new medical techniques or stay in Dodge—a city that truly needs him. John Dehner, Virginia Gregg, Vic Perrin, Ralph Moody, James Nusser and Sam Edwards guest star.

Note: The last original episode of the radio show.
Letter of the Law (6/18/61)
Rerun

SELECTED TV GUEST ROLES

The Ed Sullivan Show (8/21/1955) A salute to radio episode which also features Jack Benny, Edgar Bergen, Gertrude Berg, Gene Autry, Eddie Cantor, and Eve Arden.
Bat Masterson (10/29/1958) "Stampede at Tent City" Director: David Friedkin, Ziv TV (NBC) Early episode of the Gene Barry series about a gentleman lawman and his adventures. Conrad plays Clark Benson the head of a group of men who bring a herd of wild horses to town to sell—however, Bat believes that some of the horses were stolen.
The Rough Riders (11/6/1958) "The Governor" Director: Monroe Askins, Ziv TV (ABC) Conrad leads an outlaw gang that kidnaps the governor and demands the release of another gang member in exchange for the release of the governor.
The Man and the Challenge (10/17/1959) "Invisible Force" Director: Andrew Marton (NBC) Conrad plays a government official who asks Dr. Glenn Barton (George Nader) to organize a prison break behind the iron curtain to rescue three Americans. Debra Paget also appears.
Tombstone Territory (4/16/1960) "The Governor" Director: William Conrad, Ziv TV (ABC) Conrad directs and also has a small role (as Frank Banter) in this episode which stars Pat Conway, Richard Eastham and Robert F. Simon.
The Aquanauts (1/25/1961) "Killers in Paradise" Director: Jack Herzberg, Ziv TV (CBS) This adventure series starred Ron Ely (later TV's *Tarzan*), Keith Larson and Jeremy Slate as divers who make their living salvaging sunken wrecks. In addition to Conrad—Mary Tyler Moore also guest stars on this episode.

Bat Masterson (3/9/1961) "Terror on the Trinity" Director: Elliott Lewis, Ziv TV (CBS) A gold claim episode set in Northern California with Conrad the head of a gang of outlaws out to steal gold.

Have Gun-Will Travel (3/24/1962) "Man Who Struck Moonshine" Director: Andrew V. McLaglen, (CBS) Conrad directed several episodes of Richard Boone's classic western series and got a chance to act in a couple of episodes—this being the first. This is a semi-comic episode in which Conrad plays a drunkard who holds Paladin hostage in an attempt to keep him from drinking before his wife comes back home—problem is the well produces whiskey!

Target: The Corruptors (5/11/62) "Yankee Dollar" Director: William Conrad, Four Star Productions (ABC) Veteran actor Stephen McNally stars in this crime series as a crusading newspaper reporter who infiltrates the mob. Conrad directs and has a cameo appearance.

Have Gun-Will Travel (9/15/1962) "Genesis" Director: William Conrad, (CBS) Conrad directs this episode and has a fairly substantial role as Norge, a man that Paladin at one time owed $15,000 in gambling debts. The story is told in flashback and among the other guest stars is Parley Baer, Conrad's old *Gunsmoke* companion. James Mitchum, the son of Robert Mitchum, also appears.

The Alfred Hitchcock Hour (1/4/1963) "The Thirty-First of February" Director: Alf Kjellin, Revue (NBC). Veteran suspense writer Richard Matheson wrote this episode (based on a novel by Julian Symons) about a man (David Wayne) whose wife has died and when he returns to work he finds somebody is trying to accuse him of murdering her—did he? Conrad plays Sgt. Cresse and the cast also includes Dick Sargent (the second Darrin from *Bewitched*) and Bob Crane.

77 Sunset Strip (10/18/1963) "5: The Conclusion" Director: William Conrad, Warner Bros (ABC). Conrad directs and has a small role in this conclusion of a five episode arc to introduce the revamped *77 Sunset Strip* that he and Jack Webb devised. See book chapter covering the early sixties for more on this.

77 Sunset Strip (1/24/1964) "The Target" Director: Lawrence Dobkin, Warner Bros (ABC). Conrad plays a cameo in this episode directed by frequent *Gunsmoke* stock actor Lawrence (Larry) Dobkin.

The Name of the Game (12/12/1969) "The Power" Director: Lawrence Dobkin, Universal (NBC) Conrad returned to television acting with this powerful performance in this "wheel series" which takes place at a large magazine publishing company with alternate leads—this episode starring Robert Stack and dealing with union corruption among two longshoreman brothers. Broderick Crawford and John Ireland also appear.

The Brotherhood of the Bell (9/17/1970) Director: Paul Wendkos, Warner Bros Pictures (CBS) TV-movie that helped earn Conrad the part of Frank Cannon the next season. Conrad plays a sensationalist talk-show host with a cast that includes Glenn Ford, Rosemary Forsyth, Dean Jagger, Maurice Evans and Will Geer. This TV-movie is discussed in more detail in this books text.

High Chaparral (9/25/1970) "Spokes" Director: William Wiard, Warner Bros television (NBC). During the fourth of July Buck (Cameron Mitchell) visits the hard core mining town of Spokes where a young man is killed by an old skinner for cheating at cards. The old man is injured and Buck cares for him when nobody else will. The town's people tell Buck to turn the old man over to the dead man's vindictive father "China" Pierce (Conrad).

Men at Law (10/21/1970) "Survivors Will be Prosecuted" Director: Arthur Heinemann (CBS). Short lived TV series with Robert Foxworth as a lawyer who gives up his big time expensive law practice to start a non-profit firm. Conrad guest-stars in this episode along with Murray Hamilton.

DA: Conspiracy to Kill (1/11/1971) Director: Paul Krasny. Universal, (NBC). Pilot TV-movie to the short-lived "The D.A" TV-series that starred that other television Conrad, Robert, as a crusading Deputy D.A. The movie and TV-series was put together by Jack Webb's Mark VII production company and fictionalized a case by Vincent Bugliosi, the famous prosecutor of Charles Manson. This TV-movie deals with the D.A. reopening an old case due to new evidence. Conrad plays the police chief. This is the first of three pilot films that Conrad made during early 1971.

Cannon (3/26/1971) Director: George McCowan. Quinn Martin Productions, (CBS). Pilot TV-movie to Conrad's classic 1970's

TV-series. This is discussed fully in the text.

O'Hara, U.S. Treasury (4/2/1971) Director: Jack Webb, Mark VII, (NBC). Conrad's third pilot film of 1971—each pilot did become a series, but only Conrad's *Cannon* proved successful. This movie stars David Janssen as a U.S. Treasury agent who is out to break up a narcotics ring. Jack Webb directs as well as produces. The cast, in addition to Conrad, includes Charles McGraw—Conrad's old *The Killers* side-kick.

The Hollywood Squares (11/29/1971) Conrad is one of the squares in this episode of the venerable game show. Conrad also appeared on episodes on 3/20/1972 and 5/22/1972.

Rowan & Martin's Laugh-In (9/25/1972)—NBC. Conrad appears in sketches along with the regulars Dan Rowan, Dick Martin, Ruth Buzzi and other guest stars including Bob Crane and Nanette Fabray.

The Dean Martin Show (10/26/1972)—NBC. Dean and the Golddiggers welcome guests William Conrad and Olivia Newton-John.

The Sonny and Cher Comedy Hour (10/27/1972)—CBS. Sonny and Cher welcome guest stars William Conrad, Van Johnson and Rick Springfield.

The Sonny and Cher Comedy Hour (12/18/1972)—CBS. Sonny and Cher welcome guest stars William Conrad and Captain Kangaroo for this Christmas episode.

The Dean Martin Show (2/22/1973)—NBC. Dean welcomes guest stars William Conrad and Lonnie Schorr.

The Carol Burnett Show (3/17/1973)—CBS. Carol welcomes guest stars William Conrad and Peggy Lee.

The Dean Martin Show (4/12/1973)—NBC. Dean welcomes guests William Conrad and Nancy Sinatra in this Easter show.

The Dean Martin Show (10/5/1973)—NBC. Conrad is the "Person of the Week" for the celebrity roast which also features Petula Clark, Phyllis Diller, Bob Newhart, and Nipsey Russell.

The Dean Martin Show (10/26/1973)—NBC. Conrad is among those who roast Sen. Barry Goldwater (R-AZ).

CBS All-American Thanksgiving Day Parade (11/22/1973) Host: William Conrad. Featuring: Ed Asner, Bob Barker, Anita Gillette, June Lockhart, Leslie Neilsen.

The Wild, Wild World of Animals (1973-1978) syndicated nature/wild life documentary series that Conrad hosted and narrated over five years for Time-Life television and producing 129 episodes.
The Sonny and Cher Comedy Hour (12/9/1973)—CBS. Conrad guests stars with Sonny & Cher in another Christmas episode.
Hamburger (4/2/1974—NBC) A satirical look at network television with William Conrad, Jim Nabors, Sid Caesar, Charlie Callas and Bobby Vinton.
CBS All-American Thanksgiving Day Parade (11/28/1974) Host: William Conrad. Featuring: Rob Reiner, Lee Meriwether, John Amos, Esther Rolle, Jack Lord.
The Carol Burnett Show (1/25/1975)—CBS. Carol welcomes guest stars William Conrad and The Jackson 5.
The Flip Wilson Special (2/27/1975—NBC) Flip welcomes William Conrad, Sammy Davis, Jr., & Helen Reddy.
CBS All-American Thanksgiving Day Parade (11/27/ 1975) Host: William Conrad. Featuring: Lee Meriwether, John Amos, Sherman Hemsley, Isabel Sanford, Rue McClanahan, Michael Learned, David Groh.
The Rich Little Show (3/1/1976)—NBC. Impressionist Rich Little hosts this short-lived variety show with guest stars William Conrad and Bernadette Peters.
The Dean Martin Celebrity Roast: Dennis Weaver (4/27/1976)— NBC. Conrad joins a dais including Mike Connors, Nipsey Russell, Red Buttons, Milton Berle, Shelley Winters, George Hamilton, Rich Little, Amanda Blake and Milburn Stone in roasting TV's "Chester"—Dennis Weaver.
CBS All-American Thanksgiving Day Parade (11/25/1976) Host: William Conrad. Featuring: Loretta Swit, Richard Crenna, Isabel Sanford, Gavin McLeod, Bill Macy, Michael Learned.
The Sonny and Cher Show (1/28/1977) Sonny and Cher (now divorced) welcome guest stars William Conrad and Engelbert Humperdinck.
World Famous Moscow Circus (7/22/1977—CBS) William Conrad hosts part one of a special featuring the famous Russian circus.
The Dean Martin Roast: Dan Haggerty (11/2/1977—NBC) Dean roasts *Grizzly Adams* star Dan Haggerty along with William

Conrad, Foster Brooks, Red Buttons, Rich Little, Roger Miller, Denver Pyle, Abe Vigoda, Orson Welles—among others.

CBS All-American Thanksgiving Day Parade (11/23/1977) Host: William Conrad. Featuring: Pat Harrington, Loretta Swit, Kevin Dobson, Linda Lavin, Bess Armstrong, Jack Lord.

Night Cries (1/29/1978) Director: Richard Lang, (ABC) TV-movie starring Susan St. James as a grade school teacher who loses her baby soon after its birth, and is haunted by nightmares—with Conrad cast as the dream psychoanalyst (Dr. Whelan), who attempts to decipher her dreams.

Keefer (3/16/1978) Director: Barry Shear, Columbia TV—David Gerber Productions. TV-movie casts Conrad as a U.S. Army Colonel who leads a group of secret agents operating behind enemy lines during WWII in German occupied France.

CBS All-American Thanksgiving Day Parade (11/23/1978) Host: William Conrad. Featuring: Linda Lavin, Valerie Bertinelli, Judy Norton-Taylor, Sherman Hemsley, Loretta Swit, Lyle Wagonner, Victoria Principal.

CBS All-American Thanksgiving Day Parade (11/22/1979) Host: William Conrad. Featuring: Jack Lord, John Schneider, Victoria Principal, Judy Norton-Taylor, Loretta Swit, Tim Reid, Howard Hesseman.

Turnover Smith (6/8/1980) Director: Bernard L. Kowalski, Wellington Productions, (CBS). TV-movie casts Conrad as Thaddeus "Turnover" Smith a private detective who is investigating a serial killer who strangles young women. The mystery has an intriguing premise involving chess. The cast includes Belinda Montgomery, James Darrren, Michael Parks, Cameron Mitchell and Nehemiah Persoff. Conrad also served as Executive-Producer.

Return of Frank Cannon (11/1/1980) Director: Corey Allen, Quinn-Martin Productions, (CBS) Conrad returns to his most famous TV role only four years after the end of the series in this TV-movie that finds Cannon investigating the murder of an ex-girlfriend. The cast also includes Diana Muldaur, Ed Nelson, Joanna Pettet and Arthur Hill.

CBS All-American Thanksgiving Day Parade (11/27/1980) Host: William Conrad. Featuring: Charlene Tilton, Gordon

Jump, Joan Van Ark, Vic Tayback, Linda Lavin, Loretta Swit, Gregory Harrison.
CBS All-American Thanksgiving Day Parade (11/26/1981) Host: William Conrad. Featuring: Robert Reed, Joan Van Ark, Danielle Brosebois, Jamie Farr, Susan Howard, Donna Mills, Patrick Duffy, Beth Howland.
Police Squad (7/8/1982) "Testimony of Evil: Dead Men Don't Laugh" Director: Joe Dante, Paramount Television (ABC). Conrad has a cameo as a stabbed man.
Shocktrauma (10/27/1982) Director: Eric Till, Glen Waren Productions, Telecom (Syd). TV movie featuring Conrad along with Scott Hylands, Leslie Carlson and Kerrie Keane. The film was produced in Canada and syndicated thru the United States by General Foods. Conrad stars (in this true story) as Dr. R. Adams Crowley, a heart surgeon who became the "Father of Trauma medicine."
Murder, She Wrote (12/16/84) "Death Takes a Curtain Call" Director: Allen Reisner, Universal (CBS) it was inevitable that Conrad would be invited to guest-star on an episode of *Murder, She Wrote*, a TV series which utilized many old-time movie and TV actors. Conrad plays a KGB Major who is a fan of mystery writer Jessica Fletcher's books. The cast also includes Claude Akins, Tom Bosley, Paul Rudd, Hurd Hatfield, and Dane Clark.
In Like Flynn (8/14/1985) Director: Richard Lang, 20th Century-Fox (CBS). Filmed in Canada, Conrad joins a cast including Robert Webber, Maury Chaykin, Eddie Albert, and Jenny Seagrove in this TV-movie about a young couple who investigate murders in the Caribbean.
Hotel (1/8/1986) "Shadows of Doubt: Part One" Director: Bruce Bilson, Aaron Spelling Productions (ABC). There are three story lines involved in this episode with Conrad cast as Art Patterson, the hotels long-time Chief of Security who thinks his ambitious assistant is after his job. Patterson takes desperate actions to protect his turf. Also in the cast are James Brolin, Connie Sellecca, Anne Baxter, Audrey Landers, Heidi Bohay, Michael Spound and Peter Scolari.
Hotel (1/15/1986) "Shadows of Doubt: Part Two" Director: Bruce Bilson, Aaron Spelling Productions (ABC). See above summary.

Matlock (10/28/1986) "The Don: Part One" Director: Leo Penn (CBS) This two-parter on *Matlock* featuring Bill Conrad led to Conrad's own series *Jake and the Fatman* and interestingly enough features each of the core cast of *Jake*: Conrad, Joe Penny and Alan Campbell. See text for more.

Vengeance: The Story of Tony Cimo (11/1/1986) Director: Marc Daniels. Nederland Television Productions (CBS). Fact based TV-movie about a young man who seeks justice for his murdered parents in South Carolina. The film also stars Brad Davis, Roxanne Hart, Frances McDormand, and Michael Beach. The director, Marc Daniels, is a veteran who directed most of the first season of *I Love Lucy*.

Matlock (11/4/1986) "The Don: Part Two" Director: Leo Penn (CBS)—the conclusion of the previous week's episode.

Selected Television Directing Credits

Mackenzie's Raiders
"The Pen and the Sword" (1958-Sydnicated, assorted air dates)
Highway Patrol
"The Trap" (January, 1959-Sydnicated, assorted air dates)
Bold Venture (note: Based on a 1951-1952 radio show starring Humphrey Bogart and Lauren Bacall)
"Go Fight Sidney Hall" (1959)
"Dial M for Mother" (1959)
"The Glittering Skull of Irving Tezcula" (1959)
"The Last Angry Man" (1959)
"Oh Kaplan, Our Kaplan" (1959)
"One of Our Friedkins is missing...Fine" (1959)
The Rifleman
"Three Legged Terror" (4/21/1959) (Note: This episode features Dennis Hopper as a reckless youth).
The Rough Riders
"Deadfall" (5/21/1959) (Note: James Coburn guest-stars)
This Man Dawson (Conrad also narrated this series)
"The Assassin" (10/22/1959) (Note: The guest cast includes Raymond Bailey, who went on to play banker Mr. Drysdale on *The Beverly Hillbillies* & that superb character actor L.Q. Jones).

"The End of Kalmine" (10/29/1959)
"Doubt of Evidence" (1959)
"Copkiller" (1959)
"Short Circuit" (1960)
"Get Dawson" (1960)
"Plague" (1960)
"The Deadly Young Man" (1960)
"Loose Cannon" (1960) (Note: This episode features Leo Penn, the father of actor Sean Penn, in an acting role. He would later become a director and direct three episodes of *Cannon*).
Lock Up
"Poker Club" (3/12/1960) (Note: This episode features veteran character actor John Carradine).
"So Shall Ye Reap" (5/28/1960)
Tombstone Territory
"Marked for Murder" (3/20/1959)
"The Black Diamond" (4/17/1959) (Note: This episode features the prolific character actor Burt Mustin)
"Silver Killers" (2/26/1960)
"Memory" (3/25/1960)
"The Governor" (4/16/1960)
"Betrayal" (6/3/1960)
Men into Space
"Mission to Mars" (5/25/1960)
"Mystery Satellite" (9/7/1960)
Klondike
"Klondike Fever" (10/10/1960)
"Saints and Stickups" (10/31/1960) (Note: Again Conrad directs James Coburn, who was a co-star on this series. Also in the cast is Conrad's old friend actress Virginia Gregg).
Bat Masterson
"Wanted: Dead" (10/15/1959)
"The Reluctant Witness" (3/31/1960)
"The Good and the Bad" (3/23/1961)
"Ledger of Guilt" (4/6/1961)
The Aquanauts
"The Stakeout Adventure" (5/24/61) (Note: This episode features Ken Curtis (later Festus on TV's *Gunsmoke*) and Donna Douglas

(Elly Mae of *The Beverly Hillbillies*).
Route 66
"First-Class Mouliak" (10/20/1961) (Note: Conrad could boast of directing a young Robert Redford, who appears in this episode along with veteran actors Martin Balsam and Nehemiah Persoff).
Naked City
"A Kettle of Precious Fish" (5/31/1961)
"The Day the Island Almost Sank" (6/14/1961)
"Bridge Party" (12/27/1961)
Ripcord
"Crime Jump" (1961—no exact air date) (Note: Burt Reynolds appears in this episode).
"The Silver Cord" (1962—no exact air date)
Target: The Corruptors
"Prison Empire"
"Play It Blue"
"Babes in Wall Street"
"My Native Land"
"A Man's Castle"
"Journey Into Mourning"
"A Book of Faces"
"Yankee Dollar"
Saints and Sinners
"A Night of Horns and Bells" (12/24/1962) (Note: Cloris Leachman and future director Paul Mazursky appear in this episode as does the veteran Edward Everett Horton).
Have Gun—Will Travel
"One, Two, Three" (2/17/1962)
"Don't Shoot the Piano Player" (3/10/1962)
"Darwin's Man" (4/21/1962)
"Genesis" (9/15/1962) (Note: one of the best episodes of the series also featuring Conrad as Norge).
"A Miracle for St. Francis" (11/17/1962)
"The Black Bull" (4/13/1963)
GE True (Note: Conrad directed 22 episodes of this Jack Webb produced and hosted true-based anthology series, and he also starred in the first outing which was directed by Webb).
"Harris vs. Castro" (10/14/1962)

"The Handmade Private" (11/4/1962) (Note: This dramatic episode features two comic actors—Arte Johnson and Jerry Van Dyke).
"The Last Day" (11/11/1962)
"Man with a Suitcase" (11/18/1962) (Note: This episode features Werner Klemperer, the future Col. Klink of *Hogan's Heroes*).
"Mile-Long Shot to Kill" (11/25/1962) (Note: This episode guest-stars Russell Johnson, the Professor of *Gilligan's Island*).
"The Wrong Nickel" (12/16/1962)
"The Amateurs" (12/30/1962)
"Open Season" (1/6/1963)
"Defendant Clarence Darrow" (1/13/1963) (Note: Robert Vaughn guest-stars)
"O.S.I." (1/20/1963)
"Firebug" (1/27/1963) (Note: Interesting episode featuring Victor Buono as an arsonist).
"Escape: Part 1" (2/10/1963)
"Escape: Part 2" (2/17/1963)
"The Moonshiners" (2/24/1963)
"Security Risk" (3/3/1963) (Note: This episode features Parley Baer)
"The Black-Robed Ghost" (3/10/1963)
"Ordeal" (3/17/1963)
"Pattern for Espionage" (3/24/1963)
"The Tenth Mona Lisa" (3/31/1963)
"Heydrich: Part 1" (5/5/1963)
"Heydrich: Part 2" (5/12/1963)
"Commando" (5/19/1963)

77 Sunset Strip
"Never to Have Loved" (6/14/1963)
"5: Part 1" (9/20/1963)
"5: Part 2" (9/27/1963)
"5: Part 3" (10/4/1963)
"5: Part 4" (10/11/1963)
"5: Part 5" (10/18/1963)

Temple Houston
"Billy Hart" (11/28/1963)
"Thy Name is Woman" (1/9/1964) (Note: This episode features character actors Mary Wickes and Charles Lane).

"A Slight Case of Larceny" (2/13/1964)
"The Gun That Swept the West" (3/5/1964)
"The Town that Trespassed" (3/26/1964) (Note: Connie Stevens, who Conrad would direct in the big screen Two on the Guillotine appears in this episode)

Gunsmoke
"Panacea Sykes" (4/13/1963) (Note: Conrad directs this episode based on one of the radio scripts)
"Captain Sligo" (1/4/1971) (Note: a mostly comic episode featuring Richard Basehart as a sea captain who gives up the sea and moves to Kansas).

Side Show (6/4/1981) TV-movie featuring Lance Kerwin, Connie Stevens and William Wildom about a boy who runs away and joins the circus and then witnesses a murder—leading to his life being in danger. Conrad returned to directing after a ten year hiatus—but this would be his directorial swan-song

Cannon Episode Log

Season One Episodes

1. The Salinas Jackpot (9/14/1971)
Written by: Ken Trevey. Directed by: George McCowan
Guest Stars: Tom Skerritt, Sharon Acker, Vincent Van Patten, Lucille Benson, Charles Bateman.
Synopsis: When an insurance company hires Cannon to track down the thief's who stole $100,000 from a rodeo, he befriends a fatherless boy (Van Patten) and his mother (Acker), the widow of a former rodeo clown—who at first wants nothing to do with Cannon—and must protect them from murderers (Tom Skerritt & John Perak) There are tender scenes between Conrad and Van Patten who comes to see Cannon as a father figure
Trivia: George McCowan, the director of the March pilot film, was given the responsibility of directing the first episode of the series. McGowan specialized in directing episodic television programs, but on occasion he directed for the big screen including two 1972 films *Frogs*, a cult horror/sci-fi film which starred Ray Milland, Sam Elliott

and Joan Van Ark and *The Magnificent Seven Ride Again*, one of the lesser sequels to the classic 1960 western and starred Lee Van Cleef, Stephanie Powers, and Michael Callan.
Review: "Discriminating viewers…maybe amused by Conrad's hamming in the final struggle scenes. 'Cannon' isn't the best detective show around, but the rotund Conrad has a certain physical appeal that might overcome some of the basic silliness involved."—*The Milwaukee Journal*, 9/14/71

2. Death Chain (9/21/1972) Written by: David Moessinger & Paul Playdon. Directed by: Jerry Jameson.
Guest Stars: William Windom, Sorrell Booke, Don Gordon, Stewart Moss, June Dayton, Elaine Princi, Christopher Dark.
Synopsis: Cannon is hired to investigate the killing of a bank secretary who is run down by a car (driven by Gordon). It turns out that the secretary is also the mistress of the banker (Windom), who doesn't want to involve the police—lest his wife finds out. Why she was murdered and by who is what Cannon must figure out.
Trivia: Jameson at age 26 was a relatively new director at the time he directed "Death Chain." He would go on to direct a total of 4 episodes of *Cannon* and several episodes of such diverse series as *The Mod Squad, The Six Million Dollar Man, Dallas* and *Murder, She Wrote*.

3. Call Unicorn (9/28/1971) Written by: E. Arthur Kean, David Moessinger, Paul Playdon. Directed by: Allen Reisner.
Guest Stars: Wayne Rogers, Charles Cioffi, Patricia Smith, Joe Maross, Jenny Sullivan, Karl Lukas.
Synopsis: Cannon becomes a truck driver trying to outwit hijackers at their own game. To accomplish his mission, Cannon poses as the new husband of the trucking company dispatcher and works his way into the confidence of the hijackers. Complications arise when his 'wife's' young sister arrives unexpectedly.
Trivia: Wayne Rogers was a busy actor who appeared numerous TV shows when he appeared on this episode of *Cannon*. He was one season away from his star making role as Trapper John on *MASH*. (This episode would be the first episode of "Cannon" to be rerun on December 21, during Christmas week).

4. Country Blues (10/5/1971) Written by: Ronald Austin & James D. Buchanan. Directed by: Allen Reisner.
Guest Stars: Clu Gulager, Joan Van Ark, David Huddleston, Mark Hamill, Robert Hogan, Diane Varsi.
Synopsis: An insurance company calls upon Cannon to investigate the death of a country singer who is killed in a plane crash which seems suspicious (why would the cords of the one parachute on board be cut?). The investigation is stymied by his family which would rather see the case closed.
Trivia: Allen Reisner (1924-2004) was another hard working television director whose credits go back to *Studio One* in 1954 all the way up to *Murder She Wrote* in 1989. He directed four episodes of *Cannon*. He directed few feature films, but one he did direct has become a family classic—often shown at Christmas, *All Mine to Give* (1957).

5. Scream of Silence (10/12/1971)
Written by: Robert L. Collins. Directed by: Jerry Jameson.
Guest Stars: Tim O'Connor, Jason Evers, Jean Allison, Whit Bissell, Gregg Palmer.
Synopsis: A millionaire's (who is also a candidate for Governor) son is kidnapped but manages to escape, but the trauma of the event causes him to become mute. Not wanting to involve the police, the family hires Cannon (for the price of a few bottles of rare wine) to find out who was behind the kidnapping. Again Cannon forges a close and trusting relationship with a child.
Trivia: Robert L. Collins (1930-2011) was a distinguished writer-director. He was nominated for an Emmy Award for writing a 1975 episode of the anthology series *Police Story*. He was nominated for a Directors Guild Award for directing an *Hallmark Hall of Fame* TV-movie "Gideon's Trumpet" (1980) which starred Henry Fonda. "Scream of Silence" is considered one of the best episodes of *Cannon*.

6. Fool's Gold (10/19/1971) Written by: Edward Hume & Bill Stratton. Directed by: Don Medford.
Guest Stars: Andrew Duggan, Mitchell Ryan, Max Gail, L.Q. Jones, Ron Harper, Vic Tayback, Pamela Payton-Wright.
Synopsis: Cannon finds himself unwelcome in a ghost town where the suspects in an armored car robbery are holed up. Andrew Duggan

plays a frightened townsman.
Trivia: Don Medford (1917-2012) was another prolific television director who did his time on *Cannon*. While he directed only one episode of *Cannon*, he would later direct William Conrad in two episodes of his subsequent series, *Jake and the Fatman*.

7. Girl in the Electric Coffin (10/26/1971)
Written by: Robert M. Young. **Directed by:** Jerry Jameson.
Guest Stars: Andrew Prine, Bill Erwin, Kim Hunter, Frank Aletter, Signe Hasso, Lynn Marta.
Synopsis:
Trivia: The Swedish born Signe Hasso (1910-2002) appeared in such interesting 1940's films as *Heaven Can Wait*, *The Seventh Cross*, *The House on 92nd Street*, and *Johnny Angel*. Kim Hunter (1922-2002) won the Best Supporting Actress Oscar of 1951 for her role as Stella in *A Streetcar Named Desire*, and later played Dr. Zira in *Planet of the Apes* and two of its sequels. This is writer Robert M. Young's only episode of *Cannon*. He is known for his work as a writer and/or director of such cult horror films as *Trauma* (1962) and *The Crawling Hand* (1963).

8. Dead Pigeon (11/9/1971) Written by: Ronald Austin, James D. Buchanan & George Kirgo. Directed by: Don Taylor.
Guest Stars: Brooke Bundy, Barnard Hughes, James Wainwright, Martin E. Brooks, John McLiam.
Synopsis: A cop (John McLiam), who is an old friend of Cannon's, is framed for murder—there is evidence of his involvement due to the cop daughter (Brooke Bundy). Cannon, of course, has to clear his friend, and find the real killer before the daughter is a victim.
Trivia: Don Taylor (1920-1998) began his career as an actor and appeared in such films as *Song of the Thin Man*, *Naked City*, *Father of the Bride* (as the groom to Elizabeth Taylor's bride), *Stalag 17* and *I'll Cry Tomorrow*. He turned to directing in the late 50's (with an occasional acting job here and there) and directed two episodes of *Cannon*. He directed an occasional feature film including *Jack of Diamonds*, *Escape from the Planet of the Apes*, and *Damien: The Omen Part II*, which starred his old friend William Holden with whom he worked with as an actor in two films.

9. A Lonely Place to Die (11/16/1971)
Written by: Jack Turley. Directed by: William Hale.
Guest Stars: Harold Gould, Rose Hobart, Felice Orlandi, R.G. Armstrong, Carol Rossen, Eric Christmas.
Synopsis: Cannon is investigating a triple murder and discovers that a mob boss (Harold Gould) may be the next victim.
Trivia: Rose Hobart (1906-2000) was a stage and screen actress who had prominent roles in such films as *Liliom, Dr. Jekyll and Mr. Hyde* (1931), *Tower of London* and *Susan and God*. She was later blacklisted. William Hale is another prolific television director who would helm three episodes of *Cannon*.

10. No Pockets in a Shroud (11/23/1971)
Written by: Ken Pettus. Directed by: William Hale.
Guest Stars: Roy Scheider, Arthur O'Connell, Linda Marsh, Paul Mantee, Paul Comi, Kelly Thordsen.
Synopsis: Murder and embezzlement go hand in hand in this story about a millionaire hermit and his missing heir.
Trivia: Ken Pettus (1915-1992) was a prolific television writer who in addition to two episodes of *Cannon*, wrote several episodes of *The Big Valley, Mister Roberts* (one of the series that William Conrad helped launch at Warner Brothers as a TV-producer), *The Wild Wild West, Bonanza* and *Mission: Impossible*. Arthur O'Connell (1908-1981) was a TV and movie veteran who was nominated twice for the Best Supporting Actor Oscar for *Picnic* (1955) and *Anatomy of a Murder* (1959).

11. Stone Cold Dead (11/30/1971) Written by: Paul Playdon & David Moessinger. Directed by: Seymour Robbie.
Guest Stars: Lou Antonio, Richard Anderson, Dack Rambo, Robert Doyle, Don Chastain, Anne Barton, Richard Carlyle.
Synopsis: A young salesgirl drowns mysteriously. At the marina where her body is found, Cannon dons scuba diving gear for an underwater search for a missing bicycle that could be an important clue—besides the bike he runs into a surprise diver.
Trivia: Seymour Robbie (1919-2004) directed six episodes of *Cannon* as well as numerous episodes of *The F.B.I, The Streets of San Francisco, Ellery Queen, Barnaby Jones* and *Murder She Wrote*. He

was also known by Bill Conrad for his work at Warner Brothers during his tenure there in series like *Mister Roberts* and *F-Troop*.

Portions of this episode was filmed in the Pacific Ocean off of Oxnard, California.

12. Death is a Double-Cross (12/7/1971) Written by: George Eckstein & Edward Hume. Directed by: Richard Donner.

Guest Stars: Ed Nelson, Marianne McAndrew, Roger E. Mosley, Simon Scott, Leif Garrett, Dawn Lyn.

Synopsis: Cannon takes on a routine bodyguard assignment that eventually finds him chasing down a gang of counterfeiters. He agrees to escort a wealthy stockholder's daughter and her three children by train from Chicago to Los Angeles. The assignment turns dangerous when Cannon discovers the woman's estranged husband is involved with the counterfeiting.

Trivia: Richard Donner was a busy television director at the time he directed his four episodes of *Cannon*. By 1976 he became a highly successful film director for a time with *The Omen, Superman, The Toy, Ladyhawke, Lethal Weapon, Scrooged* and *Maverick*. Real life siblings Dawn Lyn and Leif Garrett appeared in this episode as siblings. At the time Dawn was the most prominent due to her role as Dodie on *My Three Sons*. It would be a few years to go before Leif broke out both as an actor and a teenage heart throb/rock star. It's the Christmas season and earlier in the evening this episode was aired CBS showed the perennial favorite "How the Grinch Stole Christmas."

13. The Nowhere Man (12/14/1971)

Written by: Micheal Gleason. **Directed by:** George McCowan.

Guest Stars: Fritz Weaver, Lynn Carlin, Robert Webber, Jeanne Cooper, Richard O'Brien.

Synopsis: Cannon is called in by a chemical company president (Robert Webber) and hired to track down an employee (Fritz Weaver) accused of running off with the company payroll. Cannon finds out the fleeing employee has done something far more serious. He's disappeared with a canister of deadly nerve gas which he has threatened to use to protest the company's production of it.

Trivia: Writer Michael Gleason wrote 44 episodes of the prime time soap classic *Peyton Place*. He also created and wrote 12 episodes of the 80's hit *Remington Steele*. His writing was nominated for two Emmy Awards for the *McCloud* TV-series. Jeanne Cooper (1928-2013) was best known for her Emmy Award winning role as Katherine Chancellor on the daytime soap *The Young and the Restless* (1973-2013). On the night that "The Nowhere Man" was telecast Christmas specials dominated on rival NBC which led the evening with "The Little Drummer Boy" followed by "Bing Crosby and The Sounds of Christmas" and "The Andy Williams Christmas Show" which was on opposite "Cannon." ABC countered with a made-for-TV movie "The Trackers" which starred Ernest Borgnine and Sammy Davis, Jr.

14. Flight Plan (12/28/1971)
Written by: Robert C. Dennis. Directed by: Richard Donner.
Guest Stars: Cesare Danova, Barbara Luna, John Fiedler, Joaquin Martinez, Victor Millan.
Synopsis: Cesare Danova plays a refuge from Cuba, with government agents out to kill him. Cannon has a reputation for finding missing persons, so the Cuban reasons, he can thus reverse the process and devise a perfect plan to help him disappear. Cannon does, then for reasons I won't disclose (get the DVD) he has to find the man—and it's not nearly as easy.
Trivia: Robert C. Dennis (1915-1983) wrote more than 500 television scripts including 30 episodes of *Alfred Hitchcock Presents* including the Hitchcock directed episode "Dip in the Pool." He also helmed 22 episodes of *Perry Mason* and 19 episodes of *Dragnet* (1967-1970). He was known to Conrad during his Warner Brother years for his work on *77 Sunset Strip*, *The Fugitive* and *Mister Roberts*.

15. Devil's Playground (01/4/1971)
Written by: Ken Trevey. Directed by: Marvin J. Chomsky
Guest Stars: Martin Sheen, Daniel J. Travanti, Collin Wilcox Paxton, Ned Glass.
Synopsis: An ex-motorcycle cop who was injured chasing after a holdup suspect hires Cannon to try and find the robber, who was assumed to be dead—but the ex-cop is now having his doubts.
Trivia: As a director for television Marvin J. Chomsky won four prime time Emmy Awards for his work in *Holocaust, Attica, Inside*

the Third Reich & Peter the Great. In addition he was nominated for an Emmy for his directing of the acclaimed mini-series *Roots.* The Polish born Ned Glass (1906-1984) was a top character actor in movies and television. Among his films are *Experiment in Terror, Kid Galahad* (with Elvis Presley), *Charade, Papa's Delicate Condition* and *Blindfold.*

16. Treasure of San Ignacio (01/11/1972) Written by: Bill S. Ballinger, Paul Playdon. Directed by: Allen Reisner.
Guest Stars: Tab Hunter, Alejandro Rey, Victoria Racimo, Paul Petersen, Warren Stevens, Judson Pratt.
Synopsis: Thieves steal valuable religious relics belonging to a priest (Alejandro Rey), a friend of Cannon's. Tab Hunter plays the lead heavy—a one-armed thief.
Trivia: For a time in the 50's and early 60's Tab Hunter was a top movie star with films like *Battle Cry, The Burning Hills, Damn Yankees,* and *The Pleasure of His Company.* By the time he did this guest gig on *Cannon,* Hunter's career largely consisted of appearances on episodic television programs and summer stock/dinner theater. He would make a brief comeback in the mid 80's in the cult western-comedy *Lust in the Dust.* Argentina born Alejandro Rey (1930-1987) was best known for his role as Carlos Ramirez on *The Flying Nun* (1967-1970) opposite Sally Field. Paul Petersen was best known for playing Jeff Stone on the TV family favorite *The Donna Reed Show* (1958-1966).

17. Blood on the Vine (01/18/1972) Written by: Stephen Kandel & Ken Pettus. Directed by: George McCowan.
Guest Stars: Theodore Bikel, Katherine Justice, Christopher Connelly, Ross Elliott, Ivor Francis.
Synopsis: A case right up Cannon's alley (as well as William Conrad's) because it takes place in part in a winery. Cannon is called in to investigate after several suspicious accidents take place which nearly kill the winery's owner (Theodore Bikel).
Trivia: The Austrian born Theodore Bikel was a distinguished stage, screen and TV actor who was nominated for a Best Supporting Actor Oscar for his work in the film *The Defiant Ones* (1958). He created the role of Captain Von Trapp in the original Broadway production of *The Sound of Music* opposite Mary Martin. This was the first of two

appearances on *Cannon* for Christopher Connelly (1941-1988) who was best known for playing the role of Norman Harrington in 386 episodes of *Peyton Place*. Ross Elliott (1917-1999) had worked in radio, films, and TV since the 30's and was a member of the Orson Welles Mercury Theatre radio group and was in the landmark radio production of Welles' *The War of the Worlds* (1938).

18. To Kill a Guinea Pig (02/01/1972)
Written by: Hal Sitowitz. Directed by: Allen Reisner.
Guest Stars: Vera Miles, Michael Strong, Robert Mandan, Geoffrey Lewis, Stephen Hudis.
Synopsis: A prison medical researcher (Vera Miles) is being harassed by thugs and prisoners and Cannon is brought in to find out why they want to scare her off.
Trivia: Vera Miles who appeared in the *Cannon* pilot movie returns for this guest starring appearance. Hal Sitowitz (1933-2004) wrote two episodes of *Cannon* as well as several episodes of *The Rookies* and *Gunsmoke*. One of his most highly regarded credits was the 1977 TV-movie, based on a true story, *In the Matter of Karen Ann Quinlan* which dealt with the matter of parents deciding whether or not to turn off life support for their comatose daughter. Sitowitz was also a producer of the TV-movie.

Parts of this episode were filmed on location at the Terminal Island Prison. Producer Harold Gast recalls, "It was a very chilling atmosphere. We had to be very careful whee we went, what we did. Sometimes the inmates would howl and make noise when we were filming."

19. The Island Caper (02/08/1972)
Written by: George Bellak. Directed by: Lewis Allen.
Guest Stars: Keenan Wynn, James Olson, Jacqueline Scott, H.M. Wynant.
Synopsis: Cannon tries to help an ex-con (Keenan Wynn) who he had previously helped put away, when he is forced to aid in a bank robbery.
Trivia: H.M. Wynant had one of those faces that TV viewers could recognize, if not his name. He would appear on three episodes of *Cannon* and also on an episode of William Conrad's *Nero Wolfe* series.

Keenan Wynn (1916-1987), the son of comedy legend Ed Wynn, was a consistently dependable character actor of films and TV in his own right. Jacqueline Scott was another favorite of Quinn Martin productions appearing in many episodes of *The Fugitive* (as Richard Kimble's sister), *The FBI, Barnaby Jones, The Streets of San Francisco* among others. This would be, however, her only appearance on *Cannon*. English born director Lewis Allen (1905-2000) directed some superb films during the 1940's including *Those Endearing Young Charms, The Unseen, So Evil My Love, Chicago Deadline* and especially the superb 1944 film *The Uninvited*, one of the very best haunted house films ever made.

20. A Deadly Quiet Town (02/15/1972)
Written by: Robert Lenski. Directed by: Seymour Robbie.
Guest Stars: John Rubenstein, John Larch, Louise Latham, Keith Andes, Dianne Hull, Anne Lockhart.
Synopsis: A father hires Cannon because he is concerned that his college age daughter is involved in a dangerous/murderous cult with a charismatic leader.
Trivia: Robert W. Lenski (1926-2002) is another distinguished *Cannon* writer. He would end up writing six episodes of the series. He was nominated three times for an Emmy Award for his writing of the TV-movies *The Dain Curse, Decoration Day* and *Breathing Lessons*. His final credit, broadcast the year he died, was the TV-movie *A Death in the Family*, based on the James Agee novel.

21. A Flight of Hawks (02/22/1972)
Written by: Stephen Kande. Directed by: Charles S. Dubin.
Guest Stars: Martin Sheen, Joyce Van Patten, Gerald S. O'Loughlin, Arch Johnson, Percy Rodrigues.
Synopsis: A former fighter pilot dies in a mysterious crash on a canyon road and Cannon is hired by the insurance company to prove it was suicide—something Cannon may not be able to do.
Trivia: For his second appearance on *Cannon*, Martin Sheen reprises the character he played in the earlier episode Jerry Warton. Young Willie Aames, four years from his role as Tommy Bradford on the TV-series *Eight is Enough*, has a small part. Charles S. Dubin (1919-2011) was another top-notch director hired for *Cannon*. He would

helm four episodes of the series. Dubin directed 44 episodes of *MASH*—earning three Emmy nominations.

22. The Torch (02/29/1972) Written by: Ronald Austin & James D. Buchanan. Directed by: Michael O'Herlihy.

Guest Stars: Larry Blyden, Anthony Zerbe, Richard Carlson, Sheilah Wells.
Synopsis: Larry Blyden plays an insuance investigator involved with a married woman who is accidentally killed by an arsonist (Anthony Zerbe)—the woman's husband (Richard Carlson) is the police suspect and it's up to Cannon to clear him and get the real culprit.
Trivia: Irish born Michael O'Herlihy (1928-1997) would direct two episodes of *Cannon*. His most notable directing jobs during the sixties was directing eleven episodes of the high school drama *Mr. Novak* and two interesting but not especially successful Disney films, The One and Only, Genuine, Original Family Band and *Smith!* By the 70's he was chiefly directing TV episodes and TV movies and was nominated for an Emmy for his directing of the mini-series *Backstairs at the White House*.

23. Cain's Mark (03/07/1972)
Written by: George Bellak. Directed by: Don Taylor.
Guest Stars: Bradford Dillman, Tom Drake, David Birney, Carmen Mathews. Andrew Rubin.
Synopsis: Cannon is hired by a concerned mother (Carmen Mathews) whose 'bad' (Bradford Dillman) has disappeared. The investigation leads to the 'good' brother (David Birney), and soon Cannon is being framed for a variety of crimes.
Trivia: This was writer George Bellak's second episode of *Cannon*—he would write one more. He had a long line of credits going back to the 1950's on television including many episodes of *The Trials of O'Brien* (a lawyer series starring Peter Falk), *Brenner* and *Doctors and Nurses*. He was nominated for a writing Emmy Award in 1970 for an episode of *CBS Playhouse*. Tom Drake (1918-1982) was once earmarked for stardom by his studio, MGM, and given the plum role of 'The Boy Next Door' to Judy Garland in the classic film *Meet Me in St. Louis*. However, stardom never really materialized though he did work pretty steadily in movies and TV almost up to

the time of his death. Among the other films he appeared in are *Mrs. Parkington, The Green Years, Courage of Lassie, Cass Timberlane, Words and Music* (given a big chance playing composer Richard Rodgers), and *Raintree County.*

24. Murder by Moonlight (03/14/1972)
Written by: Karl Tunberg. **Directed by:** Seymour Robbie.
Guest Stars: Mitchell Ryan, Julie Gregg, Burr DeBenning, Jimmy Lydon, Biff Elliot, Frank Marth, Linn McCarthy.
Synopsis: The Attorney father of a young convict attending college on a study-release program hires Cannon because he suspects his son is being used as a message carrier for a prison mastermind.
Trivia: This was the first of three episodes that Conrad's good friend and producing partner Jimmy Lydon appeared in (he also had a small part in the pilot film). This is also the second episode of the season to feature tough guy character actor Mitchell Ryan. He would appear only once more, in 1975. Writer Karl Tunberg (1909-1992) was nominated twice for writing Oscars for *Ben Hur* (1959) and *Tall, Dark & Handsome* (1941). Tunberg had avoided television writing until 1972 when he wrote an episode of Bonanza. He would spend the remainder of the 70's writing 13 scripts for various TV-shows, including one more episode of *Cannon* before retiring. On rival NBC opposite "Cannon" was the James Garner western series "Nichols" which had an unusual episode in an attempt to revive its ratings. Nichols up to this time had been a rather conventional western so the character of Nichols was killed off and his twin brother (also played by Garner) shows up for the funeral and becomes the new focus of the series. This new 'Nichols' is more in the old 'Maverick' vein.

Season Two Episodes

25. Bad Cats and Sudden Death (9/13/1972)
Written by: Robert Lewin. **Directed by:** Philip Leacock.
Guest Stars: Michael Tolan, James Luisi, Marj Dusay, Severn Darden, Larry Linville.
Synopsis: A District Attorney (Michael Tolin) is accused of the murder of his wife, and calls in Cannon to find the real murderer. Cannon gets additional help from the D.A.'s secretary (Marj Dusay).

Trivia: Writer Robert Lewin (1920-2004) would scribe four episodes of "Cannon." He spent most of his career writing for television despite being nominated for the Best Screenplay Oscar for the 1956 film *The Bold and the Brave*, which was based on his own experiences during World War II. He would be nominated only once for an Emmy for his writing for a 1979 episode of *The Paper Chase*. This would be director Philip Leacock's (1917-1990) only directing credit for "Cannon." Leacock would be nominated for an Emmy for his directing of *The Waltons* episode "The Thanksgiving Story." Larry Linville (1939-2000) is best known for his role as Major Frank Burns for five seasons on *MASH*, of which the first episode would air four days after his performance on "Cannon."

26. Sky Above, Death Below (9/20/1972)
Written by: Hal Sitowiz. **Directed by:** George McCowan.
Guest Stars: Leslie Charleson, Richard Hatch, Ken Lynch, Elaine Devry, Norman Foster.
Synopsis: Cannon is in the ski country of Silverton and Durango, Colorado, where he is investigating the death of a union leader whose daughter says he was murdered.
Trivia: Norman Foster (1903-1976) was an actor-director, who was once married to Claudette Colbert and then enjoyed a long marriage to actress Sally Blane, a sister of Loretta Young. Foster directed several *Charlie Chan* films including two of the series best (*Charlie Chan at Treasure Island* and *Charlie Chan in Panama*). He also directed Orson Welles' *Journey into Fear* and two *Davy Crockett* films for Walt Disney starring Fess Parker. On television Foster directed several episode of his sister-in-law's, Loretta Young, TV-series. This episode of "Cannon" was Foster's first acting job since 1938. Orson Welles also used him in his unreleased film *The Other Side of the Wind* as an actor.

27. Bitter Legion (9/27/1972)
Written by: George Bellak. **Directed by:** Michael O'Herlihy.
Guest Stars: Lloyd Bochner, Scott Hylands, Irene Tsu, James Watkins, Micky Dolenz.
Synopsis: The wife (Irene Tsu) of a Vietnam veteran hires Cannon to find her missing husband—he may have been involved in a plot to steal munitions from a National Guard Armory.

Trivia: Micky Dolenz was best known for being a member of the musical group "The Monkees" as well as one of the stars of the campy television show which enjoyed a two-season run in the late 60's on NBC. Beyond that he was also a child star on the television show *Circus Boy*. Lloyd Bochner (1924-2005), like William Conrad, had a long career in radio and also appeared in one of the best episodes of TV's *The Twilight Zone*, "To Serve Man" (1962).

28. That Was No Lady (10/4/1972)
Written by: Dick Nelson. Directed by: George McCowan.
Guest Stars: Jessica Walter, Robert Webber, Stacy Harris, Don Hamner, Biff Elliot, Clete Roberts.
Synopsis: Jessica Walters plays an attorney who receives threats on her life after an associate is killed in a car bombing. She brings in Cannon to help protect her, and trace the sources of the threats.
Trivia: This was Biff Elliot's (1923-2012) second of three appearances on "Cannon." He also had a small, un-credited, role in the William Conrad directed thriller/noir *Brainstorm* in 1965. Dick Nelson wrote only this episode of "Cannon" and would go on to write individual episodes of Conrad's subsequent series *Nero Wolfe* and *Jake and the Fatman*. Newscaster Clete Roberts, plays a TV newsman in this episode, and was, of course, a very old friend of Conrad's who helped him get into radio.

29. Stakeout (10/11/1972)
Written by: Harold Gast. Directed by: Leo Penn.
Guest Stars: Patrick O'Neal, Belinda Montgomery, Mike Farrell, Sheree North, Charles Bateman.
Synopsis: Cannon is in a bar when it is held up. A young woman (Belinda Montgomery) with the holdup man (Mike Farrell) is shot. She is the daughter of a powerful private eye (Patrick O'Neal) and suddenly everything that Cannon saw happen, apparently didn't.
Trivia: Leo Penn (1921-1998) is the father of actors Sean and Chris Penn and was a very talented television director (and occasional actor) in his own right. He wrote multiple episodes of such series as *Ben Casey, Dr. Kildare, Judd for the Defense, Bonanza, Marcus Welby, M.D., Barnaby Jones* and a whopping 27 episodes of the Andy Griffith legal/mystery series *Matlock*. This is the first of five episodes of *Cannon*

that Penn would direct. In the 40's when he was an actor, Penn was blacklisted, despite his heroism during World War II as a pilot who flew 37 bombing missions over Germany—7 more than was required. His son, Sean Penn, would recall his father as "a patriot to the core." Mike Farrell, who plays the hold-up man was three seasons away from playing good guy Dr. B.J. Hunnicut on *MASH*.

30. The Predators (10/18/1972)
Written by: Arthur Heinemann. Directed by: George McCowan.
Guest Stars: Phyllis Thaxter, Robert Pine, David Sheiner, Pamela Franklin, Eddie Firestone.
Synopsis: A sheep rancher is accused of negligence when a man is killed on her property by a trap that is used to capture coyotes and calls on Cannon for help.
Trivia: The first of three episodes written by Arthur Heinemann, a former animator who helped design *Fantasia* for Walt Disney. As a writer Heinemann wrote several episodes of *Star Trek, The Virginian* and *Bonanza*, before tackling "Cannon." Later he wrote 15 episodes of *Little House on the Prairie* and 5 episodes of the prestigious *ABC Afterschool Specials*, for one of which he won an Emmy Award.

Robert Pine recalls: "I remember it was a Monday morning and all of us gathered early, around 6am—cast, crew and Bill, of course, to fly to Colorado to do location work for the episode. We went to a place called Purgatory, Colorado—it was then a small ski resort—now it's considered a big one. We all stayed in the same motel. We shot the next day from something like 8 in the morning until about 6 at night. Now we were something like 8-9000 feet above sea level and Bill was a large man and he was doing all of this running around and I could tell it was taking a big toll on him. I was thinking 'this is a heart attack waiting to happen.' The next day I come on the set and Bill apologizes to me and says that he was so exhausted from the previous days filming that he didn't have time to learn his lines. I certainly understood—I was pretty tired myself. So Bill explains that because he didn't have time to learn his lines he was going to read his lines off of cards—which he did. Now cut to the next time I'm on the show and now he was using cue cards all the time—he had it down to a science."

31. A Long Way Down (10/25/1972)
Written by: Stephen Kandel. **Directed by:** George McCowan.
Guest Stars: Rosemary Murphy, Dana Elcar, Ned Romero, James A. Watson, Sandy Kenyon.
Synopsis: A doctor (James Watson) at an inner-city hospital is suspected of stealing drugs. The hospital calls on Cannon to determine the truth.
Trivia: The first of ten episodes written by Stephen Kandel. In his long career he wrote for shows as diverse as *Sea Hunt, Gidget, Batman, I-Spy, Room 222, Mannix, Wonder Woman* and *MacGyver*. He also created and produced the Dale Robertson 1966-1968 western series *The Iron Horse*. Kandel later wrote again for Conrad on his short-lived *Nero Wolfe* series.

32. The Rip-Off (11/1/1972)
Written by: Douglas Day Stewart. **Directed by:** George McCowan.
Guest Stars: George Maharis, Stephanie Powers, Robert Mandan, Gene Andrusco, Max Gail, Kathleen Freeman.
Synopsis: A thief breaks into Cannon's apartment and steals his file cabinets—that seem like it might be logical, but why would this thief also steal all of Cannon's furniture? Cannon is pretty sure who the thief is and seeks out the man's ex-wife (Stephanie Powers) for help.
Trivia: Writer Douglas Day Stewart had previously written for *Room 222* prior to *Cannon*, and would go on to write several prestigious projects including acclaimed TV-movies including *Murder or Mercy, The Boy in the Plastic Bubble*, for which he was nominated for an Emmy Award. He also wrote the screenplay to the hit Richard Gere film *An Officer and a Gentleman*, which earned him an Oscar nomination. George Maharis, whose only episode of "Cannon" this would be, was best known for his starring role on the early 60's hit *Route 66*. Stephanie Power was a hard-working TV-actress best known for her role as *The Girl from UNCLE* and would have her most successful TV-role opposite Robert Wagner on the *Hart to Hart* series. Robert Mandan appeared as Chester Tate on the funny 70's soap opera satire *Soap*. Max Gail would go on to play 'Wojo' on *Barney Miller*. Kathleen Freeman was a familiar TV and movie face, perhaps best known for her work as a foil for Jerry Lewis in such films as *The Ladies Man, The Errand Boy, The Nutty Professor, The Disorderly Orderly* and *Three on a Couch*.

33. Child of Fear (11/15/1972)
Written by: Robert W. Lenski. **Directed by:** David Lowell Rich.
Guest Stars: Clu Gulager, Julie Adams, Warren J. Kemmerling, H.M. Wynant, John Lasell, Murray McLeod.
Synopsis: Cannon is on a ranch where he is hired by the owner's wife (Julie Adams) to find the missing owner, who it turns out is being held prisoner on the ranch by the security chief (Clu Gulager) and his men.
Trivia: David Lowell Rich was another of the roster of distinguished directors to helm an episode of "Cannon." His earlier directing credits included episodes of *The Barbara Stanwyck Show, Naked City, Route 66* and *The Alfred Hitchcock Hour*. In the late 60's he had a spell as a director of feature films, none too memorable, and then came back to television. After "Cannon" he moved away from directing episodes of TV-movies and turned to directing several outstanding TV-movies including *The Secret Life of John Chapman, A Family Upside Down, The Defection of Simas Kudirka* (which won him an Emmy), *Nurse*, and *Thursday's Child*.

Julie Adams recalls: "I thought Bill Conrad was very professional, a very good actor, and I enjoyed working with him a great deal. Yes, he used cue cards, but it didn't bother me or hinder my performance."

34. The Shadow Man (11/22/1972)
Written by: Robert Lewin. **Directed by:** Robert Douglas.
Guest Stars: Lois Nettleton, Simon Scott, Bert Freed, Jared Martin, Scott Walker.
Synopsis: Lois Nettleton plays a bewildered wife of an executive who has disappeared after a fall. She hires Cannon to find her husband and Cannon eventually begins to wonder if she is as innocent as she seems.
Trivia: Beautiful Lois Nettleton (1927-2008) has a long list of TV credits. She was nominated three times for a Primetime Emmy Award for her work on the TV-movie *Fear on Trial* (1976) which dealt with blacklisting during the McCarthy era and for her work on individual episodes of the TV-series *The Golden Girls* (1987) and *In the Heat of the Night* (1989)—on which she was a regular during the 88-89 TV season.

35. Hear No Evil (11/29/1972)
Written by: Robert W. Lenski. **Directed by:** Charles S. Dubin.
Guest Stars: William Daniels, Linden Chiles, Alex Rocco, Louise Troy, Lynette Mettey, Wesley Lau.
Synopsis: An electronics expert (William Daniels) just released from prison is threatened and his former police officer wife calls in Cannon for help.
Trivia: At the time of his appearance on this episode of "Cannon", William Daniels was appearing on the nations movie screens in the big screen historical musical *1776* playing John Adams (and recreating his Broadway role). Of course Daniels would go on to win two Emmy Awards for his performance as Dr. Mark Craig on *St. Elsewhere* and also appear on the TV series *Boy Meets World*.

36. The Endangered Species (12/13/1972)
Written by: Del Reisman. **Directed by:** Robert Douglas.
Guest Stars: Carl Betz, Katherine Justice, Andrew Duggan, Billy Green Bush, Neva Patterson.
Synopsis: Cannon investigates when a friend is framed for the killing of his son while on a hunting trip.
Trivia: Carl Betz (1921-1978) was best known for playing Dr. Alex Stone on *The Donna Reed Show* (1958-1966) becoming one of TV's iconic dads. He later won an Emmy for playing a lawyer on *Judd for the Defense*.

37. Nobody Beats the House (12/20/1972)
Written by: Meyer Dolinsky. **Directed by:** Herbert Hirschman.
Guest Stars: Tom Skerritt, Paul Michael Glaser, Corinne Camacho, John Marley, Geoffrey Lewis.
Synopsis: Tom Skerritt plays a man who hires Cannon to protect him from being killed for not paying a gambling debt.
Trivia: Paul Michael Glaser was three years away from his most famous role, playing Detective Dave Starsky opposite David Soul's Hutch on the crime series *Starsky and Hutch* (1975-1979).

38. Hard Rock Roller Coaster (1/3/1973) **Written by:** Meyer Dolinsky with story by Bill S. Ballinger. **Directed by:** Charles S. Dubin.
Guest Stars: Greg Mullavey, Charlotte Stewart, John Vernon, Kathryn Reynolds, William Sargent, Fritz Weaver.

Synopsis: The mob is after a smuggler (John Vernon) and Cannon is hired by an art gallery owner (Fritz Weaver) to find him—but is the art gallery owner really out to help the smuggler or get his hands on him too?
Trivia: This was the third of four episodes directed by Charles S. Durbin (1919-2011) an above average TV director who directed several TV episodes of shows like *Ironside, Hawaii Five-O* (24 episodes), *Lou Grant*, and 44 episodes of *MASH* for which he was nominated for three Emmy Awards.

39. The Dead Samaritan (1/10/1973) Written by: Stephen Kandel with story by Robert Van Scoyk. Directed by: Jerry Jameson.
Guest Stars: Arlene Golonka, Barbara Babcock, David Hedison, Michael Witney, Beverlee McKinsey.
Synopsis: Cannon investigates when a bystander is charged after he sees a woman assaulted by a businessman, but the businessman dies of a heart attack—the question is was this set-up?
Trivia: Arlene Golonka has had a long career on TV but may be best known for her role as "Millie" on *The Andy Griffith Show* and its spin-off *Mayberry RFD*.

40. Death of a Stone Seahorse (1/17/1973)
Written by: Anthony Lawrence. Directed by: William Wiard.
Guest Stars: Sondra Locke, David Soul, Tim O'Connor, Malachi Throne, Don Eiter.
Synopsis: Cannon investigates when a marine biologist is stabbed while on an island conducting research.
Trivia: Sondra Locke was best known for her appearances in several Clint Eastwood films (at one time she had a romantic relationship with the actor as well): *The Outlaw Josey Wales, The Gauntlet, Every Which Way But Loose, Bronco Billy*. In 1968 she was nominated for an Oscar for the film *The Heart is a Lonely Hunter*.

41. Moving Target (1/31/1973)
Written by: Worley Thorne. Directed by: Lawrence Dobkin.
Guest Stars: Susan Oliver, Richard Carlson, Gordon Pinsent, Keith Andes, Charles Bateman, Richard Roat.
Synopsis: Cannon's client (Gordon Pinsent), a writer who has turned

out a biography of a major industrialist, which is revealed to be a hoax. The writer's collaborator dies during a TV interview show and the writer is sure he will be next. Cannon is hired to protect him.
Trivia: This episode was inspired by recent headlines in which writer Clifford Irving claimed he ghost wrote Howard Hughes' autobiography under direction of Hughes, who later denounced Irving and the whole scheme was found to be an elaborate and for a time convincing hoax.

This was the first of nine episodes of *Cannon* directed by Lawrence (Larry) Dobkin, who was a member of the *Gunsmoke* stock company on radio and worked with Conrad innumerable times on *Gunsmoke* and other radio shows.

42. Murder for Murder (2/7/1973)
Written by: Arthur Heinemann. Directed by: Herschel Daugherty.
Guest Stars: Dick Van Patten, Jason Evers, Don Chastain, Mary Frann, Noam Pitlik, Charles Bateman.
Synopsis: Cannon is hired to delve into a closed murder case. The father (Dick Van Patten) of a girl who, it was said, fell from a window while on drugs is out to kill the man (Don Chastain) that he believes was responsible.
Trivia: Veteran actor Dick Van Patten began his career as a child actor and, as such, shared the stage with Fredric March and Tallulah Bankhead in the 1942 Pulitzer Prize winning play *The Skin of Our Teeth*. But he is best known to TV fans as the father on *Eight is Enough*.

43. To Ride a Tiger (2/14/1973)
Written by: Robert W. Lenski. Directed by: Virgil W. Vogel.
Guest Stars: Christine Belford, Ramon Bieri, David S. Cass, Sr, John Larch, Scott Marlow, Paul Lukather, Stewart Moss, Donovan Jones.
Synopsis: A lawyer is kidnapped because he knew who killed a man, Cannon is brought into the case to locate the kidnapped man—but has his hands full with a cop who doesn't like Cannon's snooping.
Trivia: Virgil W. Vogel (1919-1996) began his career as a film editor and was then given an opportunity to direct in the 1950's. One of his most famous films was the sci-fi cult classic *The Mole People*

(1956). However, he spent most of his career directing for television including some 80 episodes of *Wagon Train*, 48 episodes of *The Big Valley* and 29 episodes of *The Streets of San Francisco*.

44. Prisoners (2/21/1973)
Written by: Robert Lewin. **Directed by:** Charles S. Dubin.
Guest Stars: Geraldine Brooks, Harold Gould, JimMcMullan, John David Carson, Julie Cobb.
Synopsis: Cannon is given the difficult assignment of trying to free a man held prisoner in a Turkish prison.
Trivia: 21 year old John David Carson (1952-2009) was a busy young actor at the time of his "Cannon" appearance. He had a significant role in the Rock Hudson-Angie Dickinson film *Pretty Maids All in a Row* and was featured in guest appearances on shows like *Room 222, The Partridge Family, Owen Marshall, Medical Center* and *Lucas Tanner*. Later he had a recurring role on *Falcon Crest* (as Jay Spence). His final role was in the movie *Pretty Woman*.

45. The Seventh Grave (2/28/1973)
Written by: E. Arthur Kean. **Directed by:** John Badham.
Guest Stars: Barry Nelson, Jim Davis, Robert Donner, Lou Frizzell, Shelley Duvall.
Synopsis: Cannon is called in to investigate a series of murders involving young women in a small town.
Trivia: This was an early showcase for Shelly Duvall, who had already had roles in *Brewster McCloud* and *McCabe and Mrs. Miller*. This episode of "Cannon" was her first TV work and she was only a year or so from her breakthrough movie roles in *Thieves Like Me* and *Nashville*. Her most famous film would cast her as Jack Nicholson's wife in *The Shining*.

46. Catch Me If You Can (3/7/1973)
Written by: Douglas Day Stewart. **Directed by:** William Hale.
Guest Stars: Anthony Zerbe, Dana Wynter, Jack Riley, Jay W. MacIntosh, William Sargent.
Synopsis: An intriguing woman about a man who hires Cannon to keep him from killing again, because he can't control his blood lust.
Trivia: While "Cannon" ordinarily didn't have supporting characters

it did from time to time have recurring characters. This is the third and final appearance by veteran actor William Sargent as Police Lt. Driscoll. Prior to "Cannon" he had made guest appearances on such shows as *The Twilight Zone, Alfred Hitchcock Presents, Ripcord, Dr.Kildare, Mission: Impossible* and *The FBI*. He seemed to specialize in playing doctors or cops.

47. Press Pass to the Slammer (3/14/1973)
Written by: Meyer Dolinsky. **Directed by:** Leo Penn.
Guest Stars: Stuart Margolin, Ron Hayes, Marlyn Mason, Geoffrey Horne, Hanna Hertelendy, Harrison Page.
Synopsis: A reporter is threatened with jail unless she reveals a source, she can't do this without ruining her professional standing so she hires Cannon to prove her story without using the source.
Trivia: Marlyn Mason was a pretty young actress with lots of TV guest shots on shows like *Ben Casey, Dr. Kildare, I Spy, Perry Mason* (the last episode of that series), and *Longstreet* (actually appearing in 23 episodes of this James Franciscus series). She only appeared on one *Cannon*, but also made a guest shot on Conrad's later series, *Jake and the Fatman*.

48. Deadly Heritage (3/21/1973)
Written by: Robert Lewin. **Directed by:** Seymour Robbie.
Guest Stars: Beverly Garland, John Anderson, Lynne Marta, David Macklin, Kathryn Reynolds, Glynn Turman.
Synopsis: A wealthy patron of the arts (Beverly Garland) hires Cannon to locate her missing stepson. In the course of the hunt, Cannon uncovers what appears to be a plot to eliminate the woman.
Trivia: Beverly Garland (1926-2008) had a long & active career without really becoming a big star. She was one of the first women to headline a dramatic police series with *Decoy* (1957-1959). She went on to play Bing Crosby's television wife on the short-lived *The Bing Crosby Show* (1964-1965) but had more luck as Fred MacMurray's TV wife in the final three seasons of *My Three Sons*. She later went on to play Kate Jackson's mother on the 80's hit *Scarecrow & Mrs. King*.

Season Three Episodes

49 & 50. He Who Digs His Grave (9/12/1973)
Written by: Stephen Kandel. Directed by: Richard Donner.
Guest Stars: Anne Baxter, David Janssen, Barry Sullivan, Murray Hamilton, Tim O'Connor, Lee Purcell, Royal Dana, Robert Hogan.
Synopsis: An old war buddy of Cannon's is arrested on two counts of murder in a small cattle town and it's up to Cannon to get him off.
Trivia: This was a star-studded two-hour third season premiere episode which had location scenes filmed in Grass Valley, California. In one incident just as Conrad was about to start a scene with Anne Baxter a cloud of some 300 pigeons came down out of the sky. This was actually part of the script! According to one contemporary news report of the scene being shot, "After six abortive scene takes, much wing flapping, and several beak passes perilously close to the actor's eyes, (director) Donner settled for a raven landing on Conrad's arm. When asked later if he ever wanted to work with ravens again, Conrad replied, 'Never more.'"

51. Memo from a Dead Man (9/19/1973)
Written by: Robert C. Dennis. Directed by: Richard Donner.
Guest Stars: Martin Sheen, Sheila Larken, Robert Webber, Dennis Redfield, John Carter, Regis Cordic, Lee Paul.
Synopsis: A business tycoon who dies in an auto crash leaves a will asking Cannon to conduct an investigation into his own death.
Trivia: Character actor John Carter often specialized in playing lawmen including a recurring role as Lt. Biddle in 94 episodes of *Barnaby Jones*. He also played a cop opposite Henry Fonda on *The Smith Family*. One of his more recent roles gave him a promotion to being a Judge on *Law & Order*.

52. Hounds of Hell (9/26/1973)
Written by: Jack Turley. Directed by: Lawrence Dobkin.
Guest Stars: Geoffrey Deuel, Joel Fabiani, Jim McMullan, Ford Rainey, Bill Zuckert, Nancy Piddy.
Synopsis: When two former Vietnam combat member units are killed by dog attacks, Cannon is called in to find who is behind the attacks and to prevent any others from occurring.

53. Target in the Mirror (10/3/1973)
Written by: Robert Blees. **Directed by:** Gene Nelson.
Guest Stars: Claude Akins, Alex Rocco, Frank Marth, Julie Gregg, Paul Carr, Laura Campbell.
Synopsis: A woman wants to hire Cannon , but he turns her down. She is later found murdered, and Cannon investigates both her murder and the reason why she wanted to hire him.
Trivia: Writer Robert Blees, a former fighter pilot during WWII, began in movies, writing scripts for such films as *All I Desire, Magnificent Obsession, Cattle Queen from Montana, One Desire* and *Autumn Leaves*, before alternating between TV and movies. In later years he wrote the screenplays for three horror films: *Frogs, Whoever Slew Auntie Roo?* And *Dr. Phibes Rises Again*.

54. Murder by Proxy (10/10/1973)
Written by: Robert W. Lenski. **Directed by:** Robert Douglas.
Guest Stars: Anne Francis, Linden Chiles, Marj Dusay, Ross Hagen, Charles Bateman.
Synopsis: Anne Francis is Cannon's client, a publicist who has been framed for the murder of a client, a movie producer—but the real culprits are the producer's wife (Marj Dusay) and her boy toy (Linden Chiles).
Trivia: This is the fifth and final episode that Charles Bateman plays Lt. Tarcher, Bateman had played another lawman in the first episode of the series as well. Bateman would go on to appear in two popular TV daytime soaps, *Days of Our Lives* and *Santa Barbara*.

55. Night Flight to Murder (10/17/1973)
Written by: Carey Wilber. **Directed by:** Michael Caffey.
Guest Stars: David Hedison, John Vernon, Jamie Smith-Jackson, Norman Alden, Robert Patten, Barney Phillips.
Synopsis: Cannon investigates the disappearance of a small plane which was carrying $3 million in negotiable bonds. Later the airplane turns up abandoned in the wilds of Mexico with the body of the co-pilot on board.
Trivia: This was David Hedison's second episode of "Cannon" and his favorite.

56. Come Watch Me Die (10/24/1973)
Written by: Herb Meadow. Directed by: George McCowan.
Guest Stars: Michael Tolan, Meg Foster, Will Kuluva, John Larch, Ahna Capri, Don Stroud, Eugene Peterson.
Synopsis: Cannon is hired to find a convicted murderer who escaped from a mental hospital before the police do.
Trivia: Meg Foster played Detective Chris Cagney in six episodes of *Cagney and Lacey* before CBS replaced her with Sharon Gless. The reported reason? They wanted someone more feminine.

57. The Perfect Alibi (10/31/1973) Written by: Ray Brenner & Jack Guss. Directed by: Robert Douglas.
Guest Stars: L.Q. Jones, Richard Anderson, Whit Bissell, William Watson, Tom Troupe, Burton Gilliam, Rutanya Alda.
Synopsis: Cannon visits a small southern town where he runs into a gang of crooks and a red neck sheriff (L.Q. Jones) who early on bangs heads with Cannon before coming to rely on him.

Richard Anderson recalls: "Bill Conrad was pretty much to himself and knew who he was and just went and did it. He didn't seem to do a lot of visiting with people and between scenes spent most of his time in his dressing room."

58. Dead Lady's Tears (11/7/1973)
Written by: Steve Fisher. Directed by: Virgil W. Vogel.
Guest Stars: Dabney Coleman, Peter White, Charles Haid, John Considine, Amanda McBroom.
Synopsis: A model is murdered in her apartment and Cannon is hired to clear her boyfriend of the charge.
Trivia: Dabney Coleman at the time of this appearance was a hard working journeyman actor with many credits to his name, but without many people knowing his name. That would change a few years alter with his roles in the films *On Golden Pond*, *Tootsie* (as the amorous TV soap opera director) and *Nine to Five* (as the sexist boss of Jane Fonda, Lily Tomlin and Dolly Parton). He would star in three critically acclaimed but little watched TV series: *Buffalo Bill*, *The Slap Maxwell Story*, and *Madman of the People*.

59. The Limping Man (11/14/1973)
Written by: Shirl Hendryx. Directed by: Michael Caffey.
Guest Stars: Jason Evers, Richard O'Brien, Barbara Stuart, Anthony Zerbe, Vic Tayback, Dick Dinman.
Synopsis: Cannon's old friend (Jason Evers)—a cop— is in trouble because he has not given his all in the capture of a suspect.
Trivia: Vic Tayback (1930-1990) is best known as the cook and owner of Mel's Diner on the 70's TV series *Alice*. Prior to that he played many TV and film roles mainly as cops or heavies. Among the films he appeared in are *Papillon, Emperor of the North, Maxie, Thunderbolt* and *Lightfoot*, as well as the role of Mel in the film version of *Alice Doesn't Live Here Anymore*.

60. Trial by Terror (11/21/1973)
Written by: Larry Brody. Directed by: Robert Douglas.
Guest Stars: Mark Miller, Ray Danton, Stewart Moss, Simon Scott, Keith Andes, Anne Randall, Kelley Miles, Francesca Hilton, Arlen Stuart.
Synopsis: Cannon tries to find the kidnapped daughter of a judge whose case involves a mob boss.
Trivia: Kelley Miles is the daughter and in real life is the daughter of Vera Miles. Francesca Hilton is the daughter of Zsa Zsa Gabor and Arlen Stuart (a probation officer in the episode) is the sister of Jean Peters.

61. Murder by the Numbers (11/28/1973)
Written by: Robert Blees with story by Michael McTaggart. Directed by: George McCowan.
Guest Stars: Dina Merrill, Glenn Corbett, Burr DeBenning, Jane Merrow, William Swan, Quinn K. Redeker.
Synopsis: Two brothers (Glenn Corbett & Burr De Benning) kill a blackmailer. The wife of the blackmailer seeks Cannon's help which leads him to a wealthy Mrs. Hawthorne (Dina Merrill).
Trivia: This was Dina Merrill's first role after the boating death of her son the previous September. At this time Miss Merrill was married to the Academy Award winning actor Cliff Robertson.

62. Valley of the Damned (12/5/1973)
Written by: Carey Wilber. Directed by: Lawrence Dobkin.
Guest Stars: Leslie Nielsen, Corrine Camacho, Jay Silverheels, Kaz Garas, Wesley Lau, Harry Lauter.
Synopsis: When an Indian is accused of murder an Indian Center hires Cannon to clear him—if he can.
Trivia: Leslie Nielsen at the time of this appearance was best known for his dramatic TV appearances, but all of that would change in 1980 with the film *Airplane* in which he lampooned his image and found new life as a comedian on TV and films, most notably in the *Naked Gun* films. Jay Silverheels, of course, is best known as 'Tonto' on TV's *The Lone Ranger*.

63. A Well-Remembered Terror (12/12/1973)
Written by: Robert I. Holt. Directed by: Seymour Robbie.
Guest Stars: Robert Goulet, Robert Pine, Davey Davison, Michael Strong, Eric Server, Lou Frizzell.
Synopsis: A couple (Robert Pine & Davey Davison) hire Cannon to find out who is blackmailing them, and Cannon discovers it goes back to an unsolved hijacking from years earlier.
Trivia: Singer Robert Goulet (1933-2007) often appeared in dramatic roles on TV shows (in addition to "Cannon" he would appear on *Mission: Impossible, Police Woman, Matt Houston, Fantasy Island* and *Murder, She Wrote*). In films he is best known for his role in *Beetlejuice* (1988) and *The Naked Gun 2 ½: The Smell of Fear*.

64. Arena of Fear (12/19/1973)
Written by: Meyer Dolinsky. Directed by: Marc Daniels.
Guest Stars: Nick Nolte, Jess Walton, Reta Shaw, John Marley, Pat Renella.
Synopsis: The strange behavior of a heavyweight boxing contender, who threatens to leave the country just before a fight that could lead to the championship, puzzles his girlfriend who asks Cannon for help.
Trivia: A prolific director since the early days of television, Marc Daniels (1912-1989) directed the entire first season of *I Love Lucy*. He later returned to direct six episodes of Ball's final series *Life with Lucy* (1986-1987). Twice he was nominated for a prime time Emmy Award for episodes of *Alice* and *Fame*.

This was an early showcase for Nick Nolte who would gain hit pay dirt three years later with the popular TV mini-series *Rich Man, Poor Man*. Jess Walton was a busy young actress at the time of this first of three appearances on *Cannon*. Today she is best known for her Emmy Award winning role as Jill Abbott on the popular CBS soap opera *The Young and the Restless*.

65. Photo Finish (01/02/1974)
Written by: John Hawkins. Directed by: George McCowan.
Guest Stars: Jack Cassidy, Herb Edleman, Lenore Kasdorf, Anthony Eisley, Kathryn Reynolds, Gerald McRaney, Hal Williams.
Synopsis: Cannon is hired by a General (Jack Cassidy) to find details of the death of his brother, dead for several years. The case takes an intriguing turn as Cannon delves into and finds out who the real killer is.
Trivia: This is considered one of the series finest episodes. Singer-actor Jack Cassidy (1927-1976) seemed to specialize in playing suave villains during the 70's including on three excellent episodes of *Columbo*. He was twice nominated for an Emmy (for his role on the TV series *He and She* and the TV movie *The Andersonville Trial*). He memorably played John Barrymore in the 1975 movie *W.C. Fields and Me*. He was at one time married to Shirley Jones and is the father of David Cassidy.

66. Duel in the Desert (1/16/1974)
Written by: Robert C. Dennis. Directed by: William Wiard.
Guest Stars: Joan Van Ark, James Wainwright, Denver Pyle, Paul Brinegar, David Lewis, Les Lannom.
Synopsis: While he is delivering the ransom to free a kidnapping victim, Cannon suffers amnesia.
Trivia: Denver Pyle (1920-1997), who often played rural characters, hillbillies and mountain men, was a trained stage actor who often appeared in westerns on TV and movies (*The Man Who Shot Liberty Valance, Cahill: US Marshal*), but his most memorable film is that of the handcuffed hostage Texas Ranger in the film *Bonnie and Clyde*. On television he is best known for two roles: Uncle Jesse on *The Dukes of Hazzard* and Briscoe Darling on *The Andy Griffith Show*.

67. Where's Jennifer (1/23/1974)
Written by: Robert and Phyllis White. **Directed by:** Gene Nelson.
Guest Stars: Pamela Franklin, Christopher Stone, Ann Doran, Russ Conway, Bill Quinn, Michael Rupert, Russ Conway, Keye Luke.
Synopsis: Virginia McKeller (Pamela Franklin) hires Cannon to find her sister Jennifer, who reportedly died five years earlier in a drowning, but Virginia believes that Jennifer is still alive.
Trivia: British actress Pamela Franklin began her career as one of the young wards of governess Deborah Kerr in the classic 1961 horror film *The Innocents*. Keye Luke, who plays a small but colorful role, was best known as Charlie Chan's #1 son in a series of popular "Chan" films for 20th Century Fox starring Warner Oland. On television, he later played 'Master Po' on *Kung Fu*.

68. Blood Money (2/6/1974)
Written by: Stephen Kandel. **Directed by:** William Wiard.
Guest Stars: Perry King, Diana Muldaur, Peter Haskall, Dick DeCoit, Russell Johnson, John Milford,
Synopsis: A doctor is accused of helping a prisoner escape. Cannon is brought in to find the truth.
Trivia: Guest-star Russell Johnson was best known, of course, as 'The Professor' on *Gilligan's Island*.

69. Death of a Hunter (2/13/1974)
Written by: Meyer Dolinsky. **Directed by:** George McCowan.
Guest Stars: Edward Mulhare, Sharon Acker, Ellen Weston, Herbert Jefferson, Jr., Andy Romano, Michael Alaimo, Jill Jaress, Bill Erwin.
Synopsis: When a man is killed, supposedly by a lion at the wildlife park he owns and operates, his wife hires Cannon to find out if he was murdered, as the lion was supposedly tranquilized.
Trivia: Irish born Edward Mulhare (1923-1997) was best known for two TV-series, as Captain Gregg on *The Ghost and Mrs. Muir* and Devon Miles on *Knight Rider*.

70. The Cure that Kills (2/20/1974)
Written by: Worley Thorne. **Directed by:** Seymour Robbie.
Guest Stars: Andrew Parks, Richard X. Slattery, Herman Poppe, Toni Janotta, Peter Ford.

Synopsis: A phony faith healer kills a witness to a murder he committed.
Trivia: Actor Peter Ford worked in several films of which starred his father, Glenn Ford (*The Gazebo, Pocketful of Miracles, Fate is the Hunter, The Rounders...*) but had a more substantive role in his dad's TV-series, *Cade's County*, playing a deputy sheriff.

71. Bobby Loved Me (2/27/1974)
Written by: Joel Murcott. **Directed by:** Lawrence Dobkin.
Guest Stars: Pippa Scott, Jon Cypher, Paul Stevens, Claudia Jennings, Hal Williams, Virginia Gregg.
Synopsis: When a con-man is murdered, his girlfriend hires Cannon to investigate.
Trivia: Actress Virginia Gregg (1916-1986) played many roles during her career and while she never appeared on screen she did provide the voice of 'Mrs. Bates' in *Psycho, Psycho II,* and *Psycho III*. Her voice work was equally famous and she was one of the busiest radio actresses of her time—she was a member of Jack Webb's stock company and did many radio and TV episodes of *Dragnet*.

72. Triangle of Terror (3/13/1974)
Written by: Carey Wilber. **Directed by:** George McCowan.
Guest Stars: Lloyd Bochner, Dana Wynter, David Frankham, Thalmus Rasulala, Don Knight, Maidie Norman.
Synopsis: When her father is found dead under mysterious circumstances, his daughter hires Cannon to investigate. This episode is set in the West Indies.
Trivia: British born David Frankham is best known for his roles in three Vincent Price films: *Return of the Fly, Master of the World,* and *Tales of Terror*. In addition he did numerous appearances on episodic television in shows like *Alfred Hitchcock Presents, Thriller & The Alfred Hitchcock Hour*. He also voiced the part of Sgt. Tibbs in the Disney classic *101 Dalmatians*.

73. The Stalker (3/20/1974)
Written by: Richard Newhafer. **Directed by:** Lawrence Dobkin.
Guest Stars: Luke Askew, Cindy Williams, Darrell Larson, Russell Thorson, Lew Brown, Biff Elliot.

Synopsis: It's hard for Cannon to enjoy his vacation at a remote fishing village when he has an escaped murderer stalking him.
Trivia: Cindy Williams had just made a name for herself in films the previous year with the hit *American Graffiti* (as Ron Howard's girlfriend), and was just a few years away from TV stardom as 'Shirley' on *Laverne and Shirley*.

Fourth Season Episodes

74. Kelly's Song (9/11/1974)
Written by: S.S. Schweitzer. **Directed by:** William Wiard.
Guest Stars: Stephanie Powers, James Sloyan, Frank Marth, Fred Beir, Barry Russo, Skip Ward, Janice Heiden.
Synopsis: Stephanie Powers plays an ex-call-girl that Cannon almost literally blackmails to get her help in nabbing a vice-ring chief.
Trivia: At this point in Stephanie Powers' career she was best known for playing *The Girl from UNCLE*, but a decade later she would be appearing in a more successful series, *Hart to Hart*. Between those two series she made the rounds of appearing in countless episodes of TV-series and TV-movies, mini-series.

75. The Hit Man (9/18/1974)
Written by: Robert Heverly. **Directed by:** William Wiard.
Guest Stars: Richard Kiley, Ray Danton, Christopher Connelly, Paul Stewart, Val Avery, Michael Bell.
Synopsis: A hit man hires Cannon to take his place, and to not kill the intended victim.
Trivia: Paul Stewart (1908-1986) was a founding member of Orson Welles' Mercury Theater—both on stage and radio (including the classic *The War of the Worlds*). Stewart played Charles Foster Kane's valet, Raymond, in *Citizen Kane*. Other films include: *Johnny Eager, Mr. Lucky, Champion, Twelve O'Clock High, Appointment with Danger, Kiss Me Deadly,* and *King Creole* with Elvis Presley.

76. Voice from the Grave (9/25/1974)
Written by: Robert Hamner. **Directed by:** William Wiard.
Guest Stars: Robert Webber, Jason Evers, Michael Baseleon, Madlyn Rhue, Dennis Patrick, Ford Rainey, Virginia Gregg, Milton Frome.

Synopsis: A retired detective is a target of an attempted hit, and hires Cannon to look into the probable reason—a 14-year old homicide at a nightclub.
Trivia: Tall, bald Milton Frome (1909-1989) was a well-known character actor whose name may not be known to many but his face was quite recognizable. He appeared in well over 100 movies and TV programs including as a foil to Jerry Lewis in ten films. He appears in "Cannon" as a night club owner.

77. Lady in Red (10/2/1974)
Written by: Max Hodge. **Directed by:** William Wiard.
Guest Stars: Steve Forrest, David Soul, Laraine Stephens, Claudia Jennings, Robert Emhardt, Larry Ward.
Synopsis: A husband hires Cannon to follow his wife, who is carrying negotiable bonds, and is soon led into a murder investigation.
Trivia: Steve Forrest (1925-2013) was the brother of Dana Andrews. He never equaled Andrew's success in films, but he did do quite well on television including his own hit 70's series *SWAT.*

78. The Deadly Trail (10/16/1974)
Written by: Calvin Clements, Jr. **Directed by:** George McCowan.
Guest Stars: Kevin McCarthy, Katherine Cannon, William Smithers, Ronne Troup, Whitney Blake.
Synopsis: An armament magnate (Kevin McCarthy), who doesn't have long to live, hires Cannon to locate his only daughter and heiress to his fortune.
Trivia: Ronne Troup is the daughter of trumpet player Bobby Troup and stepdaughter of singer Julie London. She also played Chip Douglas's girlfriend and later wife on the last couple of seasons of *My Three Sons.* Whitney Blake was the beautiful Mrs. B (Missy) on Hazel for its first four seasons and is the mother of actress Meredith Baxter.

79. The Exchange (10/23/1974)
Written by: Jackson Gillis. **Directed by:** George McCowan.
Guest Stars: Robert Loggia, Edward Binns, George McCallister, Suzann Arnold, Russell Thorson.
Synopsis: Cannon tries to protect a police officer (Edward Binns)

from an ex-convict (Robert Loggia) who seeks revenge for the death of his younger brother.
Trivia: Robert Loggia has had a very busy career in movies and television since the early 50's and still going strong today. To some, his most famous role might be that of MacMillan, the toy company owner, in the hit Tom Hanks film *Big* (1988) in which he dances a duet with Hanks on a foot operated electronic keyboard, performing "Heart and Soul." He was also nominated for an Oscar as Best Supporting Actor for his performance in the film *Jagged Edge* (1985).

80. The Avenger (10/30/1974)
Written by: Robert Sherman. Directed by: Corey Allen.
Guest Stars: Robert Walker, Jr., Dane Clark, Greg Mullavey, Kay Lenz, Diana Douglas, George Gaynes, David Dukes, Pat Morita.
Synopsis: Cannon enlists the aid of a policeman friend to find the runaway son of some wealthy friends. The boy's involvement with heroin leads to the policeman's death. The dead man's brother blames Cannon for the death and pretends to help him while actually setting him up for revenge.
Trivia: Robert Walker, Jr., the son of actor Robert Walker and Jennifer Jones, and a look-a-like for his dad, was a very busy actor in his own right especially during the 60's and 70's. He played the title role in the 1964 Warner Brothers film *Ensign Pulver* and later worked opposite John Wayne and Kirk Douglas in the western *The War Wagon* (1967). On television he appeared on many series including *The Defenders, Combat, Bonanza, Star Trek, Columbo, Police Woman, Dallas* and *Murder She Wrote*.

81. A Killing in the Family (11/6/1974)
Written by: Larry Alexander. Directed by: George McCowan.
Guest Stars: Peter Strauss, Robert Mandan, Jane Kean, Simon Scott, Paul Koslo.
Synopsis: The son of a wealthy business man hires Cannon to find out whether his wife's death was an accident an accident or murder.
Trivia: Jane Kean (1923-2013) assumed the role of 'Trixie Norton' in a series of "Honeymooners" sketches on the 1960's *The Jackie Gleason Show* as well as "Honeymooners" TV-specials in the 1970's.

82. Flashpoint (11/13/1974)
Written by: Robert Heverly. Directed by: William Wiard.
Guest Stars: Ruth Roman, Robert Brandon, Kristoffer Tabori, Robert Reiser, Jimmy Lydon.
Synopsis: Police arrest the wrong man for a series of rape/murders and Cannon has to help save the accused from hanging by vigilantes.
Trivia: This episode was filmed in part at Snake River Canyon and Shonshone Falls in Idaho. Ruth Roman (1922-1999) had a long career in both movies and television. Her best known film is the Alfred Hitchcock classic *Strangers on a Train* (1951) in which she plays Farley Granger's love interest. She also had good roles in *The Window, Champion* and *Beyond the Forest*.

83. The Man Who Couldn't Forget (11/20/1974)
Written by: Robert I. Holt. Directed by: George McCowan.
Guest Stars: Leslie Nielsen, Alf Kjellin, James Keach, Joan Van Ark, Alfred Ryder, John S. Ragin, John Devlin.
Synopsis: Cannon has the unsavory task of protecting accused Nazi's from Nazi hunters who don't want to bring them to justice, but want to exact revenge.

84. The Sounds of Silence (12/4/1974) Written by: Stephen Kandel, Anthony Spinner. Directed by: George McCowan.
Guest Stars: Leslie Charleson, Andrew Prine, David White, Estelle Winwood, Robert Quary.
Synopsis: A woman hires Cannon to find her fiancé, who has disappeared, leading Cannon to try and penetrate a tight security curtain of the financial institution the man worked for.
Trivia: David White is best known for his work as 'Larry Tate' on the classic TV-series *Bewitched* (1964-1972). Estelle Winwood (1883-1984) was for a long time a leading player on the London and New York stage but is familiar to TV viewers for her countless roles playing eccentric old ladies.

85. The Prisoner (12/11/1974)
Written by: Norman Hudis. Directed by: William Wiard.
Guest Stars: Peter Haskell, Steven Keats, Paul Jenkins, Edward Power, Ed Gilbert, Tim Herbert, Stanley Clements, David Mooney.

Synopsis: A rich businessman (Peter Haskell) wants a hit man to bump off a guy and Cannon goes undercover as the hit man.
Trivia: Peter Haskell (1934-2010) had a long line of TV credits going back to the early 60's and may be best known for his role as Kevin Grant in all 41 episodes of *Bracken's World* and as the adversary of Rudy Jordache (Peter Strauss) on *Rich Man, Poor Man Book II*.

86. Daddy's Little Girl (12/18/1974)
Written by: Larry Alexander. **Directed by:** Leslie H. Martinson.
Guest Stars: Leif Erickson, Kitty Winn, Vincent Baggetta, Ed Bakey, Henry Capps, Frank Christi, Jeff DeBenning, Conrad Janis.
Synopsis: The wife of a football player has kept a big secret from him—her dad (Leif Erickson) is a mob boss and now the mob wants him to do them a favor.
Trivia: Leif Erickson (1911-1986) had worked in films since the 1930's and TV since the 1950's. He was once married to the troubled actress Frances Farmer. He is best known for his role as 'Big John' on the western series *The High Chaparral* (1967-1971).

87. The Conspirators (1/1/1975)
Written by: Margaret Armen. **Directed by:** George McCowan.
Guest Stars: Tom Skerritt, Dabbs Greer, Hilly Hicks, Royce Applegate, Dick Balduzzi, Rayford Barnes.
Synopsis: Cannon travels to Texas to investigate a woman's mysterious death.
Trivia: Margaret Armen (1921-2003) made her name in the often male dominated TV writing industry from the early 1960's until she retired in the early 80's. She wrote for several western series including *Lawman, The Rifleman, The Big Valley*—as well as three episodes of the classic 1960's *Star Trek*.

88. Coffin Corner (1/15/1975) **Written by:** Robert I. Holt with story by Rick Husky. **Directed by:** George McCowan.
Guest Stars: Gary Lockwood, Jim McMullan, Patty McCormack, Noble Willingham, Karl Swenson, Corinne Camacho.
Synopsis: Cannon flies to Tampa, Florida, to find a man who abruptly withdrew a large sum of money from his bank account and then disappeared with two gunmen on his heels.

Trivia: Patty McCormack is a survivor. She had her first brush with fame on Broadway and TV as the evil little girl 'Rhoda' in *The Bad Seed* (for which she was nominated for a supporting actress Oscar). Despite the ups and downs of a child star she survived and continues to work today as a highly sought character actress.

89. Perfect Fit for a Frame (1/22/1975)
Written by: Robert Hamner. **Directed by:** William Wiard.
Guest Stars: Mitch Ryan, Kathleen Cody, Ralph Meeker, Robert Gentry, James Sutorious, Robert Donner.
Synopsis: Kathleen Cody plays a woman who literally throws her husband (Ralph Meeker) to the sharks, but when he survives she tricks her body guard, Cannon, into killing him and frames him for murder.
Trivia: Tough guy actor Ralph Meeker (1920-1988) was a busy film and TV actor, whose best film performance was as private eye Mike Hammer in Robert Aldrich's terrific 1955 film *Kiss Me Deadly*.

90. Killer on the Hill (1/29/1975)
Written by: Carey Wilber. **Directed by:** Harry Falk.
Guest Stars: Michael Tolan, Lawrence Pressman, Brooke Bundy, Ellen Weston, George DiCenzo, Milton Selzer.
Synopsis: A professional killer, hired by the top aides of a well-known political figure, keeps Cannon on guard while he works to prove that the owner of a construction company did not try to assassinate the politician.
Trivia: Veteran writer Carey Wilber (1916-1998) had been writing for television since the early 1950's on shows like *Maverick, Rawhide, The Virginian, Tarzan* and six episodes of *Cannon*, of which this was the third. To many he may be best known for writing the *Star Trek* episode "Space Seed" which inspired the popular movie *Star Trek: The Wrath of Khan*.

91. Missing at FL307 (2/5/1975)
Written by: Carey Wilber. **Directed by:** William Wiard.
Guest Stars: Bradford Dillman, Jess Walton, Mark Gordon, Eddie Barth, James Chandler, Lee Delano.
Synopsis: Cannon investigates when a former convict boards an

airliner on his way for a reunion with his daughter and is missing when the plane lands.

Trivia: Busy actor Bradford Dillman has played many roles in films, TV and Broadway. On Broadway he was part of the landmark 1956 production of *Long Day's Journey Into Night* with Fredric March, Florence Eldridge and Jason Robards. In films he was one of the young thrill murderers in *Compulsion*. On Television he worked on such diverse series as *Alfred Hitchcock Presents, Dr. Kildare, Judd for the Defense, Night Gallary, Mary Tyler Moore,* and did the round of Quinn Martin series including *The FBI, Barnaby Jones, The Streets of San Francisco* and two episodes of *Cannon*.

92. The Set Up (2/12/1975)
Written by: Robert Sherman. **Directed by:** George McCowan.
Guest Stars: John Vernon, Linda Marsh, Davey Davison, Norman Alden, Oliver Clark, Mark Allen.
Synopsis: Cannon is set up to be the victim of a mistaken identity and is almost killed in the process.
Trivia: Character actor John Vernon (1932-2005) specialized in playing villains and hard-nosed authority figures. Among his credits: the Hitchcock film *Topaz*, the crusading coroner *Wojeck*,(on Canadian TV), and multiple episodes of *Mannix, Mission: Impossible, The FBI, Kung Fu,* and four episodes of *Cannon*. He later played Dean Vernon Wormer on the short lived *Animal House* rip-off *Delta House* and played Secretary of State Seward in the TV mini-series *The Blue and the Gray*. Later in his career he did a great deal of voice work.

93. The Investigator (2/26/1975)
Written by: Robert C. Dennis. **Directed by:** George McCowan.
Guest Stars: Hari Rhodes, Cameron Mitchell, Marianne McAndrews, Keith Andes, Morgan Paull.
Synopsis: A mayor of a Midwestern city (Hari Rhodes) is beset by corruption in his police department that results in a number of burglaries when lawmen look the other way. The mayor seeks Cannon's help.
Trivia: Hari Rhodes (1932-1992) was an outstanding African-American actor who began appearing on television in the early sixties. He would make three appearances on *Cannon*, in which this is the first.

He made few movies but a stand-out is Sam Fuller's mystery-drama, *Shock Corridor* (1963).

94. Lady on the Run (3/5/1975)
Written by: Gerald Sanford. **Directed by:** George McCowan.
Guest Stars: Barbara Rush, Barbara Luna, Victor Mohica, Russell Johnson, Barry Atwater.
Synopsis: Cannon searches for the wife of an industrialist who is seeking refuge at a sanitarium after she witnessed a murder.
Trivia: Colorado born Barbara Rush began her career as in films *It Came from Outer Space, Magnificent Obsession, Captain Lightfoot, The Young Lions, The Bramble Bush*. Despite good performances and great looks she never really clicked in films and spent much of the rest of her career working quite lucratively in television including the role of Marsha

95. Vengeance (3/12/1975)
Written by: Robert I. Holt. **Directed by:** Alf Kjellin.
Guest Stars: Monte Markham, Clu Gulager, Nancy Malone, Lloyd Gough, John Lupton, Brenda Venus, Clint Young.
Synopsis: A phony CIA agent (Monte Markham) lands a man (Clu Gulager) in prison. The man's wife (Nancy Malone) hires Cannon to help her husband.
Trivia: Monte Markham was one of the busiest actors of the 1970's and is still busy to this day. In the 70's he starred in *Mr. Deeds Goes to Town* (based on the 1936 Frank Capra film playing the role that Gary Cooper played), and *The New Perry Mason*, which didn't work because memories of the old Perry Mason (Raymond Burr) were so strong, and lots of guest shots on TV shows from *Hawaii Five-O* to *Mary Tyler Moore*, as well as TV-movies.

96. Tomorrow Ends at Noon (3/19/1975)
Written by: Robert C. Dennis. **Directed by:** William Wiard.
Guest Stars: Harold Gould, Cal Bellini, Ayn Ruymen, Chalres Cioffi, Cheryl Waters, Edward Ansara, Harvey Jason.
Synopsis: Terrorists kidnap the daughter of a prominent businessman in order to win the release of a comrade from prison.
Trivia: This is the third and final episode to feature guest star Harold

Gould, who was at the time also appearing as Martin Morgenstern, Rhoda's dad on both Mary Tyler Moore and Rhoda.

97. Search and Destroy (4/2/1975) Written by: Stephen Kandel, Bob Mitchell, Esther Mitchell. Directed by: Edward M. Abroms.
Guest Stars: Dana Wynter, Alex Rocco, Lee Purcell, James Wainwright, Priscilla Pointer.
Synopsis: Cannon seeks a teen-aged witness to a murder committed by her aunt and her aunt's lover who have their own plans for the runaway.
Trivia: Lovely German born Dana Wynter (1931-2011) had some early leading movie roles in films like D-Day: *The Sixth of June, Invasion of the Body Snatchers, Something of Value* and *Sink the Bismark!* before moving almost exclusively to guest roles on TV shows. Among the many series she appeared on in addition to *Cannon* were *Wagon Train, Gunsmoke, The Alfred Hitchcock Hour, The FBI, Ironside, Magnum P.I.* Her final TV acting role was as Mrs. Robert Ironside in the *The Return of Ironside* (1993) with Raymond Burr.

Fifth Season Episodes

98. Nightmare (9/10/1975)
Written by: Robert W. Lenski. Directed by: Paul Stanley.
Guest Stars: John McMartin, Elizabeth Allen, John McLiam, Janet Ward, Harry Townes, Robert Doyle.
Synopsis: An emotional episode to launch the fifth season which Conrad, in an interview, described, "As Cannon I hear the deathbed confession of a hit man who says he murdered my wife and child 14 years earlier. This confession shakes me up to begin with, but then the hit man claims that my wife was a lady of loose morals. Now I start on a trail that has many unexpected angles…"
Trivia: The sixth and final episode written by Robert W. Lenski (1926-2002). Lenski went on to write several outstanding TV-movies including *Decoration Day, Breathing Lessons, A Season in Purgatory, Remember Me, A Death in the Family.* He was nominated three times for an Emmy for his writing.

99. The Deadly Conspiracy (9/17/1975)
Written by: Stephen Kandel. **Directed by:** Michael Caffey.
Guest Stars: Buddy Ebsen, Charles During, Barry Sullivan, Sharon Acker, Diana Douglas, Murray Hamilton, James Carroll, Jennifer Bishop, Michael Bell.
Synopsis: Cannon is hired to clear the name of a liquor store deliveryman framed for rape and murder. Meanwhile fellow private eye Barnaby Jones (Buddy Ebsen) is hired to find out more about the victim and he and Cannon appear to be on opposite sides of the fence.
Trivia: This is part one of a two-part episode which was concluded two nights later on *Barnaby Jones*.

100. The Wrong Medicine (9/24/1975)
Written by: Norman Lessing. **Directed by:** Paul Stanley.
Guest Stars: David Birney, Richard Jaekel, Don Gordon, Marianne McAndrews, Ed Peck, Janice Whitby, Bob Basso.
Synopsis: A doctor is accused of malpractice and Cannon is brought in to investigate.
Trivia: Richard Jaeckel (1926-1997) was a prolific television and film actor. He was nominated for an Oscar for his performance in *Sometimes a Great Notion*. Among his other films are *The Dirty Dozen, 4 for Texas, Flaming Star, The Devil's Brigade,* and *The Drowning Pool*. Jaeckel later was a regular on the TV series *Spenser: For Hire* and *Baywatch* (as the captain).

101. The Iceman (10/1/1975)
Written by: Larry Alexander. **Directed by:** William Wiard.
Guest Stars: Robert Foxworth, Andrew Parks, Dennis Patrick John Milford, Margaret Impert, Paul Lambert.
Synopsis: Cannon reluctantly reopens the case of an Assistant D.A. who was convicted of killing his wife several years earlier. Suddenly a series of new murders occur which seems to indicate that the D.A. was not guilty.
Trivia: Robert Foxworth is probably best known for his role as Chase Gioberti on *Falcon Crest* (1981-1987).

102. The Victim (10/8/1975)
Written by: Jimmy Sangster. **Directed by:** Lawrence Dobkin.
Guest Stars: Donna Mills, Joel Fabiani, Jess Walton, James Callaghan, Bernard Fox.
Synopsis: A singer makes a claim that her friend is being held captive, and Cannon is brought in to discover the truth.
Trivia: British actor Bernard Fox is probably best known for his work as 'Dr. Bombay' on the classic television series *Bewitched*.

103. The Man Who Died Twice (10/15/1975)
Written by: S.S. Schweitzer. **Directed by:** William Wiard.
Guest Stars: Leslie Nielsen, Leslie Charleson, Paul Stewart, James Gregory, Michael Baselon.
Synopsis: A corrupt cop who has been presumed dead for 8 years is suddenly the top suspect in the murder of a loan shark.
Trivia: This is the second episode written by S.S. Schweitzer, who wrote for such other series as *Daktari, The Bold Ones, Search,* and *The FBI*. He also wrote the screenplay for the final acting role of Elvis Presley's film career *Change of Habit* (1969).

104. A Touch of Venom (10/22/1975)
Written by: Larry Alexander. **Directed by:** Chris Robinson.
Guest Stars: Sondra Locke, Gregory Rosakus, Katharine Burns, Robert F. Simon, Leo Gordon.
Synopsis: Cannon has to contend with a group of political radicals who ultimately try to get their way by poisoning the big guy and withholding the antidote unless he does their bidding.
Trivia: Robert F. Simon (1908-1992) played many roles often as military men, politicians, cops, and doctors. He also played Darrin's father in several episodes of *Bewitched*.

105. Man in the Middle (10/29/1975)
Written by: Richard H. Landau. **Directed by:** Allen Reisner.
Guest Stars: Christine Avila, Abel Franco, William Jordan, Chris Robinson, James McCallion, Michael Pascal, Lou Peralta.
Synopsis: Cannon travels to Mexico to find the remains of the supposedly dead son of Cannon's friend (James McCallion). When he gets there he discovers the son (Chris Robinson) is alive and

responsible for a lot of other deaths.
Trivia: This is the fourth and final guest appearance of actor James McCallion (1918-1991),who was born in Scotland, and appeared in such films as *Vera Cruz, Kiss Me Deadly* and *Coogan's Bluff.* He stayed busy during the 70's appearing in a variety of TV crime series including *Barnaby Jones, The FBI, Ironside, Police Woman, The Streets of San Francisco, Mannix,* and *Harry O.*

106. Fall Guy (11/5/1975)
Written by: Howard Dimsdale. Directed by: Lawrence Dobkin.
Guest Stars: Vera Miles, Alan Feinstein, John Lehne, Kelley Miles, Denny Miller.
Synopsis: An accountant discovers fraud in company records and suddenly disappears—and made to look like the embezzler. Cannon is called in to investigate.
Trivia: This is the wonderful Vera Miles' third and final appearance with William Conrad as Cannon (this includes the pilot film) and in this episode she gets the opportunity to work with her daughter, Kelley Miles.

107. The Melted Man (11/12/1975)
Written by: Norman Lessing. Directed by: Leo Penn.
Guest Stars: Diana Hyland, Victor Mohica, Jenny Sullivan, Key Luke, James Fong, Kaz Garras.
Synopsis: A wealthy woman sees a snowman with a hatchet embedded in its head on her estate in the desert? Is this a warning? She calls in Cannon.
Trivia: Lovely Diana Hyland (1936-1977) was a hard working TV actress who was reaching the apex of her career (winning an Emmy Award for her performance opposite John Travolta in the TV-film *The Boy in the Plastic Bubble*) and appearing as the mother in the first few episodes of the popular TV series *Eight is Enough* before she died of a recurrence of cancer.

108. The Wedding March (11/19/1975)
Written by: Brad Radnitz. Directed by: Leo Penn.
Guest Stars: James Olson, Julie Adams, Paula Kelly, Vic Tayback, Tina Louise, Jack Ging.

Synopsis: Cannon is brought in to try and find a psychopath who beats women to the strains of 'The Wedding March.'

109. The Hero (11/26/1975)
Written by: Irving Pearlberg. Directed by: William Wiard.
Guest Stars: Dean Stockwell, Lee Purcell, Dierdre Lenihan, Laurie Walker, Morgan Woodward, Carl Weathers, Philip Pine.
Synopsis: The son of a distinguished war hero is implicated in the murder of a cult leader.
Trivia: This was the only episode guest starring Dean Stockwell, who got his start as a popular child actor in films like *Anchor's Away, The Green years, Song of the Thin Man, Genleman's Agreement, The Boy With Green Hair* and *Kim*. He was one of the child actors to survive and continue an active adult career in films like *Compulsion, Sons and Lovers, Blue Velvet, Married to the Mob*, and *Inferno*—as well as numerous TV shows including the role of Admiral Al Calavicci on *Quantum Leap*.

110. To Still the Voice (12/3/1975) **Written by: S.S. Schweitzer with story by Schweitzer and Robert Heverly. Directed by: Leo Penn.**
Guest Stars: Herb Edelman, Carl Franklin, Elain Giftus, Richard Denter, Robert Puttin, Pamela Bellwood.
Synopsis: Cannon investigates the assassination of a civil rights leader who was about to come forward to expose a scandal.
Trivia: The fifth and final episode to be directed by Leo Penn.

111. The Star (12/10/1975)
Written by: Margaret Armen. Directed by: William Wiard.
Guest Stars: Joan Fontaine, Jack Carter, Lynden Chiles, Richard Hatch, David Hedison, Dana Elcar, John Vernon.
Synopsis: The son (Richard Hatch) of a famous actress has photos that connect a federal officer to the mob which incriminates the man to murder and leads to a hit being placed on the young man.
Trivia: The star is, of course, Joan Fontaine (1917-2013) who won an Oscar for her starring role in *Suspicion*. Other films include *The Women, Rebecca, The Constant Nymph, Jane Eyre*, and *Letter from an Unknown Women*. Naturally she gives the part she plays on "Cannon" authority.

112. The Games Children Play (12/17/1975) Written by: Albert Aley with Story by Jack Turley. Directed by: William Wiard.
Guest Stars: Fritz Weaver, Kirby Furlong, Paul Jenkins, Norman Fell, Janet G. Montgomery, Charles Drake.
Synopsis: A young boy tries to convince people that he saw the kidnapping of a foreign prince, but nobody (except Cannon) takes him seriously.
Trivia: Young Kirby Furlong plays the boy who witnesses the kidnapping of the sick prince and at the time he was known for his role as young Patrick opposite Lucille Ball in the movie version of the Broadway hit *Mame*. He also played James Stewart's grandson for a season on *The Jimmy Stewart Show*. This episode of "Cannon" was one of his last acting roles.

113. The Reformer (1/7/1976)
Written by: Larry Forrester. Directed by: Lawernce Dobkin.
Guest Stars: Tim O'Connor, Lawrence Pressman, Patricia Smith, James Nussen, Wallace Rooney, Maila Carlis, Ramon Bieri, Reid Cruickshanks.
Synopsis: Cannon helps a corruption combating journalist defend himself against a murder frame-up.
Trivia: This was the fourth and final appearance on *Cannon* of durable and prolific actor Tim O'Connor. O'Connor appeared in over 300 episodes of *Peyton Place* (as Eliot Carson) and appeared on such 70's TV dramas as *Dan August, Hawaii-Five O, The FBI, Gunsmoke, Columbo, Medical Center, Columbo, The Streets of San Francisco, Barnaby Jones*. He played Dr. Elias Huer on the 1979-1980 cult sci-fi series *Buck Rogers in the 25st Century*.

114. The House of Cards (1/14/1976)
Written by: Larry Forrester. Directed by: Lawrence Dobkin.
Guest Stars: Pernell Roberts, Katherine Justice, Robert Pine, Dabney Coleman, Michael Anderson, Jr., Martine Bartlett.
Synopsis: A man who has evidence that a track of land being sold is worthless turns up dead.
Trivia: Pernell Roberts was best known for his two TV roles: Adam Cartwright on *Bonanza* (1959-1965) and Dr. John McIntyre on *Trapper John, M.D.* (1979-1986).

115. Revenge (1/21/1976)
Written by: Gene Thompson. Directed by: Paul Stanley.
Guest Stars: Gary Merrill, Hari Rhodes, Frank De Kova, Bert Freed, James Lydon, Jesse Dizon.
Synopsis: The son of a mob boss frames Cannon for the murder of his father, who thinks that it was Cannon who was responsible for his father's disgraceful discharge from the Army during the Korean War.
Trivia: This is one of the final credits for actor Gary Merrill (1915-1990) who was best known for playing director Bill Sampson in the classic film *All About Eve* and then spending ten years married to Bette Davis.

116. Cry Wolf (1/28/1976) Written by: Stephen Kandel, Carey Wilber. Directed by: Lawrence Dobkin.
Guest Stars: Ralph Bellamy, James David Carson, Gary Lockwood, James Keach, Emilio Delgado, Carl Benson, Michael Ebbert, Laura Hippe.
Synopsis: A grandfather (Ralph Bellamy) thinks that the kidnapping of his grandson is actually a ruse to get money, so be hires Cannon to investigate. It seems the grandson has done something like this before, but this time it appears to be the real thing.
Trivia: Ralph Bellamy (1904-1991) was a distinguished stage, film and TV performer. He could play in many different genres and perhaps is best known for his 'other man' roles in films like *Hands Across the Table, The Awful Truth* and *His Girl Friday*. He also played Ellery Queen in four B movies in the late 30's and early 40's. Later he played Franklin Roosevelt in the Broadway and film versions of *Sunrise at Campobello*—as well as the TV miniseries *The Winds of War* and *War and Remembrance*. He won an Honorary Oscar in 1987.

117. The Quasar Kill (2/4/1976) Written by: Terence and Karl Tunberg. Directed by: William Wiard.
Guest Stars: Andrew Duggan, Eric Braeden, Keene Curtis, Ellen Weston, Joshua Bryant, Peter Brandon.
Synopsis: A scientist is killed by an experimental laser beam and Cannon investigates.
Trivia: This is the third and final appearance of Andrew Duggan (1923-1988) on "Cannon." He played a wide variety of roles during

his career. He was the original John Walton in the pilot film to *The Walton's* "The Homecoming: A Christmas Story." He played such real life characters as President Lyndon Johnson (*The Private Files of J. Edgar Hoover*), Dwight Eisenhower three times (*Backstairs at The White House, J. Edgar Hoover, Tail Gunner Joe*) and Gen. Maxwell Taylor, Army Chief of Staff in *The Missiles of October*. Hard to believe that despite his consistently good work he never was nominated for an Emmy Award.

118. Snapshot (2/11/1976)
Written by: Leonard Kantor. **Directed by:** Michael Caffey.
Guest Stars: Robert Loggia, David Opatoshu, Madlyn Rhue, Hari Rhodes, Michael J. Margeta.
Synopsis: A former hit man whose wife may have been killed in a hit meant for him hires Cannon to find out who is stalking him and why.
Trivia: This is the second and last episode with actor Hari Rhodes (who appeared in the fourth season episode 'The Investigator') to appear as police Lt. Dexter.

119. Point After Death (2/18/1976)
Written by: Robert I. Holt & Mann Rubin with story by Holt. **Directed by:** Chris Robinson.
Guest Stars: Scott Hyland, Richard Dysart, Antoinette Bower, Frank March, Richard O'Brien.
Synopsis: Cannon investigates the murder of a football quarterback's (Scott Hyland) girlfriend.
Trivia: Actor Robert Dysart was a founding member of the San Francisco Conservatory Theatre and is best known for his role as Leland McKenzie in *L.A. Law* (1986-1994) for which he won an Emmy. He also played President Harry S Truman on two occasions—in the TV movie *Day One* and the mini-series *War and Remembrance*.

120. Bloodlines (2/25/1976)
Written by: Robert C. Dennis, Anthony Spinner, Gene Thompson with story by Dennis. **Directed by:** David Whorf.
Guest Stars: Nancy Mehta, Picos Van Dies, Frank Aletter, Joe Morass, Robert Drivas, Robert Hays, Leslie Moonves, Pricilla Barnes.
Synopsis: A young man (Robert Hays) jumps to his death on one of the famous cliffs of Acapulco. His family wonders why and hires Cannon.

Trivia: Director David Whorf (born in 1934) began his career as an actor in film and TV including the films *On Our Merry Way* and *PT 109*, before becoming an assistant director on television of such shows as *Batman, The FBI, Felony Squad,* and 29 episodes of *Cannon*. This is the only episode that he actually got to direct, though he did go on to direct several episodes of the TV series *Spenser: For Hire*. His father was Richard Whorf (1906-1966) also an actor turned director who helmed 67 episodes of *The Beverly Hillbillies* and 37 episodes of *My Three Sons*.

Leslie Moonves, the president and CEO of CBS television since 1998 began his career as an actor—with his first job being a small part (as Pascual) on this episode of *Cannon*.

121. Madman (3/3/1976)
Written by: Larry Forrester. **Directed by:** William Wiard.
Guest Stars: Simon Scott, William Watson, Peter Mark Richman, Charles Aidman, Allan Bergman, Quinn Redeker.
Synopsis: Cannon comes to the aid of an old friend, an Army scientist, whose behavior is becoming irrational—he wants to find out why the sudden change.
Trivia: Simon Scott (1920-1991) is a character actor who had been working steadily on television since the early 50's. Among his more prominent roles are that of Major Wilson in the *Twilight Zone* episode "The Last Flight", Chief Metcalf on *Mod Squad* and Arnold Slocum on *Trapper John, M.D.* In all he appeared on five episodes of *Cannon*.

Nero Wolfe

Episode Log

The Golden Spiders (1/16/1981) Written by: Peter Nasco, David Karp. **Directed by:** Michael O'Herlihy.
Guest Stars: David Hollander, Liam Sullivan, John Petlock, James R. Parkes, Penelope Windust, Carlene Watkins and Katherine Justice.
Synopsis: Based on one of Stout's most famous mysteries, a boy reports to Wolfe that he witnessed a woman's abduction and this nearly gets him killed.

Trivia: One of the differences between the plot of this episode and the book is that the boy (Pete) is killed in the novel, but not in this TV adaptation. Director O'Herlihy, was a known to Conrad having directed two episodes of *Cannon*. Robert Coote (1909-1982), who plays Theodore, the orchid specialist that Wolfe spars with had a long and distinguished career and created the role of Col. Pickering in the original Broadway production of *My Fair Lady*. Nero Wolfe turned out to be Coote's final acting role.

2. Death on the Doorstep (1/23/1981)
Written by: Stephen Downing. Directed by: George McCowan.
Guest Stars: Walter Mathews, Stephan Parr, Arlen Dean Snyder, Alan Bergmann, Nick Angotti, Irene Miracle, Tim Thomerson, Frank Coppola.
Synopsis: One of Archie's best friends is gunned down on Wolfe's brownstone doorstep.
Trivia: George McCowan, who directed several episodes of "Cannon" and with whom Conrad was very comfortable, ended up directing nearly half the episodes of *Nero Wolfe*, 6 of the 14 outings. The Czech-American actor George Voskovec (1905-1981), who played live-in chef Fritz, was best known perhaps as Juror #11 in the classic film *12 Angry Men*. Voskovec died of a heart attack shortly after *Nero Wolfe* ceased production.

3. Before I Die (1/30/1981)
Written by: Alfred Hayes. Directed by: Edward M. Abroms.
Guest Stars: John Ericson, Kale Browne, Ramon Bieri, Eddie Fontaine, Tarah Nutter, Char Fontane, H.M. Wynant.
Synopsis: When a mobster and a woman posing as his daughter are gunned down, Wolfe must locate the man's real daughter.
Trivia: The German born John Ericson (born in 1926) was under contract to MGM in the 1950's appearing in such films as *Teresa, Green Fire, Bad Day at Black Rock* and *Rhapsody*. He had his biggest success on television appearing in many episodic episodes and starring opposite beautiful Anne Francis in the cult classic *Honey West* (1965-1966). British born writer Alfred Hayes (1911-1985) wrote scripts for *Alfred Hitchcock Presents* and *The Twilight Zone*, as well as being nominated twice for an Academy Award for the Italian film Paisan

(director Roberto Rossellini) and *Teresa*(director Fred Zinnemann) which, as mentioned, had co-starred guest actor John Ericson. Among the other screenplays that Hayes wrote include *Clash by Night, Human Desire, The Left Hand of God* and *These Thousand Hills.*

4. Wolfe at the Door (2/6/1981)
Written by: Lee Sheldon. **Directed by:** Herbert Hirschman.
Guest Stars: Edward Bell, Joey Forman, Mary Frann, Fred Sadoff, Flloyd Levine, Eugene Peterson, Jenny Sullivan, Richard Schaal.
Synopsis: A small green box belonging to a client has been stolen from a lawyer's office. Wolfe is hired to find the box, of which nobody seems to know what was in it, but that it was extremely valuable. Archie is sent to interview the owner of the box, who is shot dead during their conversation.
Trivia: Director Herbert Hirschman's (1914-1985) career goes back to the early fifties where he directed the game show *The Name's the Same.* He moved on to direct episodes of *Playhouse 90, Perry Mason, Dr. Kildare,* one episode of *Cannon* and several episodes of *The Waltons.* Mary Frann (1943-1998), was best known for playing Bob Newhart's TV-wife on *Newhart* (1982-1990). She also had worked with Conrad on a 1973 episode of *Cannon.*

5. Might as Well Be Dead (2/13/1981)
Written by: Seeleg Lester. **Directed by:** George McCowan.
Guest Stars: Karen Montgomery, Michael Currie, Stephen Elliott, Bruce Gray, A.C. Weary, Gail Youngs, Lana Wood.
Synopsis: A man receives an anonymous call telling him that a friend is being beaten by her abusive husband. The man goes to the woman's flat only to find the woman's husband dead. Naturally the police arrive and arrest him for murder. It's up to Wolfe to find the real culprit.
Trivia: Lana Wood is the younger sister of actress Natalie Wood, and is best known for a recurring role on the 60's primetime soap opera *Peyton Place.* She also was a "Bond Girl" playing opposite Sean Connery's 2007 (as Plenty O'Toole) in *Diamonds are Forever.* Writer Seeleg Lester (1913-2004) wrote 20 episodes of *Perry Mason* as well as several episodes of *The Millionaire, The Outer Limits* and *Hawaii Five-O.*

6. To Catch a Dead Man (2/20/1981)
Written by: Peter Allen Fields. Directed by: Edward M. Abroms.
Guest Stars: Frank Christi, Titos Vandis, Charles Cioffi, Cesare Danova, Kelly Harmon, Edward Stoiber, Lee Paul.
Synopsis: Nero investigates the disappearance of a shipping magnate's right hand man—which leads to a disaster for Wolfe—the destruction of his beloved orchid greenhouse.
Trivia: Director Edward M. Abroms directed several episodes of such series as *Tarzan, Ironside, Ellery Queen* and *Columbo*. He also directed such landmark TV-movies as *My Sweet Charlie, That Certain Summer and Crash: The Mystery of Flight 1501*. Abroms was nominated four times for an Emmy Award, winning twice (*My Sweet Charlie* & an episode of *Columbo*, "Death Lends a Hand"). As a film editor, Abroms was nominated for an Oscar (with Frank Morriss) for the film *Blue Thunder*.

7. In the Best of Families (3/6/1981)
Written by: Alfred Hayes. Directed by: George McCowan.
Guest Stars: Diana Douglas, Juanin Clay, Alex Rodine, Linden Chiles, Robert Loggia, Burr deBenning, Lawrence Casey.
Synopsis: A wealthy woman's husband always demands money of her, which she won't give him. But yet he always seems to have money and she hires Wolfe to find out where he is getting his money from.
Trivia: Diana Douglas (born in 1923) was the first wife of Kirk Douglas and is the mother of Michael and Joel Douglas. While most of her work has been on television she did work with her then ex-husband in his production of the western film *The Indian Fighter*, and in the popular Steve Martin-John Candy comedy *Planes, Trains & Automobiles*.

8. Murder by the Book (3/13/1981)
Written by: Alfred Hayes & David Karp. Directed by: Robert Kelljan.
Guest Stars: David Hedison, Delta Burke, Jennifer Leak, Elizabeth Halliday, John Randolph, Ed Gilbert, Walter Brooke.
Synopsis: A lawyer on his way to visit Wolfe has a car accident and dies—police label it a suicide. However it turns out there is a connection between the lawyer's death and manuscript of a book—and a manuscript reader who seems to know a lot more than she should.

Trivia: At the time of *Nero Wolfe*, Delta Burke was a former Miss Florida who was relatively new to the acting game. Over the next few years she would rack up several appearances on episodic television before getting her big break of playing Suzanne Sugarbacker on the popular TV-series *Designing Woman*, for which she was nominated twice for an Emmy Award. John Randolph (1915-2004) was a well-regarded movie, TV, and stage actor who was blacklisted during the McCarthy era. He came back strongly in the 60's with films like *Seconds* (where he is the Rock Hudson character prior to his transformation), *Pretty Poison, Little Murders, Serpico,* and *Prizzi's Honor*—as well as scores of TV guest-appearances. Director Robert Kelljan (1930-1982), a former actor, began his directing career in low-budget horror films like *Scream Blacula Scream* and *Count Yorda, Vampire*.

9. What Happened to April? (3/20/1981)
Written by: Stephen Downing. Directed by: Edward M. Abroms.
Guest Stars: Gavin Mooney, Mario Roccuzzo, Julie Carmen, Richard Anderson, Deborah Fallender, Thaao Penghlis, Robert Carraway.
Synopsis: A dead body, a night club singer, is found in the East River. The woman is a friend of Wolfe's associate, Saul. Naturally, Saul becomes a suspect and it's up to Wolfe to prove Saul's innocence.
Trivia: Of his appearance on *Nero Wolfe*, Richard Anderson recalls, "It was just a routine job—I don't recall anything about the show itself, but I was happy to work with Bill again. He was his usual self—a bit quick tempered and yet able to regale the cast and crew with helpless laughter. I always liked him—he was a pro."

10. Gambit (1/3/1981)
Written by: Stephen Kandel Directed by: George McCowan.
Guest Stars: Darren McGavin, Patricia Davis.
Synopsis: A paroled electronics expert with a grudge against Wolfe bugs his bownstone. The grudge goes back to WWII where the man believes that it was Wolfe turned him in as a spy who sold secrets to the Nazi's.
Trivia: Stephen Kandel was another veteran TV writer with a long list of credits and multiple episodes of shows like *Sea Hunt, The Rogues, Batman, I Spy, It Takes a Thief, Mission: Impossible, Mannix*—all the

way up to *MacGyver*. He was at Warner Brothers in the 60's at the time when Conrad was in charge of its film division and wrote a picture called *Chamber of Horror* which was very much in the tradition of such Conrad shockers as *Two on a Guillotine, My Blood Runs Cold* and *Brainstorm*.

11. Death and the Dolls (4/10/1981)
Written by: Gerald Sanford. **Directed by:** Gerald Mayer.
Guest Stars: Christine Belford, Ben Piazza, John McLiam, E.J. Andre, Len Birman, Robin Stand, Maria Mayenzet.
Synopsis: When a man dies in an explosion on his yatch, his daughter seeks Wolfe's help. She believes it was her stepmother and her lover who executed the crime and wants Wolfe to prove it.
Trivia: Director Gerald Mayer (1919-2001) had a long career in television but began in movies including the gritty low-budget crime drama, *Dial 1119*, which had featured a colorful supporting performance by William Conrad (as 'Chuckles' the bar tender). Other interesting films followed including the noir, *Inside Straight*, *The Sell-Out* and *Holiday for Sinners* before devoting most of his time to television.

12. The Murder in Question (4/17/1981)
Written by: Merwin Gerard. **Directed by:** George McCowan.
Guest Star: Ted Hartley, Lucinda Dooling, Dale Rbinette, Diane Shalet, Noran Alden, John C. Reilly.
Synopsis: Wolfe's new client, the wife of a prosecutor, believes that her husband's life is in jeopardy—and describes what she believes to be two murder attempts against him. Shortly after meeting with Wolfe she seemingly dies in a fiery car crash.
Trivia: Writer Merwin Gerard (1917-1995), whose final writing credit *Nero Wolfe* would be—spent most of his time writing for television, but he did write one motion picture, the 1952 Warner Brothers film *The Winning Team* which starred Ronald Reagan and Doris Day, and told the story of the major league ball player Grover Cleveland Alexander. On television he was the creator, producer and frequent writer of the paranormal suspense anthology series *One Step Beyond*.

13. Blue Ribbon Hostage (5/5/1981)
Written by: Dick Nelson. Directed by: Ron Satlof.
Guest Stars: Bobbie Jordan, David Young, Michael Pataki, Kenneth Tigar, Simone Griffeth, Fil Formicola, Barry Nelson.
Synopsis: Wolfe is outraged when a prize orchid is stolen from his collection. When the culprit confesses that he is the thief he asks Wolfe for help—in exchange for returning the orchid.
Trivia: Director Ron Satlof spent most of his career writing for television, but he was nominated for an Oscar, for Best Short Subject in 1972 for *Frog Story*. He was also nominated for an Emmy for an episode of *McCloud* he directed in 1975. In his later career he directed Raymond Burr in several of the *Perry Mason* TV-movies of the 80's & early 90's. He also directed Conrad in five episodes of *Jake and the Fatman*.

14. Sweet Revenge (6/2/1981)
Written by: Ben Roberts. Directed by: George McCowan.
Guest Stars: Roz Kelly, Eddie Firestone, Paul Koslo, Anthony Costello, Dick Ryal, Ed Lauter, David Hollander.
Synopsis: After five years in prison, put behind bars by Wolfe, a bank robber hires two killers to get even with Wolfe.
Trivia: At the time that *Nero Wolfe* was televised, guest-star Roz Kelly was best known for her role as "Pinky" Tuscadero, Fonzie's girlfriend on the hit TV-series *Happy Days*. Writer Ben Roberts (1916-1984) ended his career writing for such TV-series as *Mannix* and *Charlie's Angels*, which he also created. But Roberts also wrote the screenplays of such films as *White Heat* (with James Cagney), *Captain Horatio Hornblower R.N., Green Fire, Band of Angels, Man of a Thousand Faces* (his screenplay was nominated for an Oscar) and *Portrait in Black*. He also served as Executive Producer of the Conrad *Nero Wolfe* series.

Jake and the Fatman
Episode Log

Each episode is titled after a song—usually a standard and gives a hint of that week's plot.

Season One

Happy Days are Here Again (9/26/1987)
Written by: Tom Lazarus with story by Mitch Paradise, Dean Hargrove, Joel Steiger. **Directed by:** E.W. Swackhamer
Guest Stars: John Rubinstein, Robert Reed, Bridget Hanley, Clare Wren, Warren Stanhope, J. Jay Saunders, Anthony Winters.
Synopsis: The mistress of a senate candidate (Robert Reed) is killed after she threatens to go public about their affair. His speechwriter (John Rubinstein) is the actual killer, and threatens his boss to cooperate or he will frame him for the murder.
Trivia: Director E.W. Swackhamer would direct 8 episodes of *Jake and the Fatman* from 1987-1990. Swackhamer, a working director since the mid-sixties directed shows as diverse as *I Dream of Jeannie, Bewitched, The Flying Nun, McCloud, Family* and *Law and Order*. He was nominated for an Emmy Award for his direction of James Coburn in the 1978 mini-series *The Dain Curse* based on the Dashiell Hammett novel.

The song "Happy Days are Here Again" with music by Milton Ager and lyrics by Jack Yellen was published in 1929 and included in the 1930 film *Chasing Rainbows* which featured Jack Benny. But the songs true claim to fame was when it became the campaign song of Franklin D. Roosevelt during his first 1932 presidential campaign against the dour incumbent, Herbert Hoover. Roosevelt wanted a song which emphasized the positive in contrast to the economically challenging times. "Son long sad times/Go long bad times/We are rid of you at last/...So let's tell the world about it now/ Happy Days are Here Again". Barbra Streisand made a big hit of it again in the 1960's.

John Rubinstein is a Tony Award winning actor on Broadway (*Pippin, Children of a Lesser God*) in addition to making numerous guest appearances on episodic TV over the years. Robert Reed, of course, is best known as Mike Brady on The Brady Bunch, but appeared in numerous dramatic TV shows and TV-movies/mini-series including his run on *The Defenders* during the 1960's. He was nominated three times for an Emmy Award (*Roots, Medical Center, Rich Man, Poor Man*).

Review (from AP): "Jake and the Fatman." CBS. William Conrad as an obese, profane district attorney whose supposedly X-rated dialogue is "bleeped" in one of the more tasteless gimmicks of recent seasons. Joe Penny ("Riptide") co-stars.

Fatal Attraction Part 1 & 2 (9/29/1987)
Written by: Stefen Borghi. Directed by: Ron Satlof.
Guest Stars: Kim Ulrich, Karen Austin, James Karen, Allan Rich, Rebecca Bush, Eugene I. Peterson, James Avery, Perla Walter, Stu Nahan, Robert Benedetti.
Synopsis: The husband of the Deputy Mayor is murdered, and an arrest is made, but things just don't add up to McCabe who pursues a further investigation.
Trivia: Rebecca Bush played the character of Katie Grant, playing a police liaison, friendly to Jake and McCabe, in four early episodes of the series before she departed the show. Joe Penny later recalled, "There wasn't much for her to do. Bill, Alan and myself were taking up most of the screen time."

Laura (10/6/1987) Written by: Tom Lazarus with story by Dean Hargrove & Joel Steiger. Directed by: E.W. Swackhamer.
Guest Stars: Robert Pierce, Brynn Thayer, Larry Hankin, Jay Ingram, Rick Telles, Matt Roe, Lillian Adams, Freddie Dawson, Claudio Martinez, Lu Leonard.
Synopsis: A woman kills her fiancée (who was Jake's former partner) in an alley way. She claims that it was an accident and a case of mistaken identity.
Trivia: The "Laura" theme from the classic 1944 Otto Preminger directed film noir *Laura* was written by David Raskin. Later lyrics were added by Johnny Mercer and the song was recorded by artists as diverse as Spike Jones and Frank Sinatra.

Character actress Lu Leonard (1926-2004) would portray McCabe's wise-cracking secretary, Gertrude, in ten episodes of the series, most of which aired during the shows first season. She had previously had a guest shot on Joe Penny's *Riptide* series.

The Man That Got Away (10/13/1987)
Written by: Michael Genelin. Directed by: E.W. Swackhamer.
Guest Stars: Robert Culp, Julie Cobb, Mitzi Hoag, William Edward Phipps, Mary Gregory, Lloyd Gordon.
Synopsis: A revengeful lawyer (Robert Culp) murders his ex-wife's new lover and has her framed for the murder. When she is arrested—he takes on the job of representing her to make sure that she is duly convicted.
Trivia: "The Man that Got Away," written in 1953 with music by Harold Arlen and words by Ira Gershwin, was performed in spectacular fashion by Judy Garland in her classic 1954 film version of *A Star is Born*. The song was nominated for an Oscar for Best Original Song. Garland's performance earned eleventh place among the 'Greatest Songs in American cinema history."

Love for Sale (10/20/1987) Written by: Douglas Stefen Borghi. Directed by: Christopher Hibler.
Guest Stars: Mitchell Anderson, Claudia Cron, Scott Palmers, Deirdre Clark, Larry Hankins, Dianne Kay, Rebecca Bush.
Synopsis: A pimp uses a call girl to smuggle drugs, and when she becomes aware of this she seeks help from McCabe, but is killed before they can meet.
Trivia: Director Christopher Hibler (1942-2010) helmed two episodes of *Jake and the Fatman*, as well as over 20 episodes of *Diagnosis: Murder*. He was the son of Disney legend Winston Hibler, who was a the narrator, writer and sometimes producer and director of such outstanding Disney documentary films as *The Living Desert, The Vanishing Prairie, Men Against the Arctic,* and *White Wilderness*. Christopher also had a long career at Disney working on such films as *Bedknobs and Broomsticks, Hot Lead* and *Cold Feet* and *Super Dad*.

The song "Love for Sale" was written by Cole Porter for the 1930 musical *The New Yorkers*, and at the time was considered somewhat scandalous being sung in the show by a character playing a prostitute.

Brother, Can You Spare a Dime? (11/3/1987)
Written by: Robert Hamilton with story by Dean Hargrove & Joel Steiger. **Directed by:** Tony Mordente.
Guest Stars: Dwight Schultz, Russell Todd, Mark Drexler, Mary Ingersoll, Tim Finnegan, Efrain Figueroa, Tim Russ, Jack Fallon.
Synopsis: A series of skid-row murders look to be the work of a serial killer, but McCabe and Jake aren't so sure.
Trivia: Mark Drexler, best known for playing Roger Lombard on the daytime soap *Days of Our Lives*, recalled this of his guest appearance on *Jake and the Fatman*, "I worked with both William Conrad and Joe Penny. I don't believe William Conrad ever picked up a script before coming to work, everything was off cue cards, but he was very good at hiding that he was basically reading."

The song "Brother, Can You Spare a Dime?" written in 1930 by E.Y. 'Yip' Harburg and Jay Gorney, became one of the major anthems of the Great Depression (Say, don't you remember, they called me Al; it was Al all the time. Why don't you remember, I'm your pal? Buddy, can you spare a dime?). It became a major hit of that era for Bing Crosby and Rudy Vallee.

Body and Soul (11/3/1987) Written by: Tom Lazarus with story by Dean Hargrove & Joel Steiger. **Directed by:** Jerry Jameson.
Guest Stars: Doran Clark, Richard Karron, Robert O'Reilly, Don Stroud, Patrick Thomas O'Brien, Jeff Abbott, Bob Bralver, Al Jones, Jamie Namson.
Synopsis: Jake backs up a determined policewoman in her efforts to trap the man who killed her father.
Trivia: "Body and Soul" was a jazz standard from 1930 written by Edward Heyman, Robert Sour and Frank Eyton with music by Johnny Green and was introduced by the famous British actress/singer Gertrude Lawrence. In the U.S. it became a standard for Libby Holman in the Broadway revue "Three's a Crowd." Over the years it has been recorded by many artists from Billie Holliday to Sarah Vaughan. The title "Body and Soul", of course has significance in

the career of William Conrad since he appeared as Quinn, the manager of John Garfield's Charley Davis, in the classic 1947 film *Body and Soul.*

The Man I Love (11/10/1987) Written by: Robert Hamilton. Directed by: Michael Lange.
Guest Stars: Leigh McCloskey, Brooks Gardner, Marilyn Jones, Lu Leonard, Kimberly LaMarque, Terri Treas, Chuck Walling.
Synopsis: Jake discovers that the police officer son of a friend of McCabe's is corrupt, so Jake poses as a relative to get the goods on the corrupt cop.
Trivia: The song "The Man I Love" with music by George Gershwin and lyrics by Ira Gershwin was originally part of the 1924 score of a Broadway show *Lady, Be Good,* and over the years has been memorably recorded by such artists as Judy Garland, Ella Fitzgerald, Miles Davis and Tony Bennett in duet with Sheryl Crow.

Love Me or Leave Me (11/17/1987)
Written by: Paul Robert Coyle. Directed by: Michael Preece.
Guest Stars: Joe Regalbuto, Bobbie Eakes, Rick Fitts, Lu Leonard, Charles Lucia, Joe Mays, Branscombe Richmond.
Synopsis: There's a crooked cop who is involved in defrauding a rock star and Jake goes undercover to get the goods on him.
Trivia: "Love Me or Leave Me" with music by Walter Donaldson and lyrics by Gus Kahn became a signature song for 20's singer Ruth Etting. In 1955 Etting's story was filmed by MGM starring Doris Day and James Cagney with the title *Love Me or Leave Me.*

Writer Paul Robert Coyle remembers: "Shortly after the show began production for its first season in 1987, Phil Salzman was hired to produce about half the episodes (executive producers Dean Hargrove and Joel Steiger did the other half). I had worked for Phil on *Barnaby Jones*, so he called me in. It didn't hurt that I'd recently finished a year as Story Editor on another CBS show, *Crazy Like a Fox*, so I was approved by the network. Luckily my first script, "Love Me or Leave Me," worked out."

Smoke Gets in Your Eyes (12/1/1987) Written by: Paul Robert Coyle. Directed by: Harvey Laidman.
Guest Stars: Amy Steele, Mark Goddard, Larry Hankin, Jeremy Roberts, Henry Sutton, Henry Sutton, Joann Adell Williams.
Synopsis: A woman (Amy Steele) is blinded in a robbery and attempts revenge not only on the person who blinded her but her two-timing husband (Mark Goddard). The question is—is she really blind?
Trivia: Mark Goddard, the two timing husband of this episode, was best known for two 1960's TV series: as Detective Sgt. Chris Ballard on *The Detectives* starring Robert Taylor and as Major Don West on the sci-fi classic *Lost in Space*.

Have Yourself a Merry Little Christmas (12/8/1987) Written by: Robert Hamilton. Directed by: E.W. Swackhamer.
Guest Stars: Joan Darling, Pat Anderson, Stephen Liska, Charles Parks, Kurt Fuller, Donna Lynn Leavy, Carol Ann Susi, Lu Leonard.
Synopsis: A man being investigated by a deputy D.A. winds up dead.
Trivia: Guest star Joan Darling began her career in improve comedy, but became best known during the 1970's for her role as the office secretary on the legal drama, *Owen Marshall: Counselor at Law*. She later became a well-regarded director, helming episodes of *MASH, Mary Tyler Moore, Taxi* and *Rhoda*. Her *Mary Tyler Moore* credit is the classic episode, "Chuckles Bites the Dust" and earned Darling an Emmy nomination.

The song "Have Yourself a Merry Little Christmas" written by Hugh Martin and Ralph Blane, was introduced by Judy Garland in the classic 1944 film *Meet Me in St. Louis* (MGM) and in the years since it has become a classic Christmas standard and has been recorded by a long list of artists including Frank Sinatra, Doris Day, Bing Crosby, James Taylor, and Luther Vandross.

After You've Gone (1/5/1988) Written by: Paul Robert Coyle with story by Coyle & Philip Saltzman. Directed by: Paul Krasny.
Guest Stars: Alan Feinstein, Manada Horan Kennedy, Gary Hudson, Joseph Ruskin, Ivy Jones, Danny Masterson, Lu Leonard.

Synopsis: The hit man Sagittarius is spotted by Jake, at an airport, who follows him to find out what he is up which ultimately leads to a shoot-out between the two with Sagittarius being killed. Jake, wanting to find out more, assumes his identity.
Trivia: Twelve year old Danny Masterson, who plays Butch in this episode, began his career with his appearance on *Jake and the Fatman*. He would later become most famous for his portrayal of Hyde on the Fox-TV hit *That '70s Show*.

It Had to be You (1/12/1988)
Written by: Paul Robert Coyle. **Directed by:** Ron Satlof.
Guest Stars: James Olson, Richard Marcus, Ann Dusenberry, Lu Leonard, Kim Sebastian, Kat Sawyer-Young, Casey Sander, Mary Gregory.
Synopsis: A friend of McCabe's (Ann Dusenberry) becomes the victim of a serial rapist. There is evidence to suggest that the culprit is a loner (Richard Marcus), which is perhaps what his psychiatrist, also a respected professor (James Olson) may want people to think. (This episode is considered one of the best in the series).
Trivia: The song "It Had to Be You" is another standard, with music by Isham Jones and lyrics by Gus Kahn and was published in 1924, and initially made famous when performed by Ruth Etting in 1936. Later it has been used on the soundtrack of many films including *Casablanca, Annie Hall* and *When Harry Met Sally*.

But Not for Me (1/19/1988)
Written by: Robert Hamilton. **Directed by:** Michael Lange.
Guest Stars: Barbara Parkins, Nicholas Walker, Kelly Meadows, Kurt Fuller, Stephen Burleigh, Jay Louden, Marjorie Stapp.
Synopsis: A mobster is murdered while in the home of a star reporter (Barbara Parkins) who is interviewing him at the time. She claims that he was shot from somebody outside of her home, but McCabe is dubious.
Trivia: Beautiful Barbara Parkins worked steadily on television from the early 60's thru the late 90's including a five year stint (and over 400 episodes) as Betty Anderson Harrington on the prime time soap opera *Peyton Place*. She also played Anne Welles in the cult classic *Valley of the Dolls* in 1967. When asked if any particular episode

that he directed of *Jake and the Fatman* stood out, director Michael Lange told me, "I loved all of them. Seriously I can't really single out any one episode. Although I must confess that the episode with Barbara Parkins was a bit higher since I had a huge crush on her. Also the Hawaii episodes were a blast because of shooting in Hawaii."

The standard "But Not for Me" was composed by George Gershwin with lyrics by Ira Gershwin in 1930 for their Broadway musical *Girl Crazy* (and introduced by Ginger Rogers). It has become a standard recorded by many top singers and on the sound track of many films including the 1943 film version of *Girl Crazy* (sung by Judy Garland) and *Four Weddings and a Funeral, Manhattan* and *When Harry Met Sally*.

What Is This Thing Called Love? (1/26/1988)
Written by: Tom Lazarus with story by Lazarus & Philip Saltzman. **Directed by:** Harvey Laidman.
Guest Stars: James Watkins, John Cooke, Maggie Roswell, Jeffrey Combs, Susan Cash, Signy Coleman, David Q. Combs, Lu Leonard.
Synopsis: A courtroom, including McCabe and Derek, are held hostage by a gunman who claims that he's seeking revenge, but Jake, working to get rescue them, discovers another more ominous motive.
Trivia: Another standard written by Cole Porter, "What is this Thing Called Love" was first performed on Broadway in 1929. The song has been performed by many artists but perhaps the two very best renditions are by Frank Sinatra on his 1954 album, "In the Wee Small Hours" and Ella Fitzgerald on her album, "Ella Fitzgerald Sings the Cole Porter Songbook" (1956).

Lady, Be Good (2/2/1988)
Written by: Tom Lazarus. **Directed by:** E.W. Swackhamer.
Guest Stars: Ed Nelson, Lee Purcell, Nana Visitor, Fredric Cook, Brian Avery, Stewart Bradley.
Synopsis: A man who is about to fake his own death so his wife can collect a huge life insurance pay-off is found murdered.
Trivia: Ed Nelson is another well-known TV-actor who appeared on *Jake and the Fatman*. Nelson was best known for playing heart-throb, Dr. Michael Rossi, on the prime time soap opera *Peyton*

Place. In later years he portrayed President Harry S. Truman on stage (replacing James Whitmore in the one-man play *Give 'Em Hell, Harry*) and taught acting and screen writing at Tulane University in his native New Orleans.

The song "Lady, Be Good" is yet another Gershwin brother's standard used by the writers of *Jake and the Fatman*.

I'll Be Seeing You (2/16/1988)
Written by: Robert Hamilton with story by Peter Allen Fields, Dean Hargrove, Joel Steiger. **Directed by:** Harvey Laidman.
Guest Stars: Stacy Edwards, John Lehne, Tim Choate, Allan Miller, Matt Roe, Bill Kalmenson, Warren Stanhope.
Synopsis: A man plans to testify in court against his boss, but while on the stand he has a heart attack and is later killed at the hospital. McCabe discovers that he was blackmailing his boss so that he could leave his daughter (Stacy Edwards) an inheritance, but McCabe discovers there is something shady about her too.
Trivia: *Jake and the Fatman* frequently utilized soap opera actors, and Stacy Edwards at the time was appearing on the NBC soap opera *Santa Barbara* (as Hayley Capwell) at the time of her appearance on the show. She would later play Dr. Lisa Catera on *Chicago Hope*.

The song "I'll be Seeing You" written in 1938 by Sammy Fain and Irving Kahal with its wistful "I'll be seeing you in all the familiar places…and when the night is new, I'll be looking at the moon, But I'll be seeing you" became one of the best loved anthems of separated lovers during World War II, and was featured in the 1944 films *I'll be Seeing You*, which starred Ginger Rogers and Joseph Cotten.

Baby Face (2/23/1988)
Written by: Dick Nelson. **Directed by:** E.W. Swackhamer.
Guest Stars: Bert Remsen, Merritt Butrick, Tony Montero, Suzanne Snyder, Robert Mangiardi, Michael Paul Chan.
Synopsis: The daughter of a wealthy man plans and executes her own kidnapping—and once she has the ransom, she murders her accomplice.
Trivia: Writer Dick Nelson began as an actor, with limited success

(though he did play the small part of Franklin Roosevelt in the 1957 Bob Hope film *Beau James*. Nelson found more success as a TV writer, scribing multiple episodes of such series as *Bonanza, The Name of the Game, Medical Center, Alias Smith and Jones, Barnaby Jones,* and *Murder She Wrote*. He scribed one episode each of Cannon and Jake and the Fatman. A 1972 episode he wrote for *Marcus Welby, M.D.* earned him a Writers Guild of America (WGA) nomination.

The song "Baby Face" was written in 1926 and is a quintessential 20's song, even though artists through the years have recorded it. It is often used on the soundtracks of films and TV shows which are set in the 1920's.

Blues in the Night (3/16/1988)
Written by: Robert Hamilton. Directed by: Harvey Laidman.
Guest Stars: Susan Blakely, Stephen Burleigh, Frank Benard, Seth Jaffe, Barbara Whinnery, Gammy Singer.
Synopsis: A woman friend of McCabe's has a criminal twin (both played by Susan Blakely) who commits a crime while the one sister is with McCabe. The question is did the one twin commit the crime or are they in it together?
Trivia: The title is based on a song written by Harold Arlen with lyrics by Johnny Mercer that was in the score of the film *Blues in the Night* (1941) and was nominated for an Academy Award as Best Original Song.

Former model Susan Blakely who plays the twins in this episode was best known at this time for her roles in the popular TV-miniseries *Rich Man, Poor Man* I & II, earning Emmy nominations for each. She also played the actress Frances Farmer in a 1982 TV-movie *Will There Really Be a Morning?*, earning a Golden Globe nomination.

How Long Has This Thing Been Going On? (3/23/1988)
Written by: Tom Lazarus with story by Lazarus & Franklin Thompson. Directed by: Christian Nyby II.
Guest Stars: David Soul, Jeanna Michaels, Dorothy Parke, John Paul Gamoke, Freddie Dawson, George Delhoyo, Nancy Arnold, Vince Inneo.

Synopsis: Aware of his wife's intention to leave him Nelson Boardman (David Soul) kills her and frames her lover.
Trivia: "How Long Has This Been Going On" was composed by George Gershwin with lyrics by brother Ira in 1928 for the musical *Funny Face*, and was later sung by Audrey Hepburn in the 1957 film version of *Funny Face* (Paramount). Among the many artists who have recorded the song are Julie London, Ella Fitzgerald, Judy Garland, Jon Bon Jovi and Ray Charles. Director Christian Nyby II helmed three episodes of *Fatman*, but did much more work on the Dean Hargrove-Fred Silverman series *Diagnosis: Murder*—directing 53 episodes.

I Guess I'll Have to Change My Plans (3/30/1988)
Written by: Paul Robert Coyle. **Directed by:** Michael Lange.
Guest Stars: Anthony Franciosa, Kathryn Leigh Scott, Jere Burns, Casey Sanders, Frantz Turner, Michael Paul Chan.
Synopsis: A former cop turned author (Anthony Franciosa) will go to great lengths to get that elusive best-seller—even as far as murder.
Trivia: "I'll Have to Change My Plan" music by Arthur Schwartz and lyrics by Howard Dietz was introduced by Clifton Webb in a 1929 revue *The Little Show*, but is most popularly recalled as a duet for Fred Astaire and Jack Buchanan in the classic MGM musical *The Band Wagon*.

Rhapsody in Blue (4/6/1988)
Written by: Robert Hamilton. **Directed by:** Michael Lange.
Guest Stars: Edward Winter, Seth Jaffe, Reid Shelton, Kim Lankford, Tracy Needham, James V. Christy, Christopher Michael.
Synopsis: An executive and his wife (Edward Winter, Kim Lankford) plan to murder his boss when he is passed over for a promotion, but accidentally kill another employee instead.
Trivia: Edward Winter (1937-2001) is probably best known for his recurring role of super patriot intelligence officer Col. Flagg on *MASH*, but he played a variety of parts including the role of Clark Gable in the TV-movie *The Scarlett O'Hara Wars*. He was also the star of the Jack Webb produced *Project UFO* in 1978-1979. On the stage he was nominated twice for Best Featured Actor in the plays *Cabaret* and *Promises, Promises*.

"Rhapsody in Blue" by George Gershwin, is one of the most famous musical compositions of all-time, is the fifth Gershwin song to be utilized as a title during the first season of *Jake and the Fatman*.

Season Two

The season began late and included only ten episodes. This was due to two industry strikes: A Writers Strike and then a Teamsters Strike. And as anybody in the industry would say—you need writers and you don't mess around with Teamsters! Nevertheless, the move to Hawaii seemed to work and *Fatman*, while not a powerhouse in the ratings, improved all the way up to #33 (from #59 in its first season) with a 15.2 rating and tied with the CBS sitcom *Designing Women*.

Episodes

Wish You Were Here (3/15/1989)
Written by: Ed Waters. **Directed by:** E.W. Swackhamer.
Guest Stars: James Karen, Amy Steel, Edward Wiley, Khigh Dhiegh, Christopher Templeton, Karen Keawehawaii, Al Harrington, Jack Hogan.
Synopsis: The two-hour season premiere takes Jake to Hawaii to visit a friend, and winds up being accused of the friend's murder. He calls on Hawaii native McCabe's help.
Trivia: Khigh Dhieh (1910-1991) was actually born in New Jersey with the name Kenneth Dickerson. One of his best known roles was that of Steve McGarrett's arch villain 'Wo Fat' on *Hawaii Five-O*. He played 'Wo-Fat' on 15 episodes of *Five-O*, including the 1968 pilot. Actor James Karen (who plays the outgoing D.A. in this episode) was a Broadway veteran—including the original Broadway production of *A Streetcar Named Desire*, while Amy Steel was probably best known at the time for the film *Friday the 13th, Part 2*.

The title "Wish You Were Here" is based not on a song standard from the 1920's & 1930's like most of the first season titles were but on a popular recording/album by Pink Floyd.

I'll Never Smile Again (3/22/1989)
Written by: Gael Phillips, Rick Kelbaugh, Kevin Droney with story by Phillips. Directed by: Don Medford.
Guest Stars: David Schramm, Janet Carroll, Brigid Brannagh, John Dennis Johnston, Bill Fiddler, Joseph Panis, David Traylor.
Synopsis: A tourist tries to stop a mugging, but is grabbed from behind (by who?) and stabbed by the mugger. The tourist is alive when police arrive but the mugger is dead from a gunshot—with no sign of the third person. A clue is a gun left on the ground that ballistics shows has been used to kill several muggers.
Trivia: Don Medford (1917-2012) was a prolific TV director and directed Conrad three times (twice on *Fatman* and once on *Cannon*). He is probably best remembered for directing the final two episodes of the Conrad narrated *The Fugitive*, including the final episode which at the time received the largest viewership for any dramatic program on television.

With the title "I'll Never Smile Again" we are back to standards. The song was written in 1939 by Ruth Lowe and became famous when recorded by Tommy Dorsey's Orchestra with vocals by Frank Sinatra and the Pied Pipers.

Bewitched, Bothered & Bewildered (4/5/1989)
Written by: Jack Fogarty. Directed by: Dale White.
Guest Stars: Steven Chambers, Maria O'Brien, Karen Keawehawaii, Bill Holland, Leslie Bevis, Ray Bumati, Adam Klawe.
Synopsis: A robbery at a trucking company is investigated by Jake, which leads to romantic involvement with its owner.
Trivia: For most of his career director Dale White was a second unit or assistant director on shows like *Hill Street Blues, MacGyver, Men Behaving Badly*—and 187 episodes of *Will & Grace*, but he got his chance to be top man on two back to back episodes of *Jake and the Fatman*.

The song "Bewitched, Bothered & Bewildered" was a popular song written by Rodgers and Hart for the Broadway musical *Pal Joey* which starred Gene Kelly. Later in the film version (1957) Frank Sinatra made a big hit of it. Recently Rod Stewart did a duet of the song with Cher.

Why Can't You Behave? (4/12/1989)
Written by: Kevin Droney. **Directed by:** Dale White.
Guest Stars: Tom Isbell, Charles McCaughan, Clarence Clemons, Ben Wong, Connie Kissinger, Mark Dillen Stitham, Karen Keawehawaii.
Synopsis: McCabe and his son (Tom Isbel) had a falling out years earlier and haven't seen each other in years, when the son suddenly shows up. When McCabe and Jake investigate a plane crash which was caused by a plane having defective parts, it appears that McCabe's son may have been involved in selling those parts.
Trivia: Hawaii born singer Karen Keawehawaii was cast in the Hawaii episodes as McCabe's secretary and appeared in seven episodes in that role. She had previously appeared on two episodes of the similarly Hawaii-shot series *Magnum P.I.* While she is not a big name outside of Hawaii, on the island of paradise she is well-known for her work as a singer with performances in concerts and with the Honolulu Symphony Orchestra. For ten years she performed a Christmas show with Jim Nabors. She is also known for her charitable work including co-hosting the local Hawaii "Children's Miracle Telethon."

Cole Porter's "Why Can't You Behave" was written in 1948 for the musical *Kiss Me Kate*, and is also featured in the 1954 film. Ella Fitzgerald also recorded a superb, jazzy version of the song.

Poor Butterfly (4/19/1989)
Written by: Rick Kelbraugh. **Directed by:** Bernard L. Kowalski.
Guest Stars: Debra Stipe, Tracy Shaffer, Jeffrey Josephson, George Cheung, Thomas Rosales, Jr., Louie Elias, Bill Bigelow, Varola Tiki.
Synopsis: A prostitute is killed by her pimp because she was going to testify in court against him. Jake who urged her to testify seeks justice.
Trivia: Bernard L. Kowalski (1929-2007) was one of the most frequent directors on *Jake and the Fatman*, helming sixteen episodes. His directorial career spanned from the late fifties to the late nineties and included many episodic TV shows and TV-movies. He was nominated twice for an Emmy for his direction (1976,1977) both for episodes of *Baretta*.

"Poor Butterfly" is one of the oldest songs used as a title for *Jake and the Fatman*, having been published in 1916. Over the years it has emerged as a pop standard and been recorded many times including by The Hilltoppers, Julie Andrews, Frank Sinatra and Sarah Vaughan.

It Ain't Necessarily So (4/26/1989) Written by: Ed Waters, Rick Kelbaugh, Kevin Droney, Kimmer Ringwald with story by E. Arthur Kean. Directed by: Bernard L. Kowalski.
Guest Stars: Alex Cord, Rene Assa, Lenore Kasdorf, Maurice Roeves, James Sutorius, Jack Hogan, Karen Keawehawaii.
Synopsis: Jake and McCabe investigate when the wife of a *Penthouse* type magazine publisher is killed when they return home from vacation—and find a burglar in their home. The question is was this a simple burglary gone bad or was her murder planned?
Trivia: Rugged Alex Cord is a durable journeyman actor who began his career (mostly exclusively on television) in the early sixties. Most of his work was as a guest-star, but he did star in 55 episodes of the action series *Airwolf* from 1984-1986. His most prolific period was during the 60's thru the 80's appearing in such diverse series as *Route 66, Night Galary, Gunsmoke, Mission Impossible, Police Story, The Love Boat, Fantasy Island* and *Murder, She Wrote*.

"It Ain't Necessarily So" is another great song composed by George Gershwin with lyrics by his brother Ira, that was utilized for a title on *Jake and the Fatman*. The song was written for the landmark Gershwin opera *Porgy and Bess* in 1935 and sung by Sammy Davis, Jr., in the 1959 film.

Someone to Watch Over Me (5/3/1989) Written by: Kimmer Ringwald. Directed by: Bernard L. Kowalski.
Guest Stars: Whitney Kershaw, Ramon Bieri, Norman Parker, Allen Cole, Stephanie Reynolds, Steve Steventon, Ronald Takemori, Karen Keawehawaii.
Synopsis: A woman is found dead on the beach from an apparent drug overdose. The immediate suspect is her boyfriend, and Jake is sent to pick him up for questioning, but it appears there is a gunman who wants to get to him first.
Trivia: Writer Kimmer Ringwald (1947-2011) began his career on

daytime soaps including *Love of Life* for which he was nominated for an Emmy. He wrote for several primetime series including 14 episodes of *Jake and the Fatman* (and producing 61 of the episodes of the series). He also wrote several episodes of *Trapper John M.D.*, *Hotel*, and *Baywatch*. Ironically Ringwald passed away in 2011 while he was vacationing with his family on the island of Maui in Hawaii.

"Someone to Watch Over Me" another standard by the Gershwin brothers was introduced by Gertrude Lawrence in 1926 and is considered one of the great Gershwin songs and has been recorded over the years by Ella Fitzgerald, Frank Sinatra, Ray Conniff, Sarah Vaughan, Etta James, Barbra Streisand, and Amy Winehouse.

They Can't Take That Away From Me (5/10/1989)
Written by: Catherine Bacos Clinch. Directed by: Don Medford.
Guest Stars: Gary Swanson, Daniel Faraldo, Patricia Sill, Michele Scarabelli, Charlie Brill, Tim Ryan, Don Yesso, Ben Wong.
Synopsis: Two colleagues who helped Jake with a drug bust are found dead—Jake needs to find the killers before he is the next victim. The two dead policemen's wives feature prominently in this episode.
Trivia: Writer Catherine Clinch wrote for such shows as *Hart to Hart, Knight Rider, The Love Boat, Jake and the Fatman* and *Hunter* before leaving to raise a family, but thru the years she has kept busy writing articles and teaching. She also spent two years on the Board of Directors of west coast Writers Guild of America (WGA.)

The title "They Can't Take That Away From Me" is taken from yet another standard written by George and Ira Gershwin and was introduced by Fred Astaire (who introduced so many standards both on Broadway and in films) in the film *Shall We Dance* (1937-RKO).

Side by Side (5/17/1989)
Written by: Kimmer Ringwald. Directed by: Jackie Cooper.
Guest Stars: Robert Munic, Fredrick Coffin, Ted Sackett, Danny Kamekona, Roland Nip, Michael W. Perry, Ted Sackett, Karen Keawehawaii.
Synopsis: It seems like it will be a nice idyllic day for McCabe and the son of one of his best friends when they take a boat out fishing,

but then they discover a bomb on board and unable to diffuse it so they jump overboard (providing Conrad/or his double) with a bit of action. They wind up on an island and are presumed dead—leading Jake and Derek to seek out the bomber.
Trivia: Jackie Cooper (1922-2011) was a good actor and began his career in the early 30's as a child star with films like *Skippy* (nominated for an Oscar) and *The Champ*. He continued to act and was a presence on TV and films as an actor for many years, off and on. Like Conrad, however, he also became a TV executive (Screen Gems in the 1960's) and director. He directed two *Jake and the Fatman* episodes back to back in 1989—his final work as a director. He won two Emmy Awards for his directing of episodes of *MASH* (in 1974) and *The White Shadow* (in 1989).

The title of this episode is derived from the 1927 song "Side by Side" with lyrics by Gus Kahn and music by Harry M. Woods. The song has been used on countless TV shows and films and recorded by many performers over the years.

Snowfall (5/24/1989)
Written by: Rick Kelbaugh. Directed by: Jackie Cooper.
Guest Stars: Ben Piazza, Michael Madsen, Branscombe Richmond, Valerie Wildman, Kirk Matthews, Bill Ogilvie, Lei Maa Richmond, Karen Keawhawaii.
Synopsis: Jake assists the Secret Service in trying to capture a counterfeiter, who uses the money to buy cocaine. When a raid fails to capture the counterfeiter and leads to the death of a friend—Jake seeks revenge.
Trivia: The song used for the title, "Snowfall" was written in 1941 by Claude Thornhill and used as his theme song. It has often been recorded by various artists and used as part of Christmas albums (Tony Bennett, Carpenters and Doris Day). For this episode the 'Snow' has to do with cocaine.

Michael Madsen is one of the busiest actors around to this day and among the films he has been associated with are *Reservoir Dogs, Donnie Brasco, Thelma and Louise* and *Kill Bill: Vol 1*.

Season Three Episodes

I Only Have Eyes for You (9/20/1989)
Written by: Paul Robert Coyle. Directed by: Chuck Bowman.
Guest Stars: Moira Walley, Charles Lucia, Olga Russell, Bob Silva, Turner Pe'a.
Synopsis: When a convict is released from prison he starts seeking revenge against the woman who helped lock him up and she seeks help from McCabe, who prosecuted him.
Trivia: Moira Walley, who plays the victim, later became a producer and among her credits is producing 39 episodes of the AMC hit, and one of the most powerful dramas on television at the time, *Breaking Bad*.

"I Only Have Eyes for You" by Harry Warren and Al Durbin was written for the 1934 film *Dames* (and sung by Dick Powell and Ruby Keeler). Later the Flamingo's had a big hit with the song in 1959. It has also been included on the soundtracks of several other films including *The Right Stuff* and *My Girl*.

The Lady in Red (9/27/1989)
Written by: Kimmer Ringwald. Directed by: Bernard L. Kowalski.
Guest Stars: Mitch Ryan, Juliana McCarthy, James Hong, Gerry Okuneff, Allan Kucin, Leo Penn.
Synopsis: An ex-cop friend of McCabe's dies in an automobile accident—apparently he was driving while drunk, but McCabe isn't sure of how this happened and has Jake investigate. Jake learns that the ex-cop (now a private-eye) was investigating a cold case—the murder of a woman he may have had a relationship with.
Trivia: Leo Penn, the father of actor Sean Penn, and a well-regarded director (and who directed Conrad in five episodes of *Cannon* and two *Jakes*) had begun as an actor, and appears as an actor in this episode and a later one titled "Come Closer to Me."

The song "The Lady in Red" became a big world-wide hit when Irish recording artist Chris de Burgh released it in 1986. In the United States it reached #3 on Billboard's Hot 100.

Easy to Love (10/4/1989)
Written by: Fred McKnight. Directed by: Alexander Singer.
Guest Stars: Claudia Christian, Stan Sells, John Michael Bolger, Lily Mariye, Douglas Mossman, Dick Jensen, James Grant Benton.
Synopsis: Jake and a policeman are transporting a prisoner to Los Angeles. He escapes and the policeman is killed. The policeman's partner (Claudia Christian) goes to Hawaii to assist in the investigation into his murder—and partially blames Jake for the loss of her partner.
Trivia: Claudia Christian had her big break playing "Susan Ivanova" on the science-fiction series *Babylon 5* for which she was nominated for two Saturn (Academy of Science Fiction, Fantasy & Horror) Awards.

"Easy to Love" the song used as the title of this episode was written by Cole Porter and sung by James Stewart to Eleanor Powell in the film *Born to Dance*. The song had originally been written for the 1934 Broadway production of *Anything Goes*, but had been cut from the show.

The Way You Look Tonight (10/11/1989)
Written by: Jeri Taylor. Directed by: Leo Penn.
Guest Stars: Rosalind Chao, Robert Harper, James Shigeta, Michael Tulin, Henry Bal, Jack Hogan, Kiyoshi Kimura, Al Harrington.
Synopsis: A daughter is acquitted of murdering her mother and wants Jake to find the killer because he is going on vacation! Then McCabe denies his vacation request and Jake quits his job and accepts the daughters' assignment!
Trivia: Rosalind Chao was a busy working actress at the time of her appearance on *Jake and the Fatman* (and continues to be to this day). Her first TV guest appearance came in 1970 when she was 16 years old on an episode of *Here's Lucy*. She may be best known for two TV roles: the part of Maxwell Klinger's wife Soon-Lee on *MASH* and its spin-off *After MASH*, and her role as Keiko on *Star Trek: The Next Generation*.

"The Way You Look Tonight" is another standard written by Jerome Kern with lyrics by Dorothy Fields and first performed by Fred Astaire in *Swing Time*. It won the Best Original Song Academy Award of 1936.

Dancing in the Dark (10/25/1989)
Written by: Steven Aspis. **Directed by:** Chuck Bowman.
Guest Stars: Ray Wise, Rodney Eastman, Stewart Finlay-McLennan, Charles Cyphers, Bill Morey.
Synopsis: A former cat burglar seeks Jake's help to clear his name after a series of robberies which carry his moniker. He also wants to clear his name so he can make amends with his son.
Trivia: This title refers to the Arthur Schwartz and Howard Dietz song "Dancing in the Dark" which was written for the Broadway musical "The Band Wagon" in 1931, and later danced to by Fred Astaire and Cyd Charisse in the 1953 MGM musical—not the 1984 song written and performed by Bruce Springsteen in 1984.

It All Depends on You (11/1/1989)
Written by: David Moessinger. **Directed by:** Michael Lange.
Guest Stars: Jeff Corey, Gregg Henry, Galyn Gorg, Kenny D'Aquila, Jim Ishida, Olga Russell, Chaz Mann.
Synopsis: Derek's first case involves a drunk driver with powerful connections who assaulted a police officer. The main witness abruptly changes his testimony and a judge (Jeff Corey) dismisses the case—Jake and McCabe look into why.
Trivia: Jeff Corey (1914-2002) was a top character actor as well as an influential acting teacher (whose students included Kirk Douglas, Sally Kellerman, Anthony Perkins, Jane Fonda and Robin Williams). One of his most famous film roles was that of 'Tom Chaney' who inspires the action in the John Wayne film *True Grit*. Among the other films he appeared in are *My Friend Flicka, The Devil and Daniel Webster, Home of the Brave, The Cincinnatti Kid, Mickey One, Little Big Man* and *In Cold Blood*. Corey and William Conrad both appeared in *The Killers* and *Joan of Arc*.

Out of Nowhere (11/8/1989)
Written by: Jeri Taylor. **Directed by:** John Llewellyn Moxey.
Guest Stars: Signy Coleman, Robert Clohessy, Tom McTigue, Sandy Ward, Robin Strand, George O'Hanlon.
Synopsis: When Jake accompanies the FBI on a raid at the home of a drug smuggler—they find no drugs—but Jake does find that a woman he once proposed to is living with the drug smuggler.

Trivia: "Out of Nowhere" was composed by Johnny Green with lyrics by Edward Heyman and first recorded by Bing Crosby in 1931—it became Crosby's first big hit as a singer without the Rhythm Boys.

Sweet Leilani (11/15/1989)
Written by: Rick Mittleman. Directed by: Russ Mayberry.
Guest Stars: Ruta Lee, Peter Haskell, Marlyn Mason, Laura Leigh Hughes, William Shockley, Olga Russell, Jack Hogan.
Synopsis: A murdered girl washes up on the beach which attracts the attention of newspaper columnist Leilani Simmons—and Jake and McCabe try to find out why she is so interested as well as who the murdered girl was and who killed her.
Trivia: Director Russ Mayberry (1925-2012) was born in Glasgow, Scotland and later immigrated to the United States. A prolific director from the late sixties to the mid-nineties, Mayberry helmed episodes of such shows as *Love on the Rooftop, Bewitched, That Girl, The Brady Bunch, Ironside, Marcus Welby, M.D., The Fall Guy, Magnum P.I.*, and five episodes of *Jake and the Fatman*. Later he directed some 18 episodes of In the *Heat of the Night*.

My Shining Hour (11/29/1989)
Written by: Kimmer Ringwald. Directed by: Bernard L. Kowalski.
Guest Stars: Ernest Borgnine, Lonny Chapman, Lenore Kasdorf, Oliver Muirhead, Steven Perry, Don Lamond, George O'Hanlon.
Synopsis: A former TV star (Ernest Borgnine) whose career has declined, states he has witnessed a murder, but nobody will believe him except McCabe.
Trivia: "My Shining Hour" composed by Harold Arlen and lyrics by Johnny Mercer was written for the 1943 film *The Sky's the Limit* (sung by Joan Leslie, who was dubbed by Sally Sweetland) and was nominated for an Academy award for Best Song.

Long Ago and Far Away (12/6/1989)
Written by: Jack M. Casey. Directed by: Russ Mayberry.
Guest Stars: Jack Hogan, Cheryl McMannis, Grainger Hines, Olga Russell, Ben Wong, Sylvia McAlester, Darryl Castillo.
Synopsis: A judge begins receiving death threats after sentencing a man to twenty-years for rape.

Trivia: Veteran actor Jack Hogan played Judge Smithwood on twelve episodes of *Jake and the Fatman*, and this episode gave him one of his best showcases. Hogan appeared on numerous TV series as a guest actor but is best known for his work as Pvt. Kirby on the 1962-1967 series *Combat*. Hogan had moved to Hawaii in the early 80's and served as a casting director for *Magnum P.I.* and then acted as Judge Smithwood during his time living there.

What Child Is This? (12/13/1989)
Written by: Jeri Taylor. **Directed by:** Reza Badiyi.
Guest Stars: Mary Ward, Matt Landers, Lu Leonard, Olga Russell, Dennis Paladino, Ellen Faibanks, Colin De Silva, Joseph Panis.
Synopsis: At Christmas a pregnant woman is on the run from two killers—and seeks protection by staying at a homeless shelter.
Trivia: Iranian born director Reza Badiyi (1930-2011) directed numerous episodes of many diverse TV series from *The Doris Day Show* to *Star Trek: Deep Space Nine*. One of his most famous jobs was developing the opening montage of *The Mary Tyler Moore Show* including coming up with the iconic idea of Mary throwing her hat in the air (they were lucky that in the background was sixty-two year old Hazel Frederick passing by to give her famous scowl).

Lu Leonard, McCabe's Secretary Gertrude during the shows first season, returns for her final appearance visiting Hawaii to join in the festivities with ex-boss McCabe.

In the Still of the Night (1/3/1990)
Written by: Carol Saraceno. **Directed by:** Georg Fenady.
Guest Stars: Shannon Wilcox, Martha Byrne, Woody Brown, James Sloyan, Dennis Creaghan, Ray Bumatai.
Synopsis: Derek has a friend whose sister gets arrested for possession of drugs, who says that they were planted on her by a vindictive mother-in-law. Derek asks Jake to look into the situation.
Trivia: This version of "In the Still of the Night" was written by Cole Porter in 1937 for the MGM film Rosalie and not the classic 1956 song written by Fred Parris and recorded by the Five Satins.

You Turned the Tables on Me (1/10/1990)
Written by: Robert Hamilton. **Directed by:** Reza Badiyi.
Guest Stars: Jacqueline Schultz, Andreas Katsulas, Cliff Bemis, Oz Toronto, Darby Hinton, George O'Hanlon, Jr., Ada Jankowics.
Synopsis: A prosecutor under McCabe is having an affair with a criminal that is under investigation. She gets information about an informant and her lover has him killed. Now Jake and McCabe have to figure out how he found out and who the informant is.
Trivia: Darby Hinton (who plays Danny) is best known for his work as a child actor, specifically Fess Parker's son, Israel Boone, on *Daniel Boone*.

The title "You Turned the Tables on me" was composed by Louis Alter with lyrics by Sidney Mitchell in 1936 and introduced by Alice Faye in the film, *Sing, Baby, Sing*.

One More for the Road (1/17/1990)
Written by: Carol Saraceno. **Directed by:** Russ Mayberry.
Guest Stars: Caryn West, Vasili Bogazianos, Ed Ames, John Furey, Nova Ball, Jack Hogan, George O'Hanlon, Jr.
Synopsis: Derek is involved in a hit and run which didn't just happen, but was planned and leads to an investigation by Jake.
Trivia: Just one week after Darby Hinton from *Daniel Boone* has a guest-shot on "Fatman" we get actor-singer Ed Ames who played the Indian 'Mingo' on *Daniel Boone*, but is perhaps best known for his *Tonight Show* appearance in 1965 with Johnny Carson—trying to show Johnny how to properly throw a tomahawk.

Who's Sorry Now? (1/31/1990)
Written by: J. Michael Straczynski. **Directed by:** Reza Badiyi.
Guest Stars: Georg Stanford Brown, Paul Lieber, George Fisher, Bob Fimiani, Olga Russell, George O'Hanlon, Jr.
Synopsis: McCabe is abducted by the brother of a cop killer that he had convicted years earlier and who now is about to be executed for his crime.
Trivia: Georg Stanford Brown was famous in the 70's for his role on the police drama *The Rookies*. He was also nominated for an Emmy for his work in the mini-series *Roots*, and later became a TV director.

The song "Who's Sorry Now" was written by Bert Kalmar and Harry Ruby in 1923 and was used in the Marx Brothers film *A Night in Casablanca* in 1946, but became a huge hit when recorded by Connie Francis in 1958.

I'll Dance at Your Wedding (2/7/1990)
Written by: Paul David Dugan. Directed by: Georg Fenady.
Guest Stars: Cassandra Byram, Jay Acovone, Rhoda Gemignani, Robert Gentry, James Craven, Gianni Russo, Brendan Dillon.
Synopsis: Jake attends his sister's wedding and discovers her intended is in big trouble, he tries to help but is told by local police to stay out of it, and of course he can't.

My Buddy (2/14/1990)
Written by: Robin Madden. Directed by: Bernard L. Kowalski.
Guest Stars: Robert Jayne, Olivia Burnette, Alan Scarfe, Randi Davis, George O'Hanlon, Jr.
Synopsis: When Jake catches a young pickpocket he tries to help her home, but she doesn't want to cooperate.
Trivia: Robin Madden produced (or associate produced) some 95 episodes of *Jake and the Fatman* and also wrote three, of which this was the first. Madden later co-produced 115 episodes of *Diagnosis: Murder*. Madden briefly was in the media spotlight during the 2012 Presidential campaign when he came forward as a former classmate of GOP presidential candidate Mitt Romney to say that Romney sometimes disguised himself as a police officer—wearing a uniform and all and said Romney told him and others that he used to pull over drivers on the road, "We all thought it was pretty weird."

By Myself (2/28/1990)
Written by: Jo William Philipp. Directed by: Chuck Bowman.
Guest Stars: Polly Bergen, George O'Hanlon, Jr., Jon Gries, Marc Poppel, Corie Henninger, Olga Russell.
Synopsis: Jake tries to track down a rapist whose victims are all single women living alone.
Trivia: "By Myself" is a standard written by the team of Arthur Schwartz and Howard Dietz. Many artists have recorded it, but it is probably most famous from the film *The Band Wagon* (MGM,

1953) sung by Fred Astaire. Jerry Lewis also sang the song in his first film sans Dean Martin, *The Disorderly Orderly* (1957—Paramount).

I Ain't Got No Body (3/7/1990)
Written by: J. Michael Straczynski. **Directed by:** Georg Fenady.
Guest Stars: Kathryn Leigh Scott, Mary-Margaret Humes, John McCann, Branscombe Richmond, Stan Ivar, George O'Hanlon, Jr.
Synopsis: A woman disappears while looking into her mother's death which occurred at a health resort.
Trivia: George O'Hanlon, Jr., was a semi-regular on the shows third season appearing in 13 episodes as Sgt. Rafferty. Previously he had been Nancy Drew's boyfriend Ned Nickerson on *The Hardy Boy/Nancy Drew Mysteries*.

Put Your Dreams Away (3/14/1990)
Written by: Steven Aspis. **Directed by:** Reza Badiyi.
Guest Stars: Sal Viscuso, Lou Beatty, Jr. Behrouz Vossoughi, Kevin Lopes.
Synopsis: A flashback episode, Jake is wounded on a plane in which the pilot jumps out with the only parachute. McCabe, in the control tower, needs to keep Jake awake to land the plane, so they look back on previous cases.
Trivia: The song "Put Your Dreams Away" was written by Ruth Lowe, Paul Mann and George David Weiss. It became a hit for Frank Sinatra three times, re-recording it in 1957 and 1963.

If I Didn't Care (3/28/1990)
Written by: Kimmer Ringwald. **Directed by:** John C. Flinn III.
Guest Stars: Mark Margolis, Mary Ellen Dunbar, Rick Giolito, Tom Lupo, Norm Compton, Tara Melia Camp, Katie Ralston.
Synopsis: An old classmate of Jake's shows up with deadly intentions.
Trivia: "If I Didn't Care" was recorded by The Ink Spots in 1939 and it sold over 19 million copies, making it one of the most popular songs ever written (written by Jack Lawrence).

Veteran actor Mark Margolis was nominated for an Emmy Award for his guest shot as "Tio Salamanca' on the hit cable series *Breaking Bad*.

You're Driving Me Crazy (4/4/1990)
Written by: Michele Val Jean. Directed by: Ronald Gary Stein.
Guest Stars: Michael Goodwin, Jean Bruce Scott, Mimi Craven, Terry O'Quinn, Jack Hogan, George O'Hanlon, Jr.
Synopsis: A man stabs his wife dead, and then pleads temporary insanity, a plea which doesn't sit well with McCabe and he and Jake attempt to prove otherwise.
Trivia: Ronald Gary Stein was the stunt coordinator on 81 episodes of "Fatman" as well as many other TV-series and films (including *Star Trek III: The Search for Spock, Scarface, True Lies,* and *The Fast and the Furious*). He was given the opportunity to direct three episodes of "Fatman."

You Took Advantage of Me (4/25/1990)
Written by: Robert Schlitt. Directed by: Bernard L. Kowalski.
Guest Stars: John Mahon, Greg Mullavey, Elyssa Davalos, Marjean Holden, Olga Russell, Jack Hogan.
Synopsis: A doctor is charged with murdering his wife, but is alibied by her secretary. McCabe has Jake go undercover as his chauffeur to find out if there is any hanky-panky going on between doctor and secretary.
Trivia: Veteran writer Robert Schlitt (1933-2008) served as producer and writer on "Matlock" and supervising producer of "Father Dowling Mysteries" and wrote episodes of shows including "The Mod Squad," "Hawaii Five-O" and "The Streets of San Francisco." Earlier in his career he lived in Paris for two years where he assisted the famous French filmmaker Jacques Tati. This was his only episode of *Jake and the Fatman.*

My Heart Belongs to Daddy (5/2/1990) Written by: Douglas Benton & Daniel Benton. Directed by: Robert Scheerer.
Guest Stars: Michelle Joyner, Stephen Root, Michael Bofshever, Olga Russell, George O'Hanlon, Jr.
Synopsis: A man claims to have evidence against a crooked oil company while a woman who claims to be his daughter visits McCabe.
Trivia: Co-writer Douglas Benton (1925-2000), a former newsman, was best known as a producer than a writer, producing such shows as *Thriller, Ironside, Police Woman,* and *Magnum P.I.* He won an

Emmy in 1974 (shared with Dean Hargrove) for *Columbo*. His son, Daniel, got his start writing an episode of *Police Woman* and later was nominated for a Daytime Emmy Award for Disney's *Adventures in Wonderland*.

There have been many famous versions of "My Heart Belongs to Daddy" (written by Cole Porter) especially by Mary Martin and later by Marilyn Monroe in the film *Let's Make Love* (1960).

Danny Boy (5/9/1990)
Written by: J. Michael Straczynski. **Directed by:** Russ Mayberry.
Guest Stars: Tom Isbel, Miguel Fernandes, Amick Byram, Robert Apisa, Jesse D. Groins, Jack Hogan.
Synopsis: Another appearance by McCabe's son, Daniel, when a prison gang threatens to kill him, Daniel joins a group planning a prison escape.
Trivia: "Danny Boy" was written by an Englishman named Frederic Weatherly, and has become a kind of an anthem to the Irish. It has been recorded many times and on TV was the theme song for Danny Thomas on *Make Room for Daddy*.

Chinatown, My Chinatown (5/16/1990)
Writen by: David Moessinger. **Directed by:** Reza Badiyi.
Guest Stars: Aki Aleong, Evan C. Kim, Kim Miyori, Cary Hhiroyuki Tagawa, Rudloph Willrich, Olga Russell.
Synopsis: Jake investigates the murder of a newspaperman working in Chinatown—and gets help from the son of the local gang kingpin.
Trivia: "Chinatown, My Chinatown" was written in 1910 by William Jerome and Jean Schwartz and was recorded over the years by artists such as Al Jolson, Bing Crosby, and even Chet Atkins. Woody Allen used the song in his 1987 film *Radio Days*.

Season Four

In terms of ratings, "Fatman" ranked #44 overall (falling four notches from the previous season) but beating its time slot opposition on NBC, *Seinfeld*, which that year ranked # 45.

Episodes

God Bless the Child (9/12/1990)
Written by: David Abramowitz. **Directed by:** E.W. Swackhamer.
Guest Stars: Richard Herd, Romy Windsor, Doug Savant, Lynn Ellen Hollinger, Ramy Zada, Jack Hogan.
Synopsis: When a father threatens to disinherit two siblings—they murder their parents.
Trivia: "God Bless the Child" written by Billie Holiday and Arthur Herzog, Jr. in 1939 became one of the songs most identified with the talented but troubled Holiday.

The Tender Trap (9/19/1990)
Written by: Michele Val Jean. **Directed by:** Michael Lange.
Guest Stars: Mitch Ryan, Kim Johnston Ulrich, Hank George, Olga Russell.
Synopsis: Derek is surprised that his Uncle is going to get married to a woman whose half his age, he begins to wonder if she is a gold-digger and begins investigating.
Trivia: Jimmy Van Heusen and Sammy Cahn wrote the song for the 1955 film *The Tender Trap* which is sung by Frank Sinatra. The song (Love Is) The Tender Trap was nominated for a Best Original Song Oscar.

Exactly Like You (9/26/1990)
Written by: William Conway. **Directed by:** Ron Satlof.
Guest Stars: Bryan Cranston, Mary Cadorette, Kerrie Keane, Maria O'Brien, Jack Hogan, Olga Russell.
Synopsis: A man is murdered and Jake picks up a suspect who admits his guilt, but McCabe isn't so sure when inconsistencies show up in his statement.
Trivia: Guest star Bryan Cranston went on to play the father in the

family favorite *Malcolm in the Middle* and then found his iconic role as Walter White in the ground breaking cable series *Breaking Bad*.

The song "Exactly Like You" written by Jimmy McHugh and Dorothy Fields was published in 1930, and recorded by many artists and one of the best versions is by Nina Simone.

Round Midnight (10/3/1990) Written by: Kimmer Ringwald with story by Robert Hamilton. Directed by: Ron Satlof.
Guest Stars: Robert Miranda, Cec Verrell, Reiner Schone, Bill Ogilvie, Richard Zobel, Lee Woodd.
Synopsis: Jake is on the case when a friend's Porsche is stolen by gunpoint.
Trivia: Another Jazz standard is used as the title of this episode. "Round Midnight" written by Thelonious Monk. It was later used as a title and theme for the 1986 film *Round Midnight*.

Only You (10/24/1990)
Written by: Carol Saraceno. Directed by: Ron Satlof.
Guest Stars: Bonnie Burroughs, Martin Slacks, Jane Sibbet, Steven Perry, Tommy Fujiwara.
Synopsis: Jake goes undercover to investigate industrial espionage.
Trivia: This is the third and final episode of the series written by Carol Saraceno. At around the same time Saraceno was writing for the *Dynasty* spin-off, *The Colbys*. Earlier she had written a well-received TV-movie called *The Initiation of Sarah*.

My Boy Bill (10/31/1990)
Written by: David Abramowitz. Directed by: Reza Badiyi.
Guest Stars: Mary-Margaret Humes, Glenn Walker Harris, Jr., Michael C. Gwynne, Stanley Kamel, William Lucking, Jack Hogan.
Synopsis: McCabe assigns a case to a top prosecutor—the prosecutor is later offered a bribe to throw the case, which she turns down. Later some evidence is tampered with and the trail leads back to the prosecutor who insists she is innocent.
Trivia: The final episode of the series to feature Jack Hogan as Judge Smithwood. The song "My Boy Bill" also known as "Soliloquy" is from the landmark Rodgers and Hammerstein show *Carousel*. It

was performed in the Broadway show by John Raitt, and then memorably recorded in 1946 by Frank Sinatra.

More Than You Know (11/7/1990)
Written by: Paul Robert Coyle. **Directed by:** Bernard L. Kowalski.
Guest Stars: Laura Johnson, Richard Hatch, Tobin Bell, Susan Park, Olga Russell, George O'Hanlon, Jr.
Synopsis: An unscrupulous reporter secretly records a conversation between McCabe and Jake in which they discuss the case of a serial killer. She then kills a woman and makes it appear that the serial killer is the actual murderer just so she can get a scoop.
Trivia: At the time of his appearance on "Jake", Richard Hatch was best known for his work as Inspector Dan Robbins opposite Karl Malden on *The Streets of San Francisco* (having taken over the sidekick role from Michael Douglas) and later for his role as Tom Zarek on *Battlestar Galactica*. This was the final episode televised written by Paul Robert Coyle.

Night and Day (11/14/1990) Written by: Joyce Burditt with story by Dean Hargrove and Joel Steiger. **Directed by:** Michael Lange.
Guest Stars: Terri Garber, Mark Rolston, Barry Sattels, Glenn Cannon, Norm Compton, Peter Clark, Karen Iboshi, Ted Sackett.
Synopsis: A gold smuggler is the target of a beautiful private eye (Teri Garber) who wants revenge for her husband's murder.
Trivia: Actress Terri Garber began her career on the soap opera *Texas*, but her big break came with the popular 1985 ABC mini-series *North and South*, playing a Scarlet O'Hara type Southern Belle opposite Patrick Swayze. More recently she had a recurring role on the day time soap, *As the World Turns*. The song "Night and Day" is another standard by Cole Porter and used in the play "The Gay Divorce" and introduced by Fred Astaire both on stage and in the 1934 film *The Gay Divorcee* (RKO). It was also used as the title of a 1946 Warner Brother's film about Porter's life which starred Cary Grant.

Goodbye (11/28/1990)
Written by: J. Michael Straczynski and William Conway based on story by Straczynski. **Directed by:** Bernard L. Kowalski.
Guest Stars: Lisa Cutter, Richard Grove, Ed Nelson, Jeremy

Roberts, Francis X. McCarthy, Bill Kohne.
Synopsis: Jake discovers a body while fishing and falls in with a group of crooked L.A. cops—eventually Jake finds himself in LA having to clear himself of murder charges.
Trivia: "Goodbye" is an apt title since by the end of this episode the whole gang returns to Los Angeles as McCabe once again becomes a L.A. District Attorney. This was a special two-hour episode.

I Know That You Know (12/12/1990)
Written by: Robin Madden. Directed by: Russ Mayberry.
Guest Stars: Erin Gray, Charles Frank, Gerald Anthony, Diane McBain, Joe Bratcher, Steve Hack, Laurence Haddon, Olga Russell.
Synopsis: A wealthy woman is murdered and a known cat burglar is arrested for her murder (though he proclaims his innocence and insists he saw somebody else enter the house before he did) and McCabe prosecutes him. He is convicted, but afterwards McCabe has second thoughts and begins to think that somebody else did actually kill her.
Trivia: Erin Gray was (and still is) a busy TV actress and at the time of her appearance on "Jake" was best known for her work as Col. Wilma Deering in the Sci-fi cult series *Buck Rogers in the 25th Century* and then her role as Kate Summers in the family sitcom *Silver Spoons*. Charles Frank was equally busy especially during the 70's and 80's-often in villain roles—one of my favorite has him as the man Ruth Gordon kills on *Columbo* seeking revenge for him killing her niece.

Let's Call the Whole Thing Off (1/2/1991)
Written by: Robert Brennan. Directed by: Daniel Attias.
Guest Stars: David Groh, Jennifer Bassey, Jay Pickett, Kate Vernon, Beth Hogan, Barry O'Neill, Richard Jamison.
Synopsis: A witness who is testifying against a major crime boss is murdered on his way to court and it's up to Jake to find another witness, the man's ex-girlfriend, before the judge drops the charges.
Trivia: While he appeared on many TV shows afterward, David Groh (1939-2008) will always be best known for his role as Joe Gerard, the man who Rhoda Morgenstern marries when she moves to New York on *Rhoda*, and the man she quickly divorces when it turns out that producers didn't like Rhoda being married! "Let's Call the Whole Thing Off" is yet another Geershwin song that is utilized as

a title for *Jake and the Fatman*. It was written for the 1937 film *Shall We Dance* and sung (and danced) on roller skates by Fred Astaire and Ginger Rogers.

I May Be Wrong (1/9/1991)
Written by: Robert Brennan. **Directed by:** Leo Penn.
Guest Stars: Clarence Williams III, Patrick Kilpatrick, Antoinette Byron, Jonathan Farwell, Erica Rogers, Tony Todd, Ryan MacDonald, Olga Russell.
Synopsis: A South African diplomat is killed by a car bomb. South Africa sends a black police officer to investigate a racist group called "The Order of Blood."
Trivia: Clarence Williams III is best remembered for his role as 'Lin' on *The Mod Squad* (1968-1973), but has continued to work thru the years and was recently seen in *Lee Daniels' The Butler* in 2013.

Daddy's Home (2/6/1991)
Written by: Kimmer Ringwald. **Directed by:** Bernard L. Kowalski.
Guest Stars: Harry Guardion, Rhoda Gemignani, Anjanette Comer, Cassandra Byram, Mike Moroff, Judson Scott, Richard Molinare.
Synopsis: Jake meets up with his father (Harry Guardino) for the first time in 27 years at his niece's christening. However, all is not well when it is discovered that the father stole $50,000 from a former employer.
Trivia: Harry Guardino (1925-1995) was physically a good selection to play Jake's father with his dark, brooding good looks. Guardino alternated between movies (*Houseboat, The Pigeon That Took Rome, Hell is for Heroes*) and TV (*Dr. Kildare, Route 66, Naked City*) early on without ever becoming a big star but certainly a recognizable and respected actor. By the 70's most of his roles were on TV (including a stint as perpetual loser Hamilton Burger on the ill-fated 1972-73 *The New Perry Mason*). However, in the 70's, he did begin appearing in a string of movies starring his friend Clint Eastwood (*The Enforcer, Dirty Harry, Any Which Way You Can*).

I'm Gonna Live Till I Die (2/13/1991)
Written by: William Conway. Directed by: Alexander Singer.
Guest Stars: David Paymer, Caryn Richman, Bradford English, Tim Rossovich, Wayne Tippit.
Synopsis: An accountant witnesses a murder and wants to help Jake out with the investigation, but the case takes a twist when the man reports another murder to Jake—his own murder.
Trivia: This episode seems to be inspired by the 1950 Rudolph Mate film *D.O.A.* which starred Edmond O'Brien about a man who only has a few hours to live who seeks out his murderer. The song "I'm Gonna Live Till I Die" became a big hit in 1955 for Frank Sinatra and Capital Records.

Pretty Baby (2/27/1991)
Written by: Robin Madden. Directed by: John C. Flinn III.
Guest Stars: Casey Biggs, Leonre Kasdorf, Robert Pine, Robert Miano, Leonore Kasdorf, Suzanne Snyder.
Synopsis: Jake takes care of a baby while her mother runs an errand and witnesses a murder; she is spotted by the killer and is shot and killed. Obviously Jake will not take this lying down.
Trivia: Once again Robert Pine is a guest-star on a Conrad series. He later recalled the experience: "Conrad was older for sure—and not healthy. He was more sedentary on this show than when I worked with him on *Cannon*, but he still had a great sense of humor…and still relied on cue cards."

I Cover the Waterfront (3/6/1991)
Written by: David Abramowitz. Directed by: Harry Harris.
Guest Stars: Jason Beghe, Roxann Dawson, Scott Marlowe, Kip Gilman, Joe Flood, Beau Starr.
Synopsis: Derek's childhood friend is trying to turn his life around, however, he is found dead full of alcohol and drugs and police believe he committed suicide. Derek doesn't believe this to be the case and—along with Jake and McCabe—he begins investigating it.
Trivia: "I Cover the Waterfront" is a jazz standard composed by Johnny Green with lyrics by Edward Heyman. The song was inspired by a novel of the same name (by Max Miller) and was also the title of a

1933 film which starred Ben Lyon and Claudette Colbert. Billie Holiday had a big success with her take on the song.

You Don't Know Me (3/13/1991) Written by: Eric Estrin and Michael Berlin. Directed by: Reza Badiyi.
Guest Stars: Katherine Cannon, Nicholas Coster, Robin Sachs, Tony Todd, Marcia Cross, David Wells, Robert J. Bernard.
Synopsis: A friend of McCabe's is ousted by his company by a man he felt was a friend and protégé. He then learns that his own wife aided in his ouster—and is the protégé's lover. Later the protégé is murdered and the wife is a prime suspect.
Trivia: "You Don't Know Me" written by Cindy Walker but was based on a title and story given to her by Eddy Arnold who recorded the song in 1956 for RCA. Later Jerry Vale made a hit of it. But the biggest success of the song was by Ray Charles in 1962 where it climbed to #2 on Billboard's Hot 100.

It Never Entered My Mind (3/20/1991)
Written by: Joyce Burditt. Directed by: Bernard L. Kowalski.
Guest Stars: Dick Van Dyke, Carol Bruce, James Cromwell, Steven Eckholdt, Sam Hennings, Margaret Reed, Kristoff S. John, Gregory Itzin.
Synopsis: McCabe's doctor, Mark Sloan (Dick Van Dyke), finds himself accused of the murder of the hospital's by the books administrator, so Sloan joins forces with McCabe to clear himself.
Trivia: This episode introduces the character of Mark Sloan and gives TV great Dick Van Dyke a late career success. This episode didn't lead right away to a series, instead there were three TV movies which featured Sloan as the crime solving doctor and then the series *Diagnosis: Murder* premiered which ran from 1993-2001 which produced 178 episodes (20 more than Van Dyke's classic 1960's sitcom!).

Second Time Around (4/3/1991) Written by: Kimmer Ringwald based on a story by Paul Schiffer. Directed by: Michael Lange.
Guest Stars: Kevin Kilner, Lori Hallier, Hector Mercado, Pamela Kosh, Frank Collison, Kristoffer Tabori.

Synopsis: Are McCabe's eyes playing tricks on him? He sees a man who was supposedly murdered five years earlier. He and Jake naturally investigate.
Trivia: This is the 8th and final episode directed by Michael Lange. Lange recalls that, "Sadly, I didn't stay in touch with Bill. We had many enjoyable times together on the show and I wish I had stayed in touch. I especially feel bad that I didn't attend his funeral, although if my memory serves me (which it does sometimes) I was out of town when it happened."

I'd Do Anything (4/10/1991) Written by: David Abramowitz and William Conway. Directed by: Ronald Gary Stein.
Guest Stars: Melinda Culea, Michael Durrell, Josh Lucas, George Cheung, Nelson Manshita.
Synopsis: A psychiatrist is having an affair with a patient and manipulates him to kill her husband.
Trivia: Melinda Culea was a former model who broke into television and had high profile co-starring roles on such series as *The A-Team, Glitter,* and *Knots Landing*. The song "I'd Do Anything" was from the Broadway musical (and later movie) *Oliver!* And is an apt title for this episode.

We'll Meet Again (4/24/1991)
Written by: William Conway. Directed by: Bernard L. Kowalski.
Guest Stars: Robert Culp, Ron Karabastsos, Catherine MacNeal, Ted Neale, Olga Russell, Frank Pesce.
Synopsis: When McCabe is showing a class around the courthouse a man (dressed as a clown) tries to shoot him, but misses. McCabe has to review old cases to try and figure out who wants to do him in.
Trivia: Robert Culp (1930-2010) had his big break as the co-lead of the witty (and ground breaking) spy series *I-Spy*. He then flirted with movie stardom with the hit 1969 film *Bob & Carol & Ted & Alice*, but TV turned out to be his bread and butter genre. He also seemed to excel at playing smooth and unruffable murderers—most memorably in three episodes of *Columbo*.

It's a Sin to Tell a Lie (5/1/1991)
Written by: David Abramowitz. Directed by: Georg Fenady.
Guest Stars: A.C. Weary, Joan McMurtrey, Julie McCullough, Elizabeth Gracen, Tom Urich, Brendon Boone.
Synopsis: An older priest is having an affair with a younger woman and when she is murdered he becomes a suspect.
Trivia: "It's a Sin to Tell a Lie" was written by Billy Mayhew and later became a big hit for Fat's Waller and later still for Slim Whitman on the country charts.

Nevertheless (5/8/1991)
Written by: Robert Brennan. Directed by: Alexander Singer.
Guest Stars: Richard Burgi, Jason Beghe, Lee Meriwether, Mitchell Laurance, Warren Burton, David Wells, Monica Ferren, Olga Russell.
Synopsis: An older woman (Lee Meriwether) is murdered by her younger husband who makes it look like it was a mugging gone bad.
Trivia: Lee Meriwether, Miss America of 1954, later came known for her work on three TV series, as Catwoman (though not as famous as Julie Newmar or Eartha Kitt) on the 1960's *Batman* (and in its feature length film), as Buddy Ebsen's daughter-in-law and secretary (Betty) on the long-running *Barnaby Jones* and later taking on the role of Lily Munster in *The Munsters Today* (1988-1991).

Fifth Season

In its fifth season the show ranked #50 overall, just ahead of *Beverly Hills 90210* on Fox, and even out-performing the Silverman-Hargrove *Matlock* (which was an older show, then in its ninth season) which ranked #56. But CBS decided it was time to pull the plug on the Fatman.

Where or When, Part One (9/18/1991)
Written by: Kimmer Ringwald. Directed by: Bernard L. Kowalski.
Guest Stars: Robert Forster, Keith Buckley, Anjanette Comer, Efrain Figueroa, Constance Marie, Richard Lynch, Leo Garcia.
Synopsis: An ex-cop turned P.I. sees a man die and notifies the police, but when they arrive the body is gone. The P.I. says the body belonged to a millionaire, who is very much alive.

Trivia: Anjanette Comer was a busy actress who began on television, and then transitioned to films (The cult comedy *The Loved One, The Appaloosa, Banning, Guns for San Sebastian*) but never really made it in that medium and became a perennial and welcome presence with TV guest shots and TV-movies especially in the 70's and 80's on shows like *Columbo, Mannix, Baretta,* and *Barnaby Jones*. This two-part episode of *Jake and the Fatman* would be her second appearance on this show.

Where or When, Part Two (9/25/1991)
Written by: Kimmer Ringwald. Directed by: Bernard L. Kowalski.
Guest Stars: Robert Forster, Anjanette Comer, Keith Buckley, Donald Burton, Richard Lynch, Constance Marie, Olga Russell.
Synopsis: See above.
Trivia: Robert Forster first made a name for himself as the Army private who rides horseback nude in the John Huston film *Reflections in a Golden Eye* and the reporter in *Medium Cool*. In the 70's and 80's he did a lot of television, including a couple of short-lived series *Banyon* (for Quinn Martin) and *Nakia*. In 1997 he made a big movie comeback in Quintin Taratino's *Jackie Brown* and since has alternated between TV appearances and films.

Street of Dreams (10/30/1991)
Written by: Douglas Stefen Borghi. Directed by: Reza Badiyi.
Guest Stars: Tommy Hinkley, Wendy Fulton, Richard Romanus, Clifton Collins, Jr., Bob McCracken, Lou Cutell, Olga Russell.
Synopsis: A young graffiti artist witnesses a murder and begins an investigation of his own in hopes of winning a reward, but then finds himself in danger when the killer recognizes him.
Trivia: "Street of Dreams" is a more contemporary song than the standards usually used on the show as an episode title. Written by and performed by the British rock band Rainbow in 1983.

I'll Never Be the Same (11/6/1991)
Written by: Kimmer Ringwald. Directed by: Peter Ellis.
Guest Stars: Richard Cummings, Jr., Mary Fanarco, James McDonnell, Alyson Reed, Richard Brestoff, Stephen Root, Olga Russell, Toby Maguire.

Synopsis: Jake kills a 14-year old boy, and claims it was in self-defense, that the boy had a gun, however, no gun is found with the body.
Trivia: An early showcase for Toby McGuire who plays the 14-year old shooting victim. McGuire would go on in the late 90's to become a major film star with films like *The Cider House Rules, Wonder Boys, Spider Man* (and its sequels), *Seabiscuit,* and *The Great Gatsby.*

I Could Write a Book (11/13/1991)
Written by: Barry M. Schkolnick. **Directed by:** James Frawley.
Guest Stars: Richard Burgi, Richard Bright, Carmen Argenziano, Leslie Bevis, Julianna McCarthy, Claire Yarlett, Ellen Geer, Olga Russell.
Synopsis: Yet another friend of McCabe's is found dead in what appears to be a suicide, but McCabe is sure it's murder (during the course of the series several friends of McCabe's seem to have been murdered!). The friend was an author who apparently hadn't written anything new in ten years but has been working on an expose and McCabe is sure this is what led to his murder.
Trivia: Ellen Geer has been a busy actress since the late sixties with regular roles in such shows as *The Jimmy Stewart Show, Falcon Crest,* and *Beauty and the Beast.* But most of her 100 plus credits have come from guest shots on episodic TV series such as *Jake and the Fatman.* She is also the daughter of Will Geer, best known as Grandpa on *The Waltons.*

Two Different Worlds (11/20/1991)
Written by: E. Nick Alexander. **Directed by:** Georg Fenady.
Guest Stars: Lori Hallier, Michael Bowen, Henry Brown, Gianni Russo, Pete Antico, Conni Marie Brazelton.
Synopsis: A woman watches as a man robs a convenience store and kills the attendant. She confronts the man and tells him that she will alert the police unless he kills her sister, whose a lawyer.
Trivia: This is the second of three guest shots by Lori Hallier, who plays duel role in this episode, and who at the time was best known for her role as Yvette Dupres on *Days of Our Lives* and later as Shannon Pressman on *Santa Barbara,* as well as numerous guest shots on TV shows and appearances in TV-movies.

Every Time We Say Goodbye (12/11/1991) Written by: Michael Part and Sam Bernard. Directed by: Georg Fenady.
Guest Stars: Melody Anderson, Melinda Clarke, Steven Flynn, Kim Morgan Greene, Tricia O'Neil, Carl Ciafalio, Taylor Fry, Olga Russell.
Synopsis: A model friend of Neely's is found dead of a heroin overdose, just as she was about to quit modeling. Neely goes undercover as a model to find out what might have happened.
Trivia: This is the first episode to feature Canadian born Melody Anderson as Jake's love interest Neely Capshaw. She would appear in six episodes in total. Prior to this she had recurring roles on the TV series *St. Elsewhere* and *Manimal*. She played Edie Adams in a TV-movie on Ernie Kovacs (*Between the Laughter*) and Marilyn Monroe in a TV-movie on Marilyn Monroe (*Marilyn and Bobby: Her Final Affair*).

Come Along with Me (12/18/1991) Written by: Douglas Stefen Borghi. Directed by: Bernard L. Kowalski.
Guest Stars: Melody Anderson, Talia Balsam, Leon Russom, Robin Strand, Joey Aresco, Denise Dowse.
Synopsis: Neely joins Jake to investigate a case where bodies are found with their livers removed. Why and who is somebody committing these crimes?

Last Dance (1/1/1992)
Written by: James Kearns. Directed by: Alexander Singer.
Guest Stars: Christopher Allport, Allan Miller, Mary Kay Adams, Allan Royal, Shari Shattuck, Caryn West, Fran Bennett, Olga Russell.
Synopsis:
Trivia: Director Alexander Singer went to school with Stanley Kubrick and later was a cinematographer of the documentary film *Day of the Flight*, which was directed by Kubrick. He has directed a variety of TV shows including nine episodes of *The Fugitive*, but today may be best known for his work directing *Star Trek: The Next Generation, Star Trek: Deep Space Nine* and *Star Trek: Voyager*. He won an Emmy for his directing of an episode of *The Bold Ones: The Lawyers* in 1972. He directed five episodes of *Jake and the Fat Man* in all.

Come Closer to Me (1/8/1992)
Written by: Doc Barnett. **Directed by:** Frank Thackery.
Guest Stars: Alex Cord, Brenda Bakke, Asher Brauner, Richard Gant, Leo Penn, Bob Frank, Tom Everett, Dusty Rhoads.
Synopsis: A gang of pickpockets pick the wallet of a hit-man (not a good thing to begin with) which contains information on who his next target will be. Naturally the hit-man wants all of this back and their lives are in danger. Jake goes undercover.
Trivia: Director Frank Thackery was better known as a cinematographer, but he got his chance to direct two episodes of *Jake and the Fatman* and then 17 episodes of *Matlock* and 11 episodes of *Diagnosis Murder*. In this episode he got a chance to direct his fellow director, Leo Penn.

Since I Fell for You (1/15/1992)
Written by: Morgan Gendel. **Directed by:** Alexander Singer.
Guest Stars: Karen Garvian, Sal Landi, Barry Cullison, Dana Gladstone, Bert Ramsen, Olga Russell.
Synopsis: A woman that Derek loved and thought dead since a plane crash six years earlier reappears.
Trivia: The song "Since I Fell for You" was composed by Buddy Johnson in 1945, but had its biggest hit recording by Lenny Welsh in 1963 where it came in at #4.

Just You, Just Me (1/22/1992)
Written by: Kimmer Ringwald, Bernie Kowalski & story by Ringwald, Kowalski and Paul Barber and Larry Barber. **Directed by:** Richard Lang.
Guest Stars: Christopher Templeton, Candy Ann Brown, Stephen Quadros, Juan Del Castillo, Jr., Alma Beltran, Carlos Palomino, Robert Jayne.
Synopsis: A wheelchair bound shopkeeper heads a battle against a local gang after she refuses to comply with the gang's order to closer her store.
Trivia: A Tour-de-force performance by Christopher Tempeton (1952-2011), who was best known as playing Carol Robbins, the secretary of Jack Abbott on the popular CBS soap opera, *The Young and the Restless*. Templeton had contracted polio at six months old and wore a brace on her right leg and walked with a cane. Templeton was also an advocate for the disabled in her personal life.

Stormy Weather, Part One (1/29/1992)
Written by: Gerry Conway with story by Joel Steiger and George Eckstein. Directed by: Christian I. Nyby II.
Guest Stars: Gene Butler, Robert Clohessy, Roxann Dawson, Carmine Caridi, Dominick LaRue, Francis X. McCarthy.
Synopsis: Jake investigates a series of ritualistic murders in which a reporter seems to be one step ahead of him.
Trivia: "Stormy Weather" written by Harold Arlen and Ted Koehler was first sung by Ethel Waters in 1933, and has been a huge success for many artists over the years, particularly Billie Holiday, Lena Horne and Frank Sinatra.

Stormy Weather, Part Two (2/5/1992) Written by: Gerry Conway with story by Joel Steiger and George Eckstein. Directed by: Christian I. Nyby II.
Guest Stars: Gene Butler, Robert Clohessy, Roxann Dawson, Carmine Caridi, Dominick LaRue, Francis X. McCarthy, Bryan Clark.
Synopsis: Jake continues to investigate the murders as evidence begins to point towards McEwen (Robert Clohessy).
Trivia: Beautiful Roxann Dawson began her career as a dancer in the movie *A Chorus Line* (which she had also performed in on Broadway). However, she is best known for her role as B'Elanna Torres on *Star Trek: Voyager* (1995-2001). She is also a director with more than 30 credits on shows like *Crossing Jordan, Cold Case, The Closer* and *The Good Wife*.

You'll Never Know (2/26/1992)
Written by: Douglas Stefen Borghi. Directed by: Ritchie Forrest.
Guest Stars: Richard Gilliland, James Andronica, Deborah May, Gina Gallego, Cynthia Steele, Robert Levine, Dey Young.
Synopsis: A doctor, who was into child porn, is murdered—the question for McCabe and Jake is if there was a connection.
Trivia: At the time that Robert Levine was appearing as the murder victim on "Jake" he was appearing as C. Dennis Jackson on *Superboy*, which depicted the 'Man of Steel' during his teenage years.

There'll Be Some Changes Made (3/11/1992)
Written by: Douglas Stefen Borghi. **Directed by:** John C. Flinn III.
Guest Stars: Megan Butler, Justin Deas, Laurie Morrison, Kathleen Doyle, Sage Parker, Liz Vassey, Melody Anderson.
Synopsis: A singer planning a comeback after a year in rehab is the target of a stalker.
Trivia: The title "There'll Be Some Changes Made" was published in 1921 and written by Benton Overstreet and Billy Higgins. It became a jazz standard and Ann Reinking sings the song in a sequence of the film *All That Jazz*.

Pennies from Heaven (3/18/1992)
Written by: Douglas Stefen Borghi. **Directed by:** Reza Badiyi.
Guest Stars: George DiCenzo, Jennifer Hetrick, Eric Christmas, Don Keith Opper, James DiStefano, Taylor Fry, Melody Anderson.
Synopsis: People begin getting money for good deeds or to help them economically from somebody going by the name "The Good Fairy." However, the notes on the bills indicate that the money is from a bank robbery.
Trivia: "Pennies from Heaven" with music by Arthur Johnston and words by Johnny Burke was published in 1936 and introduced by Bing Crosby in the 1936 film *Pennies from Heaven*.

I Can't Believe I'm Losing You (3/25/1992)
Written by: Gerry Conway based on story by Joel Steiger.
Directed by: Ronald Gary Stein.
Guest Stars: Rosalind Allen, James Finnerty, Lori Hallier, Debbie Pollack, Craig Benton, Olga Russell.
Synopsis: A bomb is planted in Jake's car gravely hurting his girlfriend. Jake then gets a note from the bomber saying that they aren't through yet. To Jake the handwriting appears to be by a woman, so he reviews his files to follow up on different women who he has arrested who might be responsible.
Trivia: New Zealand born Rosalind Allen plays Jake's injured girlfriend, and at that time she was best known for her role as Gretchen Richards on the NBC soap *Santa Barbara*. Many *Seinfeld* fans will recall her as the woman that George is dating who thinks that George is a Marine Biologist from a fifth season episode of that series.

All Through the Night (4/1/1992)
Written by: Doc Barnett. **Directed by:** Frank Thackeery.
Guest Stars: David Soul, John Anderson, Melody Anderson, Michele Farr, Taylor Fry, Olga Russell.
Synopsis: A psychiatrist that Neely helped put in prison five years earlier is now free and begins harassing her.
Trivia: This is the last episode to feature Melody Anderson's character of Neely Capshaw. From here she went on to appear on several episodes of the soap opera *All My Children*.

Ain't Misbehavin' (4/8/1992)
Written by: Bruce Franklin Singer. **Directed by:** Christopher Hibler.
Guest Stars: Nell Carter, Robert Reed, Michael Ensign, Michael McGrady, Jeff Yagher, Kene Holliday, Sharon Conley.
Synopsis: McCabe has to deal with a bail bonds woman who personally tracks down people who skip out on their bail. She finds one who claims to be innocent and she believes him and begins her own investigation to clear him.
Trivia: Singer-actress Nell Carter (1948-2003) added some much needed spunk to her characterization. At the time she was best known as the no nonsense maid to a white family on the popular 80's sitcom *Gimme a Break!*

Nightmare (4/22/1992)
Written by: Christian Darren and Al Martinez based on a story by Christian Darren. **Directed by:** John C. Flinn III.
Guest Stars: Leigh McCloskey, Sam Anderson, Steven Marcus, Savannah Smith Boucher, Sandy Dell, Sherrie Rose, Zoe Trilling, Olga Russell.
Synopsis: Jake teams up with one of the top homicide detectives in LA to catch a serial killer who kills women who work for escort services.
Trivia: Julliard trained Leigh McCloskey was best known at this time for his recurring role as Dr. Zach Kelton on the soap opera *Santa Barbara* and as Mitch Cooper on the popular nighttime soap *Dallas*. More recently he has appeared on *The Young and the Restless*.

Beautiful Dreamer (5/6/1992)
Written by: David J. Burke. **Directed by:** Bernard L. Kowalski.
Guest Stars: Ray Sharkey, J. Kenneth Campbell, Lezlie Deane, Clarence Felder, Geoffrey Lower, Michael Tomlinson.
Synopsis: A cop makes it his mission to find a vile rapist and will stop at nothing to get him.
Trivia: This was one of the last works of actor Ray Sharkey (1952-1993) who had seemed destined for a huge Hollywood career thanks to his role as rock promoter Bob Marcucci in the 1980 film *The Idolmaker.* He never really made it big in films but he had a steady and durable career on TV and films unitl his untimely death at the age of 40.

BIBLIOGRAPHY

Aiello, Danny, *I Only Know Who I Am When I Am Somebody Else*, Simon and Schuster, 2014

Barabas, SuzAnne and Gabor Barabas, *Gunsmoke: A Complete History*, McFarland, 1990

Bassior, Jean-Noel, *Space Patrol: Missions of Daring in the Name of Early Television*, McFarland, 2012

Bogdanovich, Peter, *Who the Devil Made It: Conversations with Legendary Film Directors*, Ballantine Books, 1998

Buford, Kate, *Burt Lancaster: An American Life*, De Capo Press, 2000

Burgess, Anthony, *You've Had Your Time*, Vintage, 2002

Christopher, Nicholas, *Somewhere in the Night*, Simon and Schuster, 2010

Crowther, Bruce, *Film Noir*, Random House, 2011

Deane, Bill, *Following the Fugitive: An Episode Guide and Handbook to the 1960's Television Series*, McFarland, 2006

Dunning, John, *The Encyclopedia of Old-Time Radio*, Oxford University Press, 1998

Eames, John Douglas, *The MGM Story*, Octupus Books, 1975

Emery, Robert J, *The Directors: Take Three*, Allworth Press, 2003

Etter, Jonathan, *Quinn Martin, Producer: A Behind-the Scenes History of Q.M. Productions*, McFarland, 2003

French, Jack, with Siegel, David S, *Radio Rides the Range: A Reference Guide to Western Drama on the Air, 1929-1967*, McFarland, 2013

Froug, William, *How I Escaped from Gilligan's Island: And Other Misadventures of a Hollywood Writer-Producer*, UW Press, 2005

Greco, Joseph, *The File on Robert Siodmak in Hollywood, 1941-1951*, Dissertation.com, 1999

Hand, Richard J, *Terror on the Air: Horror Radio in America 1931-1932*, McFarland, 2006

Hare, William, *L.A. Nor: Nine Dark Visions of the City of Angels*, McFarland, 2004

Hayde, Michael J, *My Name's Friday: The Unauthorized But True Story of Jack Webb*, Cumberland House Publishing, 2001

Hirschhorn, Clive, *The Universal Story*, Hamlyn, 2000

Inman, David M, *Television Variety Shows: Histories and Episodes Guides to 57 Programs*, McFarland, 2001

Johnston, Lyle, *Good Night Chet: A Biography of Chet Huntley*, McFarland, 2003

LeRoy, Mervyn (with Richard Kleiner) *Take One*, Hawthorn Books, 1974

McBride, O.E., *Stout Fellow: A Guide Through Nero Wolfe's World*, iuniverse, 2003

McGilligan, Patrick, *Robert Altman: Jumping Off the Cliff*, Macmillan, 1989

McGrath, Patrick J, *John Garfield: The Illustrated Career in Films and on Stage*, McFarland, 1993

Meyers, Jeffrey, *Hemingway: A Biography*, Da Capo Press, 1985

Nachman, Gerald, *Raised on Radio*, University of California Press, 2000

Nott, Robert, *He Ran All the Way: The Life of John Garfield*, First Limelight, 2003

Rode, Alan, *Charles McGraw: Biography of a Film Noir Tough Guy*, McFarland, 2007

Romano, Frederick V, *The Boxing Filmography: American Features, 1920-2003*, McFarland, 2004

Scott, Keith, *The Moose That Roared: The Story of Jay Ward, Bill Scott, a Flying Squirrel, and a Talking Moose*, St. Martin's Press, 2000

Snauffer, Douglas, *Crime Television*, Greenwood Publishing Group, 2006

Sterling, Christopher H, *The Concise Encyclopedia of American Radio*, Routledge, 2009

Terrance, Vincent, *Television Specials: 5,336 Entertainment Programs*, McFarland, 2013

Wagner, Laura, *Anne Francis: The Life and Career*, McFarland, 2011

Williams, Tony, *Body and Soul: The Cinematic Vision of Robert Aldrich*, Scarecrow Press, 2004

Zimbalist, Efrem, Jr., *My Dinner of Herbs*, Hal Leonard Corporation, 2003

Zuckoff, Michael, *Robert Altman: The Oral Biography*, Alfred A. Knopf, 2009

SOURCES

Chapter One
1922-1951

"I remember him saying he was teased as a boy...," Christopher Conrad to author
"He loved singing...," ibid
Recollection of Conrad's introduction to KFOX Radio in Long Beach, Bassior, *Space Patrol: Missions of Daring in the Name of Early Television*
Meeting Clete Roberts, *TV Guide*, 2/21/1976
"Clete worked out a deal...," William Conrad to Leonard Maltin, 1992
"This big voice...," *TV Guide* 2/21/1976
"I took him to Redondo Beach...," ibid
"I had been poor all of my life...," William Conrad to Leonard Maltin, 1992
"I had always hoped to be a director...," TV Times, 10/9/1971
"A training ground of sorts...," Dunning, *Encyclopedia of Radio*
"And from that day I started until the day I got out of radio...," William Conrad to Leonard Maltin, 1992
"As a pilot Bill buzzed the Golden Gate Bridge...," Christopher Conrad to author
Grounded from flying due to night blindness, Sterling, *Encyclopedia of Radio*
Background on *Destination Tomorrow*, http://www.otrsite.com/logs/logd1048.htm
"Full of enthusiasm and eager to perform at the microphone...," Froug, *How I Escaped from Gilligan's Island*.

"*The Whistler* remained the great omniscient storyteller...," Dunning, *Encyclopedia of Radio*

"That is why I kept so involved in everything..." William Conrad to Leonard Maltin, 1992

"...I was very impressed with his voice and ability...," Peggy Webber to author

"I saw that he liked to look as if he were very nonchalant...," ibid

"I'd say just tell me what the character is...," Maltin, *The Great American Broadcast*

Robson, "a delightful, charming, blowhard...," William Conrad to Leonard Maltin, 1992

"Robson, "an impresario...," Peggy Webber to author

"He knew what he was doing..." ibid

"I am not one who suffers fools gladly...," http://www.goldenage-wtic.org/gaor-70.html

"Ideal for radio...," Peggy Webber to author

"There was a lot of loyalty-camaraderie...," http://www.speakingofradio.com/interviews/gregg-virginia-actress/

"Actors became close as family..." Peggy Webber to author

"There was a lot of rivalry between Bill and Stacy Harris...," Herb Ellis to author

"Bill and I would play cards with a group...," ibid

"Bill had an instinct into the characters...," ibid

"He knew everybody and everybody knew him...," Helen Frees to author

"I couldn't double to save my life...," William Conrad to Leonard Maltin, 1992

"I seem to be tied to Jack Webb...," ibid

"He made fun of actors like Bill Conrad...," Peggy Webber to author

"I used to ask Jack to use Bill...," Herb Ellis to author

"We always got along...," William Conrad to Leonard Maltin, 1992

"We lived together for fifteen years...," ibid

Chapter Two: Films
1946-1952

"I played a lot of heavies and the leading man's best friend...," *Toledo Blade*, 7/10/73

"The most American film genre...," Roger Ebert, "A Guide to Film Noir," 1/30/95

"That's the guy," *St. Petersburg Times*, 5/20/74

"With time and typecasting...," Rode, *Charles McGraw*

"The only good picture ever made of a story of mine," Meyers, *Hemingway*

"Universal was certain to recoup...," Greco, *The File on Robert Siodmak*

"One picture that didn't turn out as well as I had hoped...," LeRoy, *Take One*

"Hemingway always considered *The Killers* the best of the many films...,"

"Pretentious twaddle," Hirschhorn, *The Universal Story*

Chapter Three: Gunsmoke
1952-1955

"Of course there was no Matt Dillon...," Conrad to Chris Lembesis, *Spotlight on a Star*, 2/15/69

"We made a list of every western cliché..." *Reading Eagle*, 5/5/57

"...big wide, open sound to it...," Dunning, *Encyclopedia of Radio*

"As I thought of Dillon first..." *Reading Eagle*, 5/5/57

"They auditioned everybody in town...," *Spotlight on a Star*, 2/15/69

Naming Chester, Dunning, *Encyclopedia of Radio*

"It was a time of shooting and fighting...," Maltin, *The Great American Broadcast*

"Kitty is just someone Matt has to visit every once in a while..," *Time*, 3/23/53

"Neither a hero nor a villain, just a human being...," *TV Radio Mirror*

"Bill is one of the warmest people I know...," *Radio-TV Mirror*, Jan-June, 1957

"Bill Conrad created the role of Matt Dillon...," Ray Kemper to author

"Parley Baer...was a consummate actor..." ibid

Baer, "brought a unique quality to every character he played," Herb Ellis to author

"We felt that he was always a middle-aged man...," *Spotlight on a Star*, 2/15/69

"Howard...seemed to know instinctively...," Ray Kemper to author

"In all the years that I've been in the business...," *Spotlight on a Star*, 2/15/69

McNear, "A complete joy to work with...," Herb Ellis to author

"Gunsmoke became a Labor of Love to us...," Parley Baer to Chuck Schaden, *Speaking of Radio* 3/22/84

"They took complete and deliberate time in setting up the sound effects...," *Spotlight on a Star*, 2/15/69

"Tom Haney and I were assigned as the sound effects men...," Ray Kemper to author

"When Dillon and Chester rode the plains...," Dunning, *Encyclopedia of Radio*

"The atmosphere surrounding the radio show...," Barabas & Barabas, *Gunsmoke: A Complete History*

"I played all kinds of things...," ibid

"Let the words do the work...," ibid

"Matt Dillon was first of all a human being...," ibid

"What made *Gunsmoke* such an important series...," Herb Ellis to author

Meston, "short on words...," Ray Kemper to author

"Both Tommy and I had written for radio...," ibid

"I never heard a cross word...," ibid

"When *Jason* began...," Herb Ellis to author

"Bill liked working...," ibid

"I went out and got Bill Conrad, who I think is a fascinating actor...," Peter Bogdanovich, *Who The Devil Made It: Conversations with Legendary Film Directors*

"Bill Conrad came in one Saturday morning with a terrible hangover...," *Gunsmoke: The Complete History*

"I don't look like Matt Dillon, god dammit!," Maltin, *The Great American Broadcast*
"Sure, he wanted to play Matt Dillon on TV...," Herb Ellis to author
"Bill Conrad trimmed down to a slender 170 or so...," Ray Kemper to author
"I got talked into making a test...," Maltin, *Great American Broadcast*
"I don't think there ever really was a six-foot-seven marshal in the west...," *Gunsmoke: The Complete History*

Chapter Four: The Ride Back
1956-1961

"June was a very nice lady...," Herb Ellis to author
"Susan was more out-going...," ibid
"I produced a film, *The Ride Back*...," Williams, *Body & Soul*
"Everytime I listen to that I smile, I cry...," Christopher Conrad to author
Details of Conrad's contracts and work for Ziv Television, Ziv-TV Production Files, Wisconsin State Historical Society Archives.
"Directing in TV is at best constantly settling for something less than you would like...," *Miami News*, 9/1/1973
"The recording sessions were the happiest time of everybody involved...," Scott, *The Mouse that Roared*
"When he did the narration...," *People*, 2/28/1994

Chapter Five: Warner Brothers
1962-1969

"I gave up acting...(because) I felt it was not honorable work...," *Lakeland Ledger*, 5/2/73
"My first impression of Bill was this great big guy who had this commanding voice...," Jimmy Lydon to author
"Bill and I would go into Jack's office...," ibid
"The show was successful but junk...," Jimmy Lydon to Tom Weaver, *Films of the Golden Age*, 2009

"I had the pleasure of firing the little prick…," William Conrad to Leonard Maltin

"Transformed into a civilian Sgt. Friday…," Zimbalist, *My Dinner of Herbs*

"We panicked because it was impossible to have scripts…," ibid

Jeffrey Hunter, "a lovely man…," Jimmy Lydon to author

Hunter, "a dear friend of my mom's…," Christopher Conrad to author

"William Conrad had this voice that shook the world," Etter, *Quinn Martin, Producer*

"I'll say to you today it's a lousy idea…," *Miami News*, 9/1/73

"It was comfortable…," Christopher Conrad to author

"You have to realize I grew up around all this…," ibid

"I know we had a black maid…," ibid

"Mom had boyfriends and dad had girlfriends…," ibid

"He was in love, but…," Jimmy Lydon to author

"Cesar Romero, "a thorough professional…," ibid

"The kid from Disney…," Jimmy Lydon to Tom Weaver, *Films of the Golden Age*, 2009

"After she falls…," ibid

"That's what Bill would call a 'plot scene'…," ibid

"Bill was doing a very sentimental scene with her…," ibid

"Dana Andrews was a pro…," ibid

"One of the brightest directors I've ever worked with…," Wagner, *Anne Francis*

Brainstorm, "A minor masterpiece of the 1960's," Crowther, *Film Noir*

"Just as *Kiss Me Deadly*…," Christopher, *Somewhere in the Night*

"An interesting psychological movie…," Crowther, *Film Noir*

"He collected pipes, shot guns…," Christopher Conrad to author

"For reasons I still don't fully understand…," ibid

"When I threaded them up to check what might be on them…," ibid

"At one point we were seeing three sets of rushes every day…," Jimmy Lydon to author

"Whitman was sort of a second level leading man…," ibid

"This was on our time...," ibid
"It has been written and directed by some fellows from television," Kael, *Kiss Kiss Bang Bang*
"I mean a guy wouldn't push his wife out a window in Los Angeles...," Lennon, *Conversations with Norman Mailer*
"Nobody believed a first time director cold have such a big hit...," McCarthy, *Howard Hawks*
"Nyby had a lot of experience...," Jimmy Lydon to author
"We thought we had done a very good war picture...," ibid
"Lamont Johnson came from radio and was a very good director...," ibid
"Bill and I thought *The Cool Ones* had great potential...,' ibid
"*Chubasco* is probably the worst picture we made...," ibid
"We liked the idea of using real locations...," ibid
"I told Bill that the guy was never on budget in his life...," ibid
"You can't hire that person," Zuckoff, *Robert Altman: The Oral Biography*
"A couple of weeks into the picture...," Jimmy Lydon to author
"So in the movie we have a way we figure we can get Jimmy...," Zuckoff, *Robert Altman*
"That fool has actors talking all the time...," ibid
"Bill Conrad took the picture away from him at the end...," ibid
"There's a lovely scene...," Roger Ebert, *Chicago Sun Times*, 7/1/77
"A true actor, in that he knew Shakespeare," Burgess, *You've Had Your Time*
"I really loved Bill...," Jimmy Lydon to author

Chaper Six: Cannon
1969-1976

"I had a little money...," *Harlan Daily Enterprise*, 9/13/71
"Fred Silverman flipped over my role...," *Toledo Blade*, 6/10/73
"Quinn had called Fred Silverman...," Etter, *Quinn Martin, Producer*
"Quinn Martin was a classy guy...," David Hedison to author

"One thing about Quinn Martin Productions...," Robert Pine to author

"Quinn...was a writer primarily...," Richard Anderson to author

"Quinn...was on the set a lot...," Julie Adams to author

"Quinn was a very shy man...," Etter, Quinn Martin Producer

"The production team was like a family...," ibid

"George was the only director who wasn't there...," ibid

"Bill Conrad was probably...," ibid

"William Conrad is a familiar voice...," *Evening Independent*, 3/26/71

"Cannon is the type of role I enjoy...," *TV Times*, 10/9/71

"It's a great school...," *Eureka Times-Standard*, 5/6/1973

"He...was strict, but he never raised a hand to me...," Christopher Conrad to author

"Bill didn't think he was a good father...," Herb Ellis to author

"Part of the pleasure I get from my role...," *Times-Union*, 6/9/72

"Believe me, I consume very little...," *Lakeland Ledger*, 5/2/73

"This is the only way I know of taking a chance...," *Eureka Times Standard*, 9/12/71

"The other day someone asked me how it feels to be a star...," *Waycross Journal Herald*, 9/23/72

"Bill was an incredible guy...," Jonathan Etter, Quinn Martin, Producer

"The first season, Bill was a dream-boat...," ibid

"To Bill, this was filmed radio...," ibid

"I would visit him when he was doing Cannon...," Jimmy Lydon to author

"Many actors used cards...," Robert Pine to author

"Sure Bill used cue cards...," Richard Anderson to author

"I was never close to him...," Robert Pine to author

"I had a tough time on that series...," Jonathan Etter, Quinn Martin, Producer

"Bill Conrad the actor...," *Sarasota Herald-Tribune*, 6/4/72

"The ridiculous thing was we got to be a hit...," *Waycross Journal Herald*, 9/23/72

"I remember it was a Monday morning...," Robert Pine to author

"I thought Bill Conrad was very professional...," Julie Adams to author

"I was meant to be heavy...," *Miami News*, 9/1/73

"I have seen too many shows ruined...," *St. Joseph News-Press*, 5/6/73

"You no longer have to be seven feet tall and handsome...," *Leader Post*, 6/1/73

"After six abortive scene takes...," *The Robesonian*, 9/9/73

"He was a hard-nosed tough individual...," Jonathan Etter, Quinn Martin, Producer

"I liked the one where I played...," David Hedison to author

"Bill Conrad was pretty much to himself...," Richard Anderson to author

"I first met Mr. Conrad in Manhattan around 1978...," Kevin Butler to author

"Bill swore like a seaman...," Jonathan Etter, Quinn Martin, Producer

"Skewering the cast and crew...," Christopher Conrad to author

"Jimmy had to look like Bill in profile...," Jonathan Etter, Quinn Martin, Producer

"Why, Mr. Kempfer...," *Milwaukee Sentinal*, 10/18/76

Fire on the soundstages of Cannon & Barnaby Jones, *TV Guide*, 7/13/74

"The Cannon people would be happy if I didn't do anything else...," *TV Guide*, 3/3/73

"I loved working with Leo Penn...," Julie Adams to author

"We started to shoot this scene going into a police station...," Robert Pine to author

"Television is a business...," *Calgary Herald*, 9/17/76

Chapter Seven: Nero Wolfe
1977-1986

"I'd wanted to do a play for a long time...," *Chicago Daily Herald*, 8/27/76

"Conrad's portrayal is a living advertisement...," *Miami News*, 8/11/76

"William Conrad put forth a great effort...," *Boca Raton News*, 8/11/76

"Conrad's substantial stage debut...," *Chicago Tribune*, 8/23/76

"I'll never do it again...," *Calgary Herald*, 9/17/76

"Conrad took us all out for dinner...," Danny Aiello, I Only Know Who I Am When I Am Somebody Else

"She could be a very vain, socially conscious and very proud woman...," Christopher Conrad to Author

"My mother's illness was very hard on my dad...," ibid

"My dad came to the conclusion...," ibid

"Yes, she was frightened and didn't want to die," ibid

"Her long suit is fashion, beauty and the undeniable fact...," *Washington Post*, 10/23/10

"She sat in my lap or something corny like that," ibid

"Bill was at her door the next day...," Peggy Webber to author

"He called me after he married Tippy...," ibid

"It was a very happy marriage," Jimmy Lydon to author

"Tippy was a very large woman...," Christopher Conrad to author

"William Conrad's a rough gruff man...," Rome (NY) *News-Tribune* 6/19/92

"When Nero says so-and-so did it...," *Star-News*, 1/16/81

"Wolfe is the 'brightest and rudest...,'" *Lewiston Morning Tribune*, 1/23/81

"I could never stand doing another series..." *Star News*, 1/16/81

"I never get outside of my brownstone...," *Lewiston Morning Tribune*, 1/23/81

"I despise orchids...," *Windsor Star*, 2/5/81

"Nero is constantly telling Fritz...," *Lewiston Daily Sun*, 1/16/81

"I think Nero Wolfe is one of the best drawn detectives...," ibid

"Obesity—obviously...," *Windsor Star*, 2/5/81

"I got all excited because, it being so early in my career," Interview with Lee Horsey by Brian Sheridan, *The Gazette: The Journal of the Wolfe Pack*, spring, 2008

"Conrad...could be 'brusque and demanding at times,'" ibid

"I remember the days when he would shoot the final scene...," ibid

"Listen, we're all gambling...," *Lewiston Daily Sun*, 1/16/81
"I know, I know, the show pales next to The Rockford Files," *Press Courier*, 2/20/81
"How the hell should I know what makes a hit TV series...," *Toronto Sun*, 11/30/91

Chapter Eight: Jake and the Fatman
1987-1994

"I loved his voice...," Fred Silverman, interview Archive of American Television
"I thought he was an excellent actor...," Michael Lange to author
"Everybody had the impression he was a gruff guy...," Joe Penny, *The Hollywood Show*
"This gave Bill a lot of teachable moments...," Alan Campbell to author
"He had his 'buttons' things that would set him off...," ibid
"Joe could also be unpredictable...," ibid
"Once Bill said he was going to show me the use of star power...," ibid
"He and Tippy kept to themselves...," ibid
"I did some research on this mutt...," *The Miami News*, 9/11/1987
"It's a shame we can't say words...," ibid
"It's a gamble...," ibid
"The shooting schedule was 7-days...," Michael Lange to author
"When I was a young boy, I used to pretend...," ibid
"The type of stories they wanted was set by the pilot...," Paul Robert Coyle to author
"I worked with both William Conrad and Joe Penny...," Mark Drexler, http://www.jason47.com/days/bromkadrexler.html
One particularly interesting thing happened that I have Bill Conrad to thank for...," Paul Robert Coyle to author
"My second episode involves a young girl on the witness stand...," Michael Lange to author
"Once when Tony Franciosa...," Paul Robert Coyle to author
"We had Anthony Fanciosa in an episode I directed...," Michael Lange to author

"It's a shame we cannot use words that are used every day by virtually everybody...," *Chicago Tribune*, 8/25/87

"I can't tell you the reason behind the move...," *The Angus Press*, 4/21/89

"I want the show to get a little more realistic...," *Victoria Advocate*, 7/5/89

"CBS had always been successful with shows operating from Hawaii...," Alan Campbell to author

"I was down to 242 from 290 pounds...," *Milwaukee Sentinel*, 8/15/89

"I pitched, like 5 stories—none of them worked...," J. Michael Stracynski, Interview Archive of American Television

"He was tricky to direct...," Michael Lange to author

"I believe the main reason the show moved back from Hawaii...," ibid

"He loves shows that I don't...," *TV Guide*, 10/20/90

"His health made him impatient...," Alan Campbell to author

"I would often..., stay to do Bill's off camera lines...," ibid

"Does a guy like me need a 32-inch waist?...," *People*, 2/28/1994

"He was perpetually on a diet...," Christopher Conrad, KCJJ Radio, 4/9/12

"I was against being identified as Bill Conrad's kid...," ibid

"I was in school studying photography...," Janet Conrad to author

"He was gracious, kind, easy to talk to...," ibid

"Bill loved singing and always loved the fact...," Alan Campbell to author

"We stayed up talked until 3 in the morning...," Herb Ellis to author

"Tippy told me, 'Please don't come over...,'" Jimmy Lydon to author

"We hung out and watched movies...," Christopher Conrad to author

"People accepted him as the gruff, rough curmudgeon...," *People*, 2/28/94

"You get a guy like Bill...," ibid

"I was honored to work with him for the years we had together...," *St. Louis Post-Dispatch*, 2/12/94

"I went to his funeral...," Herb Ellis to author

"I'm not sure she had anyone there to advise her...," Christopher Conrad to author

"You'll be a happier man...," Christopher Conrad, KCJJ Radio, 4/19/12

"When she heard my response to that...," Christopher Conrad to author

"If I died tomorrow...," ibid

Epilogue

"There was always a danger thing in my voice...," William Conrad to Leonard Maltin, *The Great American Broadcast*

"All I thought about was the money that it was possible to make...," ibid

Inducted into Radio Hall of Fame, 1997, http://www.richsamuels.com/nbcmm/rhof/rhof97sc.html

INDEX

Adams, Julie, 9, 139, 147-148
Adventures of Sam Spade, 189
Aiello, Danny, 152
Aldrich, Robert, 64
Alfred Hitchcock Hour, The, 292
All-American Thanksgiving Day Parade, 142-144
Altman, Robert, 99
American Dream, An, 92-93
Anderson, Richard, 129, 135, 136-137, 141, 216
Arness, James, 58, 59, 151
Assignment to Kill, 98

Baer, Parley, 10, 32, 33, 35-37, 41, 44, 45, 54, 57, 67, 74, 187, 195, 196, 205, 206, 207, 210
Barnaby Jones, 140, 142, 146, 147, 171
Bartell, Harry, 10, 38-39, 57, 192, 195, 210
Basehart, Richard, 22
Bat Masterson, 291, 292, 299
Body and Soul, 19-21
Brainstorm, 87-90
Brinkley, David, 154
Brotherhood of the Bell, 125-126, 293

Butler, Kevin, 143-144
Byrnes, Edd, 76-77

Caan, James, 99-101
Campbell, Alan, 168-169, 177-178, 180, 182, 184
Cann, Ida (mother), 5-7
Cann, John (father), 5-6
Cannon, 126-131, 133-142, 144-149, 158, 302-348
CBS Radio Workshop, The, 66-67
Chubasco, 97-98
Clark, Marion, 43, 72-74
Conqueror, The, 52-53
Conrad, Christopher (son), 5-6, 8-9, 62, 78, 79-81, 85, 91-92, 132, 153-154, 156, 161-162, 163, 182-183, 184, 185, 186
Conrad, Janet, 183-184
Conrad, June (Nelson), 8, 9, 62
Conrad, Susan (Randall), 62,78,80,81-82,91-92,132,133,153-154
Conrad, Tippy, 154-156, 184, 185, 186, 188
Conried, Hans, 70-71
Cool Ones, The, 96-97

Countdown, 98-102
Covenant with Death, A, 95-96
Coyle, Paul Robert, 171-173, 174-176, 179
Crime Classics, 190
Crutchfield, Les, 42, 62, 210
Cry Danger, 24-25
Cry of the Hunted, 46

Dean Martin Show, The, 294-295-296
Dehner, John, 8, 10, 38, 50, 67, 211
Dial 1119, 23-24
Dobkin, Lawrence, 38, 67, 207
Donahue, Troy, 85-87
Druxman, Michael B, 164-165
Duval, Robert, 99

Ebsen, Buddy, 140, 142, 147
Edwards, Sam, 38, 40, 67
Ellis, Anthony, 42-43, 63, 66
Ellis, Georgia, 33, 36, 42, 44, 51, 54, 57, 132, 195, 197, 207
Ellis, Herb, 10, 36, 37, 40, 45, 46, 56, 62, 184, 195, 196, 207
Escape, 28, 38, 47-49, 190-197
Everett, Chad, 95

Family Theater, 197-198
Favorite Story, 12-13, 198-200
Fiddler on the Roof (play), 163-164
First to Fight, 93
Fontaine, Joan, 148
Foray, June, 71
Franciosa, Anthony, 175-176
Frees, Paul, 12, 70-71, 190, 192, 207, 211

Fugitive, The, 78-79, 126

Gardner, Ava, 18
Garfield, John, 19-21
GE True, 75-76, 300-301
George, Lynda Day, 129, 130-131
Gist, Robert, 93-94
Gregg, Virginia, 10, 38, 62, 67, 84, 85, 210
Griffith, Andy, 167
Gunsmoke (radio), 27-46, 221-289
Gunsmoke (TV), 58-59, 302

Hackman, Gene, 95, 103
Hanley, Tom, 35, 37-38, 41, 44, 51
Harris, Stacy, 67, 194, 196, 216
Have Gun Will Travel, 292, 300
Hayward, Susan, 52, 53
Heatherton, Joey, 85-87
Hedison, David, 128, 141
Hellinger, Mark, 17-18
Hermit's Cave, The, 7-8
Heston, Charlton, 51-52
Highway Patrol, 298
Horsley, Lee, 156-157, 158, 159-160
Hotel, 297
Houston, Lou, 6
Hunter, Jeffrey, 77-78, 88-90
Huntley, Chet, 9, 154-155

Jake and the Fatman, 128, 168-182, 355-398
Jason and the Golden Fleece, 45
Johnny Concho, 62-62
Johnson, Lamont, 96
Jones, Christopher, 97-98
Jones, Dean, 83, 84

Karlson, Phil, 55, 56
Keefer, 296
Kemper, Ray, 35, 36, 37-38, 41, 44, 51, 56-57
Killers, The, 16-19
Klondike, 299
Koury, Rex, 8, 30-31, 45

Lancaster, Burt, 16, 18, 21
Lange, Michael, 168, 170-171, 175, 176, 179-180
Lee, Canada, 19-21
Leigh, Janet, 93
Let George Do It, 200-201
Lewis, Joseph H, 46, 51
Lockhart, June, 187-188
Lux Radio Theater, 201-206
Lydon, Jimmy, 76, 81, 82-103, 136, 156, 184, 187

MacDonnell, Norman, 28-35, 40, 44, 49, 56, 58, 59, 69, 192, 210
MacDowell, Roddy, 96-97
Martin, Quinn, 78, 126-127, 128-129, 136, 137, 138, 142, 145
Matlock, 167, 298
Mayer, Gerald, 24
McGraw, Charles, 16, 17, 216
McNear, Howard, 10, 32, 33, 36-37, 44, 54, 57, 195, 205, 207, 210
Meston, John, 28-31, 40-41, 42, 49, 54, 56, 58
Mikado, The, 162-163
Miles, Vera, 128, 130, 131, 135, 148
Miller, Allan, 158-159, 160
Miner, Allen, 64, 65, 97
Mitchum, Robert, 25, 26

Mohr, Gerald, 11-12
Moonshine County Express, 152-153
Moore, Kevin, 163-164
Moorehead, Agnes, 52, 53, 67, 93
Mr. President, 206-207
Murder She Wrote, 297
My Blood Runs Cold, 85-87

Naked City, The, 300
Naked Jungle, The, 51-52
Name of the Game, The, 293
Nero Wolfe, 128, 156-162, 348-354
Night Beat, 207-208
Night Cries, 296
Nyby, Christopher, 95

Parker, Eleanor, 51-55, 93, 94
Parrish, Robert, 24-25
Penny, Joe, 168, 169, 173, 174, 176, 177, 179, 180, 181-182
Perrin, Vic, 38, 44, 57, 58, 67, 191, 193
Pine, Robert, 128-129, 136-137, 138-139
Police Squad, 297
Purdum, Herb, 42, 43

Quinn, Anthony, 63-65

Railroad Hour, The, 209
Return of Frank Cannon, The, 296
Richard Diamond, Private Eye, 208-209
Ride Back, The, 63-65
Rifleman, The, 298
Roberts, Clete, 7, 9
Rocky the Flying Squirrel, 70-71
Romance, 209-210

Romero, Cesar, 83-84
Rossen, Robert, 20-21
Rough Riders, The, 291, 298
Route 66, 300
Rowan & Martin's Laugh-In, 294

77 Sunset Strip, 76-77, 292-293, 301
Sinatra, Frank, 61-62
Siodmak, Robert, 17-18
Six-Shooter, The, 210-211
Stanwyck, Barbara, 21-22
Sorry Wrong Number, 21-22
Stevens, Connie, 83, 84
Stewart, James, 210
Strange Wills, 211
Strasberg, Susan, 97-98
Sullivan, Barry, 22, 46, 128, 131, 141, 145
Suspense, 47, 49, 67, 211-216

Temple Houston, 77-78, 301-302
Tension, 22-23
That Championship Season (play), 151-152

This is Your FBI, 216-217
Thompson, Marshall, 23-24
Tombstone Territory, 291, 299
Two on a Guillotine, 82-85

Van Dyke, Dick, 181
Voyage of the Scarlet Queen, 217-218

Walsh, George, 32
Ward, Jay, 70-71
Wayne, John, 52, 53, 58, 80
Webb, Jack, 10, 71-72, 75-76, 191, 193, 194, 198, 200
Webber, Peggy, 10, 71-72, 75-76, 191, 192, 211
Whistler, The, 10-12, 218-220
Whitman, Stuart, 93

Yours Truly, Johnny Dollar, 220-221

Zimbalest, Jr, Efrem, 76-77, 129
Ziv, Fredeerick, 68
Ziv Productions, 68-70

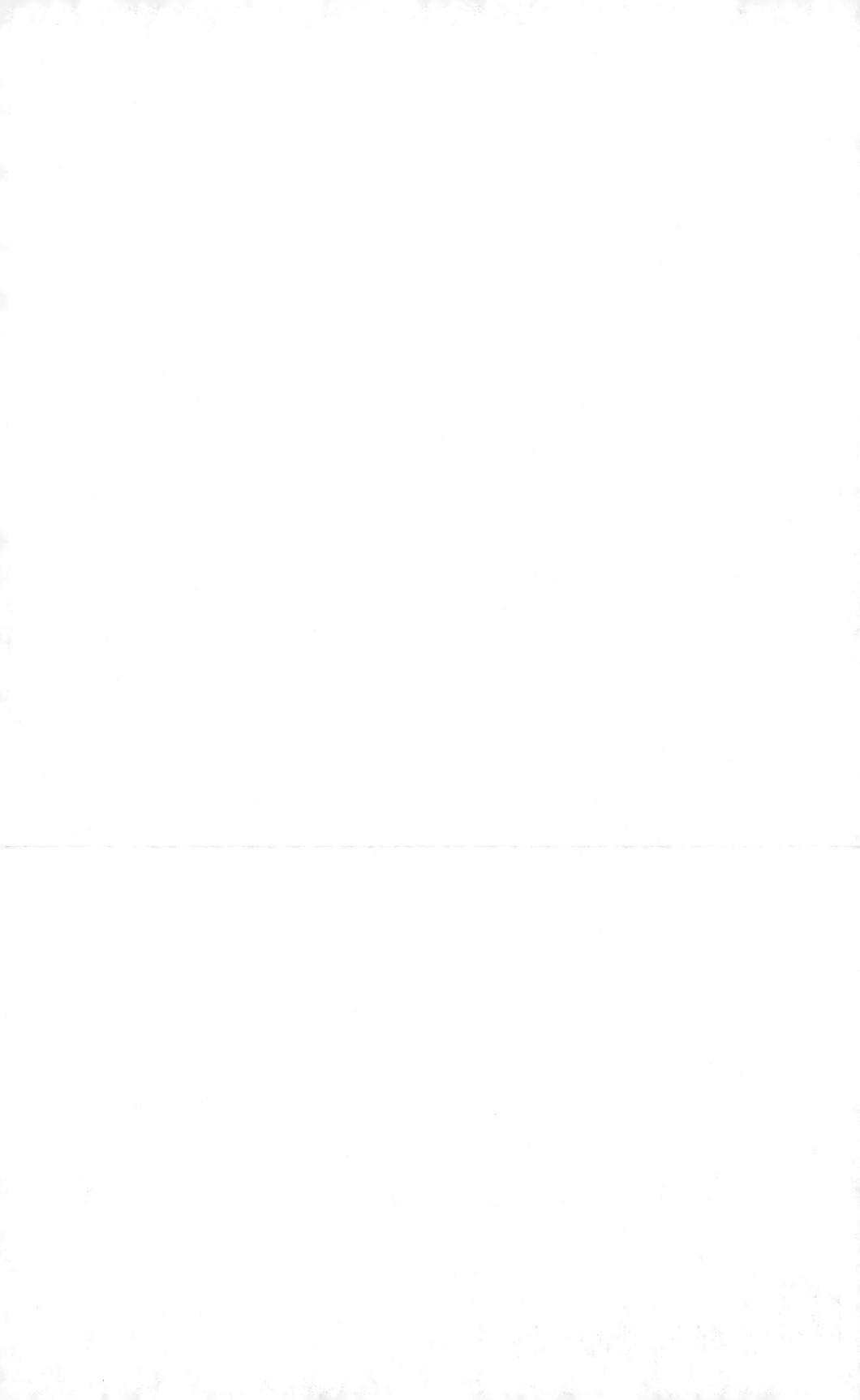

www.ingramcontent.com/pod-product-compliance
Lightning Source LLC
Chambersburg PA
CBHW060547230426
43670CB00011B/1721